A Light
for your way

Victor Maxwell

Rom 8:31

A Light for your way
© Copyright Victor Maxwell 2017

ISBN 878-1-909751-72-9
For further copies please contact:
ACRE INTERNATIONAL
30 Carnglave Manor
Spa
Ballynahinch
Co.Down
Northern Ireland
BT24 8XE
Telephone: +44 (028) 97563200
Email: acregospelmission@hotmail.co.uk

Printed by
JC Print Ltd
BELFAST
Telephone 07860 205333
email: info@jcprint.net

photography by Andrew Linden
email: andrew.linden@sky.com

ACRE GOSPEL MISSION

A Light for your way

MEDITATIONS ON GOD'S WORD AND REFLECTIONS OF GOD'S WORK

Victor Maxwell

A word from the author

The Scriptures are replete with occasions when God spoke with those who took time to wait on Him. He is the speaking God who desires to speak with you. We do not expect to hear His voice in burning bushes or by a thunderous voice from heaven. However, we can meet with Him in His Word.

We live in a pressurized world where the things that matter most are too frequently pushed aside, especially time with God. We all need time to clear the debris that clutters up our lives and make more time for Him, time to meditate on His Word.

So much positive feedback followed the publication of the first volume, *A Word for Your Way*, that I decided to write another daily devotional. Like the first, these daily readings alternate between mediations on God's Word and reflections from God's work; what God says to our hearts and how He works in our lives.

I am grateful to all who patiently helped in collating and correcting these devotional thoughts and personal anecdotes. My prayer is that God will bless them as He has blessed us.

Victor Maxwell

January

Ballymoney, Co Antrim

The Bible's First "Fear Not"

"After these things the word of the LORD came unto Abram in a vision, saying, Fear not, Abram: I am thy shield, and thy exceeding great reward."
Genesis 15:1

I remember working with men who had returned from World War II and the Korean War. Some spoke of amazing escapes from sinking ships. Others spoke of hand-to-hand combat and some of the horrors of Japanese prison camps. Many shared that even years after the war they still suffered nightmares and fears. Their greatest fear was that a World War should ever start again. Dr. Donald Barnhouse said, "Cowards fear before the war, heroes fear after the war."

In Genesis 15 Abram had just returned from the war in which he had defeated five kings. He had refused a reward from the King of Sodom. However, he was vulnerable, for he lived in a hostile environment, perhaps fearing that war should come again. It was then that God came to him with reassurance. I find it amazing how God did not wait for Abram to go to Him.

God's reassurance to Abram gives us the first *"Fear not"* of the Bible. This was God's promise to Abram to reassure him who God is, what God said and what God will do.

We need not fear when God is our refuge. "I am thy shield..." God was his protection. God is a real shield for troubled hearts in troubled times.

We need not faint when God is our reward. "Thy exceeding great reward." God was his provision. Abram had refused the riches of the King of Sodom. Christians are coheirs with Christ. All that God has is ours.

We need not fail when God is our righteousness. God has given His promise. "Abram believed in God and it was counted unto him for righteousness."

We need not fret when God is our ruler. God gave to Abram a foresight of what would happen to the nation - the nation's sojourn and sufferings in Egypt, their salvation from Egypt and inheritance of the land.

Who God is, what He said and did for us in Christ, is sufficient.

It Matters to God

"Cast thy burden upon the Lord, and he shall sustain thee." Psalm 55:22

During recent summers we have been blessed and privileged to share in the ministry of Portrush Baptist Church where we have thoroughly enjoyed the fellowship. Besides ministering the Word of God we have been enriched and blessed by the prayer times with the church members.

At a recent Sunday morning service I preached on 1 Peter 5:7; *"Casting all your care upon him; for he careth for you."* By way of illustration, I related the story of George Mueller who built many orphanages in Bristol, England. We told how that without a personal salary, he relied wholly on God to supply the funds and food to support hundreds of children. Mueller wrote of the secret of his ministry, "For many years I have kept a motto on my desk that has brought comfort, strength, and uplifting confidence to my heart. It reads, *'It matters to Him about you,'* which is a more literal rendering of the last half of the well-known text, 'Casting all your care upon him; for he careth for you.' In other words, our Lord is concerned with our problems."

Later that day Ronnie McMullan, a long-serving member of the church and a gifted servant of God, slipped me a piece paper on which he had written some lines of his meditations on the story;

> It matters to Him about you!
> It matters to Him about you!
> On Calvary He died, was for you crucified,
> For it matters to Him about you!
>
> And there on that old rugged Cross
> He suffered your pain and your loss,
> Atonement was made, your debt was all paid
> 'Cause it mattered to Him about you!
>
> In love, He makes offer to you
> Of salvation so rich and so true.
> Accept now His grace, your sins He'll erase,
> For it matters to Him about you!
>
> Does it matter to you about Him,
> The One who has paid for your sin?
> He waits still today to cleanse sin away
> Cause it matters to Him about you!

You are always on His mind.

Serving the Lord

"Fervent in spirit; serving the Lord."
Romans 12:11

Because of World War II Willie and Margaret McComb and Mollie Harvey could not return home from Brazil. Nine straight years in the interior of the Amazon ended when they finally arrived in Belfast in 1946. Meagre rations, exposure to disease and primitive conditions had taken its toll on their health and prohibited Willie and Margaret returning to the Acre. When Mollie Harvey went back to the Acre again in 1948 she was the only missionary of Acre Gospel Mission.

Although ill health had weakened his body, this could not and did not lessen Willie McComb's passion to serve his Saviour and Lord and reach the lost. Nearby to where he lived was Everton Hall. The hall is located at the top of the Cregagh Road, Belfast, and maintained a witness to that area since 1934. At that time several Christians felt constrained to establish an evangelistic thrust to reach the growing community on the edge of the city's boundary. Mr. McKeown from the nearby Hillfoot Road and Fred Backley teamed up with other believers to lay the basis of a non-denominational witness in the upper Cregagh district.

These Christians acquired a site in the new housing development that bridged the Cregagh and Mount Merrion communities, and subsequently a new hall was erected, and an evangelistic work was established. Everton Hall was not designed to replace any church, and for that reason, no Sunday morning service was arranged until later years. It was essentially meant to be a Gospel outreach with prayer meetings, Bible studies, children's meetings and Sunday School. Initially, the work grew until the outbreak of World War II when many people were evacuated out of the city.

By the end of the War the congregation had greatly diminished until it was suggested that the Hall should be closed. Willie, challenged by the need of the area, saw this as an opportunity to serve His Lord. With the same zeal and enthusiasm that characterised his missionary service, Willie and friends re-opened the Hall and revived the evangelistic outreach.

Today Everton Hall has been re-established as Cregagh Baptist Church.

"Where He may lead me, I will go."

Greatly Beloved

"And he said unto me, O Daniel, a man greatly beloved."
Daniel 10:11

The greatest assurance we can enjoy is to know that God loves us. Daniel certainly needed that confidence as he lived through turbulent times while exiled in Babylon far from his Jerusalem home. Three times God's angel brought the message from heaven assuring Daniel that he was greatly beloved: *"At the beginning of thy supplications the commandment came forth, and I am come to shew thee; for thou art greatly beloved"* (9:23); *"And he said unto me, O Daniel, a man greatly beloved"* (10:11); *"And said, O man greatly beloved, fear not: peace be unto thee, be strong, yea, be strong"* (10:19).

His peers and colleagues might have loved Daniel, but his comfort and strength were drawn from the assurances that he was supremely loved by God in heaven. Reading through the twelve chapters of his prophecy Daniel's love for God is evident right from the opening verses. Although he lived in Babylon and served a variety of kings in a pagan society, yet his primary allegiance was to the God of heaven, the God of Israel. Because of Daniel's love and loyalty to his God, he was opposed and severely persecuted, but it was not his love for God that saw him through those difficult days. Rather, Daniel rested and was reassured to know that God loved him.

We also can rest in the assurance that our heavenly Father loves us. According to the prayer and promise of the Lord Jesus, He loves us as He loves His Son (John 17:23, 16:27). The greatest demonstration of that love was at Calvary. For love of sinners like us, ungodly, weak and rebellious, God sent His Son to the cross to provide forgiveness and redemption for us.

You can almost sense the amazement of the apostle Paul, formerly a persecutor, a blasphemer and the chief of sinners when he was overcome with the fact that Jesus Christ was *"the Son of God who loved me and gave Himself for me."* Truly this is "love divine, all loves excelling", love that is immeasurable, indescribable, inexhaustible and interminable.

God's love is as great and infinite as He is.

Rescued

"Is not this a brand plucked out of the fire?"
Zechariah 3:2

Sammy Spence of the Coalmen's Mission was one of East Belfast's best-known characters. His conversion to Christ was genuine and radical. During the political upheaval following the 1916 Easter Rebellion in Dublin and the partition of Ireland, Sammy Spence was very quick to enter the fray of street fights, riots and shootings to defend what he felt was the right for Ulster to remain British. It would be wrong to say Sammy was a terrorist, but he certainly was a terror on the streets agitating and inciting mobs to violence. These activities not only frequently endangered his life, but they also resulted in Sammy being thrown into the Crumlin Road jail on many occasions. He was imprisoned more than sixty times before his conversion, and he used to say that he had more friends inside the prison than on the outside.

He related that on one occasion as he made his way home from the Belfast Coal Quay he was accosted by the Harbour Police, generally nicknamed by Sammy as "The Bulkies." It was obvious that Sammy had something stuffed up his coat, something he wanted to conceal from these law-enforcing officers. When they suggested searching him, Sammy said, "You lay a hand on me, and you will have to deal with the hard men at Bridgend. I live in a street filled with hard men. The farther you go up the street, the harder they get, and I live in the last door." "The Bulkies" never touched him.

Sammy and his wife lived in a small terrace house in Newfoundland Street at Bridgend in East Belfast. It defies imagination to understand how they raised twelve children in such a small house. Sammy admitted that he made life even more distressing for his wife and family because of his drunken escapades. He openly admitted that the only weekends he was sober were those he spent in jail.

Through all this his wife never gave up praying for him. It was a great night at Memel Street when Rev. Redmond led Sammy to faith in Christ. This East Belfast character became more zealous for Christ than he had ever been for the devil.

Rescued and redeemed by the power of the Gospel.

Delayed Doors

"For a great door and effectual is opened unto me..."
1 Corinthians 16:9

In 1939 Willie and Margaret McComb, founders of the Acre Gospel Mission, travelled down the River Acre to Boca do Acre, hoping to go to Sena Madureira, but those plans changed. Willie wrote of that journey:

We intended to be travelling for six weeks, but the opportunities were so many and the needs so great that we did not return for nearly three months. Sadly, we were unable to enter all the doors that were open to us … but time did not permit us to do so.

After four days we reached Boca do Acre only to find that we had missed the boat for Sena Madureira. We had to content ourselves to wait for the next one. This delay was in the Lord's hand, for we were able to conduct meetings each night. The mayor proved to be a gentleman and gave us permission to have a meeting in the main square and even provided seats from the school.

We had a splendid meeting, with about 250 present, including all the leading men from the town. Although we felt much power in the meeting, we were conscious, too, of the presence of the enemy of souls. Boca do Acre is about as evil a place as one could find on the face of the earth.

We had a great sale of Scriptures in the town, and after the open-air meetings, some asked for as many as four or five New Testaments. Our great regret was that we were unable to supply all the demand.

In Boca do Acre they met a young woman, Dona Nené Ale, who was married to a Syrian immigrant. She was the only believer in town and appealed for the McCombs to remain in Boca do Acre. They were grieved to decline her invitation but prayed that one day the Lord would send someone to that needy town. The answer to that prayer was delayed fourteen years until God sent James and Dorrie Gunning to the Boca do Acre in 1952.

God's timing is always on time.

Why We Ought to Pray

"Men ought always to pray and not to faint."
Luke 18:1

Sammy Spence worked at the Belfast Coal Quay on the County Down side of the River Lagan. Every day coal boats berthed at the quayside to unload hundreds of tons of coal for the Ulster population. Kelly, Kingsberry, Craig, and Harcourts were the leading coal importers at the time. These companies employed hundreds of men who, by the nature of their work, were often as black as the stuff they handled. Mountains of dirty and dusty coal heaps rose up from quayside as horse-drawn carts lined up to draw precious fuels to homes all over the city.

The miracle of God's grace that had transformed Sammy Spence's life changed him from being a slave and addict of sin to become a dedicated servant of the Saviour. Sammy and his friend Pop Stewart met every lunch hour to pray that God would also save their work colleagues. God answered those prayers, and one by one the Lord opened the hearts of Mick Martin, Sam Dunnon, Alex Small, Sam Dunlop, and many others.

These new converts joined Sammy and Pop Stewart to maintain a vital witness for their Lord at the docks. They conducted open-air meetings and were invited to churches and mission halls to testify of their Saviour. Soon they became known as the Coalmen's Testimony Band. Their witness for Christ resulted in many souls trusting the Saviour.

With the outbreak of World War II in 1939, emergency conditions were imposed on all British ports. Consequently, the activities of the Coalmen's Testimony Band were suspended. However, in 1947 several Christians approached Sammy and Pop Stewart and asked them to revive the former testimony band.

Each day at lunch time up to ten men crammed into in a small tea hut to pray for God's guidance and blessing. Surrounded by the blackened implements and tools used to unload the coal boats, these men removed their caps and bowed their heads to pray passionately. Those prayers were answered by the founding the Coalmen's Mission in nearby premises. Hundreds of people were converted to Christ during the next twenty-four years of existence.

When we pray, God answers.

Master of the Universe

"So the sun stood still in the midst of heaven, and hasted not to go down about a whole day."
Joshua 10:13

Four miracles occurred during Joshua's campaign to conquer the Promised Land. The first was the crossing of the Jordan when God parted the waters allowing over a million people to cross over on dry land. The second was the walls of Jericho falling flat after seven priests gave a long and loud blast on their trumpets, and the people gave a mighty shout.

The second two miracles occurred when Joshua was confronted by five kings who tried to overthrow Israel's campaign. Armed with the promise of victory, Joshua discomfited the enemy, and as they fled, God rained large hailstones from heaven upon them.

Perhaps the most remarkable of these miracles was when God caused the sun and the moon to stand still, thus prolonging the day and allowing Joshua and his army to destroy Israel's enemies.

Sceptics might mock these miracles as they do other miracles in the Scripture. But they waste their time, for they leave out God. Like a little boy said, "They are "myth-taken.""

I am reminded of a legend about Strasburg Cathedral's famous astronomical clock. Its mechanism was so intricate and complicated that many thought it was a work of superhuman skill and not that of the man who claimed to be its maker. Even more insulting was that while still unpaid, people abused and ridiculed him. One day he decided to touch the clock's secret springs so that it stopped. All the ingenuity of the nation's best mechanics failed to restore the clock's mechanism and set it in motion. Finally, the injustices against the maker were redressed, so he came again, touched the inner springs, and set the clock in motion again. All the multiplied cogs and wheels seemed to be subject and obedient to the great creator's will. By a touch, he suspended and then restored the clock's complicated movements, proving beyond doubt that he was the maker and master of this masterpiece.

The Divine Maker is still the Master of His great creation.

A Stirred Heart

"Oh that Thou wouldst bless me indeed..."
1 Chronicles 4:10

When D. L. Moody returned to Glasgow for a six-month evangelistic mission in 1882, John George Govan was already in his early twenties and had established his own commercial enterprise. Although he was very busy, he made sure to be present at many of these large evangelistic rallies.

John George was the fourth son in a godly home where his parents blessed their children by daily prayer and Bible instruction. Twelve-year-old John George trusted the Saviour after listening to his father preach the Gospel at an open-air meeting on the Isle of Arran.

Mr. Govan Sr. was also a very successful businessman and a prominent member of Glasgow Town Council. He had been enthusiastically active in Glasgow's spiritual awakening when the American evangelists, Moody and Sankey first visited the city. Those meetings greatly contributed to the fact that five of the six Govan sons became preachers of the Gospel, and the six daughters also faithfully followed their Saviour.

Night after night he listened to Moody's passionate preaching, and as he observed the evangelist's soul-winning zeal, young Govan was deeply stirred. At the same time a battle constantly raged within his heart: although he was a Christian, he was very dissatisfied with the inconsistencies of his up-and-down spiritual experience and longed for a holy and victorious Christian life instead of the mediocrity that constantly dogged and defeated him.

That all changed one night when his brother James invited him to pray. John George later said, "I felt I had to decide there and then. Either I must refuse to pray, or I must trust the Lord to give me the blessing of a clean heart as I prayed. It happened in almost an instant . . . I went down on my knees and prayed, yielding my all to God, and trusting Him to cleanse me there and then … When I got home that night and went down before the Lord, then I knew the difference. The glory of God flooded my soul and it has been different ever since."

Melt my heart and fill my life, give me some souls for Thee.

In Jeopardy

"And this I do for the Gospel's sake..."
1 Corinthians 9:23

Mollie Harvey, the only missionary of the Acre Gospel Mission in 1947, wrote of her uncomfortable river trip to the distant Acre at that time:

"I found great difficulty in getting a boat to take me up river to Sena Madureira, a month's journey of 1,500 miles. Things have changed for the worse since we first did journey ten years ago. I was promised a passage on a boat for part of the way and had even called for a man to transport the baggage, but at the last moment the owner decided not to take any passengers. That meant I had to unpack my luggage and wait another month.

At last we found a boat that was willing to take me. After three days we were met by a small paddle steamer for the rest of the journey to Boca do Acre. I have never seen a boat so overcrowded. We were not long on the river when a five-year-old boy fell into the water. Thankfully, he was rescued in the nick of time.

I had many opportunities to witness on the paddle steamer. The captain was very nice, but somewhat embarrassed by the poor conditions and the inferior food. Twice a week I had meetings on the lower deck. With my portable organ we sang choruses and I told the Gospel using flannel-graphs. Many people soon learned the choruses, and I spent numerous happy hours with them. I discovered that of more than 100 passengers, only one man had ever heard the Gospel before. Another man asked me, "Please come to our town so we can learn more." Pray for them and for the Gospel booklets they took home.

The paddle steamer only took me as far as the Boca do Acre. I saw no spiritual life in that town. It is a real Sodom where we felt the power of the enemy. During our four days there I had three meetings that were very well attended.

Five years later Mollie moved to Boca do Acre and remained there for the next sixteen years.

Maybe in jeopardy, but there is great joy in serving Jesus.

Two Generations

"The book of the generations of Adam ...
The book of the generation of Jesus Christ."
Genesis 5:1; Matthew 1:1

There is a noticeable contrast between the early chapters of Genesis and the first verse of the New Testament. Genesis 5:1 draws our attention to the generations of Adam whereas the New Testament opens with the generation of Jesus Christ. This contrast reveals that there are two families on the earth: the family of Adam and the family of Jesus Christ.

Proceeding through Genesis 5 is comparable to travelling through Death Valley. Like the tolling of a funeral bell, one phrase repeatedly occurs eight times in the chapter: "and he died ... and he died ... and he died ... and he died ... and he died." These repeated phrases remind us of the *brevity of life, the certainty of death* and *the nearness of the great eternity*.

Right to the end of the Old Testament the consequence of Adam's disobedience overshadows and blights the generations that followed him in a perpetual march to death. Consistent with this morbid legacy it is worth noting that the last word of the Old Testament is "curse".

Opening the first page of the New Testament is like opening a window and letting a breeze of fresh air pass through a gloomy room. Death and sin flowed from Adam, but Jesus Christ came that we might have life in abundance. He came to give His life that we might have life through Him.

Paul emphasized this contrast between being *"in Adam"* and being *"in Christ"*: "For as in Adam all die, even so in Christ shall all be made alive" (1 Corinthians 15:22). Death came through Adam, but life came through Jesus Christ.

Entrance into both families is by birth--into the family of Adam by physical birth and into the family of Jesus Christ through the new spiritual birth. By physical birth, we are members of the human family, but by a new birth, we are members of God's heavenly family.

The monotonous toll of death in Genesis 5 suddenly stops when it comes to Enoch, for he did not see death, God took him home to heaven.

Lord, abide with me until I abide with Thee.

Lifting Jesus Up

*"And as Moses lifted up the serpent in the wilderness,
even so must the Son of man be lifted up: That whosoever believeth
in Him should not perish, but have eternal life."*
John 3:14, 15

The Coalmen's Testimony Band was composed of Christians who were as zealous for the Lord at work as they were at their meetings. Billy Stewart, a brother of Pop Stewart, delivered coal all over Belfast, first by horse-drawn carts and later by a lorry. He seldom missed an opportunity to witness for his Lord. One day while delivering coal on Belfast's Antrim Road he became aware that the family to which he was delivering coal was Jewish. As he tramped back and forward from his lorry to empty the sacks of black coal into the "coalhole" under the stairs, he not only counted the number of bags, he also prayed that the Lord would give him an opportunity to witness of the Saviour to this gentleman. After emptying the last bag, Billy began to write an invoice for the coal.

No obvious opportunity had arisen for Billy to speak about Christ, so he made his own opening. Deliberately turning to the unsuspecting Jew, Billy said, "Sir, I promised my Saviour that I would speak a word of testimony for Him wherever I went, and I would like to tell you about Jesus. Do you remember when you fellas were going through the desert and snakes came out from every place to bite you?"

The gentleman incorrectly assumed that Billy was referring to an incident during the recent World War II when Rommel was locked in battle with Montgomery in the North African desert. Billy continued unabashed, "There was no healing for you Jews until Moses made a serpent of bronze and lifted it up to the people and whoever looked at that bronze serpent was saved. Jesus said that just as Moses lifted up the serpent for the salvation of the sick and dying, He also was lifted up on the cross to be our Saviour, and now He is able to save Jews and Gentiles." The stunned man could hardly answer a word.

This uplifted Lord Jesus Christ is still able to save.

Master And Lord

*"A certain Jew named Apollos... an eloquent man,
and mighty in the Scriptures... being fervent in spirit,
he spake and taught diligently the things of the Lord."*
Acts 18:24, 25

Apollos, the preacher, was highly respected by his peers, but he humbly sat at the feet of two tentmakers who taught him the Scriptures. Misguided Corinthians mistakenly became infatuated with his eloquence, but he refused their plaudits by indicating that his work and words were primarily given to lead people to Christ.

John George Govan, the founder of the Faith Mission in 1886, truly was a man highly respected by his colleagues and greatly used by the Lord. One of the early Pilgrims wrote of "the Chief," as he was affectionately referred to by his Mission colleagues:

"Mr. Govan had great natural gifts, and great grace was upon him. I can recall him in those days. He read a passage slowly, thoughtfully – almost hesitatingly, you would say, he would begin to speak slowly with the book open. Then, as he kindled to his subject, he would close the book, and soon the words and ideas of his address would be like a rushing torrent of eloquence, which carried all before it and bowed the hearts and heads of his audience like corn before the wind. Like Apollos, *'he was an eloquent man, and mighty in the Scriptures.'*

And what power and scorn he had for all that was false and hypocritical, and what dramatic power of description! One address I will never forget. I think the text was, 'Behold the Man.' After a moving description of Christ's sufferings - Gethsemane, the sleepless night, the mock trials, the scourging, the purple robe in mockery, the crown of thorns, the tired face smeared with blood, and the spitting of the cruel Roman soldiers, he paused for quite a while and then said quietly – 'My Master!'

If I had not crowned Him King and Lord of my life before, I would have certainly done it then. How anyone who was present could have refrained from doing so, I do not know. 'My Master!' that was the secret of his life."

King of my life I crown Him now.

You Can Trust God

"Commit thy way unto the Lord; trust also in Him; and He shall bring it to pass."
Psalm 37:5

With an open Bible in hand, members of Bible Study Fellowship groups meet weekly in several locations in Northern Ireland. Each year they study a different book or section of the Bible chapter by chapter and verse by verse. The aim is to give people a better understanding of the Scriptures and a personal and deeper relationship with the Lord.

The Bible Study Fellowship had its beginnings through English missionary, Audrey Johnson. Miss Johnson had served God in China until she and other missionaries were forced to leave the land they loved in 1950 when Mao Tse-Tung's Communist forces overran the country. Audrey loved China deeply, and her heart was torn when she moved to the United States. In 1958 five ladies asked her to teach a Bible study. This is what she said, "My heart fell! What had I come to? In China, there are millions who have not even heard His name. Am I to give more to those who already have so much?"

Reluctantly Miss Johnson promised to pray about leading the study. She did say "yes" but told them she would not spoon-feed them from the Scriptures. She prepared her lessons with questions to help the ladies dig deeper into God's Word for themselves. That small group eventually became the Bible Study Fellowship, which has grown to over 1,000 classes with more than 200,000 members in more than thirty-eight nations on five continents.

Miss Johnson could never have foreseen that when her plans were thwarted, and her heart was torn because of a closed door God had greater plans for her. Our dashed hopes are often God's way of introducing us to greater avenues of service for Him.

When we choose to trust our Lord, He gives us reason to trust Him more and more for every step. Even though we may come up against disappointments, we soon learn that His way is always best, even when we may not understand it.

When we trust in God, He promises to direct our paths.

Worshipping Faith

*"Take now thy son, thine only son Isaac, whom thou lovest,
and get thee into the land of Moriah; and offer him there
for a burnt offering upon one of the mountains..."*
Genesis 22:2

In Genesis 22 we have God's seventh and last appearance to Abraham. After this trial of faith, there was nothing more costly that God could ask Abraham to do. This is the supreme test of Abraham's love, faith and hope.

The particular time is indicative. "And it came to pass after these things, that God did test Abraham..." Abraham's story reveals his growth in grace. In Genesis 12 he took his first steps in learning to *walk by faith.* Later he entered into conflict against the heathen kings and had to *war by faith.* Patience was difficult when he had to *wait by faith* for the fulfillment of God's promise. His prayers and intercession for Lot's family involved his important *work of faith.* Here we meet Abraham on a mountaintop where he finally had to learn to *worship God by faith.*

This painful test was incisive. "Take now thy son, thine only son Isaac, whom thou lovest, and ... offer him ... for a burnt offering." There are times when God prompts us to let go of some dear and precious things. Full surrender to Him is vital. The hymn says:

> Our souls are held by what we hold
> Slaves still are slaves in chains of gold
> To whatsoever we may cling
> We make it a soul-chaining thing.

Here is a test of Abraham's *love.* This is the first time love is mentioned in the Bible. Although Isaac was the son of his love, by obeying God, Abraham displayed his love and allegiance to God.

Here is a test of Abraham's *faith.* Isaac was the son of God's promise. To sacrifice him was a display of Abraham's confidence.

Here is a test of Abraham's *hope.* Isaac was the embodiment of Abraham's hope, for God's promises would be fulfilled in him. This was a display of Abraham's obedience.

Only by full surrender to God can we enjoy the fullness of His blessing.

Living for Jesus

"Grace be unto you … we give thanks to God always …
remembering without ceasing your work of faith, and labour of love,
and patience of hope in our Lord Jesus Christ…"
1 Thessalonians 1:1-3

Our missionary colleague James Gunning was one of the most selfless Christians I have ever known. Perhaps that selflessness was demonstrated in a very simple incident. While travelling on an old river steamer making its way up the River Purus, James sat on his hammock chatting to a few other passengers whose hammocks were slung alongside his.

Just as James rose from the hammock to move towards the front of the boat his rubber flip-flop caught on the uneven deck and fell into the muddy river. James reacted immediately, not to dive in after the lost footwear, he removed his other flip-flop and threw it into the churned up waters quipping, "One flip-flop is of no use for anyone. If someone finds one flip flop I hope they find the other and that will give them a pair."

Four words from Thessalonians 1 sum up James Gunning's exemplary life; *grace, faith, love* and *hope*.

James was saved by grace. During special meetings in Newtownards in 1932, he recognised he was a lost sinner who needed to be saved and called upon God for mercy.

James lived by faith. His was a life of faith. James' namesake in the New Testament said that faith without works is dead. James had a faith that not only worked but also enabled him to walk with God.

James served in love. Christ-likeness is not measured by the words we speak or even the labels we wear. True love is expressed in how we serve our Lord. The Saviour set the example; *"Even as the Son of man came not to be ministered unto, but to minister, and to give his life a ransom for many."* James's life was one of sacrificial service.

James died in the blessed hope of the Gospel. This living and lasting hope in Christ wipes away our tears, helps us sing in our sadness and clears our vision to eagerly look for our soon-coming Saviour.

Those who live for Jesus look for His coming.

Saved to Serve

"Come with me, and see my zeal for the Lord."
2 Kings 10:16

Sammy Spence was undoubtedly a unique character. He often made the Saturday night congregation roar with laughter when he gave out the prayer requests. Quite innocently Sammy announced, "Prayer is requested for a brother up the country who has a very severe pain in his leg, and he takes it on and off every day." Another request went; "We need to pray for these young people who are passing through the walls of the Bible Colleges." It sounded like a very painful experience for the young people.

When no musician was available, Sammy used to call out, "We've no piano tonight, so we'll just fut it." With that Sammy burst into song and kept the timing of the music by loudly stamping his foot on the platform as the people heartily sang.

Although Sammy was a small man, he had a big heart and never forgot what the Lord had done for him. He often provided meals and clothing for down-and-outs on the street, visited known criminals at the local jail and led many of them to Christ. Each evening Sammy scanned the classified columns of the local newspapers and picked up bargains to pass on to the poor and needy.

The local auctioneers knew Sammy who always had a keen eye for a bargain. On one occasion, he spied a single-decker bus that would be suitable for the Coalmen's Testimony Band. He alerted other dealers not to dare to bid for it. On the sale day there were no opposing bids, so Sammy drove away in his newly acquired bargain, secured at a ridiculously low price.

Sammy knew most of the long-term prisoners, and when they were released, they came to the Coalmen's Mission looking for their former inmate and friend. He even bought several unwanted grave plots and reserved them for prisoners who died in jail or for the poor who died without next of kin to bury them. On several occasions, only Sammy, the Governor of the prison and the undertaker stood around a graveside to bury the remains of long-term and forgotten prisoners who had died in jail.

Sermons should be seen as well as heard.

Root And Fruit

"Those that be planted in the house of the Lord shall flourish in the courts of our God. They shall still bring forth fruit in old age..."
Psalm 92:13, 14

Early in the ministry of John George Govan, founder of The Faith Mission (FM), God gave him a promise: *"I will be as the dew unto Israel: he shall grow as the lily, and cast forth his roots as Lebanon. His branches shall spread..."* (Hosea 14:5, 6). The young Scotsman, whose life God had touched, could not have known how much his ministry would grow through the work of The Faith Mission or how far its branches would spread or how much fruit it would bear for God's everlasting Kingdom. God also taught His servant how deep those roots must go for he and the Mission to be able to withstand the numerous storms that would inevitably rage against it.

Within a few decades, those fruitful branches not only spread their reach all over Scotland and its islands, but they also extended across the Irish Sea. Devoted FM Pilgrims zealously preached in churches, mission halls, community halls and other public venues with a passionate endeavor to lead souls to Jesus Christ. In Scotland and in the Emerald Isle, their labours were not easy and at times were greatly opposed, but God mightily used them in the salvation of the lost, the blessing and sanctifying of His people and to establish Prayer Unions all over the land.

John George Govan said, "If the FM ceases to be a soul-saving agency, it doesn't deserve to exist." He later said, "There is a right sense in which we can become all things to all men, without sacrificing principle. We seek to keep clear of controversy about nonessentials, for it is a great mistake to treat nonessentials as if they were principles. Our chief business down here is to get souls saved, and we are willing to lay aside our own ideas about minor things in order to join in this. Arguments do little good, and up in heaven we shall not bother about those non-essentials."

One hundred and thirty years later the FM is still bearing fruit.

Help Arrives

"Come over into Macedonia, and help us."
Acts 16:9

James and Dorrie Gunning turned their backs on the comforts of home and the security of their jobs to step out in faith to serve God in far-off Brazil. After arriving in Manaus, 1,000 miles up the Amazon, they still had to travel another 1,500 miles farther up river to join Mollie Harvey in Sena Madureira. They wrote of that journey not long after arriving in Sena:

We were told on leaving Manaus that it would take thirty days for the boat to reach Sena ... Instead, it was forty-five days before we arrived at our destination, largely due to the river level having fallen rapidly.

People on board were very kind and did everything to make our journey as comfortable as possible even though conditions were far from ideal. Fifty passengers shared one bathroom and toilet. The captain even brought tea on the journey for his "English passengers."

Although we could not speak Portuguese, we were able to witness in a small way for our Lord. A young lady saw us trying to read our Portuguese Bible, so she offered to read a chapter each day in order to help us. This attracted the attention of many other passengers who listened to the reading of God's Word.

We spent two days in Lábrea and have been greatly burdened about this little place ever since. From the Boca do Acre to Sena was the worst part of the journey. We had to change into a smaller boat that had very few comforts and fewer conveniences. Notwithstanding all this, we had perfect peace in our hearts.

We shall never forget Sunday, 19th June when our boat drew near to Sena and we could see dear Mollie in the distance and then hear her shouting "Hallelujah." As soon as the plank was put in place we were off immediately and what a reunion we had. Many of the believers came down to the riverside and gave us a great welcome. Words fail us at this moment to describe our meeting.

Over the next fifty years this dedicated couple led hundreds to Christ.

Hallelujah, the messengers of grace have arrived.

A Miracle of Grace

"But I obtained mercy."
1 Timothy 1:13

I wrote a book for Rev. Thomas Martin in which he related the following:
Early one Monday morning I was startled by the roar of Police Land Rovers outside our house. It sounded as though an army had set siege around our home. I was terrified. My blood ran cold as I lay motionless and paralyzed with fear.

Suddenly there was an abrupt hammering at our front door. I heard dad struggling down the stairs shouting, "All right! All right! I'm coming." He was overwhelmed by a barrage of armed policemen. "Does Thomas Martin live here?" an officer shouted.

"Yes, he does," dad replied. "What do you want him for?" The leading policeman shoved dad to one side and mounted the stairs. They forcefully pushed open my bedroom door. "Are you Thomas Martin?" he gruffly asked.

"I am," I answered quietly.

"Thomas Martin, I am arresting you under the Prevention of Terrorism Act."

During the next few days, I was interrogated before being remanded in Belfast's Crumlin Road Prison. I was charged with possession of illegal weapons and membership of a proscribed organization. When I signed up to 'defend our wee country' I did not expect to end up behind bars.

I was assigned the Loyalist Wing of the Maze Prison where I met many fellow inmates who were as rebellious as I was. I also noticed a small group of prisoners who were different. They were regarded as loyalists but were not disorderly. When I inquired about them, I was told they were Christians. Since coming into the Maze, each one of them had been converted.

That initial contact with these Christians was the beginning of a long six-month process in which I began to read the Bible and attend their Bible studies. One night, lying on my cell bunk I closed my eyes and prayed silently, but sincerely, "Lord Jesus, I am a sinner. You know I am a sinner. I believe that You died for me on Calvary's cross to put away my sin. Please come into my heart and save me now. In Jesus name, I pray, Amen. Thank God He did.

Thomas Martin is now a preacher of the Gospel.

Grace indeed.

Come and Help Us

"Truly, the harvest is plenteous, but the labourers are few."
Matthew 9:37

Boca do Acre is located at the confluence of the Rivers Purus and Acre. The low-lying land is surrounded by swamps that flood the town each rainy season. Large river vessels from the coast, 2,500 miles and more than a month's journey away, ply these rivers transporting tons of rubber latex and Brazil nuts.

The lively trade attracted people from all walks of life. Travelling merchants and crews combined to corrupt the town with all the vices associated with loose and licentious living. As a result, Boca do Acre became a byword for gambling, drunkenness, violence and immorality.

One lady in Boca do Acre, Dona Nené, had a heavy heart because of the worsening moral climate and earnestly prayed that God would send someone to preach the Gospel to her people. Although a believer for many years, she did not possess a Bible. She had a hymnbook page that she greatly treasured, and when any friend died, Dona Nené went to the house and read to the family from that page.

Meanwhile, two days journey away, James Gunning shared with his missionary colleagues how he sensed God was speaking to him to branch out to another needy area. He and his wife, Dorrie, were waiting for God's time and His direction.

Just then a government official visited the Gunnings and showed great interest in the Gospel. He encouraged James to think of going to his town, Boca do Acre, two days down river. Later, James received a letter from this friend saying he had trusted Christ and wanted the Gunnings to come soon as he had a place for them to stay. That letter convinced James that the Lord was leading them to Boca do Acre.

Local religious authorities forbade the people to receive the missionaries. Notwithstanding, one woman was determined to use her simple wooden house for a meeting. She removed all her furniture and made room for the Gospel. Six people turned up at the first meeting and Dona Nené was grateful that at last someone cared enough to come to Boca do Acre.

How many still wait for the Gospel?

Keep Going On

"Ye did run well; who did hinder you …?"
Galatians 5:7

Although slimming programmes are very popular, it is acknowledged that there is a very high turnover. Many well-intentioned-slimmers begin with great gusto and enthusiasm, but alas, too soon they succumb to tempting delicacies and consequently become drop-outs along the way.

A similar fate can happen to runners. I have never run a marathon, but I am reliably informed that the most difficult stretch of that gruelling race is the "middle mile." The exhausting race seems to take its toll on many runners, and because of weakness, exhaustion or even boredom, they drop out around the middle distance.

It seems that is what Paul has in mind when he writes to the Galatian Christians, *"Ye did run well; who did hinder you"* (Galatians 5:7)? Paul speaks of their initial enthusiasm for the Gospel and God's servants when he writes, *"I bear you record, that, if it had been possible, ye would have plucked out your own eyes, and have given them to me"* (Galatians 4:15). Now they were in danger of giving up. They had lost the blessedness and joy of following Christ because of legalistic Judaisers who had seduced them by introducing *"another gospel."* This brought them into the legalistic bondage of observing days, meats and rituals, which ignored the centrality of Christ and the redeeming work of His cross. Paul took a pen in hand, and with large letters, he boldly confronted and exposed this heresy and convincingly expounded the glorious liberty of free grace through Jesus Christ.

As he drew his letter to a close he urged these Christians not to give up in following after Christ or serving Him: *"And let us not be weary in well doing: for in due season we shall reap, if we faint not"* (Galatians 6:9).

What happened to the Galatians can happen to Christians in any generation. Too often we can grow weary and even faint and become spiritual dropouts. It was for that reason the writer to the Hebrews drew believers' attention to Christ, *"Consider him that endured such contradiction of sinners against himself, lest ye be wearied and faint in your minds."*

He will never give up on you.

Known to Him

"Behold, I have graven thee upon the palms of My hands."
Isaiah 49:16

"Operation Nachshon" was the name given to the Jewish military operation to open the highway from the Mediterranean coast to Jerusalem during the 1948 War for Israel's Independence. Palestinian troops had blockaded the road preventing supply convoys from reaching the isolated and besieged population of West Jerusalem. On 31st March 1948, a sixty-vehicle Jewish convoy was ambushed and forced to turn back with the loss of many lives and vehicles. Israel's first President, David Ben-Gurion, therefore launched Operation Nachshon to break the siege of Jerusalem and open up the city. The two-week operation was successful, but 274 soldiers died in that advance.

Today a plaque stands where that old road started in memory of those brave pioneers. It reads, *"Not by might, nor by power, but by my Spirit, saith the Lord of hosts"* (Zechariah 4:6).

Nahshon was the first man to step into the Red Sea when the Hebrews escaped from slavery in Egypt and is mentioned ten times in the Scriptures. He was a descendant of Judah and a brother-in-law of Aaron. According to the New Testament genealogy of our Lord, he was also the father-in-law of Rahab.

According to Numbers he was at least twenty years old during the census in the Sinai Desert that was taken after the Exodus. He did not survive the forty-year sojourn in the wilderness or enter the Promised Land.

At God's command Nahshon was appointed by Moses to be prince and military commander of the Tribe of Judah, and although his tribe was fourth in the order of the Patriarchs, at the dedication of the Tabernacle he was the first to bring his dedicatory offering.

Nahshon was a direct ancestor of David, exactly halfway between Judah and King David. He is also mentioned in the New Testament genealogy of our Lord Jesus, the Saviour and Messiah.

Israel honoured Nahshon in their early and pivotal battle in 1948, but to be included in the lineage of our Lord's ancestry was a far greater honour. The same Lord Jesus who chose His ancestors has graven your name on the palms of His hands.

You are known to God.

Introducing Jesus

"The beginning of the Gospel of Jesus Christ, the Son of God."
Mark 1:1

There is a lot to be said for being brief. Mark most certainly majored in brevity. This is evident, not only because his is the shortest of the four gospels, but he was able to sum up in a few effective and expressive words what took the others almost a whole chapter to cover. This was evident when he introduced Christ with a conspicuous absence of any genealogy such as in Matthew and Luke.

Genealogies were important for Jews to trace the royal priestly roots. However, a servant did not need such a lineage or birth certificate. All a servant needed was a reference. His abilities and accomplishments were better credentials than his ancestors. Mark presented the credentials of Jehovah's Servant, Jesus Christ, in words that brim with meaning: "The beginning of the Gospel of Jesus Christ, the Son of God."

This was not the beginning of the Lord Jesus. John stated, "In the beginning was the Word." This goes back to the dateless beginning in eternity and before the inception of time. Christ is the Eternal Son of God.

"Gospel" was a familiar term in Roman times. When a ruler began his reign or a ruler's son was born, the announcement was called "gospel" - good news. The Gospel of Jesus Christ is the news that God loves sinners and that Jesus paid their debt on the cross. That really is good news.

Mark presents the credentials of our Saviour, *"Jesus Christ, the Son of God."*

"Jesus" denotes His identity. Jesus was a historical person, and Mark portrays the unfolding drama of His life, climaxing with His death on the cross and resurrection from the dead.

"Christ" signifies His authority. "Christ" means "the anointed One." Priests, prophets and kings were anointed on inauguration to their office. Jesus was "the Anointed One Whom God had promised. He was a Priest like Melchisedec, a Prophet like Moses and a King like David.

"Son of God" indicates His divinity. Mark climaxes Christ's credentials by declaring that He is the Son of God--God manifest in the flesh.

Begin each day with Jesus Christ.

Be Aware

"Ye also helping together by prayer for us."
2 Corinthians 1:11

It is a well-known fact that many missionaries do not survive more than one term on their field of service. This may be for a multitude of reasons: family responsibilities, ill health, lack of support or failure to adapt to conditions and culture. We should not be surprised at this; nor should such Christian workers be discouraged. It happened to a well-known New Testament character – John Mark.

Perhaps it was because of the influence of his uncle Barnabas that Mark was able to accompany Paul and Barnabas on Paul's first missionary journey. He was commended to this pioneer missionary enterprise knowing that it called for sacrificial service. Sadly, Mark did not stick the pace and rigours of the work at that stage. There were several factors that possibly contributed to Mark's early departure from the work.

Illness. Life in a foreign climate can be difficult. The crossings of choppy and pitching seas may have left Mark seasick. Furthermore, it was known that the coastal area of Perga was rife with malaria and other diseases to which the young man may have been exposed.

Homesickness. This can be a common experience. Perhaps John Mark thought of his widowed mother at home and longed for the family and comforts he had left behind in Jerusalem.

Incompatibility. Living and working in close proximity to other people often takes its toll. Some people just cannot get along with their colleagues. This can happen to even the most gifted Christian workers. Maybe Mark found Paul's regime too strict and arduous.

Insecurity. The "life of faith" may seem too insecure for some workers. Most mission agencies run on a slim budget. Mark might have wrestled with thoughts of an uncertain future since he had always been used to security.

Prejudice. Those who try to impose their own prejudices on other cultures without Biblical foundations often don't stay long. Some suggest that Mark's inflexibility may have resulted in not wanting to work in Gentile cities.

We are not told why Mark returned home, but God still had a future for him. That is why we have Mark's Gospel.

Your prayers help your missionary friends.

26th January

Saved

"Believe on the Lord Jesus Christ and thou shalt be saved."
Acts 16:31

There has been nothing more thrilling in our lives than pioneer evangelism: having the privilege of presenting the glorious message of the Gospel to people who have never heard it before. Often those meetings were conducted in the most primitive of conditions, but notwithstanding the difference in culture, climate, language or race, the need of the human heart is still the same--without Christ, sinners are lost.

This privilege of presenting the Gospel in such circumstances is also accompanied by a great challenge and responsibility. This may be the first time for these people to hear the Gospel, but it could also be the last time. Therefore, it is incumbent on the missionary to present the Gospel in such simplicity so the people can understand it and yet with such impact that they will never forget the good news of God's love in Christ.

There are many wonderful Bible texts that we have sown into the hearts of countless numbers of people, but there is one word that sums up the message of the Gospel, a word that is at the heart of the Gospel but is sometimes misunderstood or misrepresented. "Saved," that's the word.

The necessity – of every person to be saved. We all need to be saved, for all have sinned and come short of the glory of God. Like lost sheep, we have all gone astray.

The inadequacy - no person can save themselves. Paul wrote, "Not by works of righteousness which we have done but according to His mercy, He saved us." There is no church we can join, no deed we can do, no ritual we can observe or money we can pay that will ever save us.

The possibility – it is possible to be saved because of the cross of Christ. Christ died for our sins according to the Scriptures. The Lord Jesus took our place and died for us that we might be saved.

The simplicity – the way of salvation is very clear. The Bible assures us that any sinner can be saved when they call upon the name of the Lord.

Oh, how sweet the glorious message simple faith may claim.

27th January

Hospitality

"They made Him a supper; and Martha served…"
John 12:2

Looking after the Mission headquarters in Brazil was enjoyable and at times challenging. Besides teaching at Bible Schools we always had the enjoyable task of looking after many missionaries who were passing through. That meant the kitchen was always a busy place. A plaque on the wall read: "Heavenly Father bless us and keep us all alive. There's ten of us for dinner but not enough for five."

Luke 10 provides a page on hospitality. First our Lord instructed His disciples about their conduct in homes where they would stay. Those instructions are still valid for missionary candidates: "Travel light, don't be aggressive, eat what is set before you and preach the Kingdom of God."

Jesus then told the classic story of the Good Samaritan who freely gave his time and generously provided for a stranger at his own expense.

The chapter ends with our Lord's visit to Bethany where the spotlight focused on Mary and Martha, the latter's name always synonymous with service.

Martha's home. Jesus received hospitality in many homes, but it was at Martha's home in Bethany that He more often resided. She must be commended because she shared her home with friends and served them generously.

Martha's harassment. Probably as a perfectionist Martha wanted the best meals, but during Jesus visit everything seemed to go wrong. The more she tried, the more flustered she became. Even worse, her sister Mary was sitting at Jesus' feet. It was all too much for Martha, *"Lord, dost thou not care that my sister hath left me to serve alone? Bid her therefore that she help me."*

Jesus knew all about her stress, *"Martha, Martha, you are worried and upset about many things, but only one thing is needed"*. The Saviour was teaching her about priorities; physical food is important, but spiritual nourishment is more valuable and enduring.

Martha's hope. The final glimpse of Martha is in John 12 when Martha was still in her element, serving a dinner to honour Jesus. As she served, Lazarus reclined at the table while Mary poured out her devotion to the Lord, and this time there is no protest from Martha.

A hospitable heart is a blessing.

Progress

"I Paul, the prisoner of Jesus Christ, … who am less than the least of all saints, is this grace given, that I should preach … the unsearchable riches of Christ."
Ephesians 3:1, 8.

Before his conversion Saul of Tarsus was the foremost and most notorious persecutor of the early church. After his conversion the Apostle Paul became the foremost preacher of the Saviour he had previously blasphemed, and consequently he was constantly persecuted and opposed by his former associates. He not only spent more than five years in various prisons in Asia and Europe, he was finally beheaded in Rome for his forthright and steadfast preaching of the crucified and risen Christ. During those prison years Paul's captors became his congregation as he witnessed to them of Christ and led them to the Saviour. Not only so, his prison cell became a sanctuary where he sounded praises to God in heaven, and from those cells he enriched the world with his inspired prison letters.

300 years ago John Bunyan was in a similar situation. God had called this former tinker to preach the Gospel, but the law of that day tried to make all churches conform to the orders of the Anglican Church and all preachers submit to its authority. Bunyan was not a member of the Anglican Communion and refused to desist from preaching God's Word. Consequently, he was imprisoned three times, but this did not silence the man of God. Walls, locks and keys could not stop the pen of this servant of the Lord. During his longest imprisonment, which lasted twelve and a half years, he wrote several books, including *Pilgrim's Progress*, his most famous work and a true classic. For the last three centuries, outside of the Bible, *Pilgrim's Progress* has been the most read book in the world.

Although Bunyan had little education, his works and sermons were scholarly, inspiring and widely read. On one occasion King Charles II asked John Owen, one of the greatest theologians of the church, why he appreciated so much the sermons of that unknown tinker. Without hesitation Owen replied, "Could I possess the tinker's ability for preaching, I would willingly relinquish all my learning."

God will not be silenced.

Faithful to the End

"I have fought a good fight, I have finished my course, I have kept the faith."
2 Timothy 4:7

Fred Orr was converted to Christ when he was eighteen years old. Instead of pursuing a career in sports or following his father into secular business, Fred obeyed God's call, and with his wife, Ina, sailed to Brazil in March 1954 as missionaries with Acre Gospel Mission. This talented couple stepped out in faith and seemed to have a promising future serving God in the Amazon Valley. Alas, in less than three months, their world was turned upside-down when tragedy struck. Ina was only twenty-nine years old when she fell ill of a fever while travelling on a river steamer on the river Purus. Several days later she passed into the presence of her Lord.

Although bereaved in losing his darling wife, Fred found grace to continue in the work to which God had called him. Fred remarried Zeni in 1969 and remained in Brazil until his homecall. During that time, he impacted multiple lives for God. He founded the Cruzada Amazonica, the Hebrom Evangelical Church, and the Hebrom Theological Seminary.

Fred was possessed by a passion that helped him remain faithful to his Lord until he triumphantly reached his journey's end on 29th January 2011. Zeni and their two children, Fred and Florence continue serving God in Manaus.

He fought the great fight. "*I have fought a good fight.*" The Christian life is not a picnic. Serving God involves a constant conflict against the world, the flesh, and the devil. Although he suffered and sacrificed much, Fred triumphed through Christ.

He forged a great finish. "*I have finished my course.*" Throughout those years God's servant did not grow "weary in well doing." His Bible ministry continued until his last week. He died with his boots on, sprinting toward the finish line.

He faithfully kept The Faith. "*I have kept the faith.*" To keep the faith we must give it away. Fred committed to faithful men the faith he had loved and the precious truths gleaned from God Word. He was ready when the Lord said, "Well done, thou good and faithful servant."

Fight, run and keep going on.

Majesty on the Mountain

"We ...were eyewitnesses of His majesty."
2 Peter 1:16

Many great experiences in the Bible happened on mountains. Just think of Moses. He stood before the burning bush on Mount Horeb, received the stone tablets of the Law on Mount Sinai and was buried by God on Mount Nebo. Also in the ministry of our Lord mountains seemed to be His favourite place. He preached the famous "Sermon on the Mount", He often resorted to mountains to pray, and of course, we speak of "Golgotha" as "Mount Calvary". We should not forget that it was on an exceeding high mountain that He was tempted by the devil, and yet on another high mountain, Mount Hermon or Mount Tabor, the Lord Jesus displayed the greatest manifestation of His glory and majesty.

The Mount of Transfiguration and the greatest conference of history. The Saviour's countenance and clothing shone with His inner glory. Two visitors from heaven were present: Moses who received the Law, and Elijah who was representative of God's prophets. Three Galilean fishermen were present and the Father's voice was heard. What an awesome gathering! The disciples were speechless and so overwhelmed that they fell asleep!

The Mount of Transfiguration and the greatest conversation of history. Jesus talked with Moses and Elijah about His imminent exodus - His departure. Moses led the great exodus out of Egypt, and Elijah had experienced a personal exodus from earth when he was caught up in a whirlwind into heaven. These men knew what they were talking about, for the Law and the Prophets had long pointed to the coming Messiah and His death.

The Mount of Transfiguration was a great contrast to Calvary. One was a mountain of glory, but the other was a place of grief. In one His clothing could not hide His glory, but at Calvary, clothing did not cover His shame. On one Jesus stood between two worthies of history, but at Calvary, He was crucified between two thieves of infamy. In one His brightness outshone the sun, but at Calvary the darkness hid the sun. In one the Father's voice of approval was heard, but at Calvary the Father's voice was silent.

We shall behold Him in all of His glory.

Nothing Impossible

"For with God nothing shall be impossible."
Luke 1:37

God's unchanging attributes reassure us every day. His omnipresence assures us that He is with us everywhere and at all times even as He has promised. His omniscience confirms that our heavenly Father knows everything about us; He knows our physical frame, the number of our hairs, the burdens of our heart and everything we need. His omnipotence gives us the confidence that there is nothing too hard for the Lord. He is the Almighty God, and there is nothing impossible for Him. Consider the following:

God can furnish a table in the wilderness (Psalm 78:19). During Israel's forty years in the wilderness, God sent manna from heaven and birds to sustain His people every day. Sadly, although His loving kindnesses were new every morning and His faithfulness was unfailing, it was met with ingratitude and unfaithfulness.

God can feed a multitude with lives yielded to Him (John 6:9). Thousands of people flocked to a solitary place to hear Jesus. After three days, their need for food was urgent. Our Lord graciously accepted a boy's lunch, blessed it, and fed a multitude of hungry people. That boy might have sold his lunch or shared it with someone else. He surrendered it all to Jesus who fed the hungry multitude.

God can find a way in a storm (Acts 27:26). In Acts 27 Luke gave graphic details of how he and Paul were caught in a raging northeasterly storm: *"And we being exceedingly tossed with a tempest ... lightened the ship ... And when neither sun nor stars in many days appeared, and no small tempest lay on us, all hope that we should be saved was then taken away. "* While all on board were despairing, Paul was praying. He confidently stood up in their midst, and declared, *"Be of good cheer ... I believe God ... we must be cast upon a certain island."*

Paul recognized that God was his Pilot on the storm-tossed vessel. He can see in the dark, always knows what He is doing and where we should go.

Be of good cheer; He will still your Pilot be.

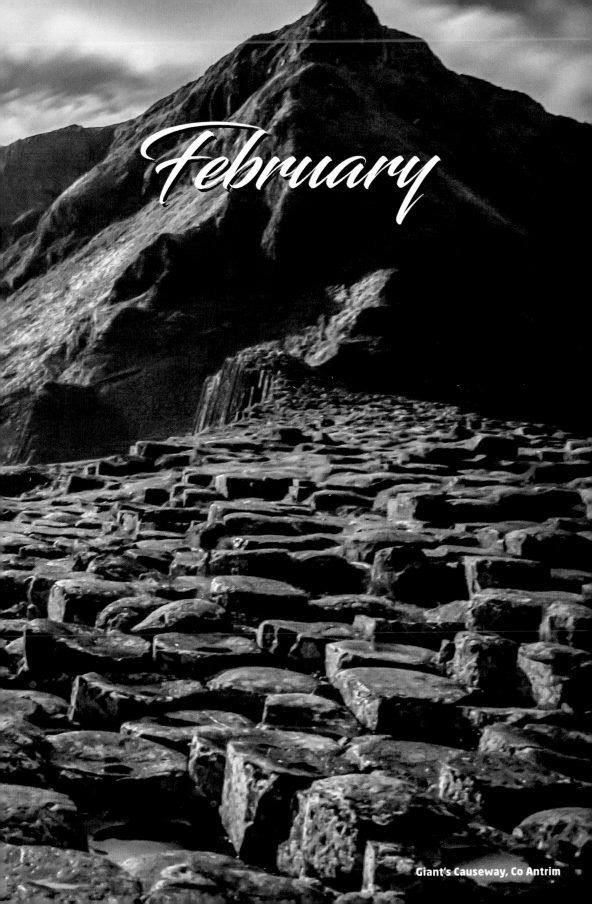

February

Giant's Causeway, Co Antrim

Feeding the Multitudes

"Give ye them to eat."
Luke 9:13

In 2015 Audrey and I led a touring group to Washington DC where we visited many of the American Capital's famous sites, most of which are located between the magnificent Capitol building at one end of the Mall to the imposing Lincoln Memorial at the other. The most memorable episode of that visit was when we arrived at the National Cathedral.

We were welcomed by the chief guide who began to give us details about this remarkable building, the sixth largest Gothic cathedral in the world. He told us that Theodore Roosevelt was president of the United States in 1907 when the Cathedral's first foundation stone was laid at Mount Albans, overlooking Washington.

Eighty-three years later, on September 29, 1990, President George Bush gave an oration to thousands who gathered to witness the official completion of the construction.

The guide began to explain about the rich stone carvings and beautiful stained-glass windows. He then asked why we had come and if there was anything we wanted to see. When we told him that we would like to see the "Saint Windows," he was taken aback, and tears began to run down his face. He said, "Few people know about these windows. Most of the guides don't even know about them. How did you hear?"

We told him that we had read the story of missionary pilot Nate Saint who had been martyred by Auca Indians in Ecuador on 8th January 1956 and that his father had made these famous Saint windows when Nate was only a boy. Also, Mr. Saint's daughter, Rachel Saint, had given her life to serving the same Indians.

When Mr. Saint directed the work on the cathedral's stained glass windows he chose scenes from the ministry of the Lord Jesus and included members of his family to feature in some of those windows. At one of the Saint Windows, we saw the image of a young lad surrendering his lunch to the Lord Jesus to feed the hungry multitude. The boy in the window was Nate Saint who gave his all to Jesus in Ecuador.

Across the window was written, *"Give ye them to eat."*

This lad surrendered his lunch to the Lord, but Nate Saint surrendered himself.

The Best Place

"Mary, which also sat at Jesus' feet, and heard His word."
Luke 10:39

Mary of Bethany is one of the best-known women to appear in the Gospels. Together with her siblings Lazarus and Martha, she lived in the village of Bethany near Jerusalem. On each occasion she is mentioned, she was found at the feet of Jesus.

Mary sat at Jesus' feet to grow. We do not know when Mary first met the Lord but clearly, she was one of His most devoted followers. It seems she never missed an opportunity to sit at the Master's feet and learn all she could about the Kingdom of God. Her choice brought criticism from her sister whose priorities were different. *"Martha,"* said Jesus, *"you are worried about many things...Mary has chosen the better part."*

Mary fell at Jesus' feet to grieve At their Bethany home the sisters were mourning the death of their beloved brother, Lazarus. To make matters worse they felt that their best Friend had let them down, for Jesus had not come to them immediately

The two days of waiting seemed endless, but at last, word came that the Lord Jesus was on His way. Typically the sisters reacted differently. Martha immediately went out to meet Him while Mary stayed at home. Martha returned saying, *"The Master is come and is calling for you."* Mary hurried to meet the Lord and fell at His feet where she found comfort.

We have no details of Mary's reaction to her brother's resurrection, but it is not difficult to imagine her joy. Not only had her beloved brother been restored, her faith had also been revived.

Mary knelt at Jesus' feet to give. The raising of Lazarus had wide repercussions. Because of Lazarus many of Mary's friends put their faith in Jesus, but the Pharisees stirred up more enmity against Christ. However, the Bethany family prepared a dinner in honour of Jesus.

While Martha served and Lazarus reclined at the table with Jesus, Mary poured out her most treasured possession on Jesus' feet, a flask of pure nard, an expensive perfume usually reserved for a marriage or a burial.

Give of your best for the Master.

3ʳᵈ February

Three Wise Men

"Who then can be saved?"
Matthew 19:25

Here is a story about an Englishman, a Scotsman and an Irishman from our missionary colleague Mark Loney.

"An Englishman e-mailed me several weeks ago asking, "Do you believe that Jesus is the only way?" I replied with an absolute "Yes" and several supporting Scriptures. Next Sunday at church he explained that he had been reading the Bible and consequently was looking for people who believed that Jesus was the only way to God. Last Sunday after church he gave his life to the Lord.

The Scotsman is a retired GP whose wife is a born-again Christian. They spend most of their winters in the Algarve and return to Scotland each summer. For many years his wife had been praying for his salvation, but he told her that though he enjoyed the messages each Sunday he just couldn't believe that the Gospel was so simple. He told his wife, "I won't believe unless God gives me a sign".

In Scotland last summer he travelled weekly to his nearest pub for a quiet read. One day a man sat nearby and asked what he was reading. This weekly meeting developed into a friendship. There was something about this man that fascinated the doctor. One day he suddenly asked this friend, "Are you a Christian?" The man replied affirmatively and then began to witness to the doctor about Jesus. The doctor was surprised he was hearing that same thing in such a remote part of Scotland as he had heard in the Algarve. Finally, the friend asked the doctor, "Why don't you accept the Lord Jesus?" To this, he replied, "I'm waiting for a sign." The friend persisted, "Do you not think I am your sign?"

Two weeks ago I had the joy of praying with the doctor who asked the Lord into his life. A few days later he and his wife were distributing Gospel tracts on the sea front.

The Irishman has lived nearby in the Algarve for twenty years. His mother was originally from Belfast. He arrived at church looking for friendship. On Sunday he prayed to give his life to the Lord Jesus.

They shall come from every nation.

Eternity in our Hearts

"He hath made everything beautiful in His time:
also he hath set the world in their heart."
3:11

God has put eternity in our hearts. It is for that reason that the instinct of heaven nags at the heart of every human being. Hindus speak about karma, the consequence of deeds in past reincarnations. Muslims have strange views of paradise, and heathen animists adapt many strange practices in preparation for the afterlife. God has put eternity in their hearts.

Only the Bible gives us a revelation of heaven in a sure word of prophecy. Not only did our Saviour speak with authority and clarity of the Father's House where He has gone to prepare a place for His children, but He also came from heaven that He might go to the cross, and He returned to heaven after the resurrection.

The Bible also provides us with witnesses who went to heaven and returned to earth. The apostle Paul was caught up to the third heaven; he was not sure if it was in the body or out of the body, but he knew he saw things of which he was not permitted to speak (2 Corinthians 12:1-4). The apostle John, at an advanced age, was also caught up into heaven and wrote of what he saw in the unfolding revelation of God's plan for this world (Revelation 4:1f).

John Lennon wrote, "Imagine there's no heaven. It's easy if you try. No hell below us, above us only sky…" Imagine? Heaven may grab the imagination, but it is not imaginary. It is not "pie-in-the-sky" or mere speculation. Heaven is for real, more real than the material things we touch and see. Christian, you are nearer heaven than you have ever been before.

The thought of heaven puts a song in our mouths. For that reason, heaven is sometimes called, Beulah land because it is the marriage place. It is also called the New Jerusalem for its capacity for people of all ages, all tribes, tongues, and nations. Heaven is called Paradise for its beauty and a Kingdom for its royalty. Heaven is also known as the Father's House, for it is our heavenly home.

You must be heaven-born to be heaven-bound.

Precious Word of God

"The law of Thy mouth is better unto me than thousands of gold and silver."
Psalm 119:72

William Hunter was only nineteen years old when he was burned at a stake in Brentwood, England, in 1555 for wanting to read the Bible. In William's days, it was illegal to own a Bible. The only Bible in Brentwood was chained to the pulpit in the parish church away from the non-clergy. William was so determined to read God's Word that he entered the church and opened the Scriptures to read for himself.

When William was caught, he was arrested and spent nine months in prison. At his trial, he was given a chance to recant and go free if he promised never to attempt to read the Bible again. This brave teenager refused the offer, even when the Bishop offered him a bribe to start his own business.

On 26th March 1555, William Hunter was burned at a stake for one crime -- refusing bribes and threats to refrain from reading the Word of God. He was the first Essex martyr of Mary Tudor's reign. There is a memorial in Brentwood to the memory of William Hunter. The inscription reads, *"William Hunter, Martyr. Committed to the flames, March 26th 1555. Christian reader, learn from his example the value and privilege of an open Bible."*

Alexander Duff was only twenty-three years old when he sailed for India in 1829. During their six-month voyage to the sub-continent, they suffered two unforgettable shipwreck experiences. The first happened off the coast of Cape Town. Their ship hit a reef and split in two. Through that night twenty-two passengers and crew clung to a portion of the ship that had precariously settled on rocks. They were all rescued early the next morning, but the ship's cargo was lost.

Looking out sadly at the reef where they had almost lost their lives, Dr. Duff saw a small package bobbing in the water. He waded out to retrieve it. It was his Bible and Psalter. These became the instruments Dr. Duff used to win the lost for Christ and establish a theological school that spread the Gospel all over India.

Treasure this precious Book.

Who is Jesus Christ?

"But whom say you that I am?"
Matthew 17:15

During our trips to Israel, we always visit Caesarea Philippi, which currently forms part of the Golan Heights. Today the location, at the foot of Mount Hermon, is known as Banias. Prior to the time of Christ, it was called Paneas, a name derived from the pagan worship that took place at a cavern out of which cold water pours and gives rise to the River Jordan. This place was out of bounds to Israel because the Canaanites worshipped Baal there, and the Greeks erected a shrine to their god, Pan. Herod Philip, son of Herod the Great, erected a marble temple in honour of the deified Emperor, Caesar Augustus. All this combined to make Caesarea Philippi a place of pagan deities. Appropriately, it was here that Jesus Christ posed two great questions, *"Whom do men say that I, the Son of man, am?" "But whom say you that I am?"*

"Who is Jesus Christ?" This is a question that was frequently asked about our Lord, a question that echoes as loudly today as it did when Jesus probed His disciples. Perhaps it is a question we do not ask often enough, nor do we take enough time to answer. There is no other person as majestic, as mysterious or as meaningful as the Saviour.

Who was Jesus Christ according to people's opinion? Some heard His preaching and teaching and concluded, as did Herod, that He was John the Baptist. Others witnessed His miracles and were sure He was Elijah. Still, others were impressed with His compassion and saw in Him the weeping prophet Jeremiah. Public polls are never a good guide to what the truth is, but truth has only one voice.

Who was Jesus Christ according to Peter's confession? We often blame Peter for saying the wrong thing. Here he spoke with courage and conviction when he openly confessed, *"Thou art the Christ, the Son of the living God."* Peter's response was not formed by public opinion. It was based on the revelation God the Father had given him, the fundamental confession of the Christian faith.

There is no one like Jesus, never was and never will be.

Our Heavenly Home

"For we know that if our earthly house of this tabernacle were dissolved,
we have a building of God, an house not made with hands,
eternal in the heavens."
2 Corinthians 5:1

While living in Canutama, we left town to travel for two days by mission launch on the Rivers Purus, Mucuim, and Içuã to leave Wycliffe missionary Arne Abrahamson at a settlement where he was working among the Juma Indians. Just as we arrived, we received a radio message informing us that Mollie Harvey had arrived in Canutama to pay us a surprise visit. Not to disappoint Mollie, Audrey and I turned around immediately and headed back down-river. It was a frightening journey through that dark and cloudy night as we negotiated the bends of the river. When dawn finally broke, we discovered we had lost our way. We had entered a large lake, and it took quite a while to find our way back to the river. Helped by the current, we continued our homeward journey. When at last, we got a glimpse of Canutama in the distance, we were relieved to know that we were nearly home.

Christians may face many twists and turns in life and feel at times they are travelling in the dark. There may be times when they feel bewildered, and they might be tempted to give up. It is then that we need to keep our eyes on the lights of our heavenly Home.
.

Heaven is it not the figment of someone's imagination or created as a forlorn hope of some troubled soul. Our knowledge and assurance of heaven are given by the revelation from God in His Word, the Bible. The Scriptures do not tell us everything about heaven. Our finite minds could never understand it all. However, the Bible tells us all we need to know about heaven.

Multiplied millions of Christians have rested their entire future on the Saviour's promises about the Father's house. The Apostle Paul wrote, "I am in a strait betwixt two, having a desire to depart, and to be with Christ; which is far better" (Philippians 1:21, 23).

Keep your eyes on the Light of that city so bright.

Intelligence and Confidence

"We are not ignorant of his devices."
2 Corinthians 2:11

One of the most engaging books I have read is *Our Man in Damascus,* the story of an Israeli spy in Syria who was eventually caught and publicly hanged in Damascus. Although a Jew, Ari Cohen was an Iraqi by birth, and, among other languages, he spoke Arabic and Spanish fluently. After a purge of Jews in Iraq, he and his family were repatriated to Israel where he was recruited by the Mossad. At the request of the Israeli intelligence agency, Ari went to live for a while in Argentina where he posed as an affluent businessman. In his line of business, he imported large amounts of goods from Syria and as a result was invited to visit Damascus.

Through his contacts, he became very friendly with top members of the Syrian government and was even taken on a tour of the military bases of the Golan Heights when they were still in Syrian hands. He indicated to the head of the Syrian army that he would like to donate a gift of eucalyptus trees from Argentina to be planted at army bases all over the Golan Heights providing shade for the soldiers in this region, which was greatly exposed to the hot sun. The offer was welcomed as a brilliant idea and a magnanimous gesture.

During the Six Day War, the clandestine information sent by Ari Cohen enabled the pilots of Israeli fighter jets to identify the enemy's bases on the Golan Heights and quickly destroy them. His bravery and sacrifice paid off with Israel's rapid victory over Syria.

While the accuracy of intelligence may be decisive in the conflict and conquest of an enemy, ignorance of that enemy can also prove perilous and costly. It was exactly this that Paul had in mind when he wrote that he was not ignorant of the devil's devices. Paul's way of confronting those devices was to be confident in Christ's glorious victory at Calvary. This confidence was evident when he followed with, "Now thanks be unto God, which always causeth us to triumph in Christ" (2 Corinthians 2:14).

Thank God for the sweet sound and savour of victory through Christ.

Crowns

"Henceforth there is laid up for me a crown of righteousness, which the Lord, the righteous judge, shall give me at that day: and not to me only, but unto all them also that love His appearing."
2 Timothy 4:8

Repeatedly in his epistles, the Apostle Paul made reference to athletics and competitions. He not only likened the Christian life to a race that must be run to finish the course, but he also alluded to the crowns that follow victory. Crowns in the Greek world were not regal headpieces studded with diamonds and precious stones. They were simple wreaths made from palm or olive leaves, woven together and placed upon the victor's head as a prize for winning a race or after the conquest of war.

Paul contemplated receiving a victor's crown from the Saviour's hand at the end of his earthly course.

A crown of rejoicing for those who reach the lost. "For what is our hope, or joy, or crown of rejoicing? Are not even ye in the presence of our Lord Jesus Christ at his coming? For ye are our glory and joy" (1 Thessalonians 2:19).

A crown of life for those who resist temptation. "Blessed is the man that endureth temptation: for when he is tried, he shall receive the crown of life, which the Lord hath promised to them that love Him" (James 1:12).

A crown of glory for those responsible for the flock of God. "And when the chief Shepherd shall appear, ye shall receive a crown of glory that fadeth not away" (1 Peter 5:4).

A crown of righteousness for those who rally to the fight. "Henceforth there is laid up for me a crown of righteousness, which the Lord, the righteous judge, shall give me at that day: and not to me only, but unto all them also that love His appearing" (2 Timothy 4:7,8).

On that day, victorious saints will join the four-and-twenty elders who fall down before Him to *"cast their crowns before the throne"* (Revelation 4:10).

Shall I wear a golden crown when I get home?

Be in Time

"Boast not thyself of tomorrow;
for thou knowest not what a day may bring forth."
Proverbs 27:1

In Luke's story of the conversion of Zacheaus everything happened in a hurry; Zacheaus came running to Jesus; the Saviour said to him, "Make haste and come down." To this Luke said that Zacheaus made haste and came down from the tree. Salvation is an urgent matter.

At a Saturday evening open-air meeting in Boca do Acre I got speaking to a man who showed interest in accepting Christ. When I pressed upon him to trust the Saviour that night he said he would go to church the next day and become a Christian. When pressed further he admitted that he could not become a Christian that night as he had already arranged for a *festa* that night, the hall was booked, the people invited and the liquor was bought. He left assuring me that he would be at church the following morning.

Later that night there was a fracas in which our friend became involved in a fight with an underage youth, João de Deus, who tried to gate-crash the *festa*. Our friend was arrested, but the young man escaped. At daybreak the next morning, two policemen took the man from his rough cell, frog-marched him up the dusty street, down the riverbank and into a canoe. They were on their way to identify João who lived at the edge of the forest across the river. João's two brothers saw the policemen approaching and shouted to warn him that the police were coming to arrest him. Instead of fleeing into the forest, João grabbed his rifle, cocked it to take careful aim from the window of his mother's home. One solitary bullet whistled through the air before smashing into the prisoner's temple; the man who said, "I'll get saved tomorrow." He immediately fell into the River Acre. His body was never recovered.

There was a solemn air at the Sunday meetings when news broke that the man who had intended to trust the Lord that day had already passed into eternity, the victim of a cold-blooded murder.

Procrastination is always a thief of time and of souls.

A Missionary Postcard

"Because that for His name's sake they went forth."
3 John 7

Dorrie Gunning was such a prolific letter writer that some people still treasure her warm-hearted and chatty letters. With the advance and proliferation of modern communications, perhaps we have lost the art of those treasured letters.

Missionary letters are not a modern phenomenon. All the New Testament epistles were written by missionaries. All the churches to which the letters were addressed were missionary-founded churches. That said, I think we could say that Philemon, 2nd and 3rd John and even Jude are more like Bible postcards.

3rd John is largely taken up with three church members, Gauis, a commendable Christian who was hospitable in the work, Diotrephies, a contentious Christian who hindered God's work, and Demetrius, a consistent Christian who was a great helper in God's work.

This Bible postcard also gives us a backdrop to the great missionary movement of that time:

Advance of the missionary movement - "They went forth…" The mathematics of the early church is very interesting. In Acts 2 and 4 we read how the Lord *added to the church daily* those who were saved. In Acts 6 and thereafter we read how *"the church was multiplied."* The expanding and advancing church is seen in Paul's words of Colossians 1:23 when *"every creature under heaven had heard the gospel."*

Anonymity of the missionary material - "They went forth…" We don't know who they were or how many there were nor even where they went. We do know they went forward. Thank God for all those in the ranks of the great missionary movement who have given their lives for the advancement of God's Kingdom. Many never hit the headlines on earth, but all of them are known to God in heaven. He has no anonymous servants.

Allegiance to missionary motives - "For His name's sake…" We can have no greater motive than the Lordship of Jesus Christ and no greater constraint than the love of our Saviour.

Appeal for missionary means - "Fellowhelpers…" Gaius opened up his home; some opened their purses, and all engaged in praying.

Be sure to be going forth with the Gospel.

All The Way to Heaven

"Blessed are the dead which die in the Lord from henceforth:
Yea, saith the Spirit, that they may rest from their labours;
and their works do follow them."
Revelation 14:13

I was invited to speak at a Missionary Convention for the *Paul of Tarsus Mission* in Boa Vista, Roraima, Brazil. Besides working all over the Amazon region, these Brazilian missionaries are reaching into nearby southern Venezuela. Before the first meeting began, Abraão approached me. "Pastor Victor, do you have any contact with Senhor Paulo Mayner?" I told him that Paul was a deacon in a Baptist church, and I had conducted his wife's, Reta's, funeral six years previously. To this, he ventured, "I remember Paulo when he lived in Canutama more than forty years ago, for he led me to the Lord there when I was ten-years-old." I thought this was wonderful, for Paul did not know that, when he led this little boy to the Lord years previously, he would eventually become a missionary. Furthermore, Reta had gone to be with the Lord without knowing the outcome of that conversion.

After the meeting, another member of the Mission spoke with me. Like Abraão earlier, he asked about Paul Mayner. When I assured him that I knew Paul, he said, "Paul led me to the Lord in Canutama when I was only five years old." I was amazed to learn of another of Paul's converts who was serving the Lord. Even more so since Paul and Reta's service in Brazil was cut short due to family illness.

Next morning the President of the Mission, Senhor Ranulfo, asked me if I knew Paul Mayner. He went on to tell me that he had been an altar boy, but Paul had led him and his mother to faith in Christ in Canutama. Later that day yet another missionary, Raimundo, who works among an Indian tribe, asked me about Paul. He was another convert who Paul had led to Christ.

What Paul and Reta had sown by faith decades earlier is not only producing a harvest on earth, but Reta's works follow her to heaven.

So live to store up treasure in heaven.

Soles for Souls

"If I then, your Lord and Master, have washed your feet;
ye also ought to wash one another's feet."
John 13:14

While Bill Woods was studying medicine in Manaus, Brazil, Pastor Francisco Poderoso accompanied him to a seminar where several American nurses demonstrated a newly developed shoe to prevent foot ulcers in leprosy patients. This Plastisol-lining insole would give protection to their mutilated and deformed feet. By distributing the pressure of the foot, it relieved the most vulnerable pressure points, which often became gruesome ulcers. These plantar ulcers were caused by lack of sensation when the sufferer could not discern they were stepping on thorns, glass or nails. These resultant injuries soon became infected ulcers. A custom-made shoe with a Plastisol lining offered greater protection for the damaged feet for each patient.

Bill procured funds from the sale of a house he was building to send Francisco to Carville in the United States to learn the technique of making these orthopaedic shoes. In the meantime, God provided premises at a Baptist Church for consultations and the necessary machinery to make the shoes.

When Francisco returned from Carville, he immediately went to work. The front part of the small building was a waiting room with educational posters on the walls enlightening the patients about the advantages of the treatment. Gospel leaflets were also available, and Bible texts were posted on the walls. An evangelist was often present to offer Gospel literature to the patients.

Next to the waiting room was a small area for consultations where the patient's feet were washed in disinfectant. Bill then examined the feet, and an impression was taken of each foot on the heated Plastisol mould. Once the impression was finished, Francisco made the leather upper for the boot or shoe. Further appointments were made for the patient to return for fitting and periodic inspection.

The results were dramatic. People who had been confined to their homes and not able to walk because of chronic ulcerated feet were soon able to walk, and they often returned to their employment. Better still, the workshop became a place where these patients heard the Gospel, and many received Christ as Saviour.

Stooping to wash feet is Christ-like.

14th February

Twists

"These are parts of his ways: but ... who can understand?"
Proverbs 26:14

When Keith and Karen Lindsay went to Accrington, Lancashire for Faith Mission meetings they had hospitality with Edna, a very godly lady. Edna's parents were well known locally for their home-made-pie industry, but they had passed away, and she was left alone, a senior citizen and a spinster.

Edna enjoyed Keith and Karen's visit so much that she quickly developed a close bond with them. She had already been praying for Karen and other Faith Mission Bible College students. To meet Karen gave her added pleasure. In subsequent visits, Edna became dependent on Keith and Karen's counsel and company and confided much in them.

One day not long after she had legalised her will, leaving her house to Christian work, she shared with the Lindsays that while reading the Scriptures, she felt God had told her that she would soon be leaving her house. Because she already suffered from angina and was seventy-one years old, she concluded from her Bible reading that she was going to die soon and go to heaven. Keith and Karen listened quietly and were quite concerned for Edna lest she should become morbid and depressed.

Not long afterward, Keith got a telephone call from Edna. He was stunned when she announced that she was going to be married and asked if he would "give her away!" During a hurriedly-arranged visit, Edna explained that fifty years previously she had had a crush for the assistant pastor of her church. Alas, that did not develop into anything, but ironically, he married Edna's "best friend, " and afterward they went to serve God in South Africa.

Edna told the couple that out of the blue she received news that her former "best friend" had died. Before her death, she told her husband she wanted him to marry again and would love for him to marry Edna. In an unexpected phone call from the widower, he proposed marriage and Edna readily accepted the offer. Edna's house was donated to the Lord's work; all her belongings were distributed to her friends, and Keith "gave her away."

There are many bends on life's road.

When God Speaks

"I will hear what God the Lord will speak."
Psalm 85:8

On Easter Tuesday 1962, Mr. James Cardoo invited his son Victor to accompany his parents to the Missionary Meeting at the Faith Mission Easter Convention in Bangor. At first, he told them that he did not want to go. God had been speaking to him about being a missionary, but his audio deficiency seemed to be an obstacle blocking his way. This disappointment created some personal resentment as to how God was leading him. However, at the last minute, Victor consented to accept their invitation.

At the church, his parents chose to sit downstairs, but Victor escaped upstairs to the church's huge gallery. He found a corner where he felt he would be left alone. Due to his resentment, he had deliberately left his hearing aid at home for he was in no mood to listen to more sermons or missionary challenges.

In spite of Victor feeling sorry for himself, God broke through in his life and awakened him that afternoon. Three missionary reports passed over his head for he could not hear what was said. However, when a Church of Scotland minister, a former missionary, rose to give the closing message, his resonant voice was like a roar of thunder vibrating through the building. Victor could not avoid the message for he had no difficulty hearing this man's booming voice.

In loud and distinct tones, the former missionary preached about Jonah, the reluctant missionary prophet who ran away from what God wanted him to do. Victor not only heard every word the minister spoke, but felt that God was speaking directly to him. Like Jonah, Victor was down in the doldrums and was resisting God in his life.

At the closing appeal for people to dedicate or rededicate their lives to Christ, Victor was up like a shot. He made his way downstairs and then up the aisle to the front of the church. There he prayed, "Lord, I am willing to dedicate my whole life to You, to be whatever You want me to be and go wherever You want me to go."

Be sure to have open ears to hear God's call.

16th February

Saved

"For by grace are you saved."
Ephesians 2:8

The skirl of the bagpipes fascinated Duncan Campbell as a young man and he quickly earned the name of *the Red Piper.* Clad in kilt and sporran, bonnet and ribbons, his belt and buckles shone as he stood tall to play familiar and favourite Scottish airs while revellers danced their reels.

While he was playing at one of these concerts he was so struck with a deep sense of guilt that he withdrew even though friends tried to persuade to stay. The Holy Spirit had gripped Duncan's heart, and he could not resist. "I'm going home to get right with God," he announced.

During the three-mile walk home carrying his pipes and swords, a battle raged in his heart between Christ and the world. He turned a corner and noticed a light in the small Memorial Hall. He could hear a voice passionately praying. Cocking his ear to the keyhole, he was startled to hear his father praying for his eldest son, Duncan.

Duncan quietly slipped into the hall to sit beside his dad and listen to the Gospel message. He began to shake with fear, and, afraid he might make an embarrassing scene, Duncan picked up his bagpipes and swords and left the meeting for home.

He fell to his knees at the side of the road and pleaded with God for mercy. Finally, arriving home at two o'clock in the morning, he slowly opened the door to discover his mother on her knees by the kitchen fire. Without restraint, Duncan poured out his burdened heart to her. She showed her son the simple way of salvation and suggested that he go out to the barn and call upon God.

Duncan said, "I entered the barn, and falling on my knees among the straw prepared for the horses in the morning, I began to pray … in Gaelic! 'Lord, I know not what to do. I know not how to come, but if You'll take me as I am, I'm coming now,' and in less time than I can take to tell it I was gloriously saved kneeling in the straw."

Wonderful grace of Jesus.

Touching Jesus

"She said, If I may touch but His clothes, I shall be whole."
Mark 5:28

Dr. Bill Woods has devoted decades bringing help and healing to thousands of leprosy patients in Brazil. In the course of treatments and clinics, he often came upon other dermatological conditions for which he could find no cure. One of these was Jorge Lobo disease, a rare fungal condition, which is manifested by large unsightly cauliflower-like growths on the skin. Even if they are surgically removed, they grow again. An amazing development happened with Bill. While treating one of his leprosy patients who also suffered from Jorge Lobo disease, he discovered that the leprosy treatment reduced the growth of this fungi. Subsequently, a whole new line of investigation and treatment is being pursued to establish a cure for this horrendous condition.

A cursory read through Mark 5 has been likened to a visit to an infirmary which might rightly have been called "The House of the Incurables." Here are cases which our Saviour encountered and were beyond human help.

At first, we find a man who society could not reform, a demonized and deranged man from Gadarra. A legion of demons controlled him and he was beyond human help.

Next was the pitiful case of a lady who was terminally ill. All the conventional and perhaps unconventional medicines had been used on her, but without any lasting benefit. Not only had she spent all her money on physicians, but she was worse off than before she started.

Finally, there is a twelve-year-old girl who had suddenly died. She was probably ready to be embalmed for burial, and no one could help her grieving parents. Humanly speaking all of these cases are hopelessly impossible - impossible without Jesus Christ.

Against this backdrop of human plight stands the Saviour's divine might. With Him, there are no impossibilities. He stilled the storm in an hour of danger. He demonstrated His power and authority to confront demons, cure any disease and even conquer death itself. All were subject to His command.

There were no maladies Jesus could not match, no problem He could not solve and no soul He could not save.

The Great Physician always makes a difference.

Always Abounding

"He worketh the work of the Lord, as I also do."
1 Corinthians 15:58

Early in the twentieth century W. E. Tocher and his wife arrived on Ulster's shores from Broughty Ferry in their native bonnie Scotland. For years they traversed the length and breadth of Ulster in a horse-drawn caravan as true ambassadors for Christ preaching the Gospel in the Province's remotest areas. Mr. Tocher's Bible preaching and evangelistic zeal made a considerable impact on the evangelical life of Ulster.

Besides his powerful preaching, Tocher's wit and humour and sometimes his eccentricity made him a compelling character. Taking up residence in East Belfast he exchanged his horse-drawn caravan for a motorcycle and side-car which he aptly named "Nearly-a-car." Early in his life polio had left Mr. Tocher lame on both feet. Because of this handicap, he could not throw his leg over a saddle so the motorbike was custom made for him, and this untiring servant of God used it regularly in his continuing evangelistic efforts.

He certainly was unconventional in his evangelism, and these unorthodox ways attracted hundreds of people to hear him preach at "The Winkie," the old Willowfield Cinema on the Woodstock Road. Encouraged by the response of the Christian public to these meetings Mr. Tocher and his friends formed a new assembly, and no time was lost in erecting a new functional building in which they constituted "The Templemore Hall Christian Brethren" in June 1934.

Pastor Tocher was probably best known for his prophetic conferences in the days leading up to and during World War II. Comparing the political developments alongside his Bible, he made some bold predictions. Some of these were fulfilled in later years, while others were grossly inaccurate. Among the predictions he foretold were the independence of all nations and a European single currency before the Second Coming of the Saviour.

One Monday night of each month was devoted to questions regarding prophetic matters, and Tocher was prolific in his comprehensive answers to all queries. Often when closing some of those prophetic meetings Tocher would shout, "Jesus is coming! No surrender!"

How can we keep silent about Jesus?

19th February

Trusting God

"But she of her want did cast in all that she had, even all her living."
Mark 12:44

Everything seemed to be working out very well when Victor Cardoo applied to the Missionary Training College in Glasgow and was accepted. However, one night before leaving, God challenged him about living by faith and what it really meant to trust in the Lord. Until then, Victor had been saving every penny to make sure he had enough money for his first year at college. It seemed to be a reasonable and responsible thing to do. However, on his knees, Victor wrestled with God on this point. *Does God want me to give this money to Him? Was this not God's supply for me to go to college? Lord, what am I to do?*

He shared his thoughts about the life of faith with his dad who was fully behind Victor entering Christian service. He told his father that he had enough money to pay for the first year at college, but was wondering if it was wrong to save that money or should he be trusting God for his fees. His father answered, "Son, you'll have to learn to trust God for all your needs. Don't rely on your money. Do what you feel God would have you do. The life of faith is a life of obedience."

A few nights later God challenged Victor again: *Did you not surrender your life to Me?* Victor readily agreed with the Lord. The thought came again, *If you surrendered all to Me, did that not include your money as well as your plans?*

Before sleep would come that night, Victor accepted that he would have to give God all that he had, step out in faith and trust the Lord for everything.

Over the next few days, he cleared out his bank account and sent gifts to various missionary agencies. Although still a little anxious, Victor had the quiet assurance that this was what God wanted him to do.

That first step took Victor to Brazil where he served God faithfully for the rest of his life, trusting God moment by moment.

In God we trust.

Sowing Mustard Seed

"The kingdom of heaven is like to a grain of mustard seed…"
Matthew 13:31, 32

At the turn of the twentieth century, John Govan and his wife arrived in Ulster from his native Scotland. Like his full cousin, John George Govan, founder of The Faith Mission, John had trusted Christ early in life and shared the same concern to win the lost for the Saviour. Secular business helped to provide for his family, but John was also busy in his heavenly Father's business.

After the Govans had taken up residence on the Crumlin Road, John was struck by the spiritual needs of the surrounding community. Always a man of action, he decided to do something to reach these neighbours with the Gospel. At his own expense, he took an extended lease on two terrace houses in Vistula Street and converted them into a plainly-furnished meeting place. He called the hall, "The Mustard Seed."

If ever there was an appropriate name for a Mission Hall it was this one. John's mustard-seed faith in a great God resulted in many blessings on the community, and scores of neighbours were brought to Jesus Christ. Under John's leadership, The Mustard Seed was a refuge for fellowship and a centre for evangelism. The hall also supported missions for almost six decades.

Alex and Anna Todd regularly attended the Mustard Seed Hall. For many years they were associated with an American soul-winning organisation known as "Christians in Action." Often Alex and Anna and Marie embarked on "Faith Treks" which was an exercise of dedicated shoe leather to win the lost. Armed with an abundance of gospel literature they set off on a trek to various parts of Ireland or towns and villages in England.

Besides giving leadership to the Mustard Seed, the Todds conducted "soul winning" clinics and then sent the recruits out to engage in evangelism. Through the ministry of the Mustard Seed and many evangelistic treks, hundreds of people were converted.

A grain of mustard-seed faith can bring a great harvest.

Church Building

"I will build my church; and the gates of hell shall not prevail against it."
Matthew 16:18

The Crescent Church on Belfast's University Road has a rich spiritual heritage. The building was first opened as the Crescent Presbyterian Church on Sunday 11th September 1887 at the cost of little more than £8,000. The premises only came into the possession of the present congregation in December 1975.

Conversion and change are perhaps the most appropriate words when speaking of this fellowship. Since its beginnings in the 1870's the assembly has changed its meeting venue and name several times.

It had its beginnings in the aftermath of the 1859 Ulster Revival when the Brethren movement enjoyed rapid growth throughout the British Isles and beyond. Several Brethren evangelists from Britain visited Ulster and were instrumental in founding various assemblies. Initially, they met with several Christian families in a private home in King Street where they conducted Bible studies and celebrated the Lord's Supper. When their numbers increased they rented the Abercorn Rooms at 101 Victoria Street, Belfast.

During the first year at this new venue, the numbers rose from around fifty believers to well over 100, and it became necessary to move to the larger Victoria Room at 63 Victoria Street in October 1874.

Over the next forty years, the assembly continued to outgrow its capacity in Victoria Street, and in October 1916 they acquired the Belfast Music Hall which afterward was renamed "The Victoria Memorial Hall." Bible teachers from all over the world expounded the Scriptures at the Victoria Hall, and the Assembly also provided some of the best Bible scholars of their time.

Special evangelistic endeavours extended to preaching the Gospel at the Grand Opera House, Barry's Amusement grounds, the Plaza and Maxim's Ballrooms, the boxing ring at the Ulster Hall, Queen's Island Shipyard and Crumlin Road Prison. These fruitful enterprises resulted in many conversions and more growth at the Victoria Hall Assembly.

Throughout changing decades this Assembly has been rich in fellowship, zealous in evangelism, faithful in Bible ministry, fervent in missionary enterprise, and diligent in Christian work--all to the glory of God while impacting generations of people.

His truth goes marching on.

Weak but Willing

"The weakness of God is stronger than men."
1 Corinthians 1:25

At the end of the nineteenth century, outside of the ranks of the Salvation Army, lady preachers were virtually unheard of in Scotland. Nevertheless, John George Govan and his colleagues discounted public opinion and reasoned, *'If Mary Slessor can go from Scotland to Africa to successfully serve God, why not welcome dedicated sisters who are prepared to serve God in Scotland?'*

This viewpoint prompted two lady Pilgrims, Annie Martin and Miss Mitchell, to go to Rothesay on the beautiful Isle of Bute for an evangelistic mission in 1888. Even though few people attended the initial meetings the two ladies continued to preach the Gospel night after night and the Holy Spirit began to move on the people. Miss Martin wrote to her friends:

"Hallelujah! Last night we had a glorious meeting. The hall was crammed with four hundred people and five souls professed. The Lord was present in power, and many went away deeply convicted, some with tears running down their cheeks. Keep believing! We are having splendid open-airs, and last night we had a proper march along the main streets with a great crowd following us."

For several weeks the two ladies were constant in their work. They visited, prayed, marched, sang and preached the Gospel. Their prayer meetings continued for hours. This was more than another mission; a heaven-sent revival had come to Rothesay. So many people travelled from all over Bute to hear the Word of God that larger premises were needed to accommodate the increasing numbers. Soon the girls were preaching to 800 people each night and on Sunday evenings to 1,500 people.

Those meetings continued to be well attended every evening for three months, and people were converted almost every meeting. Mr. Govan and other preachers arrived to help the two lady Pilgrims as the blessings flowed.

So great was the influence of the "Rothesay Revival" on the whole community that Rothesay's chief magistrate attributed that the crime rate in the town had fallen significantly because of those Faith Mission workers. Hundreds of people professed conversion in those meetings.

Our weakness finds sufficiency in the mighty power of God.

People Need the Lord

"I have much people in this city."
Acts 18:10

Charles Lepper, a descendent of the French Huguenot Le Pere family, was born in the middle of the nineteenth century. His father sent Charles to study law at Trinity College, Dublin, and while there, he trusted Jesus Christ as personal Saviour.

Charles felt a deep constraint in his heart to serve his Lord, and devoted all his zeal and energies to that end. Following his graduation, Charles moved to Belfast where he entered the family's Tea Merchants business. Although he and his new wife bought a house on the outskirts of Bangor, they travelled to Belfast for fellowship at the newly formed Victoria Rooms Assembly.

His uncompromising fidelity to his Lord and his knowledge of the Word of God made Charles a great witness for the Saviour. He also employed his developing talents to spread the Gospel, and through his instrumentality, many people were led into the glorious light of the Gospel.

His frequent travel between Bangor and Belfast made Charles aware of and concerned for the spiritual needs of those who lived in East Belfast. His concern prompted him to start a Sunday School in the Mountpottinger Orange Hall to reach the many impoverished boys and girls of that area. Encouraged by the success of the Sunday School, Charles embarked on a series of evangelistic meetings for adults. He looked on the streets of terraced houses and saw multitudes of souls who needed Christ. This made him work more fervently, and consequently, so many people were converted that it became necessary to start a regular programme of weekly meetings.

The development of this *new* outreach constrained Charles to seek a permanent home for this growing number. The Victoria Hall Assembly helped him purchase a plot of ground at the corner of Thorndyke Street, on Templemore Avenue in March of 1890. On this site, he erected a corrugated-iron building which, for obvious reasons, became known as "The Iron Mission Hall".

Charles Lepper arrived in Belfast as a Tea Merchant, but that business eventually closed. Charles had a vision and burden for a greater and longer lasting work, leading souls to Christ.

Lead me to some soul today.

Longings

"David longed, and said, Oh that one would give me drink
of the water of the well of Bethlehem."
2 Samuel 23:14, 15

"Oh James, I would love a drop of Guaraná," said Dorrie Gunnning to her husband James. Dorrie had been ill for several days and could not retain any food in her stomach. She thought that this Brazilian soft drink might help settle her digestive system. Her desire put James in a little dilemma. Their monthly mission allowance had not arrived, and James lived by the principle of not borrowing or buying on credit. *Without money how could he get Guaraná for his wife? If we were at home there would be no problem.* James had no other alternative but to compromise his personal policy and ask credit at a local shop. Dorrie's health mattered a lot more than James's personal preferences.

When he arrived at the shop a little girl from the church was already being served. Ironically, she was buying a bottle of Guaraná. After James greeted the child, her little face lit up with a smile. "Senhor James," she said, "my mummy sent me to buy a bottle of Guaraná for Mãe (mother) Dorrie." James was humbled to think that a family cared for them, and he was rebuked that he inhad not trusted God in this situation.

Have you ever longed for your childhood home or even for food of your childhood? It seems that was the case when David and his band of refugees were hiding from the King Saul. In the cave of Adullam he longed for the sweet water of his childhood memories in Bethlehem.

Three of David's mighty men heard the king's impulsive comment. They immediately rose to the challenge, broke through the camp of the Philistines and drew water from the well by Bethlehem's gate. They ran the perilous gauntlet again in returning with the precious commodity for their king.

David refused to drink the water. Instead, he poured it out as an offering to the Lord, saying, "Far be it from me, O Lord, that I should do this! Is this not the blood of the men who went in jeopardy of their lives?"

God is mindful of every sacrifice His children make.

Stand Up for Jesus

Put on the whole armour of God, that ye may be able
to stand against the wiles of the devil."
Ephesians 6:11

Dudley Tyng was a young and uncompromising Episcopalian preacher in Philadelphia during the great spiritual awakening in the middle of the nineteenth century. Periodically he organised noonday meetings at the downtown YMCA. Great crowds flocked to hear the dynamic young preacher. At a meeting on Tuesday, March 30, 1858, over 5,000 men gathered to hear Tyng preach from the text, *"Ye that are men, go and serve the Lord"* (Exodus 10:11). At the end of the service over 1,000 men committed their lives to Jesus Christ.

During the course of his sermon the young preacher exclaimed, "I must tell my Master's errand, and I would rather that this right arm were amputated at the trunk than that I should come short of my duty to you in delivering God's message."

A week after this event Dudley Tyng visited the Pennsylvanian countryside and watched men work at a corn threshing machine in a barn. Accidentally the young preacher's loose sleeve was caught between the cogs of the machine. As a result of the severe injuries, blood loss, and shock, Dudley Tyng died.

A group of sorrowing friends and ministers gathered at Tyng's deathbed and one of them asked him for a final statement. Mr. Tyng feebly whispered, "Let us all stand up for Jesus."

On the following Sunday his close friend and fellow worker, the Rev. George Duffield, minister at Temple Presbyterian Church in Philadelphia, preached the morning sermon as a tribute to his ministerial colleague. He concluded his sermon by reading a poem that he had just written in tribute to the final words of his great friend, Dudley Tyng.

> Stand up, stand up for Jesus; ye soldiers of the cross;
> Lift high His royal banner -- it must not suffer loss.
> From victory unto victory His army shall He lead,
> 'Till every foe is vanquished and Christ is Lord indeed.
>
> *Stand up for Jesus; the strife will not be long;*
> *This day the noise of battle-the next, the victor's song.*

Tough Labour

"Salute Persis who laboured much in the Lord."
Romans 16:12

Increased numbers and regular conversions in Boca do Acre demanded that James Gunning should construct a suitable building. Their small missionary allowance certainly did not allow any surplus to build a church. Their tithes and offerings had already been used up to purchase a site for a church, but what remained was insufficient to employ workmen or buy the raw materials. This dilemma helped James and his colleague Jack Finlay to decide to go into the forest and cut down the trees to provide the wood.

At daybreak each morning both men headed down river in a large dugout canoe. In the forest they identified the best quality trees that would provide long planks for the church's structure. After the tree was chopped down, the men tied thick ropes around their waists, attached these ropes to the tree trunk and then hauled it to a previously erected platform on which they suspended the log. A hole was dug under the platform and the log put in place. While James stood in the hole below Jack stood above on the log and then they began to move the large double-handed woodcutter's saw up and down, always following the straight carbon line they had drawn with the aid of a tight string soaked in ash. The up and down rhythmic movement of the saw went on for hours each day in the sweltering heat. It was exhausting and very dangerous work, but the Lord protected His servants.

In the afternoon the men had to trail the sawn boards to the river's edge and down the steep bank to be loaded into the canoe. With the canoe fully loaded, they paddled back up stream against the swift current to Boca do Acre where Dorrie had a good meal ready for them. The boards were placed in an upright position and left for two months to dry. They then had to be trimmed and planed by hand.

James and Jack preached in the evenings and weekends and were woodcutters each day before they were able to construct the first church building in Boca do Acre.

In it all they served the Lord with gladness.

Trust and Obey

"I will be as the dew unto Israel: he shall grow as the lily, and cast forth his roots as Lebanon. His branches shall spread..."
Hosea 14:5, 6

Today's verse is the promise God gave to John George Govan when he forsook his business interests and obediently stepped out to found The Faith Mission. At that embryonic stage of the work the young Scotsman, whose life God had touched, could not have known how much that plant would grow, how far its branches would spread or how much fruit it would bear for God's everlasting Kingdom. Over the following years, God also taught His servant how deep those roots must go for the Mission to be able to withstand the numerous storms that would inevitably rage against it. Paradoxically, the storms served to deepen the Mission's roots even more.

Those fruitful branches not only spread their reach all over Scotland and its islands, but within a few years they extended across the Irish Sea. Devoted Pilgrims zealously preached in churches, mission halls, community halls and other public venues with a passionate endeavor to lead souls to Jesus Christ.

As in Scotland, so also in the Emerald Isle, their labours were not easy and at times were greatly opposed, but God mightily used these dedicated workers in the salvation of the lost, the blessing and sanctifying of His people and to establish Prayer Unions throughout the whole of Ireland.

Dozens of those Prayer Unions continue to this day. These are like multiple branches that stem from that tiny seed of faith which initially germinated in Mr. Govan's heart. These fruitful boughs have produced the sweet fruit of God's grace in countless lives, and the impact continues to this day.

The old hymn expresses the pattern that Mr. Govan followed and is still good for us today: *"Trust and obey for there's no other way...."* Obedient faith is not only pleasing to God, it is productive. Noah's obedience to God in building the ark still blesses us today. Because Abraham stepped out in faith on God's promise, all the ends of the earth are blessed.

Trust and obey – there still is no other way.

28th February

Zeal

"A peculiar people, zealous of good works."
Titus 2:14

The Coalmen's Testimony Band was a zealous cluster of rough diamonds. When they regrouped soon after World War II they were swamped by invitations to conduct meetings in many places. Sammy Spence and Pop Stewart requested the use of the weighbridge shed at the entrance to the Coal Quay for prayer and fellowship meetings on Wednesday and Thursday nights. The request was readily granted, and the lively and bright meetings began in that old shed.

People who had no connection with the docks came to enjoy the warm fellowship of these dedicated coalmen. The increasing numbers forced Christian coalmen to look elsewhere to accommodate the crowds.

Their attention was directed to a larger shed that had been used by His Majesty's Custom and Excise when American ships dropped anchor in Belfast during the war. St. John's Ambulance used the building afterward. Sammy Spence, ever an opportunist, appealed to the brigadier of the St. John's Ambulance, for permission to use the shed on Saturday nights. Consent was granted, and for the nominal fee of one shilling per year, the Harbour Commissioners leased the building to the coalmen. The old shed accommodated about 400 people, and very soon it was not only packed, but people also queued outside long before the hall was opened to ensure they got a seat.

Pop Stewart and Sammy Spence enthusiastically led those meeting while David Sinclair was at the piano and Tommy Hunsdale played his violin. Preachers from many places preached the Gospel each Saturday night. Week after week people were converted, and lives were transformed.

These meetings were unconventional. Although they had no theological training, the coalmen communicated the Gospel in a way that ordinary people could understand. One night Sammy was stressing that we are all sinners and need salvation. A good-living woman protested to him, "Mister, my name is on the church roll, and that is good enough for me."

To this, Sammy replied, "Missus, you might as well have your name on a sausage roll as on the church roll. Without Jesus Christ, you can never get to heaven."

True Christian zeal causes the light of the Gospel to shine.

All We Need

"Blessed be the God and Father of our Lord Jesus Christ, who hath blessed us with all spiritual blessings in heavenly places in Christ."
Ephesians 1:4

Because Boca do Acre was so far inland in Brazil it was difficult and expensive to have holidays at the shore. Therefore, Hazel and Mollie decided to travel to Rio Branco, capital of the Acre for a deserved rest from their busy programme.

For that week in the Acre capital they booked into the *Shui Hotel*, the only decent one in town at that time. To minimize their expenses, they bought food from local stores, furtively cooked on their paraffin Primus stove and ate on the verandah of their hotel suite.

When they went to check out of the hotel at the end of the week the receptionist asked if they had been satisfied with their stay. Mollie assured the lady that they had enjoyed a wonderful time. The receptionist then said, "It is a pity you didn't have meals in the dining room. Are you both on a special diet?"

It was only then they discovered that they had paid for full board but had missed the meals. Both ladies nearly fell over laughing at the thought that they had spent the whole week living on scraps while they could have been living it up.

This incident reminds me that although God has richly endowed all Christians with all heavenly blessings in Christ, yet at times we live on scraps. Paul indicated that God has freely and fully bestowed upon every believer a treasure of dazzling blessings, all of which are ours "in Christ"

These blessings of God are available. God has deposited Christ's whole estate of heavenly wealth for every believer in Christ. Without Christ we have nothing, we are nothing and can do nothing.

These blessings of God are adequate. Paul spans the past when we were chosen in Christ, moves through the present to the blessing of redemption and then reaches into the ages to come.

These blessing of God are from above. These riches are heavenly and not earthly, spiritual and not material, they are eternal and not temporal.

Jesus is all we need

March

Spring Flowers, Glenariff, Co Antrim

God At Work

"For we are His workmanship, created in Christ Jesus unto good works, which God hath before ordained that we should walk in them."
Ephesians 2:10

The long sandy beach just across the road from Amy Carmichael's childhood home in Millisle, County Down, was ideal for her, her brothers and her cousins to run, play and expend their childish energies. Amy also loved to ride her pony up and down the sandy stretch along the shore. Theirs was truly a happy and prosperous Christian home which provided an idyllic childhood.

Although the Carmichael children had a private education from various governesses, not all of them left a good impression. However, when Miss Eleanor Milne arrived all the Carmichael children loved her. She was virtually looked upon as another daughter in the family. Besides teaching them reading, writing, and arithmetic, Miss Milne took time to teach the Scriptures to the children and tell them stories of the great reformers and heroes of Christian history. These historical accounts of great men and women of God made an indelible mark on Amy's memory, and the story of their lives and exploits remained with her for years to come.

The arrival in Millisle of Mr. & Mrs. Beatty, missionaries from India, made another lasting impression on young Amy. For a whole year the missionary couple occupied the house next door to the manse and during that year Mrs. Beatty gathered the Carmichael children together each Sunday afternoon and held them spellbound with graphic stories of life in India. When the other children left, Amy stayed behind and begged Mrs. Beatty to tell her more about her work in India.

Miss Milne, Mrs. Beatty, and young Amy did not know that those early encounters and invested hours would be God's way of shaping Amy's early life and preparing her for her future ministry which would result in so much blessing upon thousands on a distant continent.

Every redeemed life is a monument to mercy and a miracle of grace created to be a masterpiece of God's providence. The Master Architect skilfully and silently is shaping our lives to fulfil His purpose in us.

Let the Lord have His way in your life every day.

The Servant Sings

Behold My Servant..."
Isaiah 52:13

Isaiah's prophecy was written 700 hundred years before the coming of the Messiah. Sir *Winston Churchill* was asked his opinion on the qualifications needed to succeed in politics. To this he replied, "To succeed in politics *is to have the ability to foretell what is going to happen tomorrow, next week, next month, and next year. And then to have the ability afterwards to explain why those things didn't happen.*" God's prophets never had to explain why their predictions never came true. They are always accurate *and never need* to explain away their mistakes because there are no mistakes.

Isaiah foretold the manner of the Saviour's birth and the name by which He would be called: "*Behold, a virgin shall conceive, and bear a son, and shall call His name Immanuel*" (Isaiah 7:14). Isaiah also spoke of the manner of His life and everlasting Kingdom: "*For unto us a child is born, unto us a son is given: and the government shall be upon His shoulder: and His name shall be called Wonderful, Counsellor, The mighty God, The everlasting Father, The Prince of Peace. Of the increase of his government and peace there shall be no end...*" (Isaiah 9:6,7).

The four Servant Songs of Isaiah (42:1-9, 49:1-13, 50:4-11 and 52:13-53:12) are also prophecies speaking of the service, suffering, and exaltation of the Messiah. The best known of these songs gives us a detailed portrayal of our blessed Saviour.

Behold the majesty of His glory: "*He shall be exalted and extolled, and be very high.*" He came from the excellent glory and returned to glory, from eternity to eternity.

Behold the measure of His grief: "*His visage was so marred more than any man, and His form more than the sons of men.*"

Behold the ministry of His grace: "*He shall sprinkle many nations...*" Here the risen Priest sprinkles His redeeming grace on many nations bringing many sons to glory.

Behold the message of the Gospel: "*That which had not been told them shall they see; and that which they had not heard shall they consider.*" To this the prophet adds, "*Who hath believed our report*?"

It truly is the "old, old story," yet it is ever new.

Up to Jerusalem

*"Behold, we go up to Jerusalem; and the Son of man
shall be delivered unto the chief priests."*
Mark 10:33

Jesus Christ always had a sense of purpose throughout His earthly ministry. His first spoken word was, *"I must be about my Father's business."* There certainly was a definite purpose behind His words when He said, *"Behold, we go up to Jerusalem."* In the Scriptures, Jerusalem is always up. People ascended to Jerusalem. This was true geographically because Jerusalem is elevated on a mountain, and from whatever direction you may approach the Holy City, you will always be going up.

What is true geographically, is also true spiritually. When people went to Jerusalem, they were going up to the Temple with offerings for the Lord. They went up to meet with God. The Lord Jesus went *"up to Jerusalem"* to offer Himself to His Father on Calvary's altar and to make atonement for our sins.

Christ also emphasized His Person; *"the Son of Man."* This is one of the most common names for our Lord Jesus in the New Testament. It is mentioned on eighty-two occasions. I find it interesting that it was the Lord Jesus who first ascribed this name to Himself when He spoke of how *"foxes have holes, and the birds of the air have nests; but the Son of man hath not where to lay his head."*

This name chosen by Christ had a direct reference to Daniel 7:13: *"I saw in the night visions, and, behold, one like the Son of man came with the clouds of heaven, and came to the Ancient of days, and they brought him near before him."* Although the name *"Son of* Man" identifies His humanity, this reference associates Him with His Messianic splendour and glory.

The disciples had gone up to Jerusalem many times with Christ, but to hear Him speak about going up to suffer and die. That was not in their plans. Christ, using that name, gave them visions of Messianic grandeur in a visible kingdom and an earthly reign. They had not yet learned that the only crowning glory for Christ was by the cross of Calvary.

Let us go up to Calvary.

Christ's Prophecies

*"All things that are written by the prophets concerning
the Son of man shall be accomplished."*
Luke 18:31

One of the great marvels of the Bible is its predictive voice, or as Peter calls it, *"a more sure word of prophecy."* In Psalm 22 alone there are thirty-three distinct prophecies about the death of Christ at Calvary, and all of them were fulfilled. The Bible's fulfilled prophecy in the past assures us that all prophetic predictions in the Scriptures will be accomplished.

We can marvel even more that our Saviour made so many predictions about His death and resurrection. We cannot predict the moment or manner of our death, but Christ was in control of His life and death as He followed the path of the Father's will.

Consider these progressive predictions the Lord Jesus gave concerning His impending death as recorded in Luke's Gospel:

The Lord Jesus predicted the necessity of His death: *"The Son of Man must suffer many things, and be rejected of the elders and chief priests and scribes, and be slain, and be raised the third day"* (Luke 9:22). The emphasis is on our Saviour's use of the word *"must"*. His first public utterance as a boy was that He *"must"* be about His Father's business. There was a Divine compulsion on Him. There was no other way.

The Lord Jesus predicted the certainty of His death: *"Let these sayings sink down into your ears: for the Son of man shall be delivered into the hands of men"* (Luke 9:44). The word *"shall"* puts emphasis on the fact that God was controlling the future. He was then and He still is in control today.

The Lord Jesus predicted the cruelty of His death: *"He shall be delivered unto the Gentiles, and shall be mocked, and spitefully entreated, and spitted on: And they shall scourge him, and put him to death: and the third day he shall rise again"* (Luke 18:32). The Saviour predicted not only the place of His death but also the details of the manner in which it was going to take place.

With each prediction of His death, Christ gave an assurance of His resurrection.

Wonderful Saviour!

Jesus and Jerusalem

"He must go unto Jerusalem, and suffer many things of the elders and chief priests and scribes, and be killed, and be raised again the third day."
Matthew 16:21

Although the Lord Jesus was born in Bethlehem, had fled to Egypt, was raised in Nazareth and ministered in Galilee, He always had Jerusalem in view. He was taken there as a baby, visited there as a boy, ministered there as a Servant and died at Jerusalem as the Saviour of the world. Jerusalem was the city of His sympathetic tears, the site of His scornful trial, the scene of His suffering on a tree and where He left the sublime testimony of His empty tomb.

Matthew told the story of our Saviour's last fifteen hours in Jerusalem, but John put the details of the Lord's Passion between two Gardens: the Garden of Gethsemane where He prayed and the Garden Tomb where they buried Him.

While Jesus sweated, wept and prayed in the Garden Judas was counting out thirty pieces of silver, the price of a crippled slave. Perhaps the priests bartered and bribed Judas until he settled on the price of thirty pieces of silver, but it was a very low and sad estimate of the Saviour.

Around the cross in Jerusalem, ruthless legionnaires gambled for His clothes. Religious leaders spewed out their hypocritical derision. The riotous crowd taunted the Saviour. To crucify the Lord Jesus was the greatest of all crimes, but to add to the shame, the holy, sinless Son of God was crucified between two thieves.

Undoubtedly, Calvary was the most ghastly altar when Jesus Christ, God of very God, was hanged between heaven and earth and suspended as the supreme Substitute. For six torturous hours He hung on that cross and His every movement shot searing pain through His body. Like the thousands of other lambskins stretched in the mid morning sun, the Son of God lay stretched beneath the burning skies of Judea. God's Passover Lamb was there for all to see.

Jerusalem, the city of the Great King, now awaits His coming in power and glory.

He who once was crowned with thorns, is now crowned with glory.

The Silver Coins

*"And said unto them, What will ye give me, and I will deliver Him unto you?
And they covenanted with him for thirty pieces of silver."*
Matthew 26:15

While the Lord Jesus wept, prayed and sweated great drops of crimson blood in the Garden of Gethsemane, Judas was counting his thirty pieces of silver.

The story of Judas Iscariot is beyond question the blackest page on the history of the human race. Judas is sometimes referred to as "the man who kissed heaven and went to hell." He was a misfit of history and tragedy for humanity. We still associate his name today with treachery when we speak of a Judas hole and a Judas kiss. His name has become a byword for betrayal.

When the Bible mentions our Lord's betrayal by Judas it points out the fact that he was one of the twelve. I find that so amazing. Here is one who had walked with Jesus Christ and had travelled with our Lord the length and breadth of the country. He had been there when Jesus had performed His great miracles such as feeding the five thousand or calming the raging sea. He was right there to hear everything that Jesus Christ said including the Sermon on the Mount and the Olivet discourse. He was even present when Jesus taught His disciples how to pray.

The tragedy of tragedies, here was one who had known Christ so well and yet betrayed Him for the price of a crippled slave. He was with Christ, saw the works of the Lord Jesus Christ and heard the Saviour's words, but for all that, it seemed it had no effect on him. Although he was often by the Lord's side, he was never on the Lord's side.

Caiaphas sent a cohort of Roman soldiers with arms to take Jesus captive. He was the Prince of Peace. They carried lanterns to arrest Him who is the Light of the world. Judas betrayed Jesus who is the Lover of our souls.

Judas not only sold the Saviour, he sold his soul, and with thirty pieces of silver he paid his way to perdition.

Thirty silver coins were a very poor estimation of Jesus.

The Way of the Cross

"For God so loved the world, that He gave His only begotten Son..."
John 3:16

Every Friday in Jerusalem, and especially on Good Friday, thousands of pilgrims follow a procession on the Via Dolorosa, the supposed *"Way of the Cross,"* the route that Jesus took between His condemnation by Pilate and His crucifixion and burial. Since Emperor Constantine legalised Christianity in the fourth century, the route for this religious procession has changed many times.

The Scriptures teach us that the "Way of the Cross" never changed. It did not begin at Gabbatha, Pilate's Judgement Hall in Jerusalem. The true *"Way of the Cross"* began in the heart of the Father in heaven as we learn from 1 John 4:14; *"the Father sent the Son to be the Saviour of the world.* Consider, therefore, the way of the cross:

The plan Jesus followed. We can never fully comprehend the weight of the words, *"He (God) gave His only begotten Son,"* or that *"He spared not His own Son, but delivered Him up for us all"* (Romans 8:32). There was an immeasurable sacrifice in heaven before there ever was a cross on Calvary.

The prophecies Jesus fulfilled. The Father also superintended our Saviour's path to the cross. He gave prophecies, promises and typical pictures that permeate the pages of the Old Testament. We marvel at these words; *"Jesus knowing that all things were now accomplished, that the Scripture might be fulfilled, said, 'I thirst'"* (John 19:28).

The pain Jesus felt. The Lord Jesus was aware of the path He was following. He said, *"The Son of man must suffer many things, and be rejected of the elders and chief priests and scribes, and be slain..."* (Luke 9:22). He endured the pain even though *"His visage was so marred more than any man, and His form more than the sons of men"* (Isaiah 52:14).

We are the people Jesus freed. We worship our Saviour with John, *"Unto Him that loved us, and washed us from our sins in His own blood, and hath made us kings and priests unto God and His Father"* (Revelation 1:5,6).

Make your way to the cross every day.

Crushed

*"Then cometh Jesus with them unto a place called Gethsemane …
and began to be sorrowful and very heavy."*
Matthew 26:36, 37

Anticipating His impending death the Lord Jesus said, *"The hour is come when the Son of Man should be glorified."* While we consider the passion of our Saviour we often become absorbed with His grief and the gore, whereas our Saviour focused on the joy and the glory. Death on the cross was the purpose for which He came. He was made flesh and blood that He might taste death for every man. Because of the joy that was set before Him, He endured the cross, despised the shame and is now seated on the right hand of the majesty on high.

In following the path to the cross we see our Saviour leading His disciples out from the upper room on Mount Zion into the dark night. Passing the southern entrance to the temple they crossed the Kidron Valley to the Garden of Gethsemane on the lower slope of the Mount of Olives, a place to which He often resorted to pray.

Gethsemane means "Oil Press." Olives were placed in a pit, and then a heavy lever was pressed down to crush them and extract the oil. The first crushing produced the best oil and was reserved for holy and medicinal purposes. The second crushing yielded oil for domestic use. The third and final crushing provided inferior oil that was used for burning in lamps.

Look at Him. Olives were crushed three times. Does this not parallel with our Saviour who three times prayed to His Father in agony. He was so crushed in agony as the Father laid on Him the sin of the world. The intensity caused Him to pour holy tears and soak His body in blood-drenched sweat.

Listen to Him. Sense the passion in His voice, *"O my Father, if this cup may not pass away from me, except I drink it, Thy will be done."* He drank the bitter cup of sorrow that we might drink from the cup of salvation.

Love Him. It was for me in the garden He prayed, "Not my will, but Thine."

Behold

"Then came Jesus forth, wearing the crown of thorns, and the purple robe. And Pilate saith unto them, Behold the Man!"
John 19:5

Reading about the final hours of our Lord's Passion makes us feel we stand on holy ground. Early on that day of all days, Jesus stood in the Antonia Fortress to be judged by Pontius Pilate. The events that followed were momentous and majestic.

The Scorning. Archaeologists excavated down to the original pavement where the Lord Jesus stood before Pontius Pilate in the Antonia Fortress. In the excavation, they discovered etched into the pavement the markings of a game that was commonly played by soldiers of that day. It was known as *"The King's Game"* in which the prisoner was their victim. Thus, they mocked Christ, blindfolding Him before they put a purple robe on His shoulders. These rough soldiers then pressed a crown of thorns into His brow. They put a rod in His hand and began to taunt and make fun of Him. They mocked the Lord of glory.

The Scourging: A Roman soldier lashed His back with a leather whip laced with fine, and sharp bones. Each lash tore across His flesh, ripping muscles and sinews. The scourging was so severe that His visage was more marred than that of any man until He was virtually unrecognizable. The Lord Jesus predicted this scourging.

The Spitting: Spitting on anyone is a revolting insult. Jesus Christ was adored by His Father, worshipped by angels and filled of the Holy Spirit, but Roman soldiers emptied their throats to spit on Him. They substituted the absence of anointing oil by spitting on Heaven's King.

The Spiking: Listen to hammers reverberate as iron beats on iron when they pierce the hands and feet of the Saviour. These are the hands that touched the lepers, blessed the children and broke bread to feed multitudes. His feet had walked on water and had run through the streets of Nazareth. His precious blood gushed from those open wounds.

The Spearing: When a Roman soldier shunted a spear into the side of our Lord, blood and water flowed out. From His side flowed a fountain of precious blood sufficient to cover all of the sin and uncleanness of His followers.

Look at what He did for us.

The Smiting

"Then did they spit in His face, and buffeted Him;
and others smote Him with the palms of their hands."
Matthew 26:67

After His arrest in the Garden of Gethsemane, our Saviour was brought to the High Priest's palace to face trial. This was supposed to be the highest court in the land where the most dignified leaders were supposed to administer justice. Sadly, this august body degenerated into a lynching mob.

Having arrested Him in the garden where He prayed, they falsely accused Him of blasphemy and then began to abuse Him. The mob was stirred up against Him and began to spit in His face. This is the same face that smiled when little children approached Him, the same upon which tears ran down when He wept before the tomb of Lazarus. This is the same face before which, the Bible says, one day, earth and heaven will flee.

They also buffeted Him, that is, they punched Him. See them slapping and socking the lovely face of Jesus until it begins to swell. It is amazing that the Bible predicted this would happen to the Messiah: "*I hid My not my face from shame and spitting.*" This is man at his worst spitting and smiting Christ, and yet it is Jesus at His best suffering the contradiction of sinners against Himself because He loved them.

In striking our Lord, this angry mob literally fulfilled the word of the prophet Micah, "*They shall smite the Judge of Israel with a rod upon the cheek*" (Micah 5:1). Although Peter was at the point of denial he later wrote, "*Who, when He was reviled, reviled not again; when He suffered, He threatened not; but committed Himself to Him that judgeth righteously.*"

This whole scene shows how wickedly a man can treat God, yet on the other hand, how loving God can be to man. Jesus never called for revenge, never complained to His Father, nor did He call for the assistance of holy angels. Silently He faced His suffering and death for us.

He was not guilty of blasphemy, but those who blasphemed spat in His face.

Mothers

*"They ceased in Israel, until that I Deborah arose,
that I arose a mother in Israel."*
Judges 5:7

The four-hundred-year period of the Judges went in monotonous cycles that begin with disobedience and end in disgrace. The twenty-one chapters make for depressing reading except for some great highlights. The last verse of the book, provides the key phrase that is repeated several times throughout Judges, *"In those days there was no king in Israel: every man did that which was right in his own eyes."*

It is also against the bleak and depressing background of despair and dismay that we have some of the greatest tales of devotion and heroism. There are seven such luminaries who shone in the darkness of the Judges; *Othniel, Thud, Shamga, Gideon, Jephthah, Samson, and Deborah,* who was a heroine in her nation.

Deborah was a singer with Barak. Judges 5 contains their wonderful song. Their duet was a majestic doxology of praise. No matter how dark the age, in the great purpose and plan of God, there is always time for singing, motivation and prompting for a song.

Deborah was a Judge in Israel. She was chosen, equipped, empowered, and used by God. Two heroic women stand out in Judges 4; Deborah and Jael. Deborah's name means "bee," and she was always bee-like -- busy but sweet. Jael was more like a wasp – busy, but with a sting. She invited King Sisera to her tent for a drink in her milk bar, and after the first jar, he was out cold. With Jael's help, he never recovered from the headache she gave him!

Deborah was a prophetess to her people. Deborah whose words and counsel were respected in Israel is only one of three women in the Bible known as prophetesses.

Deborah was a mother in her home. Her husband's name was Lapidoth, but we read little about her family. However, besides being a homemaker, Deborah was described as "a mother in Israel." Billy Graham said, "Let your home be your parish, your little brood your congregation, your livingroom a sanctuary, and your knee a sacred altar."

Mothers can shape lives that change nations.

The Scourging

"Then Pilate therefore took Jesus, and scourged Him."
John 19:1

S courging was the cruelest form of punishment, and it was reserved for the worst of criminals. Yet, they took the One who was innocent and scourged Him. This was not the Jewish scourging that Paul suffered five times. Jesus received the Roman scourging which was known as the "half-way death." In this scourging, the soldiers beat the victim until they brought him to the very edge of death. There were thirty-nine strikes in Jewish scourging, but with Roman scourging there were no stipulations to the number of blows. Under this kind of scourging some victims went raving mad, and some even died.

In the Antonio Fortress judgment hall, there were three thick pillars, each about three feet high. They bent the Lord Jesus over on those pillars, tied His hands and delivered Him to a trained soldier. This soldier took what was known as a flagellum, a sort of "cat of nine tails." It was a short piece of wood attached to which were strips of leather, and at the end of the leather were small pieces of iron and sharpened bone.

You can almost hear the whistle of the scourge as the soldier swung it forcefully down on the Saviour's body. The leather, bone and iron ripped across His back, tearing flesh and sinews. One lash often knocked the breath out of the victim and his legs would buckle. That was only the first blow on our Lord, but this continued as the whip wound around Him to tear into the Saviour's side and abdomen. With each lash huge chunks of flesh were torn from Him, and His precious blood flowed.

It is unbelievable that the Lord Jesus was able to endure such scourging and afterwards carry His cross toward Calvary. Is it any wonder that Isaiah said His visage was more marred than that of any man? The Scriptures predicted, *"The plowers plowed upon my back: they made long their furrows"* (Psalm 129:3). Peter also quoted Isaiah when he wrote, "For by His stripes ye were healed."

Sin scars our lives; He was scarred for our sins.

The Spitting and Stripping

"Some began to spit on Him, and to cover His face, and to buffet Him, and to say unto Him, Prophesy: and the servants did strike Him with the palms of their hands."
Mark 14:65

The Gospel writers tell us that both In the house of Caiaphas and at the hands of the soldiers, *"they spit on Him."* They spat in His face. One day we shall see that face, but on that day, vile men showed their contempt for Him when they spat on His lovely face. The spittle has ever been the foulest insult among men. Well did Philip Bliss write, "Bearing shame and scoffing rude…"

We may blush at the spitting. There was no oil to anoint Him as King in the mocking game. Instead of oil, mocking soldiers displayed their own depravity as they emptied their throats and spat upon Him. His suffering was not designed to arouse our pity but to assure us of the extent of His love for us.

Having survived the scourging, Roman soldiers took this opportunity to have their fun with Him. They stripped Him of His clothing, robed Him in purple and then crowned Him with platted thorns, and with their hands they beat Him. They were playing a cruel Roman game in which all the soldiers would show the prisoner their fists. Then they would blindfold the prisoner, and all but one would hit him as hard as they could. Then they would remove the blindfold, and if the prisoner was still conscious, he was to guess which soldier did not hit him. Obviously, the prisoner could never guess the right one. They would continue this until they had beaten the prisoner to a pulp. Can you imagine slapping the face of the Son of God.

The Lord Jesus was so mutilated that He was unrecognizable. *"His visage was so marred more than any man, and his form more than the sons of men"* Isaiah 52:14). No one could hide from Him. He knew the name of every soldier who hit Him, and He would soon bear their sins on the cross.

Such intense shame should make us love Jesus Christ more intensely.

The Sentence

"Take ye Him and crucify Him…"
John 19:16

One of the saddest faces peering out of the Gospels is that of a privileged politician, Pontus Pilate, the governor of Judea. However, privilege could not help him on this occasion. He was caught on the horns of a great dilemma. He had been acquainted with the claims of Christ, and he was impressed. He had investigated the character of Christ and had found nothing amiss. He was confronted with the crowds that opposed Christ and was fearful of displeasing them. For this reason, he asked the greatest question, *"What shall I do then with Jesus …"*

A pilot in the cockpit of a jumbo jet carries a weighty responsibility, for he has the lives of all his passengers on his hands. A judge at the bench carries great responsibility as he presides over a case and makes judgement that can put a person in prison for many years. He has the life of a man in his hands. A surgeon in an operating theatre skilfully and carefully uses a scalpel as he does surgery on the body of a patient. He has a sick man in his hands.

While all these carry awesome responsibilities, none come near to the responsibility that confronted this politician, Pontus Pilate. He had the God Man, Jesus Christ, on His hands when he grappled with this question, "What shall I do then with Jesus …" Sadly, he made the wrong decision because of:

The values that controlled him. Pilate thought more of his public image, his personal pride and lucrative position than of the Saviour. He was controlled by greed and had no value for grace. What he considered to be privileges became obstacles to him.

In spite of the voices that confronted him. He heard "a good confession" from Jesus Christ, listened to the concern of his wife and quenched his accusing conscience.

His verdict condemned him. Pilate gave the sentence to appease the crowd, and Jesus Christ was crucified. Pilate tried to wash his hands of all responsibility, but he will be forever known as the man who crucified Christ and sealed the destiny of his soul.

Jesus Christ was the only person worthy of life, but He was put to death.

The Spiking

"They pierced my hands and my feet."
Psalm 22:16

Roman soldiers stretched the blood-drenched body of the Lord Jesus on the cross. With the grim sound of iron on iron, coarse nails pierced His sinews and flesh. He must have writhed in pain as crimson blood spurted out when the spikes sank through His hands and into the tough wood. His feet were then laid flat on the wood with His legs drawn up and two more terrible spikes pierced His ankles. Like a lambskin stretched in the midmorning sun, the Son of God was stretched beneath the burning skies of Judea. This was God's Passover Lamb, nailed and crucified for all to see. Calvary was the most ghastly altar ever created when Jesus Christ, God of very God, was suspended between heaven and earth as our Supreme Substitute.

Standing around that cross were ruthless soldiers gambling for His clothes, the religious leaders spewing out their venom and hypocrisy and the riotous crowd taunting and jibing at the Saviour.

To crucify the Lord Jesus was the greatest of all crimes, but shame was added to insult when the sinless Son of God was crucified between two thieves, brigands and murderers. For six torturous hours, He hung on that cross, and His every movement shot searing pain through His body.

Those nailed-pierced hands that were once gory with His blood, still bear the marks of suffering, but they are now glorious with the blessings of salvation. Peter discovered that those hands of Christ were strong to save him when he was sinking into the sea after he took his eyes off Jesus.

The touch of Christ's hand was sympathetic to the leper who called out for healing. Jesus put His hands on children to bless them when mothers brought their little ones to Him. His is the touch of a sympathetic friend, the gentle Lord Jesus.

As the Good Shepherd. He taught His disciples that no one can snatch His sheep from His hand because the hand of the Father encircles His hand.

Cruel soldiers opened His hands to puncture them with nails. He opens His hands to satisfy the need of every living thing.

We shall know Him by the nail prints on His hand.

Prayer

"He kneeled upon his knees three times a day, and prayed."
Daniel 6:10

Prayer and prayers pervade the pages of the Bible. The Scriptures provide us with examples of people who prayed and give demonstrable evidence that God is able to do exceeding abundantly above all we can ask or think. Added to this, we have many "great and precious promises" in the Bible assuring us that God hears and answers prayer.

Amy Carmichael's life was not only productive, it was prayerful. Perhaps we should say that it was productive because hers was a prayerful life. When she was a teenager, she established "The Morning Watch" among her friends. This involved some young people, including two of her brothers, who pledged to follow a course of Bible reading and prayer and then meet at her home on Saturday mornings to compare notes and pray together. Amy organised weekly prayer meetings for a group of girls in various homes. When the numbers attending these prayer meetings became too many for a house, some of the teachers at Victoria College, Belfast, invited Amy and her friends to conduct their weekly prayer meeting at the school.

It was in answer to her prayers that God provided a sum of money to purchase the land and erect a prefabricated building for the beginning of the Welcome Hall in Belfast. It was through prayer that she heard God's call to leave home, never to return and give her life to rescue thousands of Indian girls from temple prostitution. Is it any wonder Amy wrote these lines?

> From prayer that asks that I may be
> Sheltered from winds that beat on Thee,
> From fearing when I should aspire,
> From faltering when I should climb higher
> From silken self, O Captain, free
> Thy soldier who would follow Thee.
>
> Give me the Love that leads the way
> The faith that nothing can dismay
> The hope no disappointments tire
> The passion that'll burn like fire
> Let me not sink to be a clod
> Make me Thy fuel, Flame of God.

Satan laughs at our schemes and talents, but trembles before a praying saint.

The Superscription

"A superscription also was written over Him in letters of Greek, and Latin, and Hebrew, THIS IS THE KING OF THE JEWS."
Luke 23:38

Pontius Pilate knew that the Jews hated Jesus so he inscribed on a board, "This is Jesus, the King of the Jews." Normally a soldier would carry a board in front of a victim on which would be written the crime committed by the person to be crucified. That is what they did with Jesus. His board had the accusation: "THIS IS JESUS OF NAZARETH, THE KING OF THE JEWS." That was the only crime they could find to hang on Jesus, that He claimed to be the King of the Jews.

What was written on the board was in Hebrew, Greek, and Latin. Hebrew was the language of religion. Greek was the language of philosophy and culture, and Latin was the language of law and government. People from all over the world converged on Jerusalem for Passover, and when they looked at the crucified Christ they could see the witness of the cross. These words were written for the whole world to see that He died for all, and this is the Gospel that is to be preached to the world.

The Magi sought the King of the Jews: *"Where is He that was born King of the Jews?"*

Pilate questioned if Jesus was King of the Jews: *"Art Thou the King of the Jews?"*

Roman soldiers mocked Him as King of the Jews: *"They began to salute Him, Hail, King of the Jews!"*

The watching crowd taunted Him as King of the Jews: *"If Thou be the king of the Jews, save Thyself."*

Luke called it a *"superscription"* while Matthew called it *"an accusation"*. John called it "a title". I think John was right. Jesus was not only the King of the Jews; He is the King of the world, and He is the King of the universe. Jesus Christ is the King of kings and the Lord of lords. One day every knee will bow and every tongue will confess that Jesus Christ is Lord.

King of my life I crown Him now.

People Who Came to the Cross

"And it was the third hour, and they crucified Him."
Mark 15:25

A variety of people stood around the cross. There were mourners and mockers, soldiers and civilians, religious zealots and rebels and women weeping. Mark gives us details of those who were there the day Jesus died.

Simon of Cyrene carried the cross for Christ. He came to Jerusalem for Passover but was compelled to carry the cross for the Lamb (15:21).

Soldiers brought the nails, the board, the paint and the money to gamble for His garments. It was the duty of these seasoned soldiers to be at the cross (15:20). They had never been on a campaign like this before.

Thieves brought their sins to the cross. On the cross one thief died in faith and went to Paradise. At the same execution, the other thief died in sin and went to hell (15:27-28).

Scorners brought vinegar and a sponge to add to the suffering of the victims (15:23).

John the Apostle brought Mary, the mother of the Saviour, to the cross.

Priests and scribes brought their insults to the cross. When all rational argument was exhausted and found wanting, insult and scorn were the only means left (15:31-32).

The Centurion brought the spear that punctured Christ's side. At the cross, he discovered that Christ was God (15:39).

Sympathetic women brought wine and myrrh. They came to stay at the cross (15:40-47).

People watched Jesus on the cross as a spectacle and passed by pouring out their scorn (15:29-30). It was reported that during the French Revolution ladies were able to bring their knitting to watch the executions by guillotine.

Jeremiah did well ask, *"Is it nothing to you, all ye that pass by?"*

To those who believe He is exceedingly precious.

The Sponge

"Jesus knowing that all things were now accomplished, that the Scripture might be fulfilled, saith, I thirst ... they filled a sponge with vinegar, and put it upon hyssop, and put it to His mouth."
John 19:28, 29

Early in His ministry Jesus said to a woman, "Give me to drink." On the cross, He cried again, "I thirst." Scientists tell us that thirst is the most agonizing of all pains. A pinched nerve, a wound or some bodily malfunction can result in tremendous pain, but nothing is more excruciating to bear than thirst. Every cell in the body cries out for relief, and the pain gets worse as time goes by.

They took a sponge filled with vinegar, put it at the end of a stick of hyssop and offered it to the Saviour. Sponges were not natural to that area. Roman soldiers carried sponges with them for their ablutions in bathrooms or toilets. At communal toilets, a soldier was given a piece of sponge to use, and afterwards it was washed to be used again. It was probably a piece of such sponge that was given to the Lord Jesus. How repulsive is that?

Despite their debased and vulgar actions, John records something remarkable. Jesus cried out, "I thirst," only because it was necessary to do so for Him to fulfil the Scriptures. This clearly implies that if He had not been required to fulfil Scripture He would have borne this agony of thirst without a single word of complaint. But in order to faithfully do what God had said, our Lord revealed His anguish by crying out, *"I thirst."*

Jesus was fulfilling Psalm 69:21: *"They gave me also gall for my meat; and in my thirst they gave me vinegar to drink."* Afterwards, Christ cried with a loud voice, *"Tetelestai!"* Everybody around the cross that day understood what that meant. "It is finished!" This accounting term meant "Paid in full." With His last breath on the cross Christ declared that the debt of our sin had been fully paid, and God was completely satisfied.

He said, "I thirst," yet He made the water.

Looking at Jesus

"And sitting down they watched Him there."
Mathew 27:36

Before the Father enveloped the scene at Calvary in a cloud of thick darkness, a thousand eyes must have fixed their gaze on our Saviour while He suffered on the cross. Through whose eyes would you have looked on the crucified Son of God?

Looking at Jesus through the eyes of the ruthless men. Hard Roman soldiers scourged the Saviour, mocked Him while placing a crown of thorns upon His head and treated Him cruelly. They swung the hammer that nailed the Saviour to the cross and then gambled for His garments. They saw no beauty in Christ.

Looking at Jesus through the eyes of the religious men. The chief priests and scribes were vigorously involved in the death of Jesus. They arrested, accused and condemned Him under false charges. They mocked Him as He died, for they were too blind to see who He was.

Looking at Jesus through the eyes of the ruling men. Pilate and Herod were guilty of ignoring what they knew to be true about Jesus. Pilate tried everything short of bravery to get Jesus released. Cowardly, instead of releasing Him, both rulers chose to send Him to the cross. Pride and fear blurred their vision.

Looking at Jesus through the eyes of rebellious men. The Bible tells us that Jesus was crucified between two thieves, both of whom ridiculed Jesus and rejected Him vocally. One thief looked on Him and saw a Saviour while the other rejected the Saviour. One rebel was saved, for he looked on Christ by faith.

Looking at Jesus through the eyes of riotous men. Crowds gathered in Jerusalem to celebrate the Passover, and without a doubt, many of them had hailed Christ a few days earlier as their coming King. Now, they stood with their leaders to call for the blood of the innocent Messiah. They had a fickle view of Christ.

Looking at Jesus through the eyes of a released man. Barabbas provided a great example of salvation. He was justly under the sentence of death for his crimes, but Jesus took his place on the cross. Barabbas saw Christ as his substitute

Give me a sight oh Saviour of Thy matchless love for me.

The Spear

"But one of the soldiers with a spear pierced His side,
and forthwith came there out blood and water."
John 19:34

They pierced His side with a lance. When the Roman soldier shunted his spear into Jesus' heart, it was proof that Christ had really died. It was also the fulfillment of the Scriptures; *"... they shall look upon me whom they have pierced, and they shall mourn for Him, as one mourneth for his only son"* (Zechariah 12:10). That part of Zechariah's prophecy has been fulfilled. But the prophet says that Messiah shall return again, and when He comes, then they shall look upon the One whom they have pierced, and they shall mourn for Him."

It was the custom of the Romans to leave a crucified victim on the cross for many days. The intense heat of the sun and the cold air of the night, the gnats, the flies and the raging thirst all contributed to make crucifixion the cruelest form of execution.

Old Testament law was very specific that a body should not be left on a tree overnight. In addition to this, the Sabbath day was approaching, and it was Passover Day. If the victim had not died, the soldiers would use mallets to crush the legs and thereby hasten the victim's death. When they came to the Lord Jesus, He was already dead. They did not need to break His legs, and thus they fulfilled the Scriptures that *"not one bone of His would be broken."*

As the soldiers turned to go away, one soldier plunged his spear into the Saviour's side so that blood and water gushed out. This was evidence that the Saviour's heart had already burst.

> Let the water and the blood,
> From Thy riven side which flowed
> Be of sin the double cure,
> Cleanse me from its guilt and pow'r.

That piercing by the Roman spear was an act of violence against the Lord, but when it touched the heart of the Lord Jesus, it touched the very fountain that brings salvation.

A fountain was opened for all sin and uncleanness.

Behold My Servant

"He is despised and rejected of men; a man of sorrows,
and acquainted with grief."
Isaiah 53:3

Martin Luther called Isaiah 53 "The golden chapter of the Bible." For centuries this song of the Saviour has captivated the hearts and minds of Bible scholars. Throughout church history it has been celebrated as the evangelical heart of the Old Testament. For that reason Isaiah has been correctly referred to as "The Fifth Gospel" or "The Gospel According To Isaiah."

Isaiah 53 is also the most quoted Old Testament chapter in the New Testament. Was this Apostle Paul's favourite chapter? He quoted from it or alluded to it on more than forty occasions.

It is said that while Handel was composing his masterpiece, "The Messiah," he was moved to tears when he came to this chapter. Surely, it is enough to cause tears to course down our cheeks. In some ways this Servant Song is the sad story of the creature rejecting and crucifying the great Creator. Another look reveals the sovereign hand of God planning and performing the great work of our redemption through Christ: It pleased the Father to bruise and crush Him. His soul was made an offering for sin.

An Old Testament scholar wrote, "These five matchless stanzas of the fourth Servant poem are the Mount Everest of Messianic prophecy." That great mountain stands out for its grandeur and beauty, but this chapter takes us higher than Everest. It takes us to Mount Calvary where the grandeur, the beauty and the majesty are that of the love of God displayed in Christ. Everest has been climbed and conquered, but no one has been able to scale the heights or conquer the full significance of Calvary. We do not come to Isaiah 53 to view a hill but to see the hand and the heart of the Father.

While contemplating Isaiah 53 Charles Spurgeon said, "Here is a Bible in miniature, the Gospel in its very essence." Another commentator added, "This is the most central, the deepest and the loftiest of Old Testament prophecies, and it seems as if it had been written beneath the cross upon Golgotha."

Jesus keep me near the cross.

Scarred

"I bear in my body the marks of the Lord Jesus."
Galatians 6:17

Eddie and Sadie Young were commissioned to missionary service from the Welcome Hall, and for twenty years they served God in Senegal, West Africa, with the Worldwide Evangelization Crusade. Prior to his conversion Eddie had been a champion boxer with a promising future. However, when the grace of God came into his life, he forewent any boxing ambitions. There were greater battles to fight, not with flesh and blood in a ring, but with the infernal forces of Satan.

After more than twenty very productive years in West Africa, Eddie accepted an invitation to be the pastor of his home church. Eddie was inducted as pastor of the Welcome Evangelical Church in 1980, a ministry he and Sadie maintained until his retirement in 1997. During those seventeen years, many mission halls in the surrounding area were forced to close down due to redevelopment and relocation of the population. Even then, Eddie maintained a constant witness to the Gospel and made sure that the Welcome Hall survived those times of shifting loyalties and shrinking spiritual commitment.

Any residual scars from Eddie's years as a teenage boxer are not to be compared with the invisible marks branded on his life after sixty years of Christian service.

Amy Carmichael, the founder of the Welcome Evangelical Church, asked the question, "Can we follow the Saviour far, who have no wound or scar?" Perhaps those scar marks on Eddie's life find a parallel in the famous poem Amy Carmichael penned in India:

> Hast thou no scar?
> No hidden scar on foot, or side, or hand?
> I hear thee sung as mighty in the land,
> I hear them hail thy bright ascendant star,
> Hast thou no scar?

> Hast thou no wound?
> Yet, I was wounded by the archers, spent.
> Leaned me against the tree to die, and rent
> By ravening beasts that compassed me, I swooned:
> Hast thou no wound?

> No wound? No scar?
> Yet as the Master shall the servant be,
> And pierced are the feet that follow Me;
> But thine are whole. Can he have followed far
> Who has no wound nor scar?

Christ's Submission

"As a sheep before her shearers is dumb, so He openeth not His mouth."
Isaiah 53:7

Our Lord's submission to the Father may be hard to understand. Although He is the Son of God and co-equal with the Father, for the purpose of redemption, the Father sent the Son into the world to be our Saviour. For that reason the Lord Jesus constantly referred to doing His Father's will and always doing those things that pleased the Father.

Paul spoke of the Saviour's submission when he wrote, *"He made himself of no reputation, and took upon Him the form of a servant … and became obedient unto death, even the death of the cross."* There was a compulsive constraint upon our Lord to do His Father's will, and He was always submissive to the Father's plan.

Jesus was submissive In His silence, in His suffering and in His shame. The words, *"He opened not His mouth,"* are repeated twice for emphasis. A submissive servant did not talk back; he submitted to the master's will. The Lord Jesus was as submissive as a lamb being led to the slaughter.

He was silent when human hands oppressed and afflicted Him. Though the wicked hands of cruel men punched Him, whipped Him, spiked Him to the cross and shunted a spear into His side, yet from our Saviour's lips there was no word of protest or for protection. There was no complaint against the Father's will. There was not even a command for holy angels to come to His assistance. He was absolutely silent.

He was silent before Hebrew authorities. Caiaphas, the chief priests and the elders combined to destroy our Lord on false charges. They delivered Him to Pilate.

He was silent before the heathen Roman authorities. Pilate tried to wash his hands of Christ as he found no fault in Him, and Jesus never answered a word to Herod.

He was silent when human hands led Him to the slaughter. It is amazing that He should be led anywhere. He is the incarnate Son of God, the Creator of all things with innumerable angels at His command.

His silence speaks volumes of His great love for us.

All for You

"They pierced my hands and my feet."
Psalm 22:16

Very few details are given to us in the New Testament about the actual crucifixion of our Saviour. The Gospel writers are very factual but without details. As the Gospel writers pass over Christ's death with a reverent restraint, it seems as though the Holy Spirit has drawn the veil of silence over the cross so that none of the gruesome particulars of the carnage and suffering of the Saviour are set forth. Though a hostile mob sat down and gazed on Him, we are not permitted to join that crowd. Even they did not see all, for God placed a mantle of darkness over His Son's agony.

The hymn writer had this in mind in these words:

> But none of the ransomed ever knew
> How deep were the waters crossed,
> Nor how dark was the night that the Lord passed thro'

Ere He found His sheep that was lost.

Isaiah 53 and Psalm 22 give us a more vivid account of the crucifixion of Christ than is found elsewhere in the Bible. They speak of the bruising, the piercing and the wounding of our Lord when He made His soul an offering for sin.

Nicholaus Ludwig von Zinzendorf was born into European nobility in 1700. While visiting Dusseldorf's art museum he was deeply moved by looking at Domenica Feti's famous painting, *"Ecce Homo,"* a portrait of the thorn-crowned Jesus. He read Feti's inscription below the painting: "I did this for thee! What hast thou done for Me?" Zinzendorf answered, "I have loved Him for a long time, but I have never actually done anything for Him. From now on, I will do whatever He leads me to do." His life was never the same again.

Two hundred years later, Frances Ridley Havergal saw the same painting and read the text below. She also was so deeply moved she scribbled these lines:

> My Life was given for thee
> My precious blood was shed
> That thou might'st ransomed be
> And quickened from the dead
> My life, my life was given for thee,
> What hast thou done for Me?

Good question. Is there a good answer?

When I Survey

*"He was wounded for our transgressions, he was bruised for our iniquities:
the chastisement of our peace was upon Him;
and with His stripes we are healed."*
Isaiah 53:5

Although Isaac Watts was a son of the manse, a minister of the Gospel and the author of several books, he is best remembered for the great hymns he wrote. Perhaps the greatest of all these hymns is *"When I survey the wondrous cross..."* When he wrote that hymn it was a new departure in hymnody in that era. Never before had the first personal pronoun, "I", been included in hymns for public worship. Isaac Watts' use of personal pronouns brings into focus our individual relationship to Jesus Christ in His atoning work. Isaiah made Calvary personal when he wrote, "He was wounded for our transgressions…"

The saints sing about the Saviour. However, Isaiah 52:13 introduces us to the Saviour's song, the final of Isaiah's four Servant Songs. I find it amazing that this should be called a song in view of the sorrow and suffering expressed in it. This sounds more like a sob, a lament instead of lyrics. However this is a song. In Isaiah the words "sing", "singing" and "songs" are mentioned more than forty times. Hebrews 12:2 gives us an insight as to why our Saviour sang: *"Who for the joy that was set before Him, endured the cross, despised the shame."* There was joy in the midst of the suffering.

We generally associate joy with success. This Servant song certainly is one of success: *"The pleasure of the Lord shall prosper in His hand. He shall see of the travail of His soul and be abundantly satisfied"* (53:10). However, success in God's economy is different from ours. We associate joy with a rags-to-riches story, but this song of our Saviour is more of a riches-to-rags story. He became so poor that we might be made rich.

This is the song of the Shepherd who passed through the night of deep sorrow to find the sheep that was lost. Now He comes with the sheep on His shoulders and with great rejoicing.

Love so amazing, so divine, demands my all.

27th March

What More?

"What could have been done more to my vineyard, that I have not done in it?"
Isaiah 53:4

Although Isaiah was a prophet, much of his prophecy was taken up with songs. Singing and songs are mentioned more than forty times in its sixty-six chapters. The most famous songs in Isaiah are the Songs of the Servant--the best known of which is Isaiah 53.

Isaiah 53 is more like a sob than a song. God is grieved at His people who had forsaken Him to follow the gods of the surrounding nations. In this song, God likened His people to a vineyard that He had purchased and prepared and in which He had planted the choicest vines. After all He had done, He looked for a harvest of choice fruit. Instead, the vineyard yielded briars and thorns. God lamented that after lavishing Israel with His goodness, they were ungrateful and unfaithful. They had turned their backs on Him instead of returning gratitude and praise. God cried, "What more could I have done for my people?"

God did so much for Israel. He lavished His love on them when He chose them, not because they were many, but for His love's sake. He liberated them from Egypt by the blood of redemption. With His own finger God wrote His Law on stone tablets, and then for forty years He accompanied them, fed them and clothed them during their long pilgrimage through the desert. He gave them the Promised Land where He established King David's throne. Added to this, God favoured them with priests for the Tabernacle, prophets to speak His Word and kings to occupy the throne. What more could God have done?

God's lament over Israel was reflected when the Lord Jesus wept over Jerusalem because of Israel's continued refusal to come to Him.

Sadly, too many people still refuse to come to Him for salvation. God's lament still echoes today, *"What more could I have done that I have not done?"* God so loved the world, that He gave His only begotten Son that whosoever believes on Him would not perish, but have everlasting life."

He did it all for us.

Remember Him

"As often as ye eat this bread, and drink this cup,
ye do shew the Lord's death till He come."
1 Corinthians 11:26

One of the highlights of a trip to County Donegall was to visit the Potato Famine Museum at Doagh village. It was an eye-opener of how difficult it was for those whose primary diet was the humble potato.

When Jimmy Quinn and Paddy Flanagan dug for potatoes in September 1868, they could have hardly imagined what they were about to discover. They had cleverly grown potatoes inside a ring fort near Ardagh, County Limerick, to avoid the affects of the potato blight of the Great Irish Famine. When digging between the roots of a thorn bush, the spade struck something hard. When they cleared away the earth they found a beautiful communion cup now known as the "Ardagh Chalice," an excellent example of 8th century metal work. They continued digging and came on a second and much plainer bronze communion chalice and four silver brooches.

These cups remind us of the simple remembrance service established by the Lord Jesus at the Passover Supper before His death. The elaborate chalice and its contents have no virtue. We remember Christ as we partake of these symbols of the bread and cup. When we celebrate the Communion service several things come to mind:

The Lordship of Jesus Christ. The Lord's Supper is for the Lord's people to remember the Lord's death. In 1 Corinthians 11:23-32 Paul repeats the name *"Lord"* seven times. With Lordship authority, Jesus transformed the Passover Supper into this remembrance feast.

The Love of Jesus Christ. When we sit at the remembrance table we often quote from The Song of Solomon 2:4, *"He brought me to the banqueting house, and his banner over me was love."* It is a love feast.

The life Jesus Christ gave for us. The Bible says, *"The life of the soul is in the blood."* Christ gave His life for us and through His death gives life to us.

Looking for Jesus Christ coming again. At the Communion Service, we remember Jesus until Jesus comes again when the symbols will be replaced by seeing Christ, face to face.

We will sit down with Him.

29th March

A Good Man

"For he was a good man..."
Acts 11:24

Generally speaking, Brazilians are amongst the friendliest people in the world. This congenial disposition was epitomized in José Alves Areias, a Brazilian who spent most of his life in Northern Ireland. José, born in the interior of Minas Gerais, Brazil, was the oldest of ten children whose Christian parents worked on their small farm, far from any urban influence.

Converted when he was a young boy, José felt God's call to Christian service as a teenager. He travelled far from his rural home to train at a Bible College in Londrina, Paraná, in the south of Brazil. After graduation he met and married Irish missionary, Sheila Ward who had been serving God in that country since 1964.

José and Sheila arrived in Northern Ireland in 1972 with a view of returning to Brazil, but Sheila's ill health prevented that from happening. Subsequently, José completed a theological course at Belfast Bible College. He was always a very hard-working person and was able to employ his many diverse skills to establish his own construction business. Besides his evident love for his family, José also befriended countless people of all nationalities and was always available to help them. This was particularly true with the migrant population, often providing them with employment and financial help.

José was a member of the Great Victoria Street Baptist Church for more than 40 years and a highly respected deacon in that assembly. His caring and winsome disposition made him a blessing to many. Friends will always remember his rich baritone voice singing out the Gospel while he strummed his guitar. He also was a member of a musical group, which travelled throughout Northern Ireland singing for the Saviour. Many mission agencies benefitted from José's trips to various countries to help in their building projects. He was especially keen on helping his brother Aroldo at Santo André in Portugal.

Jose's sudden death on 29th March 2017 shocked everyone who knew him. At the funeral Thanksgiving Service, his son, Rev. André Areias, gave a triumphant and clear Gospel message, affirming that Jesus Christ is the only hope of salvation.

Christian friendship carries many blessings.

The Great Destroyer

"For He is our peace, who hath made both one,
and hath broken down the middle wall of partition between us."
Ephesians 2:14

Our Lord's greatest antagonists were from the religious community, the Scribes, Pharisees and Sadducees. They accused Him of destroying the Law of Moses, but Christ replied that, rather than come to destroy the Law, He had come to fulfill it. The impeccable and immaculate life of the Saviour reflected the perfect righteousness of Christ.

The Lord Jesus was the Great Destroyer. The Apostle John wrote, *"For this purpose the Son of God was manifested, that He might destroy the works of the devil"* (1 John 3:8). The author of Hebrews wrote that the Lord Jesus was made flesh and blood *"that through death He might destroy him that had the power of death, that is, the devil."* Christ's death was the death sentence on death itself. Paul confirmed this when he wrote, *"The last enemy that shall be destroyed is death"* (1 Corinthians 15:26).

Reflect on these aspects of our Saviour's death:

At Christ's death the veil of the Temple was rent in two. This twenty-metres-high and heavy veil was a dividing wall between the Holy Place and the Holy of Holies in the Temple. The veil was indicative of the separation between God and sinners, shutting God in and shutting men out. When Christ died, that veil was torn in two from top to bottom by God's invisible hand. By His atoning death, Christ destroyed the barrier and made a way back to God. There was no more need for the temple or its offerings.

At Christ's trial, the High Priest's garments were rent in two. When Jesus spoke of His coming again in glory the High priest rent his garments, the robe of the ephod. In doing so, he rendered his priestly office null and void. His priestly office was also made redundant by Christ's death. It was no longer needed, for Christ is the only Mediator between God and man.

By Christ's death, He broke down the middle wall of partition between Jew and Gentile and made peace by the blood of His cross.

Jesus is the Destroyer and the Constructor.

An Early Easter Message

"I know that my Redeemer liveth, and that He shall stand at the latter day upon the earth: And though after my skin worms destroy this body, yet in my flesh shall I see God: Whom I shall see for myself, and mine eyes shall behold, and not another."
Job 19:25-27

Preachers tend to spend a lot of time around old books. None of these books is older than the Bible book of Job. It is not only the oldest book in the Bible, but it is also thought to be the oldest book in the world and reaches back to times predating Abraham and the great Bible Patriarchs.

At Easter, it is good to read Job's ancient writings and to identify with his assurance, *"I know that my Redeemer liveth..."* His use of the word "Redeemer" indicates that even in those earliest times, people looked and longed for a Redeemer and redemption. From the early dawn of history Job's words have reverberated with meaning even though written long before there ever was an Easter.

At that time Job wrestled with the great problems of suffering, death, and loss. His hope was so wonderful that he wanted to preserve the record, *"Oh that my words were … printed in a book! That they were graven with an iron pen and lead in the rock forever"* (Job 19:23, 24)!

Job was comforted and assured by the precious truth of Redemption. Equally, he was consoled by the prospect of resurrection for the believer. There were many things of which he was not sure, but these unshakeable foundational truths, personal and prophetical, gave him stability. Through the eyes of faith, Job looked into the future and saw that the coming Messiah would be the Redeeming Messiah.

Job was conscious of the price of redemption. Redemption is a commercial term involving a price to be paid, the redeeming blood of Christ.

Job was confident of the power of the resurrection. Once the price is paid, the Redeemer executes His power and authority. He was going to see God in his flesh.

Job was comforted by the prospect of The Redeemer's return.

Handel's Messiah echoes the melody, *"I know that my Redeemer lives."*

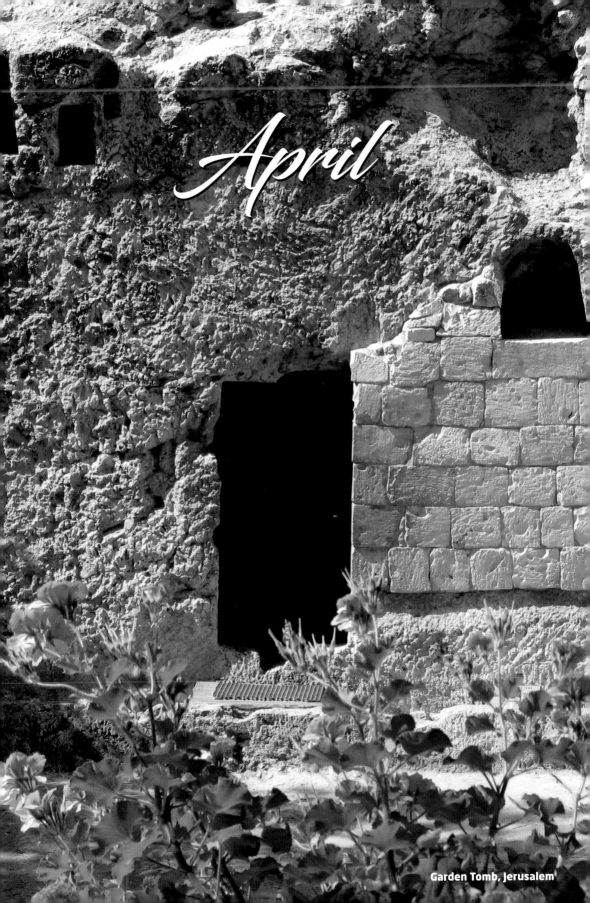

April

Garden Tomb, Jerusalem

The Empty Tomb

"The first day of the week cometh Mary Magdalene early, when it was yet dark, unto the sepulchre, and seeth the stone taken away from the sepulchre."
John 20:1

Quiet cemeteries and revered memorial parks are part of the landscape all over our world. Some of us have visited the graves and mausoleums of famous people from all walks of life. I remember seeing Korean people camping beside the grave of their family. Why do they do it? Because the last remains of their loved one are entombed in that grave.

However, there is a grave near the Old City of Jerusalem that has been visited by countless millions, not because of who is in the grave, but because of Who is not in the grave. I am speaking of the grave and tomb of the Lord Jesus Christ.

I like the story of a missionary in Northern India who was preaching in a bazaar. When he finished a Muslim gentleman walked up to him and said, "You must admit we have one thing you have not, and it is better than anything you have." The missionary said, "I should be pleased to hear what it is." The Muslim said, "You know that when we go to Mecca, we at least find a coffin. But when you go to Jerusalem you can find nothing but an empty grave."

To that, we say, "Hallelujah." We can only find an empty tomb. We do not worship someone whose decayed remains are contained in a coffin or a tomb. We celebrate a Saviour who rose from the dead and left the grave empty. Mohammed may be found in a coffin, but we will never find the Lord Jesus in a grave. Instead of being in a grave, He is in the glory. We do not worship a dead Saviour. We worship a living Lord.

When Mary Magdalene approached the Saviour's tomb in the early morning, she was shocked to find *"the stone taken away from the sepulchre."* The stone was not rolled away to let Jesus out. It was rolled away so others could see the tomb was empty.

Christ's tomb is empty, but our hearts are full.

Come and Dine

"When the morning was now come, Jesus stood on the shore."
John 21:4

If you have been to Israel you probably have your favourite place to visit. For some, it is Jerusalem's Garden Tomb and the adjoining "Skull Hill." Others carry lingering memories of the Garden of Gethsemane or the Praetorium where Christ was scourged. We even had one woman admit that she would love to have been in Cana of Galilee when Jesus transformed water into wine. That lady created some suspicions!

Most people choose the Sea of Galilee, and I stand with them. There is something awesome about the tranquil waters of this heart-shaped lake. We love the beauty of the quiet hills that surround it, but what people like most is Galilee's authenticity. It certainly puts new meaning to the words, "I walked today where Jesus walked." No religious trappings have been added to this lake, and no church has been erected to preside over it. Better still, there is no charge for standing at the shore to listen to the wind that sometimes whistles across the waves.

To quietly be at Galilee alone with your thoughts on a misty morning as the sun slowly emerges above the mountains and its reflection glistens across the water is an unforgettable experience. At times, I have tried to envisage in the distance a group of the disciples crouched down in a small circle on the shore as fresh fish is cooked on the fire. They had fished all through the night and had caught nothing. Then Jesus, Stranger of Galilee, commanded them to throw their nets on the other side of the boat. He blessed their obedience with an overabundance of fish. He then beckoned them to come to the shore where He had prepared breakfast. His invitation was for them to "Come and dine."

Those disciples had enjoyed many meals with the Saviour, but this was different. The day had begun with failure, for they had returned to fishing. Despite their failures, the Saviour gave them a miracle catch. He not only provided fish, but He also lit a fire, cooked the meal and restored the fervour of their love for Him.

This was just like our Lord.

Easter Emphasis

"Master, it is good for us to be here."
Mark 9:5

The beautiful seaside town of Bangor has long been a centre of Christian witness. As early as the fifth century, Christianity flourished in the town, and from Bangor Bay, under the leadership of the famed St Columbanus, Christian missionaries sailed to Scotland and distant Europe to preach the message of the Gospel to the lost.

When John McLean first arrived from Scotland as the Irish Director of the Faith Mission early in the twentieth century, Bangor was a thriving seaside resort. One mild summer day in 1915, John and another Faith Mission worker, were strolling past Bangor's Pickie Swimming Pool enjoying the pleasant sea breezes in their faces. John remarked to his friend, "Wouldn't Bangor be a great place to hold a holiness convention?"

John's suggestion seemed like a moment of inspiration, and his colleague heartily approved of the thought. Undoubtedly, both Pilgrims still had lingering memories of the great days of the "Rothesay Convention" which had attracted great crowds to the Scottish seaside town.

Rather than let this inspired thought die, both men decided to try to implement the idea immediately. They listened to good advice from local friends and supporters of the Mission who welcomed the idea with great enthusiasm. In the weeks that followed, local ministers were also consulted, and without hesitation they all whole-heartedly supported the Pilgrims' venture of faith.

Back in Scotland, "the Chief", John George Govan, and the Mission Council were glad to give their enthusiastic approval for this new venture.

With such widespread support for the Convention, John and his friends decided that Easter would be the most appropriate season for the convention seeing it was then that Christians majored on the fundamentals of the Christian faith: the death and resurrection of the great Lord and Saviour, Jesus Christ. Furthermore, Easter was a holiday week for most of the general public and a time when farmers were less busy.

Thus the first Faith Mission Easter Convention began on Friday, 21st April 1916 at the Good Templar Hall, Hamilton Road, Bangor. In the decades that followed thousands of people were converted, greatly blessed and called to Christian service at the annual Convention.

Meetings with the Lord Jesus are always enriching.

Take Jesus Home

"Go home to thy friends, and tell them how great things the Lord hath done for thee, and hath had compassion on thee."
Mark 5:19

For many years Billy and Ruby enjoyed the outdoor activities of fishing and camping with their family. However, both were introduced to a binding web of alcohol abuse. At first, it seemed glamorous and the sophisticated thing for couples to do.

Billy enjoyed his evenings out at several bars in East Belfast. Some nights he became so drunk that he staggered home on his bare feet without realizing he had left his shoes in the pub. On Saturday nights no one in Billy's street dared to leave their milk bottles at their doorstep for it was known that Billy smashed every milk bottle he found as he stumbled home after midnight.

Alcohol made a fool of Ruby, too. When sober, she was a cheerful, very kind and considerate person. However, under the influence of alcohol Ruby became schizophrenic and underwent a change of personality by which she became quite aggressive. As a result of this aggression in company, the family decided to bring Ruby's alcoholic beverages to her house so that she could routinely intoxicate herself at home from Thursday through to Sunday. Frequently so much alcohol was brought to their house that Billy, Ruby, their four children and visiting cousins were all totally drunk.

Although alcohol had become the most important thing in their lives, Billy would not admit that he was an alcoholic. He loved his drink and the company at the bar and felt he had it all under control.

Life changed for Billy and Ruby with the incredible news that their only daughter had been converted. Until then they had lamented her life-style, which had been a sad reflection of their own addiction to alcohol. Jesus Christ had radically changed their daughter's life, and the news of it was like a bombshell in the home. She not only had been converted, she had also brought Jesus home and introduced Him to her mum and dad.

For Billy and Ruby, this news was not only incredible, it was irresistible. Jesus Christ not only entered their home, but He came into their hearts also.

Take Jesus home with you.

Chosen

"He shall be a vessel unto honour, sanctified, and meet for the Master's use."
Acts 9:16

With the outbreak of the Great War in 1914, Duncan's Campbell's older brother was called up by the army. Two years later Duncan enlisted in the Argyll and Sutherland Highlanders and was drafted as a machine-gunner to the battle-front during the Flanders Campaign.

I remember when Duncan spoke to us at Bible College of how he was thrown into the battle and right away was overwhelmed by the enemy's force. As his horse galloped on a charge toward the enemy it was shot, and he fell, severely wounded, into deep mud. The dead and dying were all around him while rider-less horses ran wildly among them.

As blood flowed from his open wounds Duncan was sure he was dying. He felt unworthy, but was glad he had trusted Christ years earlier. Contemplating his impending meeting with Christ, he was grieved that he had accomplished so little in life.

Just then a second charge of the Canadian Horse Brigade surged across the gory and muddy battlefield. As one charge raced by, the horse's hoof struck Duncan's spine. He cried out and writhed in pain. Those cries saved his life. The Canadian, whose horse had injured Duncan, returned to where he lay, picked up the wounded soldier and threw him across his horse and then galloped to the nearest Casualty Clearing Station.

The loss of blood had weakened Duncan and it seemed death was near. As he lay across the steed's back he was still concerned of how little he had accomplished as a Christian. He prayed the words of Robert Murray McCheyne, "Lord make me as holy as a saved sinner can be."

Instantly, the power of God filled and possessed him. The Holy Spirit swept through his being like a refining and cleansing flame, purging him until he felt as pure as an angel. God felt so near that Duncan was sure he was about to be ushered into heaven, but this was not heaven. God had more work for him to do on earth. This invigorating experience was a divine visitation preparing him for future days.

Meet and prepared for the Master's use.

A Heart For God

"Thou shalt love the Lord thy God with all thine heart,
and with all thy soul, and with all thy might."
Deuteronomy 6:5

David Livingston was one of the greatest missionaries who ever lived. He was a cultured, God fearing and Christ-honouring man. He turned his back on home, family and wealth to take the Gospel to the heart of darkest Africa. For years no one knew what had happened to him. When the *New York Times* commissioned Henry Morton Stanley to search for Livingston, he did not even know where to start. He set out on an expedition that took him deeper and deeper into the heart of Africa. One day, by the providence of God, he met the famous missionary and spoke those immortal words as he stretched out his hand, "Dr. Livingston, I presume?"

In conversation Henry Stanley further said to Dr. Livingston, "Dr. Livingston, you've done a good job here in Africa, but you're sick, I want you to come home. Your books have sold so many copies that you're a wealthy man. You can come back home to wealth and to the accolades you deserve. Come back to your people. Come back and tell us what God has done here in Africa."

Livingston excused himself and answered, "I must pray." He went to his tent where he spent the night in prayer. Afterwards he told Mr. Stanley, "I cannot go. I promised God I would serve Him here, and I promised God that I would die here."

Stanley shook Dr. Livingston's hand and returned to New York. That was Livingston's last contact with the civilized world. The old missionary returned to his little hut and wrote these words in his diary, "My Jesus, my King, my life, my all, I again dedicate the entirety of my life to Thee."

After his death in 1873 at sixty years of age, Livingston's remains were returned to England for interment at Westminster Abbey. The Africans cut Livingston's heart from the body and buried it in Africa. They said, "His body may belong to England, but his heart belongs to Africa."

Both England and Africa were wrong, his heart belonged to Jesus.

7ᵗʰ April

A Royal Audience

"They shall see His face."
Revelation 22:4

Soon after leaving school I gained employment as a telegram boy at the General Post Office in Belfast. While darting around on the GPO's 125 BSA Bantam motorcycle, the vehicle boldly displayed the letters OHMS - On Her Majesty's Service.

Sixty years later we had an opportunity to visit Buckingham Palace, the Queen's residence. Lead-like soldiers stood motionless outside their sentry boxes with automatic weapons resting on their right shoulders and the famous tall black busbies almost obscuring their faces.

After we crossed the palace's inner courtyard, men in top hats, tails and smart pinstripe trousers ushered us into a plush reception area. Members of the Household Cavalry, standing at attention, lined each side of the hallway. Their gleaming swords, bright breastplates, and silver helmets reflected a galaxy of sparkling lights from several grand chandeliers. Delicate but elegant tapestries and huge oil paintings adorned the high walls on either side of the lavishly decorated corridor. The deep pile of the red carpet gave the impression that we were treading on air.

As we entered the bright and resplendent ballroom the band of the Grenadier Guards, although hidden from view in the minstrel gallery, played regal music that set the mood for the opulent surroundings.

Shortly, a procession of Beefeaters paraded through the room. They were followed by an entourage of Gurka soldiers and neatly dressed courtiers who accompanied Her Majesty as she entered the ballroom. Our eyes were fixed on the beloved Sovereign, elegantly dressed in blue. All the elegant trappings of the palace were grand, but for us to see Queen Elizabeth II in her palace was the highlight of our visit. When I saw the Monarch, I could not help but remember those days when I was On Her Majesty's Service. I never thought that one day I would see the Sovereign in her palace.

That experience cannot be compared to the day when we shall see the King of Kings and Lord of Lords in all His beauty. The streets of gold, walls of jasper, crystal river, and pearly gates will be incidental to looking upon our blessed Redeemer.

But I long to see my Saviour first of all.

Family Prayers

"For this … I prayed."
1 Samuel 1:27

Norman and Linda lived in the heart of the Woodstock Road with their only son, Gary. Gary arrived home one evening to tell his mother and father that he had become a Christian. Even though his parents had no regard for religion in their lives, they were glad their son was not following in their footsteps. Norman and Linda were at home in the pubs and social clubs of East Belfast, and sadly, like many of their friends, Thursday through to Sunday was frequently one continual binge which resulted in total intoxication.

While onlookers may have found it difficult to see any sense or satisfaction in such a lifestyle, yet for Norman and Linda, this was their idea of living. Norman enjoyed the bar scene so much that he began working in one.

Gary prayed for the conversion of his wayward but loving parents. As often is the case, God answered prayer in a way Gary could not have imagined. When Linda's mother became ill, young Gary led his grandmother to faith in Jesus Christ. Her death shortly afterward had a devastating effect on Linda. She knew no other way to drown her sorrows than by consuming more alcoholic drink. The stress and tension that followed the bereavement resulted in more drunken binges that lasted for days.

During all this time Gary did not give up on praying for his mother and father. One night he stepped into the midst of a terrible brawl between his parents and when he saw the state of his mother he told her she needed to find God and get out of the mess of drink and violence. Linda longed to abandon the drink but did not know how.

It was a happy day when Linda came to the end of her own attempts to give up this vice and discovered a new life in Jesus Christ. She recognized that her mother was in heaven and her son was serving the Saviour. She not only accepted the Saviour, she also joined Gary in praying for Norman's conversion. God answered that prayer, too.

Never give up in asking God.

God Helping

" I am helped: therefore my heart greatly rejoiceth."
Psalm 28:7

Before Victor Cardoo left for Brazil, the Mission Director said to him, "Victor, we know about your fear of being able to learn a foreign language due to your hearing difficulty. We have decided that if after six months you have not been able to learn Portuguese it would be best to bring you home and review your situation." Victor related:

To learn Portuguese was a challenge, but to do it within six months was formidable. Besides asking the Lord's help, many letters from home assured me that friends were praying.

The first three months were extremely difficult. I was becoming increasingly frustrated for I had never really given much attention to grammar in the past. Now I was learning the conjugations of verbs, regular and irregular verbs and the feminine and masculine gender of nouns. What I found most annoying was that little children who had no idea of these grammatical rules were able to speak Portuguese without any effort, and here was I wrecking my brains and virtually tongue-tied.

I was grateful for two persistent teachers who did not give up on me. They taught me to laugh at myself, for making mistakes was part of language learning. We often had a good laugh at the blunders I was apt to make. Brazilians are most kind. They did not laugh at my mistakes in my presence, but I am sure they must have doubled up with laughter afterwards. Like the rainy day when I left my umbrella at the bank by mistake. When I returned to enquire about my lost property I got the word for umbrella (guarda-chuva), mixed up with the word for wardrobe (guarda roupa).

After speaking with the bank clerk, with an expressionless face, he swung round and shouted to his colleagues, "Did anyone see this gentleman's wardrobe? He said he left it here in the bank before lunch?"

Suddenly everybody exploded with laughter.

Through much patience, trial, errors and many laughs, I got there within the time scale. The Mission was duly notified that I was speaking Portuguese quite fluently."

When we are weak, He is sufficient.

God Makes His Man

"I went down to the potter's house, and, behold,
he wrought a work on the wheels."
Jeremiah 18:3

Duncan Campbell was demobilised from the British army at the end of World War I in 1918. However, he knew that there was no demobilisation for soldiers of Jesus Christ, and there were other battles to face. Still conscious of his indebtedness to God for sparing his life on the battlefield, he waited for the Lord to open a door for Christian service. After much prayer, he finally applied to the Faith Mission. It was there under the watchful guidance of John George Govan, that Duncan was introduced to an even closer and intimate walk with God.

When his course at the Training Home ended in 1920, Duncan was assigned to evangelism in Northern Ireland. However, his time there was cut short when he was sent back to Scotland to conduct similar missions in his beloved "Highlands and Islands." This work and region were close to his heart, and God mightily used Duncan in remarkable ways across the country. Hundreds of sinners were saved, many weeping their way to Christ.

After four years of itinerant preaching, Duncan's health was so severely affected by his strenuous exertions that he was confined to bed in his lodgings. A doctor diagnosed Duncan with suspected tuberculosis. Besides this, the strains of his constant evangelistic work took their toll. Consequently, Duncan was sent to Glasgow to consult a radiologist, who told him that he had a strained heart and was not only physically ill, but he was at the point of nervous exhaustion. Because of this John George Govan invited Duncan to return to the Training Home in Edinburgh for convalescence and recuperation.

After some months of recovery, Duncan decided to attend the Keswick Convention in 1924. At Keswick, he renewed his acquaintance with Shona Gray, a young lady to whom he had been greatly attracted more than ten years earlier. His heart was smitten and after prayerful consideration and consulting with John George Govan, Duncan resigned from the Faith Mission and married Shona in 1925.

God makes and shapes the vessels He will use.

Danger, Saints at Work

"My strength is made perfect in weakness…"
2 Corinthians 12:7

Craigs Mission Hall is located between the County Antrim towns of Cullybecky and Rasharkin and has maintained a faithful Gospel witness in the locality since 1925. From early January until Easter of 1960 Bill Woods and Billy Magee conducted a very notable mission at the Craigs Mission. In spite of deep drifts of snow on the country lanes, people came from far and near to hear God's servants preach their hearts out night after night. Both of these young men enjoyed great freedom in preaching the Gospel which resulted in scores of people being converted to Christ.

The mission nearly came to an abrupt end when Bill was left with the responsibility of preparing the hall for the evening service. Besides tidying the premises and making sure it was comfortably heated, he tried to light a fire in the potbelly stove in the middle of the hall. This was the only source of heating during those cold winter nights. Bill stuffed paper and sticks into the old stove and tried to ignite them. His efforts were futile for the paper and sticks would not catch fire. Not to be outdone, Bill decided to douse the paper and sticks with paraffin oil. He then opened the stove and threw in a match.

Woof! The stove was engulfed in a blaze of fire, and before Bill could pull back, a sudden sheet of flame leaped up around him scorching his face and clothes. Disregarding his own personal welfare and alarmed that the hall might be destroyed, he frantically tried to douse the flames.

Relieved when the fire was under control, Bill then attended to his singed clothes and appearance. When he looked in the mirror he was aghast. His face was blackened, he had lost his eyelashes, his eyebrows and his hairline had receded, thus increasing his forehead by an inch or more.

Too embarrassed to venture out, Bill sent Billy Magee to do the visitation while he conveniently stayed at home and prayed. God answered prayer and souls were saved.

God delights to use weak vessels.

Full of the Holy Spirit

*"For he was a good man, and full of the Holy Ghost and of faith:
and much people was added unto the Lord."*
Acts 11:24

At the Faith Mission Easter Convention in Bangor, the gifted Ulster preacher, William Patterson Nicholson, shared his testimony. He told how that, in 1891, at fifteen years of age, he left his seaside home in Bangor to become an apprentice seaman. Although a teenager, he was as rugged and hard as the granite from the Mountains of Mourne of Northern Ireland's County Down. As a seaman, he needed to be hard. Young Nicholson spent months at sea without seeing land and often confronted horrific hurricanes and life-threatening dangers in which he sometimes thought he would die. At the same time, he said, he was fearless and bold. He often engaged in bare-fisted fights on deck and elsewhere, "all in with no holds barred."

Mr. Nicholson told that it was his mother's prayers that protected him during those perilous years at sea. God further answered those prayers when he was saved by the grace of God one morning on 22nd May 1899 at his home in Bangor. While he was waiting for breakfast, he was suddenly overwhelmed with a deep conviction of his sin and guilt. Before the breakfast could be served, he fell to his knees and called upon God for mercy. Nicholson said that in an instant he had the assurance that he was saved by the grace of God.

Although saved by the grace of God, Mr. Nicholson had a crisis experience that changed his Christian life. One evening he listened to Rev. Stuart Holden preach at a conference for the "Deepening of the Spiritual Life." At the end of that meeting, "W. P." met with God in a new way. He learned that the secret of victorious Christian living was total surrender to God, to His will and to the fullness of the Holy Spirit on his life.

With the anointing of the Holy Spirit upon him and his ministry W. P. Nicholson became a mighty instrument in the hand of God.

Let the Lord have His way in your life every day.

Learning

*"Strengthened with all might, according to his glorious power,
unto all patience and longsuffering with joyfulness."*
Colossians 1:11

New missionaries often find difficulty coping with new languages and adapting to different cultures. Victor Cardoo related his early experiences in Brazil:

It was recommended that I should travel to language school in Brasilia, the capital of Brazil and over a thousand miles away from where I lived.

The senior missionary took my belongings and me to the Recife bus station for a thousand-mile bus ride that would take at least two days. It was an unforgettable experience. Once we got beyond the city limits the old bus swayed and swerved around large potholes on the highway. Some of those craters were so wide and deep I thought the bus was in danger of being swallowed in one them.

For the next forty-eight hours we bumped our way over unpaved and dusty roads kicking up clouds of dust in our wake. The rough ride made it impossible to sleep although we did have periodic comfort and refreshment stops along the way. Although exhausted, I was excited when we finally saw the city's skyline coming into view, indicating the end of our bus journey.

When I retrieved my suitcase from the rear of the bus it was totally covered with red dust. I tried to blow the dust off the case. Later when I opened my baggage I discovered that all my clothes were covered with the same red dust gathered from those rural roads. Everything was a mess and needed to be washed several times before it could be worn.

When we got there I found that only two candidates had arrived for the language course. They had been expecting another six American candidates, but they had been refused resident visas for Brazil. I waited for two months before it was finally announced that the language course had been cancelled. I was a little frustrated at this - until I remembered that this is Brazil where people are used to programmes being cancelled at short notice and think nothing of it.

*Longsuffering and patience are not mentioned in missionary equipment lists,
but we all need these virtues.*

Building Hebrom

"I have laid the foundation, and another buildeth thereon."
1 Corinthians 3:10

In January 2017 I had the privilege of preaching at a conference to mark the 24th anniversary of the Hebrom Evangelical Church in Manaus, Brazil. What made the occasion very special was the opening of the beautiful new church building with a capacity for 300 people. The three days of meetings to a crowded congregation were filled with praise and wonder at what God had done over the years.

It all began when Fred Orr used his garage for a children's meeting. His family could not find a place of worship in their district so they also conducted Bible studies on Sunday. Evangelism and teaching the Word of God were the main emphasis at these meetings. Within a short time, neighbours drifted into the garage services, and several of them trusted the Saviour.

Missionaries Hazel Miskimmin and Jose Carlos began to visit from door-to-door in the district. People not only responded to the invitation to the garage meetings, some were led to faith in Christ on the doorstep.

When the congregation outgrew the capacity of the garage, Fred purchased a house farther down his own street. Within a short time, the house was renovated to accommodate the increasing number of converts and people attending the meetings.

On 10th January 1993, the Hebrom Evangelical Church was founded, and José Carlos was installed as pastor of the new church. Fred's and José's families along with Hazel gave themselves wholeheartedly to the work. So many people were converted that the original house had to be enlarged twice until it was finally knocked down to build a 150-seater church.

Pastor Herbeth Fernandes became pastor after Fred Orr's death, and through his work, the church continued to grow, and soon they needed a larger auditorium. Herberth, a civil engineer, was able to oversee the construction of this magnificent new church where we had the 24th-anniversary conference.

Bricks and mortar alone do not measure the building of a church. Hebrom Evangelical Church is a training base for Christian workers. It is also a missionary sending church. Their missionaries are serving God all over Brazil and abroad. Their mission is to help build Christ's church.

Living stones fitly joined together.

Humility

"All of you be subject one to another, and be clothed with humility: for God resisteth the proud, and giveth grace to the humble. Humble yourselves therefore under the mighty hand of God, that he may exalt you in due time."
1 Peter 5:5,6

It is amazing how few people admit to having problems with pride. They prefer to think that they are more humble than proud, and some may even be proud of their humility. The Scriptures have so much to say about pride and humility. Twice in the New Testament, it is stated, *"God resisteth the proud, but giveth grace unto the humble"* (James 4:6).

While humility is one of the highest spiritual virtues, pride ranks first among the seven deadly sins in Proverbs 6:16,17: *"Six things doth the Lord hate: yea, seven are an abomination unto him: A proud look…"*

There is no doubt that humility is supremely exemplified in the life of our Lord Jesus who humbled Himself and became obedient unto death, even the death of the cross. It was also seen in the life of Joseph who was humiliated by his brethren, falsely accused by a woman, and forgotten in prison before he was exalted to the highest office in Egypt.

Humility is revealed in our relationships. It is easy to be humble in a vacuum or when we are alone. *"Look not every man on his own things, but every man also on the things of others"* (Philippians 2:4). To be clothed with humility is the picture of our Lord taking a towel and washing the disciples' feet.

Humility is reflected in our attitudes. Humility is a mind-set. *"Let this mind be in you, which was also in Christ Jesus" (Philippians 2:5).*

Humility is required before God. The prophet Micah asked, *"What doth the Lord require of thee, but to do justly, and to love mercy, and to walk humbly with thy God"* (Micah 6:8)? Humility is an acknowledgement of all that God is and who I am, an appreciation of all that He has done and the availability for all that He wants from me.

Humility is rewarded by God. God honours humility with a boundless supply of His grace.

Holiness and humility are twin virtues.

Changed and Charged

"For I am not ashamed of the Gospel of Christ:
for it is the power of God unto salvation…"
Romans 1:16

Belfast's urban redevelopment undoubtedly provided many new houses to replace the streets of two-up-two-down small terrace houses. However, the once familiar names of "… Street" were transformed into "… Gardens', "... Close" or "… Court". In this regeneration programme not only did street names change, but also communities lost their local "corner shop," and many small mission halls became extinct.

Among those halls that closed was Banbury Street Mission Hall. It had a remarkable beginning. In the early 1920s, a group of fellows gathered on Sunday afternoons to play cards and gamble their money on a plot of spare ground in Banbury Street. One day in 1923 a brave and zealous Christian dared to invite these young men to attend an evangelistic Mission at a church on the Newtownards Road. The evangelist was William Patterson Nicholson from Bangor, but the name meant nothing to the lads. However, they agreed to go.

During that mission over 1,000 people professed faith in Christ. On that Sunday afternoon five young men were converted: Jimmy White, Tommy Hunsdale, Jimmy Scott, Sam Hewitt and another pal. These were the lads who had gambled their money at Banbury Street every Sunday.

After their conversion, Jimmy White involved his chums in serving the Lord and between them they acquired the spare ground in Banbury Street where they formerly had wasted time and money. Instead, they invested their meagre funds in purchasing and erecting a wooden hall for evangelistic meetings in this area. This was a forerunner of the more permanent brick building that was constructed some years later.

Out of remarkable beginnings, the Banbury Street Mission Hall was a Gospel Beacon in that part of East Belfast until urban development transformed the community.

Fret not because the place is small,
Thy service need not be,
For thou can'st make all there is
Of joy and ministry

The dewdrop, as the boundless sea,
In God's great plan has part
And this is all He asks of thee;
Be faithful where thou art.

Across the street or across the world, the Gospel is the same.

Do it Again Lord

"In that day shall this song be sung in the land ..."
Isaiah 26:1

Late in 1920 the famed Irish evangelist, William Patterson Nicholson, returned to his native Bangor to recuperate from an operation. Little time was given for his recovery. Very soon he was invited to conduct an evangelistic mission in his hometown. This was the first of many missions he would conduct all over Ulster during the next few years. Through this rugged, fearless and unconventional evangelist, God visited Ulster with revival blessing.

"W. P.", as he was commonly known, spoke the language of the people and at times was not afraid to go beyond the limit by insulting his hearers. It was in the midst of Ulster's political and sectarian strife in 1922, that W. P. began a series of Gospel missions in Belfast and other towns and villages. Such was the magnitude of blessing that Nicholson's powerful and Spirit-anointed preaching fired the souls of Christians with new zeal and expectancy of spiritual life and power.

Thousands were converted, and whole communities were touched and transformed because of what God did through this man. The impact of his powerful ministry resulted in an influx of candidates to various Bible colleges with quite a few of the converts becoming ministers of the major denominations and foreign missionaries with various agencies.

The Faith Mission Easter Convention at Bangor also enjoyed an abiding overflow of blessings in the years that followed this exceptional time of revival. The Bangor-born evangelist was invited to speak at the convention in 1923. On Easter Monday, crowds of Nicholson's young converts marched in a long procession from the Bangor Railway Station to Hamilton Road Presbyterian Church, singing as they went to the accompaniment of bagpipes and other musical instruments.

When the chairman of the meeting announced a hymn, a loud voice of one of these converts called out, "Mr. McLean, will you allow us to lead the hymn with the bagpipes?"

"Certainly," was the reply. Soon the pipes swirled to accompany the congregation joyfully singing, "Let us sing of His love once again..."

All blessings belong to God.

18th April

Welcome Home

"Whilst we are at home in the body, we are absent from the Lord."
2 Corinthians 5:6

Lily Boal's excited family gathered at Belfast docks to welcome her home. "There she is. Here comes our Lily," they shouted.

Lily was absolutely thrilled to see her family after nine fruitful years in volatile Pakistan. She had much to tell. During that first furlough she was delighted to discover that some of her neighbours had been converted and formed part of the Coalmen's Mission. The Coalmen adopted her as their missionary.

Even after those years of service abroad Lily was active in her Belfast City Mission and speaking at meetings for the WEC. When she went to be with Christ in August 1987 she whispered with her last breath, "Jesus, lovely Jesus." That was the secret of her great life. At her funeral Willie Weir, a former missionary colleague, quoted from Bunyan's Pilgrim's Progress a fitting tribute:

"I saw in my dream, that these two men went in at the gate; and lo, as they entered, they were transfigured; and they had raiment put on that shone like gold. There were also those that met them with harps and crowns, and gave them the harps to praise withal, and the crowns in a token of honour. Then I heard in my dream, that all the bells in the city rang again for joy, and that it was said unto them, "enter ye into the joy of your Lord."

I also heard… them sing with a loud voice, saying, *"Blessing, and honour, and glory, and power, be unto Him that sitteth upon the throne, and unto the Lamb, for ever and ever."*

Just as the gates were opened to let in the men, I looked … and behold the city shone like the sun; the streets also were paved with gold; and in them walked many men, with crowns on their heads, palms in their hands, and golden harps, to sing praises withal.

… And they answered one another without intermission, saying, Holy, holy, holy is the Lord. And after that they shut up the gates; which, when I had seen, I wished myself among them."

What a gathering of the ransomed that will be.

God's Call

"Then Samuel answered, 'Speak; for Thy servant heareth.'"
1 Samuel 3:10

In the years that followed C. T. Studd's death in 1931 there was a steady stream of young volunteers ready to follow the sacrifice of the founder of the Worldwide Evangelization Crusade and serve God on distant mission fields. It was then that Ernie Allen started to attend the Mustard Seed Mission in Belfast where there was a farewell service for William and Agnes Weir going to serve God in India.

In July 1936 Mr. John Govan Jr., leader of the Mustard Seed, took a party of friends to the annual Missionary Conference at the Bible College of Wales in Swansea. Ernie did not know it then, but that conference changed his life completely.

Mr. Norman Grubb, son-in-law of C. T. Studd, was the main speaker. Every day he gave challenging reports of what God was doing in the various mission fields and preached inspiring messages from the Word of God. Veteran missionaries and new candidates gave thrilling testimonies and challenging reports each day. A Mr. Pantridge, who had just returned from the Belgian Congo, recounted the moving story of his wife's death in the heart of Africa. For Ernie, the whole week was a moving and life-changing experience.

On Friday morning, 17th July 1936, the conference hall was packed to capacity for the final meeting. It had been a very emotional and impressionable week. Could Ernie Allen ever be the same again? He vividly remembered that last meeting:

God called me to give my life to His service. I knew that the Lord's return was near, and that dark times lay ahead for this world. God gave me a vision of a future worldwide ministry of blessing. The Lord spoke to me and promised, 'If you give your life to me I will give you a life of blessing.' I knelt in full and glad surrender to the Saviour.

On my return home I found that my life had been radically changed, and I had to face up to all that was involved in obeying the call of God.

God's call on Ernie Allen brought blessings to millions.

20th April

Love for the Lost

"Charity never faileth..."
1 Corinthians 13:8

Before going to the Bible College of Wales Hazel Miskimmin trained as a nurse and midwife. This was preparation for the blessings and frustrations she would encounter in Boca do Acre as she reported in 1962.

Medical work continues to open doors for the presentation of the Gospel. At the same time, our hearts are saddened by the number of people who pass into eternity without hearing the Gospel, even once.

A few nights ago some old midwives called Dorrie Gunning and I go to a confinement that was too difficult for them. The poor woman had been suffering for two days and her condition was critical. Four hours later she delivered a stillborn baby whom we believed had been dead for some time. If this mother had been left much longer, she certainly would have died.

That same night, another woman across the River Acre was in great difficulty in the birth of her twin boys. Her husband was on his way to call us when someone told him that we were already attending to another confinement. When he returned home, he was devastated to find that his wife had already died before giving birth to their second baby.

On the next day, another urgent call came to attend an expectant mother who lived upriver. Even before we boarded the dugout canoe, news arrived to say that the woman had bled to death. The grief of this family was terrible to see. Can you understand something of our burden as we wondered just how much of the Gospel that woman had ever heard? Did she, or did she not ever hear of the way of salvation?

A few nights ago a man stood up in church and said that midwifery had been a great testimony for the Lord in Boca do Acre. He referred to the first case mentioned in this report. Many friends of that family expressed their desire to attend the meetings including the young mother who was safely delivered.

The words of the hymn came to me: "See, they are looking learning of you, silently watching all that you do."

Love shows God's way.

Rescuing the Perishing

"And the common people heard Him gladly."
Mark 12:37

Although born in Londonderry, Raymond McKeown was taken to Scotland as a young boy. Following his conversion in Scotland, he was greatly influenced by the ministry of Jock Troop at Glasgow's famous Tent Hall. Raymond followed the role model of this renowned Scottish preacher but developed his own skills and abilities, which would make him one of the most gifted open-air preachers in the United Kingdom.

While working at the Govan Shipyard, he often used his lunch hour to conduct open-air meetings at the shipyard gates. These were bright and engaging and often began with Raymond playing his accordion and singing lively Gospel songs. His genial manner and ready wit were greatly enhanced by his Glaswegian accent and his use of the plain man's language. These combined qualities soon captivated his listening audience. Those who knew Raymond will always remember his famous Saturday night and Sunday afternoon gatherings at Glasgow's Toll Cross and the "Barras" market.

Quite a few Glasgow musicians were converted through Raymond's ministry, and many joined him with their trumpets, clarinets, and saxophones. The tempo was upbeat, but the message was always clear and dynamic, and many passers-by were converted as a result of those open-air meetings.

Raymond became pastor at Belfast's Templemore Hall in November 1982. Alongside all the normal duties of a busy pastorate, he immediately embarked on a vigorous open-air Gospel campaign in many unlikely places around the city. On Friday mornings he led a small group of men to the Short Strand, an area many considered to be "off limits" for Protestant preachers. However, the Short Strand residents warmly received Raymond and enjoyed listening to "the wee Scotsman with his accordion." Raymond also conducted effective open-air meetings in front of Belfast's City Hall, at the gates of Harland Wolff Shipyard, at Mackie's Factory, at Gallagher's Cigarette Factory and anywhere else he could muster up a crowd to listen to the Gospel.

Raymond also imparted to many his burden for a spiritual revival and his passion for prayer. Sadly, his effective ministry in Belfast was abruptly interrupted after two short years by his sudden death in May 1985.

Rescue the perishing, tell them of Jesus, the mighty to save.

Evangelism

"Do the work of an evangelist, make full proof of thy ministry."
2 Timothy 4:5

The Irish evangelist, W. P. Nicholson, first stepped out into Christian work when he enrolled as a student at the Bible Training Institute (BTI) in Glasgow's Bothwell Street. The Institute had opened in 1892 following the D. L. Moody and Ira Sankey's evangelistic enterprise in the city.

Although W. P.'s soul was on fire for evangelism before going to college, that zeal was greatly boosted when he engaged in open-air preaching in Scotland. It was then that he came into contact with the founder of the Faith Mission, John George Govan.

Nicholson wrote of that time: "I first came into contact with the Faith Mission, its work and workers, when I was a student at the BTI in Glasgow. Several of us were appointed for work with the Mission at the Ayr Races. What a time we had – preaching, singing and marching! … We all rested and had refreshments together, between times. During one of those intervals, I was introduced to Mr. J. G. Govan. I remember wondering at the time how one so cultured, reserved and quiet could be the founder and leader of such an out-and-out, religiously unfashionable organization. There was a quiet intensity about him – a greediness to buy up the time and lose none of it. I wondered about this at the time; for, after our meals, while we were laughing and talking about our experiences and feelings, he quietly sat in a corner, working away at his correspondence. Every now and then he enjoyed a laugh as heartily as any of us; but he had much work to be done. It was a lesson to me then, as a young convert, and has been a blessing to me ever since.

I was evangelizing for several years in Lanarkshire after that and came into contact with Pilgrims quite frequently. One of my assistants was one of the first Pilgrims – Miss Agnes Jack. What a fearless, untiring, uncompromising warrior, always ready for any unconventional, dare-devil attack on the devil and his works."

An evangelist is a good messenger of good news.

Vision and Vigour

"Those women which laboured with me in the Gospel ...."
Philippians 4:3

Nell Shannon and Dulce Robertson were two remarkable but contrasting spinsters who dedicated their lives to reach others with the Gospel in Amazonas, Brazil. Nell never forgot she was from Belfast's Shankill Road, and although she spent the greater part of her life abroad, she never lost her rich Belfast accent nor did she forsake her Irish colloquialisms. On the other hand, Dulce was from Scotland with a more refined and soft Scottish accent. Nell was a loud extrovert who was not slow to give her opinion, whereas Dulce was quiet, restrained and possibly more dignified. For all their disparities, these two combined to make an excellent and effective pair of Christian workers.

Both ladies arrived in Brazil almost simultaneously not long after the end of World War II. Although unknown to each other at that time, their intention was to be available for work amongst indigenous Indians in the Amazon. It was while studying Portuguese that they met, and their early zeal to reach the lost for Christ pitted them together. During those early months God redirected their initial intent from Indians to see the benefits of reaching Brazilians with the Gospel through Christian literature.

That zeal and conviction prompted Nell and Dulce to open an evangelistic stall at the entrance of the Municipal Central Market in Manaus. Surrounded by traders trying to make a living, the two ladies distributed literature from early morning, 6.30 a.m., until afternoon. They witnessed to the everyday traders and customers, and they spoke to travellers boarding or disembarking nearby riverboats: they saw each of these as an opportunity to engage in conversation about their Saviour. During more than thirty years they had the joy of leading many to personal faith in Christ.

When Nell had to finally return to Northern Ireland due to failing health, Dulce quietly continued that work every day. Advanced years and ill health soon caught up with Dulce, and when she had to reluctantly leave Brazil she recruited Hazel Miskimmin to take her place at the market.

Although all three ladies are now in heaven, that work continues with Raimundo Nonato still witnessing to the Gospel at the central market every day.

What rejoicing there will be in His presence.

A Delayed Harvest

"Forasmuch as ye know that your labour is not in vain in the Lord."
1 Corinthians 15:58

One Sunday in May 1956, W. E. Tocher, in his eighty-sixth year, preached his final sermon in Templemore Hall. His health had been failing, and in his latter days, he had to be carried to the pulpit and propped up between two good friends while he preached.

On that Sunday Mr. Tocher collapsed in the pulpit, and a local doctor was summoned. The aged preacher recovered somewhat, but before the physician left Mr. Tocher stood up, steadied himself on his stick and thanked the doctor for his kind attention. He finished by saying, "Young man, I have one thing to say, 'Jesus is coming. No Surrender!'"

One memorable experience in Mr. Tocher's ministry was in 1937 when Pastor George Olley invited him to Newtownards Baptist Church for an evangelistic mission. The meetings were well attended, and Tocher preached his heart out every night. However, there were no evident results at the end of three weeks, and inevitably, the evangelist searched his own heart and questioned why no one had been converted.

Seven years later, an ill Mr. Tocher received a visit from a young up-and-coming preacher. In the course of the conversation, Tocher asked the young man to tell how he had been converted. The visitor related that his conversion happened after attending Tocher's mission in Newtownards in 1937. At the time the young preacher had been a wayward prodigal and a virtual outcast of society. He went on to tell the sick but surprised pastor, how he had stumbled into those meetings, and as a result of Tocher's preaching, he had received Jesus Christ as Saviour.

That convert was the well-known Ulster preacher, Willie Mullen, who in later years would be instrumental in leading hundreds of people to Jesus Christ.

Mr. Tocher's home-call was sudden and stunning. News of his death made front-page headlines in the *Belfast Telegraph*. Before his death, Mr. Tocher confessed that the Newtownards mission was the most productive he had ever conducted even though he did not recognise it at the time.

We may plant and water, but only God can give the increase.

Fervent in Spirit

"Serving the Lord with all humility of mind, and with many tears."
Acts 20:19

When W. P. Nicholson returned to Northern Ireland from his evangelistic travels with American evangelist and Bible teacher, Dr. R. A. Torrey, he spoke of the times of blessing he experienced with the Faith Mission.

"For years after that, I was wandering over the face of the earth like an Ishmaelite, my hand was against sin and the devil and their hand against me. After that, I came home to recuperate and have a rest.

I wasn't long home until we began work in the Province of my birth and love. Revival truly broke out all over Ulster, and the most loyal and enthusiastic helpers I had were the Faith Mission workers. Wherever we went, when we met a man or a woman with a Faith Mission badge we knew we were in touch with an out-and-out worker. I had the joy here and there of speaking at their Conferences, and when I saw the results of their labours at these Conferences – fine young stalwart men and women by the score, ready to speak, sing, or pray – made my heart rejoice.

These conferences were held in the most unlikely, out-of-the-way places, where the footfall of an evangelist is never heard. Living in labourers' cottages, some of them in caravans; enduring privation and loneliness; visiting farmhouses and cottages, inviting the people to the meetings, and winning many to Christ; not going to a place for a specified time, but staying right there until something happened - such were their ways. And something generally did happen, as those Saturday Conferences proved.

Evangelists usually only go to where they are invited. If these places were only to have an evangelistic mission when they invited an evangelist they would never have one. But these workers go where neither man nor devil - and sometimes not the Church – wants them; they get an Orange Hall, or a kitchen, or a barn, anywhere, as long as they get a place, and begin their mission, and stay until God breaks out in mighty power. God bless them for their dogged determination and persistent perseverance!

There is no greater joy than serving Jesus.

Be Sure to Do Good

*"As we have therefore opportunity, let us do good unto all men,
especially unto them who are of the household of faith."*
Galatians 6:10

When Allen and Ada Loney arrived in Canutama, they were aghast to find a very high infant mortality rate. One lady said she had given birth to seventeen children, and eleven of them had died soon after birth.

One day Senhor Francisco arrived at the Mission house and begged Allen and Ada to urgently go down river to a small community where his two little daughters were seriously ill. When they arrived at the riverside dwelling, they met Francisco's distraught wife, Dona Dalha. She wept over her two beautiful little girls who lay listlessly on a bed. It was obvious to the missionaries that the older daughter, a seven-year-old, was dying and they had arrived too late to help her.

Ada, wanting to do all possible to help in this distressing situation, suggested that she and Allen would take the younger girl back to Canutama and try to treat her. At first, the girl's mother was a little reluctant to part with her sick daughter, but Francisco, the father, spoke up, "We have nothing to lose. She is going to die if she remains here, and that will mean that we will have lost both of our daughters."

Ada reassured Dona Dalha that they would do everything possible for the little girl and hoped to see her restored to the family soon. Ada soon discovered that little Eliene's distended abdomen was full of worms and as a result, she was very anaemic. They treated her with lots of tender love and diligent care. Gradually Eliene began to recover, and the colour returned to her previously pale cheeks.

It was a difficult day for Ada when she had to hand the little girl back to her parents, but there were tears of joy when the family was reunited. Subsequently, Francisco and Dalha became Christians and moved to Manaus. Now, decades later, Eliene continues to follow the Lord. One of her brothers is a Baptist pastor, and the other is a Christian lawyer.

Our service on earth will echo in eternity.

Not Counting The Cost

"Because that for His name's sake they went forth."
3 John 7

Reaching Muslim children for Jesus Christ was the burden and vision that captivated Lily Boal. Initially, she was aiming to go to Arabia, a formidable and dangerous place for Christian missionaries, more so for single ladies. Her passionate obedience to God's call meant foregoing offers of courtship and marriage, but God had called and she must follow.

The challenging story of C. T. Studd, the famous cricketer and pioneer missionary who forsook his family fortune to serve God in China, India and Africa, prompted Lily to apply to the Worldwide Evangelization Crusade to work in Arabia. After learning that Arabia was closed to lady missionaries Lily accepted the counsel of senior staff to serve God in the Kashmir region of Northwest India.

When Lily sailed down Belfast Lough en-route to Asia she did not know that she had said goodbye to her family and loved ones for nine years. World War II broke out four months after she arrived in India. Like numerous missionaries of that generation, Lily and her colleagues were prohibited from international travel during those years of worldwide conflict.

When she finally arrived in Kashmir Lily was immediately introduced to caring for children in a Christian Boarding school. Besides trying to learn Urdu, she was assigned to supervising meals, washing clothes, bathing children and looking after their general welfare. Most of these students were separated from their parents because of persecution against Christian converts. Lily took to all this responsibility quickly and capably.

Even with the inevitable language frustrations, Lily was soon able to make herself understood by her energetic gestures and increased volume of her limited vocabulary. Wrong words or mispronunciation often caused great amusement and hilarity for the children, like the time Lily told them that one of their aunties had gone to heaven when she should have said that she had gone out to the land. It was even worse when one of her colleagues said to the congregation "We are all God's monkeys." Language study can be frustrating, but Lily was where God called her and that was enough.

No sacrifice is too great when Jesus is Lord.

Do It Again Lord

"The lines have fallen unto me in pleasant places, yea,
I have a goodly heritage."
Psalm 16:6

While we might lament the spiritual dearth of our nation today and long for a great revival, we also have much to be thankful for in our generation.

It is difficult for us to imagine what life was like back in the early 19th century. At that time Belfast was a misty, damp and impoverished town with a population of about 40,000. The city boundary to the north was Boundary Street and Townsend Street, as the names suggest. Green fields stretched from the south side of Donegall Square to Donegall Pass, which was only a country lane with a few residents. These people were subjected to the foul aroma from the Paper Mill Dam, which covered most of what is now Ormeau Avenue. Cromac Street, Peter's Hill and Sandy Row were more densely populated areas and Queens Island, with its decorative gardens, amusements and bathing facilities was one of Belfast's beauty spots.

Housing was poor, and life was arduous for most families. Amenities such as running water, light and sewage were primitive. Many homes burned candles, and the very poor used rushlight, which consisted of rushes dipped in grease. Generally, the lifespan was short and miserable for many. A report written by a lady at the time is pathetic: "In a house I found a poor woman sitting picking among cinders. That was her daily employment. She said, 'I go out in the morning to gather them. Then I come home to clean them and then sell them. That is just the way I get a morsel of bread.'"

As the population increased social deprivation worsened. High unemployment resulted in increased crime and drunkenness. Police and court records indicate that juvenile delinquency was rife and increasing at an alarming rate.

Added to all this, in 1836 a terrible outbreak of cholera wreaked havoc in Belfast. Sheds were erected to accommodate and treat hundreds of cholera victims, and every day the dead were carried to the graveyards.

Such social conditions and deprivations were the backdrops into which came the great Ulster revival of 1859.

We may be more prosperous today, but our greatest need is such a revival.

We Must Preach the Gospel

"Necessity is laid upon me; yea, woe is unto me, if I preach not the Gospel."
1 Corinthians 9:19

John George Govan's passion for the lost was something he endeavored to impart to his colleagues in the Faith Mission. Speaking to the Mission's workers, he said:

"Grace, grit, and gumption are needed by Pilgrims. God has taken men and women from behind the plough, behind the counter from crofts and fishing boats, and made them mighty in prayer, and in preaching the everlasting Gospel. Academic qualifications are not to be despised, but the one indispensable qualification for soul winning is the baptism of the Holy Ghost. We have no power of our own, but living faith links us to His power. If all of us . . . . were baptized with the Holy Ghost and with fire, what an awakening and conflagration there would be! Surely such an experience is worth waiting for and sacrificing all for.

Unless we are in living touch with the Lord, we will not be equal to the task. I consider the "morning watch" one of the most important things in the life of a Faith Mission worker. Out of touch with Christ, we become powerless, formal and a burden in our work. Time needs to be set apart for special seasons of waiting upon God for spiritual renewal if we are going to be 'more than conquerors.' We need to know experimentally the "renewing of the Holy Ghost."

If The Faith Mission ceases to be a soul-saving agency it does not deserve to exist. Evangelism, the saving of souls, reaching the lost, rescuing men, women, boys, and girls from a lost hell, is at the heart of our entire ministry."

John Govan's early vision and vigour for the work of the Faith Mission has been perpetuated through dedicated workers who continued to preach the Gospel to millions of people throughout successive generations. They have been faithful to the rural population of Great Britain and have taken the Gospel across the world. Countless numbers of people, young and old, were led to Christ through its ministry.

Let us labour for the Lord of the harvest.

Foreign Faith

"O woman, great is thy faith: be it unto thee even as thou wilt."
Matthew 15:28

We live in a global village. With rapidly developing transportation people can travel to any part of our planet within twenty-four hours. How things have changed. Our voyage to Brazil in 1965 took six weeks. When Scottish missionary, Dr Alexander Duff travelled to India in 1829, the journey lasted six months having suffered two shipwrecks on the way.

The ease by which we can traverse our world is in stark contrast to our Saviour who never travelled far. He was an Infant refugee in Egypt, and the only other time He stepped outside Israel was to withdraw to Tyre and Sidon where His mercy spilled over foreign borders to perform a memorable miracle for a desperate Canaanite mother.

This Canaanite *woman overcame her obstacles*. Jesus sent out His disciples telling them to not go to the Gentiles but to the lost sheep of Israel. Mark describes this lady as a Greek born in Syro-Phoenicia. To obtain any help from Jesus she had to overcome regional and racial obstacles. We are not told how she came to know about Jesus, but she needed the help of the Saviour of the world for her demon-possessed daughter.

This woman seized her opportunity. Although Jesus requested that none tell of His whereabouts. His presence could not be hidden. This woman heard that Jesus was nearby and came crying to Him, "Lord, Son of David, have mercy on me!" Jesus remained quiet. His disciples urged Him, "Send her away, for she keeps crying out after us." Our Lord did not send her away. He simply said, "I was sent only to the lost sheep of Israel."

This woman secured her objective. Although a Gentile she addressed Jesus as "Son of David." The Saviour said, "It is not right to take the children's bread and toss it to their dogs." Her reaction was both brilliant and discerning, "Yes Lord, but even the dogs eat the crumbs that fall from the Master's table."

Jesus commended her, "Woman you have great faith." With that, Jesus sent her home with the assurance that He had cast the demon out of her daughter.

He still is the Saviour of the world.

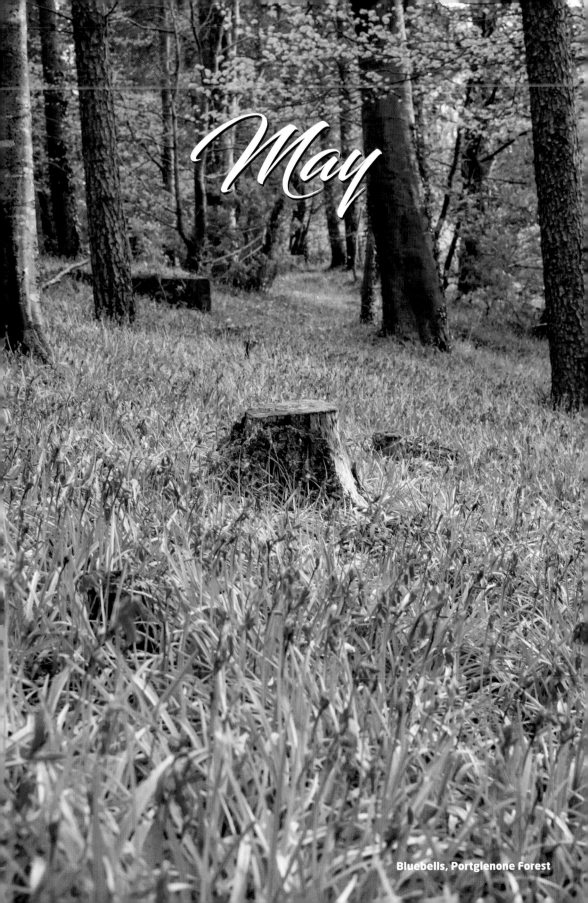

May

Bluebells, Portglenone Forest

Ready to Preach

"As much as in me is, I am ready to preach the Gospel to you that are at Rome also."
Romans 1:15

The renowned Dr. Hyman Appleman and a team of American evangelists arrived in Belfast in 1959. They came at the invitation of Ernie Allen of the Revival Movement to conduct special evangelistic meetings to mark the centenary of Ulster's great 1859 spiritual awakening. The main meetings were convened at Belfast's Wellington Hall while other evangelistic campaigns were organised in churches throughout the city.

A young Texan accompanying Dr. Appleman was Johnny Bisagno. Before his conversion Johnny had been a dance-band leader and a popular solo trombone player in the USA. Dr. Appleman recruited Johnny to use his musical talent during this tour for the glory of God.

Johnny was surprised when he was invited to conduct special evangelistic meetings at the Roslyn Street Emmanuel Mission Hall. He had arrived in Belfast to play his trombone. Notwithstanding his surprise, the young American preached fervently every night and delighted the crowds with his musical expertise.

Pastor John Proctor and friends at Roslyn Street worked hard visiting every home in the Woodstock and Cregagh Road area to invite people to this special campaign. The meetings were bright; the singing was enthusiastic, and the hall was packed with people of all ages. Amongst many who trusted the Lord as Saviour at those meetings was young Stanley Barnes. He lived only a few doors from the Emmanuel Hall, and with his seven brothers and only sister, had attended Emmanuel Hall throughout his childhood.

Following his conversion, Stanley and his wife Ina, were called to serve God as missionaries in Spain before returning to Northern Ireland where he did an outstanding work for thirty-five years as the minister at Hillsborough Free Presbyterian Church.

Furthermore, that Roslyn Street mission was a turning point for Johnny Bisagno. As a result of God's blessing on his ministry Johnny felt constrained to embark on an evangelistic ministry. This eventually led him to become pastor of the First Baptist Church of Houston, Texas, and later the President of the Southern Baptist Convention of the Untied States.

Availability is supremely important.

Faithful Fools

"We are fools for Christ's sake..."
1 Corinthians 4:10

William Patterson Nicholson enthusiastically spoke to the large congregation at the Faith Mission Convention in Bangor in 1927. He told of the day in 1900 when a "massed band" of four people marched, all of them out-of-step, down the town's main street. He said that two of the four were Salvation Army lassies in uniform, and the other two were young men, "one with a mind as keen as a razor's edge; the other hadn't enough brains to give him a nucleus for a headache." One of the men led the little parade beating on a tuneless tambourine.

Although "W. P." had vowed to God that he would go anywhere and do anything at any cost for Christ's sake, he was put on the spot that day when one of the girls asked him to stand with them at the street corner to witness for Christ.

W. P. thought how he could get himself off the hook, but not one excuse would come. He said, "Daft Jimmy, the nitwit who stood with the Sally lassies, wore a red jersey. On the back of it in white letters was written the startling non-scriptural text, 'Saved from Public Opinion.'"

Bystanders laughed at the little band marching past, but W. P. knew that public opinion was his greatest enemy. To make matters worse, it seemed that his every friend, relative, and enemy passed the corner as he stood there.

Just then, one of the Salvation Army girls suggested that they all kneel down and ask the Lord to "take over." W. P. blushed as he knelt with them. He said that something happened when he arose from his knees. He felt he had died to his reputation and to public opinion. There and then he had a public funeral of self in that street meeting.

W. P. was triumphant for he had "just lost what he never wanted to find again and had just found what he never wanted to lose." He lost his reputation and fear of man and found the joy and peace of the overflowing fullness of the Spirit.

He is no fool who stands for Christ.

Peter's First Sermon

"Peter, standing up with the eleven, lifted up his voice,
and said unto them..."
Acts 2:14

Just about every preacher can recall his first sermon--maybe with a little embarrassment. I remember in my youth the first public meeting my friends and I ever conducted. The meeting began at 8:00 p.m., and after we had sung a few hymns, had given a testimony and had preached the sermon the meeting was over by 8.30 p.m. Maybe short meetings like that would be popular with some people.

The Apostle Peter's first sermon was a memorable one. Hermeneutics deals with the principles of Bible interpretation, and homiletics deals with the art of preparation and delivery of a sermon. A study of such skills can leave the student cold and sterile. However, general observation of Peter's preaching gives us good down-to-earth and heart warming principles that are valuable, not only for all would-be preachers, but also for all who love the Word of God.

Peter's preaching was Spirit-filled. Peter was filled with the Holy Ghost when he preached. Murray McCheyne said, "There is nothing more indecent than a dead preacher bringing to dead sinners the living truth of the living God." There is a vast difference between bringing sermons and bringing God's message. Sermonising and energising are not equals.

Peter's preaching was simple and short. Too often we assume that profound preaching must be above our heads. Preaching the Word is not to be served up on high tables for giraffes but on the ground for sheep.

Peter's preaching was scripturally based. Peter preached the Word of God. He freely quoted from the prophecy of Joel and the Psalms of David. Peter not only preached the Word, he knew the Word, and he knew how to rightly divide the Word and apply it to his hearers.

Peter's preaching was Saviour-centred. Jesus Christ was the central theme of Peter's message. He majored on the Person of the Lord Jesus, His redemptive work on Calvary, His resurrection from the dead and on the promises He has given us.

Peter's preaching was specific. He preached with the authority of the Scriptures, but he also addressed the needs of sinners.

A good sermon is a feast on God's Word

Fearful But Prayerful

"And he called his ... servants, ... and said unto them, 'Occupy till I come.'"
Luke 19:13

Life for missionary Lily Boal became increasingly perilous in Northwest India after World War II. While India was finalizing its struggle to gain independence from Britain, the Muslim dominated Western Punjab was making frenzied demands for an independent homeland separate from India. After a bloody and brutal struggle in which thousands died, the Punjab State was divided to create Pakistan as a separate nation in 1947.

Just then Lily was looking forward to her first furlough after nine years absence from Northern Ireland. Before leaving colleagues in Bunyar, she travelled on the back of a horse-drawn wagon for over sixty miles of dusty roads to make some purchases and say goodbye to friends and her Kashmiri children. Unknown to her, notorious tribesmen had commandeered many trucks and were inciting violence in the region. Halfway on the journey news of these barbarous events alarmed Lily, and she decided to return.

When Lily carried her fears and anxieties to God in prayer she sensed the Lord spoke to her, "Occupy till I come." With this word, despite the imminent danger, Lily felt it was her duty to return to her colleagues in Bunyar.

By this time thousands of people were fleeing from the marauding tribesmen. Some managed to escape, but scores were slaughtered on the roadsides. Lily was anxious to find any kind of transport to Bunyar. One man she approached cried to her, "Miss Sahib, the tribesmen are fast approaching, and it is very dangerous." But Lily's desperation prevailed, and he agreed to take her part way by boat to Baramulla, fifteen miles short of Bunyar.

Already in Baramulla yells and shrieks could be heard from people being tortured and killed. Even though the streets were thronged with fleeing refugees, Lily asked a man for transport to Bunyar on his wagon. He said, "If you were to pay me a thousand rupees, I would not dare to take you there. You had better run to a safe place or you will be murdered."

With this Lily fled for shelter at a local hospital and found refuge in her Lord.

His peace passes our understanding.

The Real Saviour

"All that Jesus began both to do and teach."
Acts 1:1

During our many visits to Israel we walked the dusty highways of Judaea where Jesus walked, strolled by the beautiful shores of Galilee, moved down the steep slopes of Mount of Olives, crowded through the narrow streets of Jerusalem and explored where Jesus played as a boy in Nazareth. Like many other visitors, we often wished we could have been there when Jesus walked those roads.

If we could return to that first century during the ministry of our Lord at what incident would you like to have been present? How about the feeding of the five thousand? That's my favourite. Which sermon would you like to have heard Jesus speak? How about the Sermon on the Mount or His Upper Room discourse?

More importantly, if you could have been there, with which group would you have identified? The Scribes or the Pharisees who scrutinized and criticized Him? The disciples who followed Him? The women who helped Him? The lad who gave his all to Jesus? More than likely, we might have been like most people of His generation, having our misgivings or even have repeated some stupid remarks just like His disciples did.

We do not have to go back in time to know Jesus. Luke has lifted Him from the pages of history and brought Him to us, to where we are today. He presented the Lord Jesus as the heaven-sent Saviour with a human touch.

The Christ who identified with the real world. He toiled under the harsh sun and felt the hard earth under His feet. He understands what real life is all about.

The Christ who is touched with real needs. As the Son of Man, He touched a ragged leper, gave strength to a paralytic, gave sight to the blind and expelled demons from many enslaved by the devil. Jesus feels our pain and knows our weaknesses.

The Christ who provides real comfort. Luke tells us that Jesus was the Great Physician and the Friend of publicans and sinners, who not only sympathized with souls, but He also saves them through the power of the Cross.

He is still the Christ of the human road.

God's Template

"Ye shall receive power, after that the Holy Ghost is come upon you: and ye shall be witnesses unto me both in Jerusalem, and in all Judaea, and in Samaria, and unto the uttermost part of the earth."
Acts 1:8

The greatest work that God is doing in the world today is bringing in the redeemed and the building of His church. The political structures of the nations are similar to scaffolding around a building. When the construction is completed, the scaffolding is dismantled, and the new facility is in full view. One day God will dismantle the political systems of the nations, and there will be one glorious church--His bride and His body. For this greatest of all works consider the following:

The people God chooses -- "Ye shall be witnesses..." The Lord Jesus hand-picked His disciples. Most of them were fishermen, more acquainted with boats and nets than the trappings of religion. None of them had been trained in the great theological schools of that day. Likewise, God has enlisted every Christian to be a witness for Him.

The plan God uses -- "witnesses unto Me." In Acts, the word "witness" occurs almost thirty times. These believers were to be witnesses in the present rather than prophets of the future. Each of them was to be an individual witness for Christ.

The Person God exalts – "unto Me." The Holy Spirit was sent to testify of Jesus Christ. Our witness is not for our church or our denomination. Christian witnesses should speak of Jesus Christ. He was the theme of New Testament preaching; He was at the heart of their writings and the sole motive for their living.

The places God reaches – "Jerusalem, Judaea, Samaria, the uttermost part of the earth." Luke followed this pattern for the growth of the Gospel in the book of Acts. God still commands us to go into all the world and preach the Gospel to every creature.

The power God promised. – "Ye shall receive the promise … ye shall receive power." Before the Holy Spirit came, the disciples did not know God's power. After He had come, they were filled with His power.

Without the Holy Spirit, our witness will be ineffective and sterile.

They Came To Christ

"And they came to Him from every quarter."
Mark 1:45

Mark gives an account of a full twenty-four hours in the Saviour's life in the Galilee region. It began in the bright sunshine of a Galilean morning when Jesus walked by the lake and called fishermen to follow Him. It moved into a mid-morning visit to the synagogue in Capernaum to teach the Scriptures. In the afternoon, He visited Peter's home where He healed Peter's mother-in-law. That evening multitudes of needy people found their way to Jesus for His help and healing. Mark's account concludes in chapter 1 with the Lord Jesus on a solitary prayer-vigil in the hills during the lonely hours of the early morning. This twenty-four-hour period shows how our Lord's was life full and busy.

The Jewish historian, Josephus, tells us that at the time of our Lord there were over 200 cities and villages in the region of Galilee. Because the land was so fertile, it was a booming area for farmers; in fact, farming was the number one occupation of that day. He estimated that the smallest villages and cities contained at least 1,000 people. Galilee probably contained at least three million people.

Mark ends his first chapter with these words, *"they came to him from every quarter."*

All sorts of people came to Christ. Rich people like Zacchaeus came to Him. Religious people like Nicodemus sought Him. The rebellious like the Demoniac from the Gadarenes needed Jesus. We all need the Saviour.

All sorts of places from which they came. Matthew left his business desk to follow Christ. Fishermen left their boats and Zacchaeus came from up a tree to take Christ home. Leprous men emerged from their isolation to ask for His touch.

All sorts of problems they brought. The Bible speaks of diverse diseases. The people's problems were many. They were afflicted with diseases, tormented by demons, whipped by despair and fearful of death.

The only Person to whom they came. They did not go to the priests in the Temple. They sought Jesus--the only One who could help and heal them.

Where else can we go but to the Lord?

Decisions

"Strive to enter in at the strait gate…"
Luke 13:24

Back in July 1965 Audrey and I took our colleague, Hazel Miskimmin, to the airport for her first trip home from Brazil. Because she was making her first international flight, we gave her good instructions what to look out for. The flight was on an Air France Caravelle jet liner. The planned route was to be from Manaus to Paris and then make a connection to London where Fred Orr's father had planned to meet her.

During the ten-hour flight from Manaus to Paris Hazel was able to doze a little, but she was excited about meeting her family who she had not seen for more than four years. On arrival in Paris, things did not go as planned. Hazel got caught up with the wrong crowd at the transfer gate and boarded a flight to Frankfurt instead of London. She knew nothing about the mistake until she heard the flight attendant say, "Put your seat in the upright position and make sure your seat belt is buckled, for we are due to land in Frankfurt. It was then that the alarm bells began to ring in Hazel's mind: *Frankfurt? I am going to London. Mr. Orr is waiting for me. What am I going to do?*

The airline took care of the frustrated missionary, and Hazel arrived in London on the following morning and eventually made it home to Belfast later that day. On retracing her mistakes, she found that she had made the wrong decision, entered the wrong gate, followed the wrong crowd and ended up at the wrong destination.

Wouldn't it be wonderful if we all had a mechanism that guaranteed that we always made the right decisions? Too often we make the wrong ones. Jesus Christ urged us to make the right decision. It is the most critical decision of all, the decision about Christ and His kingdom. That ultimate choice will determine our eternal destiny. Although God is sovereign, yet He holds us responsible for the choices we make.

Joshua challenged at the end of His life, "Choose you this day whom ye will serve…"

Our decision will determine our destiny.

Persecuted

*"They laid hands on them, and put them in hold unto the next day:
for it was now eventide."*
Acts 4:3

For most of us "persecution" is just another word in our evangelical vocabulary. It is doubtful if any of us have ever suffered or are likely to suffer physical persecution for the Gospel's sake. We have never felt the searing stripes of a vicious whip as a persecutor lashes our backs for attending a prayer meeting. None of us have ever had to run through hot cinders nor felt the flames of fire lick round our feet, as did the martyrs. Thankfully, we have never had to watch our children suffer mortal wounds because we are Christians. We have never had to stare down the barrel of a gun nor feel the keen edge of a knife thrust into our bodies. We can barely imagine the loneliness of imprisonment for the Gospel's sake.

Sadly, what is true of us here is not true of all places. While we gather in safety and peace in our churches, we must acknowledge and pray for brothers and sisters, true Christian soldiers, who suffer physical hardship and have suffered martyrdom for their faith in Jesus Christ.

Such sufferings were not spared on the early church. I think we could say that Peter and John were the "pioneers of persecution" in the early church. Not only the pioneers, but they also left us a pattern to follow in times of persecution.

In Acts, we see the principle that Paul taught to the Corinthians that God had entrusted the greatest of treasures to ordinary earthen vessels. Satan cannot touch the treasure, but he buffets the vessel. The treasure is valuable, but the vessel is vulnerable.

Peter and John were tough but tender, bound but not broken, troubled but not distressed, and persecuted but not deserted. They had just experienced a tremendous miracle that gave them an opportunity to preach the Gospel. After the message finished Satan persecuted the vessels because of the treasure within.

Peter and John's testimony led to testing, and this led to a triumph of faith that glorified their Lord.

Take time to pray for saints in persecuted lands.

The Greatest

"But I say unto you, that in this place is one greater than the temple."
Matthew 12:6

Israel is an archeologist's paradise. Digs are taking place all over the country. One of the most amazing happened in 2009 just north of Tiberias and near to Capernaum, on the shores of Galilee. Bulldozers had moved in to clear a fairground that had long since outlived its usefulness and its owner's profitability. It was to be replaced with a modern ecumenical centre. The operator of one bulldozer had to stop his machine when the dozer's blade hit a solid stone that was less than a metre below the topsoil.

As is routine in Israel, archeologists were called to the scene. In the course of their dig, they discovered that the stone was part of the first-century Jewish synagogue at Magdala, the hometown of Mary Magdalene. A coin minted during Jesus' public ministry, in 29 AD, was found in a room adjoining the synagogue. We visited the restored site and saw how the synagogue was decorated with colorful frescoes and floor mosaics that were contemporary to Jesus' day. A stone pedestal that was used for reading the Torah stands in its place.

It was here that our Lord stood in this same synagogue and disputed with His critics about the disciples plucking corn on the Sabbath. The Pharisees protested that Jesus' disciples were breaking the Sabbath law.

Our Lord answered them by saying that there stood One amongst them who was greater than the Temple. Their eyes might have been fixed on the large stone in their midst that probably was the reading desk for the Torah. The carvings of the seven-branched menorah and the altar on the stone portray a model of the first-century Temple. Can Jesus be greater than the Temple?

Our Saviour astonished them even more when He proceeded to say that He was greater than the prophet Jonah and superior to King Solomon. Those words were undoubtedly met with ridicule and contempt. However, they were not lost on the most distinguished citizen of Magdala, Mary Magdalene. She discovered that He was the greatest of all--her Prophet, Priest, and King.

Jesus Christ is Lord.

Crossroads

"The path of the just is as the shining light,
that shineth more and more unto the perfect day."
Proverbs 4:18

At the Donegall Road, Belfast City Mission, we used to sing with great gusto:

> I met Jesus at the cross roads,
> Where the two ways meet;
> Satan too was standing there,
> And he said 'Come this way,
> Lots and lots of pleasures I can give to you this day.'
> But I said 'No! There's Jesus here,
> Just see what He offers me:
> Down here my sins forgiven,
> Up there, a home in heaven;'
> Praise God that's the way for me.

Crossroads are crucial places in our lives and can be painfully frustrating. That is why it is important that people make the right decisions.

As the end of Moses' life drew near, He spoke to the people: *"See, I have set before thee this day life and good, and death and evil....Therefore, choose life, that thou and thy seed may live"* (Deuteronomy 30:15-20).

When Joshua was laying down his leadership of the nation, he challenged the people to make the right choice: *"Choose you this day whom you will serve"* (Joshua 24:15).

Elijah the prophet asked the people of Israel On Mount Carmel, *"How long will you hesitate between two opinions? If the Lord is God, follow Him; but if Baal, follow Him"* (1 Kings 18:21).

Jeremiah heard the voice of God saying to him, *"Unto this people shalt thou say, Thus saith the Lord: Behold I have set before you the way of life and the way of death"* (Jeremiah 21:8).

When many people withdrew from following the Saviour, He said to His disciples, *"Will you also away?"* Simon Peter answered Him, *'Lord, to whom shall we go? You have words of eternal life'"* (John 6:68).

At Calvary, one thief made the right decision and went to Paradise. The other thief …?

Be sure to make the right choice.

Revival

"For I will pour water on him who is thirsty."
Isaiah 44:3

The chairman of the packed gathering at the Monday evening rally of the Faith Mission Easter Convention in Bangor was left stunned and almost speechless at the conclusion of another momentous meeting. After Rev. Duncan Campbell's powerful and penetrating preaching numerous people, broken and weeping, came forward seeking to get right with God during the closing hymn.

What stunned the chairman was that Duncan Campbell had turned to him and bluntly intimated, ""Brother, you will need to excuse me. The Holy Spirit has just told me that I am to go to Berneray."

"But Duncan, you can't possibly go!" protested the chairman, "You are booked to speak at the closing meeting tomorrow night. The people will be disappointed."

"I can do no other," answered Duncan, "I have just heard God repeatedly speak the name Berneray to me."

For Duncan to leave Bangor for a small Scottish island seemed absurd, but God had spoken. Duncan had no other valid reason for going other than the constraint on his heart. That night he packed his suitcase and the next morning flew from Belfast to Scotland.

He got to the Isle of Harris on Thursday, and from there, a fisherman ferried him across to Berneray. The preacher said to a boy at the harbour, "Please go and tell the minister that Duncan Campbell has arrived." The boy answered that there was no minister on the island. "Then please tell the elder that Mr. Campbell has arrived on the island," said Duncan.

Ten minutes later the boy returned saying the elder was expecting him and an announcement had already been made at church that Duncan Campbell would be preaching at the nine o'clock service that same evening.

Duncan learned that the godly elder had spent the day in his barn praying for revival and God had given him a promise in Hosea 14:5: *"I will be as the dew unto Israel."*

In the weeks that followed the whole island was shaken with a new awareness of God's presence, and scores of lives were transformed by the power of the Gospel.

Floods from above are the supreme need for today.

Type and Tell

*"That I may publish with the voice of thanksgiving,
and tell of all Thy wondrous works."*
Psalm 26:7

With the onset of World War II the normal course of lectures and studies at the Bible College of Wales (BCW) were suspended and replaced by days of prayer and fasting. This continued throughout the war years. Ernie Allen had gone to BCW for two years but remained there for eleven years of study and concentrated intercession.

Ernie took the opportunity to engage in more concentrated Bible study and the reading of church history. He was not only enriched by precious insights into God's Word but also by many biographies of great men of God. Reading volume after volume stirred his soul. He felt he was sitting at the feet of the great reformers, evangelists and Christian leaders. These spiritual giants of history made a lasting impact on Ernie's life.

Many biographies were read against the backdrop of what was going on in Europe, the Middle East, North Africa and the Far East. Ernie's soul was stretched. He longed and hungered for great revival such as God had sent in former times. This burden on his heart constrained Ernie to read only the biographies and writings of men of God who had been endued with power from on high and whose ministry had resulted in the salvation of precious souls.

The more Ernie read the more he felt that others should learn of these revivals and of the men God used. He borrowed a typewriter and soon mastered the keyboard. He typed summary accounts of the great revivals of former years and made a record of great spiritual awakenings. These summaries formed the basis of the first Revival series that Ernie produced and the beginning of The Revival Movement. Ernie sent these booklets to men involved in the ministry in Great Britain.

The unerring hand of his Sovereign Lord was pointing Ernie in a direction that would eventually develop into a worldwide ministry. Those first publications were only the embryo of millions of booklets that would follow in multiple languages. These were the early buds that would blossom into a wide and fruitful ministry.

Every seed has a potential harvest.

A Vital Contrast

*"There was a certain rich man, ... and there was a certain
beggar named Lazarus."*
Luke 16:19, 20

Electronics have revolutionized our society. We can carry in our pocket a phone or tablet that can store a larger library than most of us could house. For all that, bookstores remain very popular on the high street. We like to be able to handle a book for bedtime reading. Most popular among these books are biographies. These biographies tell the life stories of our heroes: politicians, sports personalities, royalty or characters from church history or missions.

The Lord Jesus was the greatest storyteller of all time. When He spoke, people listened. The Scriptures tell us that the common people heard Him gladly.

In Luke 16 Jesus told a true but tragic story. It is the story of a prince and a pauper--a rich man who had everything but God, and Lazarus, a beggar who had nothing in this world other than his hope in God.

Ostensibly, the story may appear to be one about a rich man and a beggar, but the real story is a contrast between a saved man at the extreme edge of poverty and a lost man who was extremely wealthy in this world. It should be noted that there is no spiritual virtue in poverty, and there certainly is no spiritual penalty for earthly possessions.

There were social, material, physical, emotional and spiritual differences between the two men. The rich man may have been important in society and indulgent in his wealth, but he was indifferent to the things of God and his eternal welfare.

Lazarus had no home, no food, no money, no health, no help and no company. But he had hope in his heart--a hope of an inheritance in heaven that was incorruptible and undefiled and would never fade.

This rich man was quite anonymous, but Lazarus' name was known in heaven. The rich man owned gold, but God owned Lazarus. The rich man was not ignorant of God; he was indifferent to what he had heard. At some point in life Lazarus made a decision to trust in God. That was the basis of his living hope.

Which man was the rich man?

The Old Serpent

"The serpent was more subtle than any beast of the field
which the *Lord* God had made."
Genesis 3:1

For simple forest dwellers, fishing and hunting are more than a hobby. They are a way of life. Most families in the forest have half a dozen dogs. These are necessary for hunting for wild animals; this hunting is best done at night or early morning. Fishing in rivers and lakes is done either by a line thrown from the water's edge or by circular nets that are weighed down with lead. The fisherman will stand on the prow of his dugout canoe to throw his net into the muddy water in the hope of making a catch.

Even when women wash clothes at the side of the river they engage in fishing. Three or four baited hooks are tied at intervals on a line. With a bottle tied to the cord's end of the line, they throw it into the river before securing the other end to a stick plunged deep into the sand. While they wash clothes, they keep an eye on the stick. Once it begins to move, they know they have a catch.

It might sound idyllic, but their lives are fraught with many dangers, especially on the river. Too many people drown on these waterways. Anacondas present one of the greatest dangers. This seven-metre-long snake can quickly pull an unsuspecting victim into the river, crush and then swallow its prey.

That is what happened to the two teenage sons of Senhor Sebastião on the River Purus. One boy's small canoe was overturned by the anaconda, and he was dragged into the muddy water. He was never seen again. Two weeks later, the other teenage son suffered the same fate on the same stretch of river.

The serpent is one of the first creatures mentioned in the Bible and one of the last (Genesis 3:1 & Revelation 12:9). This serpent is Satan, the devil, the deceiver of the world and accuser of Christians. Few animals fight with or overcome an anaconda, but Jesus Christ, the Lamb of God, overcame Satan through His precious blood, and He assures us of victory over this same enemy.

We salute the Lamb.

16th May

Jesus at Home

"It was noised that He was in the house."
Mark 2:1

Although Jesus Christ did not own a house, it is interesting to find how many homes were put at His disposal. He often resorted to Bethany with Lazarus and his two sisters, Martha and Mary. In Galilee, Peter's mother-in-law not only provided hospitality for Him, but it also must have seemed that her home resembled a hospital out-patients clinic for all the sick and infirmed gathered at her doorway to meet the Great Physician. We do not know who owned the overcrowded house where Jesus ministered. Four unknown but compassionate men tore up the roof of that dwelling to lower a paralytic man into the house to seek the Master's touch. Jesus responded to their faith and healed the paralytic. It took a lot of tolerance to accept that disruption in a home.

Another anonymous man not only provided a colt for our Lord's entry into Jerusalem, but he also furnished a room that was prepared for our Lord to celebrate the Passover Meal. After the Lord Jesus had ascended into heaven, many people continued to open their homes for prayer and fellowship meetings.

That tradition continued down through the history of the church. Many mission halls and churches had their beginnings in a house that had been used for the Lord's work.

That was the case in 1906 when Mr. and Mrs. John Galway opened their home at 51 Tamar Street in East Belfast for Alex Jardine to conduct *"cottage meetings."* This *"Wee Meeting"* continued in the same house for over a year until the house was converted to Tamar Street Mission Hall.

Mr. Jardine became the pastor of Grove Baptist Church in 1915, and Tamar Street Mission Hall became an outreach of that church. A larger building was erected on another site, and this was severely damaged on the terrible night of the Blitz in 1941. The Galways could never have known that their open home would result in over 100 years of Gospel witness at what is now "Tamar Street Baptist Hall."

"Jesus at home" is the best feature of any house.

How Great Thou Art

*"Ask now the beasts, and they shall teach thee; and the fowls of the air,
and they shall tell thee: . . . . Who knoweth not in all these
that the hand of the Lord hath wrought this."*
Job 12:7, 9

The media constantly highlight how urban development and deforestation have invaded vast regions of the Amazon rainforest, threatening to destroy our planet's greatest source of oxygen. However, when viewed from the altitude of an aircraft, the forest below looks like a brilliant green carpet stretching to the horizon in every direction broken only occasionally by meandering streams and rivers flowing to the Atlantic Ocean.

When we travelled under cloudless skies on the fast-flowing tributaries of Acre and Amazonas, we could see that the long finger of modern civilization had not touched most of these distant places. By day, crocodiles basked lazily in the sun on the sandy beaches as we made our way upstream. At night their beady orange eyes reflected the beam of our flashlight as we searched for a landing place.

Giant *tartaruga* turtles and smaller *tracajás* laid their eggs on these same sands. Fearsome and long anacondas slithered through the muddy waters or coiled their camouflaged bodies around a tree. All sorts of other reptiles darted behind the fringe of ferns and palms at the water's edge. Playful monkeys, large and small, called from the branches of giant Brazil nut or rubber-latex trees. Their cries alerted forest dwellers to the proximity of menacing pumas or wild bore. Tapir, armadillos, *capyvaras*, and deer were regularly hunted for their meat.

Red Macaws and green parrots squawked as they flew overhead while long-legged herons and cranes strutted through shallow waters where they fished with their long beaks. Although the river provides all kinds of fish for meat, the forest dwellers are aware of the dangers of electric eels and the notorious piranha fish.

The sights and sounds of the forest are something to be experienced. Not all of them were "bright and beautiful," but this close contact to God's great creation emphasized the stamp of His intelligent design and the wonder of His great handiwork.

Great is the Lord and greatly to be praised.

18th May

Revival

"Wilt thou not revive us again: that Thy people may rejoice in Thee?"
Psalm 85:6

Ernie Allen, founder of The Revival Movement, had a clear vision and great passion to win the lost for Jesus Christ. Through his literature ministry he embraced multitudes of people within and beyond the shores of the British Isles. Like Joseph, he was *"a fruitful bough, even a fruitful bough by a well; whose branches run over the wall."* Through Every Home Crusade his fruitful ministry continues to cross over the walls of cultural and linguistic frontiers to garner a great harvest of souls all around the world.

Revival was the burden of Ernie's heart. He wrote of it in the following:

We have seen the tremendous blessing revivals have been to the world. They always bring new life and power into the church; produce a new generation of soul-winning minsters, missionaries and Christian workers; extend a blessed influence far and wide. The history of revivals illustrates three things:

Prayer: Revival always begin in answer to the effectual fervent prayers of spiritually revived Christians who see the world as God sees it; and who feel the same hatred for sin, and feel the same love and compassion for sinners that God feels.

Preaching: While Christians pray in this way, preachers with the same spirit should make a balanced presentation of the Gospel to the lost. Not only preachers, but also, every church officer, every Sunday School teacher, every Christian worker and every individual Christian has a degree of influence that he is responsible to use for the glory of God and the salvation of souls.

People: All denominations have experienced revival. Whatever differences Christians may have, all evangelicals should be united on this point, that God is able to save and change men and women through the power of the Gospel.

In view of the terrible need of the world today let us all work together to promote revival and world evangelization.

Ernie lived for Jesus Christ and for a spiritual revival. He not only wrote about revival, revival was the business of his life. He endeavoured to impart that vision and passion to others.

With dry eyes in the pew and dry preaching in then pulpit – we need revival.

Delivered

"I will sing of the mercies of the Lord for ever."
Psalm 89:1

On the 19th May 1940, Neville Chamberlain was replaced by Winston Churchill as British Prime Minister. On that same day, Germany launched its fiercest attack on the Low Countries of France. Britain had sent 250,000 men of the British Expeditionary Forces to fight alongside the French. The French were taken by surprise when Nazi Panzer tanks punched through their thinly-spread lines. Within twenty-four hours the Germans reached the English Channel, trapping French and British troops in a pocket of land seventy miles from the coastal town of Dunkirk.

The options were limited for the British and French. Either they would try to make a counter-attack against the Nazis or buy enough time to be able to evacuate their men from France. When they chose the latter, "Operation Dynamo" was launched. Between 26th May and 4th June 338,226 troops were evacuated from Dunkirk. 90,000 soldiers did not make it and were taken prisoner by the Germans.

Amongst those evacuated from Dunkirk was Eddie Rutherford from East Belfast. Like many other brave Ulster men, Eddie volunteered to serve King and country in the hour of greatest need. In retreat, he scuttled across the Dunkirk sands in full uniform and waded into the sea before being hauled on board one of the hundreds of crafts that had crossed the Channel to bring the boys home.

After a brief spell back home in Belfast, Eddie was soon back in uniform. Four years later, he bravely returned to France when the Nazi forces were on the run.

That experience left an indelible mark on Eddie Rutherford. He always attributed his survival to the prayers of his family at home. One night he listened to his wife pray for him as she knelt at her bedside. He was broken. He climbed out of bed and said, "If you have prayed for me and thanked God that way, then I want to accept Christ as my personal Saviour."

In Templemore Hall, I loved to hear this old soldier pray and sing. He loved to tell how God brought him home from war to trust Christ as his personal Saviour.

A grateful heart is a big heart.

A Pinch of Salt

"Ye are the salt of the earth."
Matthew 5:13

There were times when pure salt was more valuable than gold. It was such a rare delicacy that it was often used as a medium of exchange. It is from that form of payment that we derive our English word *"salary,"* which means "salt-money." We sometimes remark, "That man is worth his salt."

During the American Revolutionary War, British sailors were ordered to intercept salt shipments to the American colonies to diminish the "rebels" ability to preserve their food. In 1812, salt brine was used to pay soldiers in the field, as the government was too poor to pay them with money.

In Temple times, people brought their sacrifices to the priests for all types of reasons. Some were thanksgiving offerings, sin offerings, peace offerings and other offerings. Besides these, there was the twice-daily sacrifice that was offered every day throughout the year. Each Temple sacrifice had its own unique set of rules, including which animals were required or qualified to be offered, but they all had one thing in common: Salt. Salt was so important that a sacrifice offered without salt was considered invalid.

Our Saviour likened His followers to sheep, stones, buildings, a body and even a bride. In Matthew 5:15, He defined them as salt and light. In the time of our Lord, both elements were extremely important. As lights, we are to shine because of the darkness of this world. As salt, we are to be a valuable preserver of God's mission because of the decadence of this world.

The Christian's relationship with the world can be difficult. We are not called to live cloistered lives that keep us separate from the world. Salt has no effect if it is kept in a saltcellar, and light is not able to penetrate the darkness if it is kept under a shade. Likewise, the Christian fails to fulfil the role our Saviour indicated if he is out of contact with the world.

Salty saints and the power of God can make a difference where we live.

People around us need "a pinch of salt."

21st May

You Can

"I can do all things through Christ which strengtheneth me."
Philippians 4:13

There are fifteen different species of toucans in Brazil. These birds are known for their flamboyant feathers and long multi-coloured bills which are thought to have a frightening effect on other birds.

The toucan's wings are short and rounded, and the tail is long. The short wings, long bills, and extended tails make toucans appear ungainly in flight. Their wings flap feverishly as they fly from one tree to another as if they are not going to make their destination. As they fly they bark out, "Tucan, tucan" and from this call, they gained their Portuguese name, "Tucano".

I often think of a lesson that comes from the ungainly flight of this colourful bird. "Tu" in Portuguese means "you". When "you" is joined to "can," it seems as if the toucan is encouraging itself as it awkwardly flies towards the tree, calling out, "You can, you can, you can make it."

We also need encouragements and assurances that we can succeed. When the future seems formidable and circumstances impossible, God's Word furnishes us with the assurances we need.

You can be saved from your sins. People asked Jesus, "Who then can be saved?" The Bible gives the answer, "*He is able also to save them to the uttermost that come unto God by Him*" (Hebrews 7:25). There are none too bad that cannot be saved and none too good that do not need to be saved.

You can be sure you are saved. The Lord assures us that "*him that cometh to me I will in no wise cast out*" (John 6:37). God has pledged His Word that whoever calls on the name of the Lord shall be saved. You can rely on that promise.

You can be strong to do God's will. God is not only the Almighty, but He also pours His strength into us so that we can do all He wants us to do.

You can stand in adversity. Paul assured Roman Christians in the midst of persecution, "*... God is able to make him stand*" (Romans 14:4). Stand up for Jesus.

You can be confident that God never fails.

The Canvas Cathedral

"They … went every where preaching the Word."
Acts 8:4

The Old Tent Evangel on Belfast's Beersbridge Road was not a Mission Hall, but it was an annual feature of East Belfast for many years. Evangelists from all over the United Kingdom preached there, and many people were converted under its roof. Some people called it "The Canvas Cathedral," and well-known John McNeill from Scotland called it the "Cloot Kirk." It was the Old Tent Evangel which in concept was the forerunner of the tent meetings Frank Knox, the famous Brethren evangelist, conducted for many summers on the "blitzed ground" in High Street after the Second World War.

The Old Tent Evangel had its beginnings during the summer months of 1922 when God graciously visited Ulster with revival. The East End of Belfast was especially blessed.

Besides the three months of meetings every year, the committee used the Canvas Tabernacle for evangelism in many provincial towns. One of the most notable campaigns outside Belfast was that conducted in Ballynahinch in June 1925.

A band of Christian workers had been praying and looking to the Lord for revival. Their eyes turned to the honoured servant of God, Rev. W. P. Nicholson. In September 1924, after listening to their case, Mr. Nicholson answered, "Boys, I would like a month down in that wee, half-damned town of yours."

When the tent was erected the rain came down in torrents, and the wind blew. The ground inside and outside the tent was just mud. On a Friday evening, Mr. Nicholson met the committee. When they prayed together, W. P. asked the Lord to bottle up the clouds and send dry weather for the month of June. God answered that prayer in a wonderful way, for throughout the five weeks of the campaign not one meeting was hindered by rain.

The crowds attending the meetings increased each night until many had to sit on the grass outside. Mr. Nicholson preached with great power, and over 500 souls passed through the inquiry room and professed conversion. That was a touch of revival in Ballynahinch.

Pray for such times of refreshing and revival to come again.

Grace, Grief and Glory

"But the God of all grace, who hath called us unto his eternal glory by Christ Jesus, after that ye have suffered a while, make you perfect, stablish, strengthen, settle you."
1 Peter 5:10

In the final chapter of Peter's first Epistle the apostle sums up his foregoing exhortations about: *ministry* (5:1-40), *humility* (5:5,6), *anxiety* (5:7), and *adversity* (5:8, 9), with a sweeping and confident doxology that embraces *grace, grief, and glory*.

We can enjoy grace each day. He is the *"God of all grace"* -- *"all kinds of grace."* Paul wrote that the *grace of God brings salvation* (Titus 2:11). He also proved that there was *"sufficient grace"* for his weakness and suffering (2 Corinthians 12:7). James added that God gives us *"more grace"* for every situation (James 4:6). To the Corinthians Paul wrote *"God is able to make all grace abound toward you; that ye, always having all sufficiency in all things, may abound to every good work"* (2 Corinthians 9:8). The fountain of God's grace will never run dry. No matter how deep the waters may be or how hot the fire may seem, there is always *"grace to help in time of need"* (Hebrews 4:16).

We may experience grief today. God's grace meets us in our earthly suffering. Our Lord said that in the world we would suffer tribulation. The Lord Jesus was a Man of sorrows and acquainted with grief. The servant is not above his Master. For that reason, Christians are not exempt from tears, pain or heartache. All over our world believers pass through the fires of hostile persecution, but Peter reminds us that we should not think this to be unusual.

We ought to express glory each day. We learn from the Westminster Shorter Catechism that *"man's chief end is to glorify God and to enjoy Him forever."* According to Hebrews 2 our Lord Jesus, who *"by the grace of God tasted death for every man,"* is *"bringing many sons unto glory."*

Join with Peter in his final doxology, "To Him be glory and dominion for ever and ever. Amen."

"Grace is but glory begun. Glory is grace perfected." J. Edwards

24th May

Fish

"And they had a few small fishes..."
Mark 8:7

In Canutama most people depended on fishing and hunting for subsistence. We often bought wild pig from the jungle, monkey meat, armadillo, tapir or other small rodents. As a boy in Belfast I paid three pence at a fair ground to see the largest rat in the world - a capybara, the world's largest rodent. I didn't know that one day I would be eating them.

Although fishing is a way of life in Amazonas, the fish most people dread was also included in our diet - piranha. The piranha generally lives near the riverbed and surfaces only at the scent of blood or the sound of something falling into the river. They travel like packs of wolves, and with their razor-sharp teeth they can strip an animal to a skeleton within minutes. Their attraction to blood makes them easy to catch, although you must be careful not to lose a finger when unhooking them. Although piranha are carnivorous, my policy is, eat them, before they eat you.

The Sea of Galilee also was a great place for fish, and most of our Lord's disciples were fishermen. Our Saviour did so much with fish.

Fish and the multitude: With a young lad's two fish and five loaves Jesus fed a large multitude.

Fish and the money: He performed an amazing miracle when He told Peter to go to the sea, cast in a hook and the first fish that would come up would have a coin in its mouth. The coin would be of sufficient value to pay the tax for Peter and the Lord Jesus.

Fish and a meal: On the shore of Galilee the resurrected Saviour lit a fire and invited His disciples to bring their fish for the meal.

Fishers of men: It was an unforgettable day when the Lord Jesus commanded Peter to launch out into the deep and let down his nets for a catch. In spite of his protestations, he did what the Lord had commanded and took so much fish that his boat began to sink. Thereafter Peter was recruited to be a fisher of men.

Jesus followers must be fishers of men.

Sowing for Generations

"He that soweth and he that reapeth may rejoice together."
John 4:36

For more than a hundred years Ballymacarrat has been one of the closest-knit communities in Belfast. Undoubtedly, one of the main contributors to this sense of community was the role of churches and mission halls in the area. The mission halls were the cement of the neighbourhood where friends met and exchanged news, and they received spiritual food for their souls. This was certainly true of the Pitt Street Mission Hall.

Pitt Street was one of a labyrinth of short streets at the lower end of the Newtownards Road and literally in the shadows of the gantries where the great Titanic was built at Harland and Wolff's shipyard. For almost seventy years the mission was one of the most productive Christian centres in East Belfast, not only in evangelism to the local community but also in providing many Methodist ministers, missionaries and Christian workers who touched regions all over the world.

The mission had its beginnings in 1893 when Mr. W. J. Dobson took a great interest in the spiritual welfare of the local young people. He started a Sunday School in a house in Scotch Row. The attendance grew so rapidly another venue had to be found in the nearby Saunders Street National School.

The leadership at Mountpottinger Methodist Church gave full support to Mr. Dobson and purchased a site in Pitt Street. The Pitt Street Methodist Mission was officially opened on 5th November 1903 and was dedicated to the Glory of God.

Captain S. J. Platt, an officer in the Royal Irish Regiment, formed the 39th Boys' Brigade Company in 1903. Captain Platt returned to active military service when the First World War broke out, and a number of his boys also became army volunteers. Some of them made the supreme sacrifice and never came home.

Due to redevelopment the Pitt Street mission was forced to close down in January 1972. The 39th Boys' Brigade Company also ceased on that date, but the 39th Old Boys continued and gained worldwide renown by producing some outstanding musicians.

The Lord of the Harvest will garner in the sheaves.

Vital Righteousness

"Having on the breastplate of righteousness."
Ephesians 6:14

After Evangelist Harold Peasley and I had a meal in a West Belfast Police station, we were invited to travel in a bullet-proof police car to view some of Belfast's interface areas. This trip took place only a few weeks after the horrendous Shankill bombing in which nine people were killed. As a precaution, we were issued bullet-proof vests for the perilous drive. This vital piece of body armour had saved the lives of many security personnel during the thirty years of terrorist violence in Northern Ireland.

Over a century ago Napoleon ordered a bullet-proof coat. When ready, the Emperor ordered the maker to wear the garment. Drawing a pistol, Napoleon fired shot after shot at the armour-clad man. Although bruised and shaken, the poor bewildered man survived the severe test and was commended by the Emperor for his skill.

No Roman legionnaire in his right mind would ever have gone to battle without his breastplate of protection. The soldier was the target of many fiery darts that were aimed at his heart and lungs. The breastplate protected these vital organs.

The Roman breastplate provided Paul with a parallel picture of the Christian's spiritual warfare. Appropriately he called it, *"the breastplate of righteousness."* Just as the breastplate was vital for the soldier, so righteousness is also vital for the Christian life.

God's righteousness is revealed in the Gospel: "For I am not ashamed of the gospel of Christ: ... For therein is the righteousness of God revealed from faith to faith (Romans 1:16,17).

Righteousness is required in man: but *"There is none righteous, no, not one"* (Romans 3:10).

Righteousness is received through faith in Christ: "To him that worketh not, but believeth on him that justifieth the ungodly, his faith is counted for righteousness" (Romans 4:5).

Righteousness is reproduced in the yielded life: "Yield yourselves unto God, as those that are alive from the dead, and your members as instruments of righteousness unto God" (Romans 6:13).

The marvel of the Gospel is that our sins were imputed to Christ, and His righteousness is imputed to us.

Jesus Thy blood and righteousness, my beauty are, my glorious dress.

27ᵗʰ May

Nuts

*"When they had fasted and prayed, and laid their hands on them,
they sent them away."*
Acts 13:3

The Amazon forest contains many unique plants. Perhaps best known among these is the humble Brazil nut. For centuries these nuts have provided the people with many of life's essential nutrients. The Brazil nut tree is one of the tallest trees of the forest--reaching up to fifty metres high. Only the top third of this tree has foliage and *castanhas* - Brazil nuts.

A surprising feature of the Brazil nut is that it grows inside a pod with a hard outer shell, giving the appearance of a coconut. Because they weigh around 2.5 kg, they fall to the ground with a thud. A falling pod is extremely dangerous and has been known to cause brain damage or even kill people.

I like to use the Brazil-nut pod for children's talks. I remind them that the nut is part of God's great creation, as we are also. Furthermore, the real nut is on the inside, just like us. God reminded Samuel, *"Man looks on the outward appearance, but God looks on the heart."* Also, to enjoy the nut we have to open up the hard outer shell. We, also, must open our hearts to let the Lord Jesus come in.

For me, the best lesson from the Brazil nut is its germination process. Each pod contains around twenty Brazil nuts arranged in segments like an orange. Each nut has the potential of becoming the seed that will grow into a tall tree. However, when that pod falls to the forest floor it is soon covered with leaves and undergrowth. During the next ten months only one nut of those twenty nuts will become the seed. All the other nuts will feed and provide the necessary nutrients for that one predetermined nut to grow out into the world above and provide another tree with more fruit. The simple lesson is this; inside that pod every nut plays its part. Either it is a sending nut, or a nut that is sent.

In God's work the same principle applies: we are either the nuts that go or the nuts that send.

Which nut represents you?

The '59 Revival

"Times of refreshing shall come from the presence of the Lord."
Acts 3:19

In 1857, even though the streets of New York were blighted by drunkenness and the nation was divided by slavery, God raised up a praying businessman, Jeremiah Lanphier. On September 23, 1857, he began a noontime prayer meeting on Fulton Street in Manhattan. Out of a city of a million, only six people showed up.

On the next week fourteen were present and by the following week twenty-three people attended. The meeting then grew to forty praying Christians. Within weeks there were thousands of business leaders meeting daily. God moved so powerfully that similar prayer meetings were organised across the nation. It is estimated that in the revival that followed nearly a million people were converted out of a total American population of thirty-five million. During a season in New York, 10,000 people were converted each week.

In November 1856, Mrs. Colville, an English lady from Gateshead, arrived in Ballymena in conjunction with the Baptist Missionary Society. She went on a door-to-door campaign to bring the Gospel to every home in the town. She was burdened and enthusiastic in her mission and had the joy of leading some people to Christ.

One day she visited a home in Mill Street, Ballymena, and found two ladies engaged in a spiritual conversation with a young man named James McQuilken. He came under conviction, and after talking with Mrs. Colville, he was converted. People saw a dramatic change in McQuilken. As a result of his testimony, his friends, Jeremiah Meneely, Robert Carlisle and John Wallace were drawn to Christ.

These men were encouraged by Rev Moore, the minister of Connor Presbyterian Church, to meet weekly for prayer and Bible study. Those meetings continued through the winter of 1857, and on New Year's Day 1858, the first conversion directly related to that prayer meeting took place. There were conversions every night after that. That was the beginning of Ulster's 1859 revival.

Before long, the revival spread to Kellswater, Ahoghill, Portglenone and soon the revival flame rapidly spread until almost the whole of Ulster was caught up in great times of refreshing.

God can do it again – when we pray.

This Same Jesus

"Ye men of Galilee, why stand ye gazing up into heaven? this same Jesus,
which is taken up from you into heaven, shall so come in like manner as ye
have seen Him go into heaven."
Acts 1:11

If given the opportunity to time travel to another age, which period would you choose? Some may choose the days of Luther's Reformation. How about the six-week period surrounding our Saviour's Passion, Burial, Resurrection, and Ascension? No stretch of time outside of the six days of Creation was so crammed with such momentous events.

In Luke's account of our Lord's ascension, he provides us with three great motives to continue in the work of missions – reaching the world for Christ. He recorded the Saviour's promise of the Holy Spirit that enabled the disciples to witness with power. Luke gave an account of the parting of the Saviour to heaven in a cloud, which encouraged His followers to walk by faith. Luke then wrote of the angels' promise that this same Jesus would return again, teaching them to wait with blessed hope for the soon coming of our great Saviour.

The ascension of our Lord is a theme we often overlook. It is the assurance that Jesus will come again.

His Departure - How He went. Jesus departed suddenly and supernaturally. The power of the grave could not hold Him, and the power of gravity could not detain Him.

Jesus was received up into glory bodily. Jesus stepped out of eternity and took upon Himself flesh and blood. He ascended back into eternity with a glorified body.

Jesus ascended into heaven visibly. The moment of His resurrection was hidden from human view but not His ascension. Although they lost sight of Him, they learned that He never lost sight of them. Clouds may still hide Jesus Christ, but we walk by faith that He lives in heaven for us.

His Destination - Where He went. On the Mount of Olives Jesus triumphantly entered Jerusalem when they cried their hosannas to Him. He also had a triumphant exit out of Jerusalem on the same mountain when He ascended to heaven as the glorified Saviour.

We look for the Lord from Heaven.

Turned Tables

"So they hanged Haman on the gallows that he had prepared for Mordecai."
Esther 7:10

Tom and Ethel Geddis' arrival in Tarauacá made a tremendous impact on the town. God was blessing at the newly-formed church, and Tom was busy every day at the local hospital and medical centre. Besides his pastoral ministry, his medical and surgical work in this isolated forest town became legendary. People even went from the state capital to seek treatment with Tom in Tarauacá.

We should not be surprised that God's work is often opposed; however, at times we are taken aback by how and from where the opposition comes. Before Tom's arrival, the local Chief of Police controlled the hospital. Although not qualified, he often engaged in surgical procedures and medical treatments and then charged exorbitant fees. Tom's arrival undermined this exploitation of the people and the Chief's unscrupulous profits.

One day Tom and Ethel prepared to travel to Rio Branco for an appointment with the State Governor who had originally invited Tom to be the doctor in Tarauacá. While waiting at the town's airstrip, six armed guards arrived and told Tom he was under arrest. Their pointed guns suggested they were expecting trouble.

At the police station, the chief questioned Tom's legitimacy for being in Tarauacá and his credentials to function in Brazil. Tom listened carefully and gave a quiet answer, explaining that it was the State Governor who had invited him to Tarauacá. The chief continued to be aggressive in his interrogation.

News of Tom's arrest spread around the small town very quickly. When Dr. Querino, the local judge, heard of the doctor's arrest he was furious. He went immediately to the chief's office and demanded Tom's release. Meanwhile, the Air Force sergeant at the airstrip notified his headquarters in Rio de Janeiro that a foreigner had been arrested on Air Force property by civilian police. That immediately alarmed the Brazilian military authorities who requisitioned an airplane to fly soldiers to Tarauacá to put down this "uprising."

As in the story of Mordecai and Haman, it was the chief who was permanently expelled from Tarauacá while Tom and Ethel served God there for another twenty years.

No weapon formed against us can prosper.

Greatly Blessed

"Fervent in spirit; serving the Lord"
Romans 12:11

Lucimar Geddis is devoted to the Gospel. Born in Tarauacá, her mother, a devout Catholic, endeavoured to provide for her little family. When she was eight years old, the first evangelical missionaries in Tarauacá, Tom and Ethel Geddis, passed by Lucimar's home calling for children to gather at the riverside for a Good News Club. She attended that first Gospel meeting in Tarauacá and on that day God touched her heart. After trusting Jesus Christ as Saviour, she faced opposition from her father, who was addicted to alcohol. He also disputed with her mother and sister when they trusted the Saviour. God was gracious, and he came to Christ years later.

Through her teenage years Lucimar was very active in children's and youth work in the church and accompanied the missionaries on their evangelistic trips on surrounding rivers. Ethel Geddis invested a lot of time teaching and encouraging her during those years. This accumulative experience equipped Lucimar for future Christian service.

After qualifying as a schoolteacher and completing the CEF course in Brazil, Lucimar was accepted as a missionary by the Acre Gospel Mission. When her mentors, Tom and Ethel, left Brazil, Lucimar went to Lábrea to work alongside the pastor. Her seven years there were bitter and sweet. Bitter because she was alone and her accommodation, next door to the jailhouse, was overrun with rats and bats. Undeterred, Lucimar devoted her time to the Lord. She rallied multitudes of children to her meetings, attracted scores of youth to the church and gave pastoral care to many adults. She was also honoured by the Lábrea Council for reorganizing the church's school, which had virtually closed.

Following her work in Lábrea, she made a similar impact on the work in Boca do Acre. All this led to her present work alongside her husband, Dr. Tom Geddis, leading a team of more than thirty workers to teach the Scriptures to thousands of children in Rio Branco's schools. One page could not contain the story of this Brazilian missionary who has led hundreds to faith in Christ and influenced countless Brazilian pastors and missionaries.

Lord, mould us to bless others.

June

Larrybane Bay, North Coast

1st June

Travelling Mercies

"The Lord shall preserve thy going out and thy coming in from this time forth, and even for evermore."
Psalm 121:8

Early on Monday morning, 1st June 2009, Keith Lindsay and I arrived in São Paulo on a flight from Natal in Brazil's Rio Grande do Norte. Audrey was due to arrive at the same airport a few hours later. The three of us were at the end of a three-week visit conduct church conferences and meeting our missionaries.

When we disembarked from our plane we were immediately struck by the inordinate flurry of activity in the airport. Television cameras and reporters were everywhere. Some people were speaking excitedly while others were wiping tears from their eyes. Just then Keith's phone rang. It was his brother-in-law, Pastor Richard Garnham, calling from Northern Ireland to check up on our welfare. Keith asked why the concern. Richard broke the news that an Air France flight had gone over the Atlantic early that morning and all on board were lost, including three Irish passengers. Richard, not knowing our travel arrangements immediately thought of us three. A cold chill went up and down our spines, for we had tried to change to an Air France flight but were unable to do so.

On the previous night, 216 passengers boarded the Air France flight 447 in Rio de Janeiro for their ten-hour flight to Paris. The flight path took them right over Natal where we had spent the previous night unaware of what was overhead. At approximately 2:15 a.m., the plane disappeared over the Atlantic Northeast of Natal. In an attempt to override a very bad head wind, the pilots lost control, and the plane plunged into the ocean. Sadly, all 216 passengers and twelve Air France crew lost their lives in the worst disaster in Air France's history. The three Irish people were young lady doctors hoping to return home.

That night our plane followed the same flight path through the same storm. It was the worst transatlantic crossing we had ever experienced, for the plane shook and bumped all night. Thankfully we arrived safely. Our thoughts and prayers were with the bereaved families.

Pray for God's protection on your going out and coming in.

Witnesses

"Ye shall be witnesses unto me both in Jerusalem, and in all Judaea, and in Samaria, and unto the uttermost part of the earth."
Acts 1:8

The task facing our Lord's disciples seemed like "Mission Impossible" when measured against their human resources. They had received the great Commission to take the Gospel into all the world and to every creature. During the forty-day period between Christ's resurrection and His ascension He equipped them for that assignment.

Jesus gave precepts to instruct them (Acts 1:2-4). "He gave commandments unto the apostles whom He had chosen." These commandments from our Lord majored on their witness in the world and waiting for the promised Holy Spirit.

Matthew and Mark's account of the Great Commission put an emphasis on the extent of the Mission – all the world. In Luke's version of the same commission he put emphasis on the content of the message -- the Scriptures. In John's Gospel the great commission was given with an emphasis on the character of the messenger in his heart (John 20, 21).

Jesus gave them proofs of His resurrection to convince them (Acts 1:3). The disciples not only needed instructions they also needed convictions. They needed to be absolutely convinced that Jesus Christ had risen and was alive. The resurrection is at the heart of the Gospel.

They received visible proofs when He showed Himself alive. He gave them time proofs -- forty days. He appeared to them many times for almost six weeks. He gave them audible proofs – For three years they had listened to His ministry. After He rose from the dead He spoke to them with the same audible voice.

Jesus gave the promise of the Holy Spirit to assure them (Acts 1:5). With the great commission our Lord gave His disciples many promises. He now spoke of the promise of the Father. The promise was that the Holy Spirit would indwell them, enlighten them, energise them, and encourage them. That promise was fulfilled on the day of Pentecost.

The winning of souls and work of conversion is by the operation of the Holy Spirit. However, we dare not underestimate the importance the Lord Jesus put on witnessing for Him.

Witnesses tell what they know.

Witnesses

"Ye shall be witnesses unto me both in Jerusalem, and in all Judaea, and in Samaria, and unto the uttermost part of the earth."
Acts 1:8

The task facing our Lord's disciples seemed like "Mission Impossible" when measured against their human resources. They had received the great Commission to take the Gospel into all the world and to every creature. During the forty-day period between Christ's resurrection and His ascension He equipped them for that assignment.

Jesus gave precepts to instruct them (Acts 1:2-4). "He gave commandments unto the apostles whom He had chosen." These commandments from our Lord majored on their witness in the world and waiting for the promised Holy Spirit.

Matthew and Mark's account of the Great Commission put an emphasis on the extent of the Mission – all the world. In Luke's version of the same commission he put emphasis on the content of the message -- the Scriptures. In John's Gospel the great commission was given with an emphasis on the character of the messenger in his heart (John 20, 21).

Jesus gave them proofs of His resurrection to convince them (Acts 1:3). The disciples not only needed instructions they also needed convictions. They needed to be absolutely convinced that Jesus Christ had risen and was alive. The resurrection is at the heart of the Gospel.

They received visible proofs when He showed Himself alive. He gave them time proofs -- forty days. He appeared to them many times for almost six weeks. He gave them audible proofs – For three years they had listened to His ministry. After He rose from the dead He spoke to them with the same audible voice.

Jesus gave the promise of the Holy Spirit to assure them (Acts 1:5). With the great commission our Lord gave His disciples many promises. He now spoke of the promise of the Father. The promise was that the Holy Spirit would indwell them, enlighten them, energise them, and encourage them. That promise was fulfilled on the day of Pentecost.

The winning of souls and work of conversion is by the operation of the Holy Spirit. However, we dare not underestimate the importance the Lord Jesus put on witnessing for Him.

Witnesses tell what they know.

4ᵗʰ June

To the Work

"I must work the works of Him that sent me, while it is day."
John 9:4

Just after dawn on Friday 4ᵗʰ June 1954, the slow-moving river steamer with Fred and Ina Orr on board finally arrived in Lábrea. This was the end of the two-week journey on the steamer and the halfway point between Manaus and Boca do Acre, the Orr's intended destination. Fred had to arrange for their baggage to be transferred to another boat for the next stage of their journey, but while he was doing these necessary things, he was much more concerned about how he was going to change from one boat to another with his very ill wife. Ina had been burning with fever for a week and seemed to be deteriorating each day.

Even though Ina was very ill, she had no sense of alarm or fear. There had been sleep for either of them during that previous week. Their waking hours were spent conversing, reminiscing, reading the Scriptures and praying.

To everyone's surprise and relief, they discovered there was a doctor in Lábrea just as the captain had said there might be. Hopes were raised when the doctor arrived on the steamer to help the young missionary. Alas, it was already too late. Ina grew weaker during that afternoon. Fred never left her side and tried to mask his real feelings of doubt and fear. Try as he might, he could not hide them from Ina. She chided him for his doubts--pointing out that to doubt was a sin. At Ina's insistence, Fred was soon on his knees beside her bunk, confessing to God his doubts and asking for forgiveness.

After he prayed, Fred looked straight up into Ina's eyes. She noticed there was a smile on his face and said, "Now that's the Fred I know. You go and get on with your work and I am going to have a little sleep."

Ina was referring to the baggage transfer, but those were her last words, and what significant words they were! She fell asleep in Christ at 8:00 p.m. that evening. Fred's work had only begun and would continue in Brazil for the next fifty-seven years.

There's a work for Jesus none but you can do.

Sharing Faith

*"Your work of faith, and labour of love,
and patience of hope in our Lord Jesus Christ."*
1 Thessalonians 1:3

When Amy Carmichael worked among the "shawlies," Belfast's mill-working girls, she met with many verbal objections and contemptuous looks from respectable churchgoers. To their relief, they learned that Amy had intimated she was looking for other premises to accommodate the increased numbers attending her Bible class.

While reading a Christian newspaper Amy's attention was drawn to an advertisement offering the sale of a spacious corrugated iron building for £500, a sizeable amount in 1886. By this time her family's assets had dwindled, and Amy had no fixed income. It was then she remembered that when she was a child, she was asked to collect donations for the Bird's Nest, a Christian orphanage in Dublin. During a visit to her grandmother in Portaferry, she took her collecting card and asked some of grandma's friends and neighbours to contribute to the cause. When one man who had just built a new house refused to donate anything to the fund, Amy felt rebuffed and disappointed. It was then that she thought, *Why not ask God to speak to those who love Him and motivate them to help those whom He loves, rather than ask help of those who don't love God?*

Amy enthusiastically told the Christian mill girls her vision to purchase the iron hall. She shared with them her burden and invited them to pray with her for God to meet this need.

Soon after the girls began to pray Amy was visiting a friend who showed an unusual interest in her work among the Belfast shawlies. Subsequently, this friend told a lady of considerable means about Amy and her zeal for these girls. The woman desired to know more about Amy so she invited her for lunch in her opulent home. Following that visit, the wealthy lady offered to buy the prefabricated iron hall for the growing work.

This direct answer to prayer not only met their need, but it was also a tremendous lesson for the mill girls, something Amy could never have taught them in a Bible class.

Faith, mighty faith, the promise sees and looks to God alone.

Yield Not to Temptation

"In all points *tempted* like as we are, yet without sin."
Hebrews 4:15

It had all the drama of a showdown in the wilderness, the battle of the ages, the Prince of Light confronting the Prince of darkness.

Following His baptism in the Jordan, the Lord Jesus Christ, filled with the Holy Spirit, followed the Spirit into the wilderness. Heaven had opened to affirm Christ. Now hell came to attack Christ. In the desert, the Lord Jesus had fasted for forty days and forty nights and was hungry. It was then that the tempter, the devil, hurled at Christ his three most devious blows: *"the lust of the flesh, the lust of the eye and the pride of life."*

Jesus Christ was not exposed to these temptations to prove to His Father that He was able to withstand the devil. He was tempted to demonstrate to us that because He underwent and overcame these temptations, He, therefore, understands our weaknesses and can undertake for us when we are tempted.

There are three ways in which Satan tempted our Lord Jesus that give us insight to how he may tempt us also.

Jesus was tempted about His dependence on the Father. After forty days fasting our Lord Jesus was hungry -- humanly speaking, He was at His weakest point. Satan tempted Him to satisfy His physical appetite. This is a reflection of Adam and Eve in the Garden of Eden. They succumbed to the serpent's temptation.

Jesus was tempted about His obedience to the Father. Satan took the Lord Jesus to the highest pinnacle of the Temple overlooking the Kidron Valley and told Him to cast Himself down. Jesus knew that this step was not in the plan of the Father. He obeyed the Father and not the enemy.

Jesus was tempted about His allegiance to the Father. Satan offered our Lord all the kingdoms of this world and the glory of them. This was Satan's shortcut to glory without the cross. Jesus answered, "Get thee behind me Satan."

Christ countered Satan's temptations by the power of the Spirit and the authority of the Scriptures.

Satan can never withstand the Lord Jesus Christ.

7th June

Mighty Messengers

"For who hath despised the day of small things?
Zechariah 4:10

1927 was a pivotal year for The Faith Mission. The famous Ulster evangelist, William Patterson Nicholson, preached with great power at the annual Faith Mission Easter Convention in Bangor and more than 100 Faith Mission workers were enthusiastically engaged in multiple missions all over the British Isles and in South Africa.

Also in 1927, John George Govan, the Chief, was the principal speaker at the Faith Mission's Convention at Perth in Scotland. It was to be his last Faith Mission Conference. During that Perth Convention, John George Govan went to be with the Lord. It was ironic if not providential that his final address was with great intensity and fervor as he preached about Elijah and Elisha travelling to the Jordan together before Elijah's translation to Heaven. That night he suffered a stroke, and after three days of unconsciousness, he passed into the presence of his Lord. He had energetically run his race, bravely fought His fight and faithfully finished his course leaving behind a legacy of blessing for generations to come.

It was a poignant coincidence that on the very day that the earthly remains of the beloved founder of the Faith Mission were being laid to rest in Edinburgh, two lady pilgrims, Helen Gibb and Phebe Rowdon, were sailing from Liverpool on their way to Canada.

As the ship, the *SS Letitia,* slowly pulled out from its moorings on Liverpool's River Mersey, Helen and Phebe were glad that Mr. Govan, who was now at home with the Lord, had got a glimpse of the Faith Mission's future work in Canada. These two pioneers were not only ambassadors for Christ, but they were also ambassadors for the Faith Mission.

When they arrived in Toronto on a Sunday morning, the minister who met them was a little perplexed for he had expected that the Faith Mission might have sent a contingent of their most stalwart young men. He was taken aback when "a bantam brigade" of two diminutive young ladies stepped off the train. He greeted them with, "You poor wee things -- you'll get lost in the snow."

These two "mighty atoms" impacted Canada for God.

8th June

Temple Mount

*"Then Solomon began to build the house of the
Lord at Jerusalem on Mount Moriah."*
2 Chronicles 3:1

Israel and Jerusalem are seldom out of the news. During the last hundred years, they have experienced more wars than any other region of the world. Of course, this territory has experienced many conflicts for centuries. At the eye of the present conflict is the Temple Mount.

Temple Mount is where Abraham offered up his son. The earliest mention of this elevation in the Bible is in Genesis 22 when Abraham and his son Isaac went to worship God on Mount Moriah. This was Abraham's greatest test of faith. Hebrews 11:17-19 reads, "By faith Abraham, when he was tried, offered up Isaac: and he that had received the promises offered up his only begotten son, … Accounting that God was able to raise him up, even from the dead." God spared Isaac and provided a ram to be slain in his place. It all happened on the Temple Mount before there ever was a Temple.

Temple Mount is where David purchased a site for worship. King David sinned against God by numbering the people. Consequently, God sent a plague on the nation in which thousands died. The plague was stopped only when the Angel of the Lord appeared at the threshing place of Araunah the Jebusite. When David desired to build an altar to the Lord there, Araunah offered the site to the King as a gift. David declined the offer, purchased it for fifty pieces of silver and made a burnt offering unto the Lord. Then and there the plague was stopped.

Temple Mount is where Solomon built the Temple. Solomon's 80,000 workmen took seven years to build the first Jewish Temple on Araunah's threshing place. The glory of God descended on this most magnificent centre of worship. It was destroyed just over four hundred years later when Judah was carried off into captivity 586 B.C.

Temple Mount is where the Lord Jesus was presented as a baby in Herod's Temple. There He confounded learned men as a boy; where He taught the Scriptures, and where the veil was rent in two when Christ died.

Pray for the peace of Jerusalem.

Commitment

"O Timothy, keep that which is committed to thy trust."
1 Timothy 6:20

Paul's New Testament epistles reveal his close relationship to Timothy and his input into the young man's life and ministry. Through Paul's preaching in Galatia, Timothy trusted Christ. Paul recruited him to be a companion in his missionary travels during which time he tutored and mentored the young servant of God. Subsequently, Timothy went on to pastor Christ's church in Ephesus. It has been well said that every seasoned "Paul" should have a "Timothy" to tutor. Likewise, every Timothy needs a role model like Paul.

Antoildson is one of the most gift young pastors I have known in Brazil. He was born and raised near the busy port in Manaus. It was this proximity to the river that brought tragedy to his family. His younger brother got into difficulties while swimming with his friends and drowned. This disaster brought heartbreak to Antoildson's family, but it also was a spiritual wakeup call to him. Until then, he was totally ignorant of the Gospel although he had been raised as a nominal Catholic. His brother's sudden death created an awareness of eternity, and he wanted to know where his brother had gone.

At school, Antoildson met twin sisters, Eliane and Eliana, who invited him to Gospel meetings at Hebrom Evangelical Church. It was there that Pastor Jose Carlos led him to faith in Christ. Following his conversion he was guided by Fred Orr. Antoildson studied for four years at the Baptist Seminary in Manaus and the Hebrom Bible Institute. He always scored the highest marks and was the top student. After graduation, he became a member of the Acre Gospel Mission and initially worked as an evangelist at the municipal market near his home.

His obvious talents were richly enhanced by his great zeal for God's work. He served God as pastor of several interior churches before accepting a call to Emanuel Regular Baptist Church in Rio Branco, the city where the Acre Gospel Mission began. Today, Antoildson is a pastor and a lawyer. He and his wife Anna, work alongside Tom and Lucimar Geddis, and he is pastor to Dr. Bill Woods.

Commitment and consecration are necessary to serve God.

Gospel Dynamics

"The Word of God increased; and the number of the disciples multiplied."
Acts 6:7

In 1922 W. P. Nicholson conducted a series of outstanding evangelistic missions in various Belfast churches. The success of those missions prompted the Kirk Session at Ravenhill Presbyterian Church, *Ross's Church*, to extend an invitation to *"W. P."* for an evangelistic crusade.

That mission commenced in February 1923, and as was his custom, Nicholson conducted several "Men Only Meetings." As a result, a large body of men who had just finished their day's work at Harland and Wolff, led by a Salvation Army Band, marched all the way from the shipyard to the church. They arrived at the church early only to find the gates were closed.

The minister, Rev. John Ross, later recalled, "When the gates were opened, the crowd was so large that the men got wedged between the pillars, and so fierce was the struggle to get in that the central pillar was moved from its place." The large crowd was eventually admitted into the building, and that night Mr. Nicholson preached with amazing power.

About halfway through his message someone threw papers over the front of the gallery. Mr. Nicholson enquired what the disruption had been about. The culprit, a notorious gambler shaking papers that were in his hand, replied, "These are gambling papers." That evening more than one hundred men passed through the enquiry room to make definite decisions for Christ, including this gambler.

On the following day one of the gambler's friends said to him, "You are a lucky fellow, those two horses you backed yesterday were winners."

"Oh," he said, "no more of that for me. I was in Ravenhill Church last night, and I put all I had on One Who is always a Winner, the Lord Jesus Christ." From that day on he lived an out-and-out life for Christ.

Like this gambler, hundreds of other shipyard men were gloriously converted. As a result Harland and Wolff Shipbuilders were obliged to open a large shed to receive heaps of stolen tools and other robbed materials. This large storage shed became known as *"The Nicholson Shed."*

The preaching of the Gospel transforms lives.

Praying Through

"As the hart panteth after the water brooks,
so panteth my soul after Thee, O God."
Psalm 42:1

In 1940 Duncan Campbell accepted a call to a United Free Church in Falkirk. He found the work in this industrial town to be hard ground and different from the Highlands where his ministry had been greatly blessed. He worked with his usual zeal but without much response. During his seven years in Falkirk, there was much soul searching. He bemoaned his barrenness of spirit and admitted that prayer had become a burden to him and that the Word of God was dull.

Duncan was due to address the Keswick Convention that year. One of the other speakers, Dr. Tom Fitch, departed from his prepared address to give his own personal testimony. Duncan felt unfit to be on the platform and cried to God where he sat, "O Lord, give me back the years that the locusts have eaten. Remake the marred vessel."

Back in Falkirk he went to his study and shut the door. Prostrate in front of the fire, he cried, "God, won't you give me again what you gave me on the battlefield?"

God answered that prayer. He said afterward, "My daughter came in at 2:00 in the morning. She got down beside me, and she said, 'Daddy, whatever it costs, go through with God.' I said, 'Sheena, I'm going through whatever it may cost.' On my face, I battled with the powers of darkness. The devil whispered that I was finished, and God had no further use for me, but the Lord put a verse into my mind: *"The Lord will not cast off His people, nor will He forsake His inheritance.'* This was followed by another word: *"Who forgives all your iniquities and heals all your diseases."*

He continued in prayer until 5:00 a.m. before the Holy Ghost came upon him again as He had done thirty years earlier on the battlefield. Once more he felt the Holy Spirit sweep over his soul like a great flood.

After twenty-three years absence from the Faith Mission, Duncan returned to the work of the Mission in 1948 to be an evangelist and God's instrument for revival.

We need revival thirst.

Baby Christians

"They that gladly received his word were baptized: and the same day there were added unto them about three thousand souls.
And they continued stedfastly in the apostles' doctrine and fellowship, and in breaking of bread, and in prayers."
Acts 2:41, 42

The arrival of a new baby is always greeted with great delight by the excited parents. However, the infant's birth is only the beginning. Caring for that little infant is an awesome responsibility. The parents have to feed the baby, clean the baby, teach the baby, and rear the baby; and that is not the work of just one day. God can make a mushroom grow overnight, a radish in fourteen days, and a mighty oak may take up to 100 years. Growing a child may not take as long as an oak tree, but it does take a lot of time and diligent commitment.

When Peter had finished preaching his first sermon on the day of Pentecost, there were 3,000 new spiritual babies to care for. Later, another 5,000 people were converted in one day. The church leaders had a very happy problem; new converts needed to be fed, cared for, sheltered and taught how to grow in grace and the knowledge of the Lord Jesus Christ.

We have no greater joy in Christian work than to see people trust Christ and be born again. We have always introduced these new converts to a "Big Brother Programme" to help them grow. The early church was geared for growth and laid foundations that we endeavoured to follow with these new Christians.

They were initially converted to faith in Christ. "They that gladly received his Word." They embraced the message Peter had preached and were saved.

They publicly confessed their faith in Christ. "Were baptized..." No new believer remained unbaptised.

They immediately confirmed their faith in Christ. "There were added unto them..." The early Church experienced immediate growth. All who believed were baptized, and they were added to the church.

They continued in the fellowship of the church. "Then they continued steadfastly in..." 2:42 Observe their four-fold programme for spiritual growth in the New Testament church: continuance in the *"apostles' doctrine -- fellowship -- breaking of bread -- in prayers."*

Be sure to encourage baby Christians.

Foundations of Faith

"The things that thou hast heard … commit thou to faithful men."
2 Timothy 2:2

In 1995 Dr. Herberth Fernandes epitomised everything that was excellent about the new generation of "Amazonenses." He had qualified in civil engineering, established his own construction business, was prosperous and had a lovely wife and family. His business partner, Mario Abraim, introduced him to Fred Orr who at that time, had established the Hebrom Evangelical Church.

Herberth's introduction to Fred was when the church was embarking on a building programme. The demand for this new building had grown out of meetings that Fred and his family had initiated in the garage at the side of their home. The congregation had grown so much that they had to purchase a dwelling in the same street and transform it into a simple meetinghouse.

When Herberth hear that Fred had already spent forty-two years in Brazil, had lost his first wife six weeks after arriving in the country, and was now in his seventies, he freely offered his professional advice about the building.

When he arrived at the site, Herberth was completely taken aback to discover that Fred was down a clay hole busily digging trenches for the foundations. The sun was hot overhead, and Fred was drenched in his own perspiration. Herberth knew this was heavy work for a younger man and articulated the same to Fred.

After some conversation and wise counsel about the building, Fred shared his testimony with Herberth. Impressed, not only by what he had heard but also the sight of this elderly missionary doing the donkeywork in the hot sun, Herberth thought the best he could do was to attend some of the meetings.

After several weeks, we were present at a Baptismal Service in Lagoa Verde Baptist Church when Pastor José Carlos, then pastor at Hebrom, baptized more than a dozen new converts. At the end of the service, he made a simple appeal for anyone to come to Christ. Herberth rose out of his seat immediately. He was converted and baptized on the same night.

Herberth was tutored by Fred and became pastor of the Hebrom Church in 2009.

Don't drop the baton. Relay God's truth to others.

All To Jesus

"Her sins which are forgiven … she loved much."
Luke 7:47

Lily Boal was born and raised near the busy Belfast docks in the times of the Great Depression. Lily was seldom depressed, although she had every reason to be; she and her older brother and younger sister suffered a great loss when their mother died. Lily was only six years old. Her father remarried, and the addition of other brothers and sisters gave young Lily a sense of responsibility for the new family. Undoubtedly, this prepared her for future days when she would rescue and care for hundreds of boys and girls in Kashmir and on the North West Frontier, today a Pakistani region bordering Afghanistan.

Like many girls of her generation, Lily found employment at a local mill where her wit and humour made her very popular. Typically, the only time she got into trouble at work was when she sacrificed her own time to help a slower mill girl reach her quota. Although raised in a church-going family Lily and other mill girls enjoyed their dancing and cinemas, filling their carefree lives with work and play.

Lily's life was dramatically changed when she and some chums decided to attend a meeting at the Mountcollyer City Mission. Although that decision was made light-heartedly and with dubious motives, the preacher was very sincere and clear in presenting the Gospel. Young Lily knew that while she had never been a criminal, she was a sinner who needed the Saviour. She saw that her popular life, good deeds and intentions mattered nothing. Only what the Lord Jesus had done for her on the cross could provide salvation. With a melted heart, Lily Boal called upon God for mercy and trusted Jesus Christ as Saviour.

When she stepped out of the City Mission that night she could never have envisaged what God had planned for her in future days. She was blessed and privileged to join a group of Christian young people that wanted to serve the Saviour. These included the Munn sisters, Emma, Jessie, Janet and Lottie, who all, with their brother Robert, went to serve God on foreign fields.

To love Him is to serve Him.

VAT Ravens

*"The ravens brought him bread and flesh in the morning,
and bread and flesh in the evening."*
1 Kings 17:6

Although the Every Home Crusade (EHC) is a non-profit registered charity, for years it was subject to Value Added Tax (VAT), which cost them lots of money. While the EHC team was praying for a better printing press, Ernie Allen and Samuel Adams thought of every means of getting the best deal possible. They knew that this hefty levy was more than they wanted to pay. Samuel phoned the VAT office to ask about their status as a registered charity. The polite civil servant explained that without the sales of literature above a certain amount the Crusade would not qualify for a VAT rebate. However, the lady said she would forward the appropriate government literature about the eligibility and requirements.

When the leaflet arrived, it affirmed that they did not qualify for VAT exemption as the lady had said. However, there was a clause that indicated that if a charity exported a large percentage of their product free of charge to Third World countries, they would qualify for exemption. That fitted the role of the EHC. Phone calls and letters shuttled between EHC and the government department until finally exemption was granted to the Crusade. That truly was a giant step as they did not like to see the Lord's money spent on anything other than literature.

Samuel decided to write again to the VAT department, and pointing out that having gained VAT exempt status, he wanted to know if the Crusade's VAT payments for the previous seven years could be refunded.

During the days that followed, telephones were buzzing and many letters were exchanged between the two parties. The staff ploughed through the Crusade's accounts of the previous seven years, and when this tedious work was completed the VAT inspectors came and combed through the accounts. After the protracted investigation was completed the inspectors found that everything was in order. It was a happy day when a cheque for more than £48,000 arrived at the EHC office. This was God's way to provide for the purchase of the new printer.

Even ravens can be God's messengers.

A Faithful Farmer

"Amos … said to Amaziah, I was no prophet, neither was I a prophet's son; but I was an herdman, and a gatherer of sycomore fruit."
Amos 7:14

Amos, a rural farmer who was called to be a prophet, was different from Amaziah, the established priest. Amaziah had sermons with no message, ceremony with no reality and position without power. Amos was a man possessed of God. Even though Amaziah told him to get out of the kingdom, Amos stuck by his task and remained faithful to God.

"Amos" simply means, "a burden bearer". Amos is a very appropriate name for this prophet. He had the burden of the Lord's message. Like Jeremiah, God's message burned like fire in his bones, and he could withhold it no longer. Motivated by a holy compulsion and a passionate urgency to speak God's Word, he did not refrain from his calling. Amos might well use the New Testament language of Paul, *"Woe is unto me if I preach not the Gospel."*

Amos looked around at the nations. He pronounced eight judgements on the surrounding nations. He said that God spoke as "a roaring lion" whose growl was heard in Damascus, Gaza, Tyre, Edom, Ammon, and Moab. He is the God of Israel, and He is the Lord over all the nations and the whole world. Nothing escapes His notice, and He holds world leaders and their nations responsible.

Amos looked within his own nation. Amos wept when he looked at Israel, God's people. Their corruption was inviting the judgement of God. They enjoyed so many privileges; they were the children "of Zion" with God's altar in the Temple, and they had the assurance of His presence with them. Despite these privileges, the people were complacent. Their self-sufficiency and spiritual apathy caused them to be lulled to sleep.

Amos looked ahead. As he closed his prophecy, Amos received five visions from the Lord indicating God's coming judgement: a vision of a plague of locusts, a scorching fire, a plumbline, a basket of summer fruit and an altar. Within a few years God used the Assyrians to carry Israel into captivity.

God is not slack concerning His promises – even His promises of judgement.

Father's Day

"Enoch lived sixty and five years, and begat Methuselah: And Enoch walked with God."
Genesis 5:21, 22

Father's Day was a smart invention. Some may suspect that it was invented by our local department stores. Like many other dates, it all began in the USA, specifically in Spokane, Washington. In 1909 Sonora Smart Dodd, a devoted daughter campaigned for a Father's Day celebration after listening to a church sermon on the merits of Mother's Day. After Sonora's mother had passed away, her father played the role of both father and mother to his six children. Sonora chose the date to be on her dad's birthday, 5th June; however, festivities were moved to June 19, the third Sunday, because there was not enough time to prepare. It was sixty-three years later, in 1972, before Father's Day was officially recognized in the United Kingdom.

One of the most important fathers of the Bible was Enoch. His life validates an old English proverb, "One good father is better than a hundred schoolmasters." Enoch's life is a lesson on the priorities that should be prized by all believers.

His family. When Enoch became a father, it changed his life. Many parents recognize their need of God by the arrival of their first child. They are not only responsible for the life of the little one they brought into the world, but they will also have the greatest influence on where that little one will go after it leaves this world. That should cause any parent to want to walk with God.

His faith. Enoch called his son "Methuselah" which means, "When he is dead it will come." This was a prophecy of the coming worldwide flood, and Enoch knew that the judgement of God was on its way. When Methuselah drew his last breath, God shut the door of Noah's ark and sent the flood.

His faithfulness. Enoch was the first prophet mentioned in the Bible. In Jude 14-15 we read of his faithful preaching to a polluted society. Because he walked with God, Enoch hated sin.

His future. It is important to see how Enoch was taken and where he went--he went to be with the Lord. For us, it is more important where we go than how we go.

Like Enoch, let us aim to please Him.

Gratitude

"Were there not ten cleansed? But where are the nine?"
Luke 17:17

The healing of the ten lepers is a familiar story. The Lord Jesus was making His way from Galilee to Jerusalem. At a village near the border of Samaria and Judea, He met and healed ten lepers at one time. Only one of them took time to turn back and thank the Lord who had performed the miracle, and he was a Samaritan. That lone Samaritan man illustrated the full meaning of true thanksgiving. The Lord Jesus used the occasion to teach a lesson about gratitude to God.

Ten unclean men. The account begins with Jesus coming to where these ten leprous men were. *Leprosy had deformed them, put them at a distance and isolated them, and they were despairing of human help. They were under a virtual sentence of death.* They must have heard of Jesus and of what He had done for others so *"they lifted up their voices, and said, 'Jesus, Master, have mercy on us.'"*

Nine ungrateful men. All ten men had received a new start in life. You would expect that all of them would have rushed back to thank the Lord Jesus. Sadly, only one returned to offer his thanks--a Samaritan. He was probably considered to be a heretic by the Jews but was the only one who exhibited genuine faith. Never neglect to say thank you for your blessings.

Charles De Gaulle is reputed to have said to Winston Churchill regarding the military aid the Allies had provided to France during World War II, "We shall stun you with our ingratitude." Even Jesus was stunned by the ingratitude of nine men who were quick to pray, but slow to praise.

One unusual Man. "And one of them, when he saw that he was healed, turned back, and with a loud voice glorified God, and fell down on his face at his feet, giving him thanks" (Luke 17:14, 15). This Samaritan's praise was prompt, personal and proper, for he glorified God. Psalm 50:23 says, *"Whoso offereth praise glorifieth me."*

Nine men were declared clean by the priest, but this grateful man was declared *saved* by the Son of God.

Now, thank we all our God.

God is Good

"The Lord God is a sun and shield: the Lord will give grace and glory."
Psalm 84:11

In 2002 a liver transplant saved the life of José Carlos, President of Missão Evangélica Amazônica, Acre International's associate Mission in Brazil. He was so close to death that the doctors did not expect him to survive the almost 3,000-mile journey from Manaus to Porto Alegre in Rio Grande do Sul, Brazil's most southerly state. They told his wife, Eurides, that his condition was critical and to be prepared for the worst. She knew that friends around the world were praying for them.

God answered those prayers, and today Pastor José Carlos and Eurides continue in their leadership role In Brazil. They not only thank God for the miracle that brought José through the precarious operation, but they can also trace God's goodness to them over many years.

José was born in the Boca do Acre. His aged grandfather, Artú, lived in a simple forest home near town. Artú recalled that in the 1930s he purchased a Bible from a colporteur who travelled on the River Purus. Later he learned that the priest in Boca do Acre made a bonfire to burn as many of the colporteur's Bibles as he could find. Artú kept his Bible and diligently read it. The Scriptures led Artú to trust Christ as Saviour even though he had never met a missionary or attended a Gospel meeting.

Soon after James and Dorrie Gunning established the first church in Boca do Acre they got to know Artú. He became a faithful member of that church and was anxious that his family should know Christ also. He took little José to the church where Hazel Miskimmin was his Sunday School teacher.

Grandfather's prayers and Hazel's early influence resulted in José trusting Christ as Saviour and Lord. I had the joy of teaching him at the Baptist Seminary. Subsequently, he worked alongside Fred Orr for many years and became the first pastor of the Hebrom Evangelical Church in Manaus. José is highly respected by the team of Brazilian missionaries who are reaching into many parts of their own country.

God holds the reins of our lives.

Apprehended by God

"I thank my God upon every remembrance of you."
Philippians 1:4

The impact of W. P. Nicholson's evangelistic campaigns in Belfast during the 1920s changed society for the better. Through the power of the Gospel thousands of lives were transformed. Many young people were shielded from the social and political unrest in Belfast's troubled streets, and integrity was restored to many work places. Besides Harland Wolff opening a special shed, *"Nicholson's Shed"*, to receive and process stolen goods that were being returned, Mr. Nicholson also received a letter from a local engineering works, Messrs. Musgrave:

Dear Sir,

We beg to acknowledge the receipt of tools returned by one of our own men, who signs himself ex-worker, and we thank you for the good influence you have used in this particular case. It will gratify you to know that we have heard of other similar cases directly attributed to your good work.

Another great outcome from Nicholson's mission was triggered on 23rd February 1923 when shipyard-worker, John Proctor, was converted. His interest was first aroused when he heard the Salvation Army Band striking up musical praise while leading the shipyard men from the yard to Ravenhill Presbyterian Church. Out of curiosity he followed the crowd to see and hear for himself what was happening. That night the Holy Spirit arrested John's heart, and he was gloriously won for Jesus Christ. From that day John Proctor sought to know and do the will of God.

In that same year Alfred Downham, a well-known Christian businessman from Great Victoria Street Baptist Church, was anxious to serve the Lord in the Sandy Row area. As a result he built a hall in Wellwood Street and named it Emmanuel Mission. That work quickly flourished, and many were saved. Encouraged with this success Mr. Downham felt he should extend his outreach to East Belfast.

Subsequently, he purchased a plot of land in Roslyn Street where he erected a wooden hall. On 1 October 1932, the hall was opened for the glory of God and for the preaching of the Gospel. On that same day John Proctor was inducted to be pastor of Roslyn Street Emmanuel Mission.

Apprehended by God and assigned to God's work.

21ˢᵗ June

Songs for All Seasons

"At midnight Paul and Silas prayed, and sang praises unto God."
Acts 16:25

We should not be surprised that so much of the Bible is given to singing. The central and the largest book of the Bible is the book of Psalms, 100-150. The Bible begins with singing. When God laid the foundation of the universe "*the morning stars sang together, and all the sons of God shouted for joy*" (Job 37:8). They sang their praises to the Creator. In the final book of the Bible, we read of an innumerable multitude blending their voices to sing the praises of the Lamb in the great song of redemption.

The Father in heaven sings over His people. Though Israel had been unfaithful, God did not fail them. He gave them this assurance: "*The Lord* thy God in the midst of thee is mighty; he will save, he will rejoice over thee with joy; he will rest in his love, he will joy over thee with singing" (Zephaniah 3:17). In Malachi 3:17 it sounds like singing when The Lord declares, "*They shall be mine, saith the Lord of hosts, in that day when I make up my jewels.*"

The Son sang on earth because of His people. Mark 14:26 indicates that after the Lord Jesus and His disciples had finished Passover supper "*they had sung an hymn, they went out into the Mount of Olives.*" That was the last hymn of the "Hallel," the Passover, which is Psalm 118. The Saviour was going to Gethsemane and Calvary, yet He sang, "*This is the day the Lord has made, we will rejoice and be glad in it.*" Jesus sang because of the joy that was set before Him.

The Holy Spirit causes singing in God's people. Paul commanded that believers be filled with the Holy Spirit. He then went on to indicate that the mark of that fullness was singing in the heart: "*Be filled with the Spirit; speaking; to yourselves in psalms and hymns and spiritual songs, singing and making melody in your heart to the Lord*" (Ephesians 5:18, 19).

Lord keep me singing 'til the day is done.

22nd June

God Stepped In

"Grace to help in time of need."
Hebrews 4:16

Although under imminent danger during the Pakistani revolt in the autumn of 1947, Lily Boal did not let those dangers dampen her zeal for the Gospel. She had taken refuge in a Catholic Mission Hospital where Hindu girls and several nuns were hiding for fear of losing their lives. Lily took the opportunity of speaking to them about the Lord Jesus and His love for them.

Lily soon found that over a hundred people had taken refuge in the hospital in the hope that even wild and violent tribesmen would respect the sanctity of its precincts. That was not to be. The Mother Superior disclosed that rioters had looted and burned the local bazaar and murdered dozens of people. Lily called the people together, Hindus, nuns and frightened children, to pray for God's help. A young Scotsman, Colonel Dykes, tried to encourage the people.

Soon the sound of shooting and screaming was heard outside the hospital before tribesmen began to scale the perimeter wall. Colonel Dykes appealed, "Don't shoot! This is a hospital." They ignored him. Through her prayers, Lily could hear tribesmen banging on doors accompanied by cries of agony from those being attacked. Lily locked the children with her in the bathroom but soon they were banging on this door too. Lily bravely opened the door only to stare down the barrel of a gun. She shouted in Urdu, "Long live Pakistan." With that, the gun was lowered but they were ordered outside. Without another command or explanation, the gunmen suddenly disappeared. Lily knew the explanation. *GOD STEPPED IN.*

Lily ran to the front of the hospital where she found the Mother Superior and another nun covered in blood. They and several other people had been bludgeoned to death. The tribesmen had cruelly shot the Colonel's young wife and had thrown her body down a well. Lily tried to make the injured Colonel comfortable, but he was mortally wounded. Lily led him to faith in Christ before he died later that day, leaving his two little children in her care.

Lily was rescued thirteen days later and allowed to travel home.

God's goodness and mercy follow us every day.

Revival Blessing

"And Jabez called on the God of Israel, saying, Oh that Thou wouldest bless me indeed, and enlarge my coast, and that Thine hand might be with me, and that Thou wouldest keep me from evil, that it may not grieve me! And God granted him that which he requested."
1 Chronicles 4:10

Revival was the longing of Ernie Allen's heart. During the eleven years he spent at the Bible College of Wales, his life of intercession deepened his passion for revival. He later wrote:

In 1936 God called me to devote my life to the evangelisation of the world. During the years that followed He led me to study the great revivals of the past and the influence they had on the spread of the Gospel. For years I studied the struggles, prayers, labours and triumphs of men like Wycliffe, Tyndale, Luther and others who followed them. I saw that the greatest days of the Church were days of revival. Every movement that God has used to bless the world originated from vital blessing in some soul.

One thing that stands out in the story of every revival is the wonderful influence ordinary well-instructed Christians exerted. Such believers, through their changed lives, testimonies and prayers, brought the presence of God and the conviction of eternal realities to powerfully bear on the minds of sinners. It was this Christian zeal that spread blessings in the world.

During this period God inspired my own heart with the vision of a worldwide army of soul-winners who could promote revivals of religion in every country, and He called me to the work of raising this army. How could this be done? He led me to publish some of the writings of Charles G. Finney in six booklets titled, "The Revival Series."

Revival was Ernie Allen's legacy. He went on to publish many more booklets in an endeavour to promote revival. Those publications eventually constrained Ernie to publish literature for every home, beginning at the street where he lived and reaching around the world.

Allowing heaven to flow through us touches the world around us.

24th June

Here He Comes

"The beginning of the Gospel of Jesus Christ."
Mark 1:1

Mark is reputed to be the earliest of the Gospel writers. Like a seamstress picking up threads that have lain untouched for a long period, he reached back four hundred years to the closing chapter of the Old Testament and picked up the golden thread of Messianic prophecy. With that thread, he interlaced a rich tapestry of Jesus Christ, the promised Messiah and the Son of Righteousness.

John the Baptist announced the Sin-bearer. In spite of his austere lifestyle, John, the forerunner who introduced our Lord, burst onto the pages of the New Testament with dynamic freshness. Christ said that John was the greatest of the prophets. He certainly preached the greatest message when he cried, "Behold the Lamb of God, who takes away the sin of the world."

The Holy Spirit anointed the Servant. The Holy Spirit descending on our Lord Jesus was a fulfilment of Isaiah's prophecy (Isaiah 61:1) to which the Saviour alluded in Luke 4:18. Our Lord was conceived by the Holy Spirit. Everything the Father sent the Son to do, He did by the Holy Spirit. He is the Spirit of Christ.

The Father declared His approval of the Son. As Jesus emerged from the River Jordan after His baptism, heaven was torn open, and the Father affirmed, *"This is my beloved Son in whom I am well pleased."* On three occasions, the Father made similar affirmations. He manifested His approval at the Jordan after Christ identified with sinners by baptism and began His earthly ministry (Mark 1:11). He spoke again to affirm the Saviour's pre-eminence at the transfiguration of the Saviour (Matthew 17:5). He testified His approval again when the Lord Jesus spoke of the glory of the cross (John 12:28).

Satan attacked the Saviour. The prince of darkness was permitted to attack the Saviour to prove to us that Christ is stronger than Satan and sin.

Angels aided the Sovereign. Holy angels followed Him from His departure from Heaven until His return. They rejoiced at His birth and announced His resurrection, but they were silent at His death.

We are loved by the Father, the Son and the Holy Spirit.

Tell Them of Jesus

"Philip opened his mouth, and began at the same scripture,
and preached unto him Jesus."
Acts 8:35

The Municipal Market in Manaus was constructed in 1880 and was designed after the style of the Les Halles Market in Paris. The building's metallic structures were built in Paris and sent to Manaus by ship. The market is strategically located at the edge of the River Negro where thousands of clients, travellers and tourists pass through every day. The traders offer fresh fruits, spices, fish, souvenirs, traditional medications and other products.

Raimundo Nonato, a converted alcoholic, arrives at the market every morning at 5:30 a.m., but not to sell any of the above commodities. He is Acre International's Port Evangelist, distributing Gospel literature to the multitudes passing through the market. Often he will strike up an impromptu solo with his smooth baritone voice and sing out the Gospel. One day he started up "Holy, holy, holy, Lord God Almighty…" Within a few moments a group of Korean tourists came over to stand with him and sing the same hymn in their native tongue.

As a result of Raimundo's witness a trader asked him to visit her family across the River Negro. Not only did Raimundo lead that family to the Lord, he goes there every Saturday morning to disciple new converts and conduct a Gospel meeting. Initially he crossed the wide river on a barge which carried many passengers and up to twenty vehicles. This gave Raimundo a captive congregation for nearly an hour. After distributing Gospel leaflets to all on board, he sang for them, gave his testimony and spoke well of his Saviour.

A few years ago the barges were made redundant when a new suspension bridge was opened. Now Raimundo travels across the river each Saturday morning by bus. He asked permission from the owner of the bus company to do what he used to do on the barge. This was readily agreed. The journey takes about forty minutes to complete. That means Raimundo still has his captive congregation every Saturday morning. Several people have trusted the Lord Jesus as Saviour, including one of the bus drivers.

He tells them of Jesus, the mighty to save.

26th June

Home and Abroad

"For from you hath sounded out the Word of the Lord."
1 Thessalonians 1:8

For over 100 years many missionaries served God at the Belfast City Mission in Island Street until the hall was demolished in 1987. In its place and under the shadows of Harland and Wolf's famous Samson and Goliath cranes, a new hall was opened on 29th October 1988. That work continues to this day.

As the bricks and mortar of the old hall tumbled down it seemed as though they were laden with numerous memories of former years. The longest-serving missionary at Island Street was David Magill who spent more than forty years serving God in that district. It was said that David wore out more shoe leather than any insurance salesman or rent collector in the city. His was a household name in East Belfast.

Perhaps the most enduring fruit of Island Street City Mission is found far beyond the boundaries of East Belfast. Back in the 1870s Samuel Bill was an active member of the fledging work at Island Street. During Dwight L. Moody and Ira D. Sankey's visit to Belfast in 1874 Samuel's heart had been greatly stirred. As a result he developed a great passion for the lost and a lasting vision for distant lands where the Gospel had never been preached.

As a result, Samuel responded to a challenge from Henry Gratten Guiness about the needs in distant Calabar, West Africa, where Mary Slessor also served the Lord. In 1887 Samuel left Island Street City Mission to travel to Nigeria where he established a mission base and the Qua Iboe Church. Mr. Bill incorporated the name of the River Qua Iboe into the church and his work when he founded the Qua Iboe Mission in 1891. Qua Iboe Mission, known today as Mission Africa, has grown to be one of the largest and most successful interdenominational missions in Nigeria. Churches affiliated with the mission and those that sprung out of the initial Qua Iboe church have grown to incorporate at least two million Christians.

The Gospel not only reaches to the end of the earth – it reaches into eternity.

God's Man

"There was a man sent from God, whose name was John."
John 1:6

To mark the hundredth anniversary of the birth of John George Govan, founder of the Faith Mission, Duncan Campbell wrote:

Seventy or eighty years ago the stream of vital Christianity was running low in Scotland. True, the spirit of McCheyne and Chalmers was still alive, but the glorious revival of the Disruption period had darkened to twilight. Moderation had given place to Modernism. Into this blighted field God sent His servant with the message of full salvation, and soon in village, strath (*valley*) and glen, the dim light became a 'great and glorious light.'

One of the early Pilgrims wrote of "the Chief," as Mr. Govan was affectionately referred to by his Faith Mission colleagues:

Mr. Govan had great natural gifts, and great grace was upon him. I can recall when he read a passage slowly, thoughtfully – almost hesitatingly, and then he would begin to speak slowly with the Book open. As he kindled to his subject, he would close the Book, and soon the words and ideas of his address would come like a rushing torrent of eloquence which carried all before it and bowed the hearts and heads of his audience like corn before the wind. Like Apollos, 'He was an eloquent man, and mighty in the Scriptures.'

And what power and scorn he had for all that was false and hypocritical, and what dramatic power of description! In one address I will never forget, I think the text was, 'Behold the Man.' After a moving description of Christ's sufferings - Gethsemane, the sleepless night, the mock trials, the scourging, the purple robe in mockery, the crown of thorns, the tired face smeared with blood, and the spitting of the cruel Roman soldiers, he paused for quite a while and then said quietly – 'My Master!'

If I had not crowned Him King and Lord of my life before, I would have certainly done it then. How anyone who was present could have refrained from doing so, I do not know. 'My Master!' that was the secret of his life.

Mr. Govan truly was a man mightily used by God.

No Turning Back

*"Jesus said unto him, No man, having put his hand to the plough,
and looking back, is fit for the Kingdom of God."*
Luke 9:62

Right from the outset of her conversion to Jesus Christ Lily Boal was thirsty for God. She happily joined other like-minded young people whose annual delight was to attend the Faith Mission Convention in Bangor. Lily was drawn like a magnet to the challenging messages of holiness through Christ and full surrender to Jesus. They touched her heart, and she was broken and melted before God until she yielded all to Him. Almost immediately Lily wanted to become a Pilgrim. Her best friend at that time, Ida Harper, was rather dismissive at the thought of becoming a soberly dressed Pilgrim wearing a bonnet. She preferred to set her sights further afield to serve God in some foreign land.

Ironically, Ida never became a foreign missionary. God mightily used her as a Faith Mission Pilgrim in the salvation of many souls in Northern Ireland. Meanwhile, Lily never got to wear the Faith Mission uniform and bonnet. God was calling her to apply to the Worldwide Evangelization Crusade for work in Arabia.

Leaving Northern Ireland to study at Bible College was one of the first hurdles Lily had to cross. Almost immediately this new Irish student with the golden wavy hair and a strange accent found it difficult to adjust to new ways and different views. Consequently, Lily felt isolated and suffered from a bad dose of homesickness. It was so bad that the Principal's wife suggested that Lily might think of returning home to Belfast on the next boat. Lily looked at her with tear-filled brown eyes and said, "There will be no turning back."

"Then dry those tears," the lady kindly said. For Lily that was one of the first victories won. During the next thirty years of missionary service, there would be many other spiritual battles she had to face, fight and conquer through Christ.

Homesickness never troubled Lily Boal again, but she never lost her Belfast wit and humour nor did she ever modify her distinctive accent.

With God, a surrendered body, mind and will can be a mighty instrument.

Heavenly Blessing

"A faithful man shall abound with blessings."
Proverbs 28:20

Ernie Allen was the founder of The Revival Movement. His Christian faith was nurtured and strengthened by studying the history of the Protestant Reformers and great revivalists. The historical accounts gave him a hunger for similar times of refreshing from the presence of the Lord. These servants of God not only left their mark on Ernie, they became his role model for future years in God's work. Ernie later wrote of these men:

These are the men who fired my soul and gave me a passionate burden for revival in our time. John Wesley and George Whitefield. Through these two men and their co-workers God stemmed the tide of sin and darkness in England in the eighteenth century. They were men endued with power from on high.

When George Whitefield was twenty-four years old he was preaching to 20,000 grim colliers at Kingswood, Bristol. Referring to these great occasions, he wrote, 'The day was fine; the sun shone very bright. and the people, standing in such an awful manner around the mount, in the profoundest silence, filled me with holy admiration. Having no righteousness of their own to renounce, they were glad to hear of Jesus, who was a Friend to publicans, and who came to call not the righteous but sinners to repentance. The first discovery of their being affected was to see the white gutters made by their tears, which plentifully fell down their black cheeks.'

For the next thirty-four years Whitefield's preaching stirred many parts of the British Isles and the American States also. His co-worker was Jonathan Edwards who also was instrumental in the New England revival.

John Wesley also joined George Whitefield at Kingswood, and there he preached his first sermon in the open air. Wesley began to look on all the world as his parish. For fifty years he preached almost daily to crowds of up to 20,000 people. During his ministry he travelled a quarter of a million miles, mostly on horseback, and preached 40,000 sermons.

Our Sovereign Lord holds the reins of history. History teaches us that His children are designed to be channels of blessing.

Pray for revival.

Beggars Belief

"One thing I know, that, whereas I was blind, now I see."
John 9:25

A poorly dressed man with an outstretched hand was begging for a few coins from people who passed him by at the Municipal Market in Manaus. His suppressed solicitation and open hand suggested that he was hesitant and possibly embarrassed to be reduced to begging in public. Although a few passers-by took pity on the beggar and tossed him a few coins, most ignored him.

Raimundo Nonato, the Acre evangelist at the market, perceived that this man was no scrounger and approached him with a kind word. Over a bowl of soup the poor soul admitted that he was begging for survival. He said that his expected pension had not been approved and because he was far from home he had no friends or family to help. This was the last resort.

Raimundo listened patiently to the man as they shared a plain meal at a market stall. At an opportune time Raimundo introduced the message of the Gospel and of God's love in Christ. He stressed to his newfound friend that the salvation of his soul and forgiveness of his sins was the greatest need he had. The deprived individual listened intently as Raimundo related his own personal experience of Jesus Christ. Formerly he had been an alcoholic and was at the point of despair when his sons arrived home to say they had become Christians. Impacted by the transformation in their lives, Raimundo had sought and trusted Christ as Saviour. The evangelist gave his friend some Gospel literature to read and assured him of his prayers.

Over the next two weeks the two men met regularly at the market until finally one day the man, still poorly dressed, but now with a beaming smile on his face, said, "Raimundo, I have asked Jesus into my heart."

News of the beggar's conversion spread round the market quickly. Better still, A week later the man accosted Raimundo to tell him his pension had been approved and he was going back to his distant home to tell his family about the Saviour.

Words fitly spoken are incalculable.

July

Ballintoy Harbour

God Can Do it Again

"The Holy Ghost fell on all them which heard the word."
Acts 10:44

Sir Leonard Tilley, one of the Fathers of the Confederation of Canada, suggested the name "Dominion of Canada" for the union of the four Colonies of Nova Scotia, New Brunswick, Ontario, and Québec. His suggestion was prompted after reading Psalm 72:8: *"He shall have dominion also from sea to sea, and from the river unto the ends of the earth."* On the basis of this Bible verse, Sir Leonard proposed the name, "Dominion of Canada", and it was accepted by all the Founding Fathers of the great Confederation.

On July 1, 1867, the Dominion of Canada was born. The words from the Latin Vulgate Version of Psalm 72:8 are emblazoned on the coat of arms of Canada: *"a mari usque ad mare"* –– *"from sea to sea."*

Five years before the founding of the Dominion of Canada, John George Govan was born in Glasgow, Scotland. He forsook his early and lucrative success in the business world to step out by faith to serve God. That step resulted in the founding of The Faith Mission in 1886 with its aim to seek first the Kingdom of God. In the succeeding years, his zealous ministry and that of hundreds of dedicated Faith Mission workers, brought blessings, salvation, deepening of the Christian life and the stirrings of revival all over the British Isles.

Through thick and thin, through evil report and good, this valiant band of Faith Mission workers has pioneered in frontier and settlement in an effort to break through the hardness of a country that has never experienced a nationwide revival. However, a gradual prayer consciousness began to take hold on individuals here and there across the nation as the years went by.

In 1964 Rev. Duncan Campbell from Scotland made his first visit to Toronto. When he spoke of the "Lewis Awakening," that mighty work of God in the Hebrides in Scotland, many hearts in Canada were stirred. Listening to the man of God who was so mightily used by God, created an intense desire for a similar revival.

"Do it again, Lord! This time let it be in …"

Olivet

*"At the descent of the mount of Olives, the whole multitude of the disciples
began to rejoice and praise God."*
Mark 14:26

The Mount of Olives played a significant role in the life of our Saviour. On its slopes, the Lord Jesus taught His disciples about His coming again. At the foot of the mountain, in the Garden of Gethsemane, Jesus prayed with such intensity that He sweated great drops of blood. Also, on this mountain, the Saviour wept over Jerusalem because of their ignorance and refusal to repent.

Our Lord's last week began with His triumphant entry from the Mount of Olives into Jerusalem on a donkey. On that occasion Christ was carried down the hillside on a colt while the people of Jerusalem shouted their praises, *"Hosanna to the Son of David; Blessed is He that cometh in the Name of the Lord."* A week later, the Lord Jesus Christ was carrying His cross through Jerusalem while the same crowds shouted. "Away with Him. Crucify Him." How fickle are the crowds. How focused was the Saviour.

The Mount of Olives had still another role in the Saviour's earthly sojourn. It was from there that He triumphantly ascended from the earth into heaven. His triumphant entry into Jerusalem is an interesting contrast to His triumphant exit from this world.

On the Mount of Olives, He was going to the cross.
From the Mount of Olives, He was going to the crown.

On the Mount of Olives, He was going to the thorns.
From the Mount of Olives, He was going to the throne.

On the Mount of Olives, He was going to be scorned.
From the Mount of Olives, He *was* going to the singing.

On the Mount of Olives, He was going to be lifted up.
From the Mount of Olives, He *was* going to sit down.

On the Mount of Olives, He was going to be crucified.
From the Mount of Olives, He *was* going to be glorified.

On the Mount of Olives, He was going to atone for sin.
From the Mount of Olives, He *was* going to mediate for sinners.

When Jesus comes again, His feet shall touch this same mountain.

Tempted

*"Then was Jesus led up of the Spirit into the wilderness
to be tempted of the devil."*
Matthew 4:1

The Prince of Life was locked in conflict with the prince of darkness, and Jesus was victorious. He always is. It is worth noting that the temptations of the Lord Jesus in the desert occurred at the beginning of His public ministry and immediately following His baptism in the Jordan.

Satan tempted our Lord with the lust of the flesh. Jesus was hungry, and Satan challenged Christ's identity by appealing to His fleshly hunger. Jesus answered by quoting the Scriptures: *"Man shall not live by bread alone, but by every word that proceedeth out of the mouth of God."* There is more to life than satisfying physical desires. We are dependent upon the Word of God for true life.

Satan tempted our Lord with the pride of life. He challenged Jesus to throw Himself from the pinnacle of the Temple in a spectacular demonstration of power to dazzle the public. Jesus again quoted the Scriptures: *"Thou shalt not tempt the Lord your God."*

Satan tempted our Lord with the lust of the eyes. He offered to give Jesus all the kingdoms of this world if He would bow down and worship him. Again, Jesus responded with Scripture; *"Thou shalt worship the Lord thy God, and Him only shalt thou serve."* Single-mindedness of worship and loyalty to God in service are paramount for every Christian.

We have the same adversary; Satan still lures people with the lust of the eye, the lust of the flesh and the pride of life.

We have the same aid; God's Word, the sword of the Spirit, is a mighty weapon.

We have the same Advocate; the victorious Christ will bruise Satan under our feet.

We also have the same assistance; Holy angels are God's ministering spirits to the saints.

When Satan tempts me to despair,
And tells me of the guilt within,
Upward I look, and see Him there
Who made an end of all my sin.

When temptation knocks, let Jesus answer.

Fishing

"Follow Me, and I will make you fishers of men."
Matthew 4:19

Fishing is a way of life in Amazonas. The great River Amazon, its tributaries and lakes contain three thousand species of fish. Many of these make favourite dishes for local people. Amongst the preferred fish is the Piraracu. It can measure up to ten feet long and can weigh five hundred pounds. Although mostly eaten fresh the Piraracu is frequently salted and left in the sun to dry. Salted and dried Piraracu has an unpleasant smell but is very popular.

Most forest dwellers engage in fishing, for they depend on their catch for their meals. Women washing clothes at the river's edge will often throw a line into the river on which there are several baited hooks. The line is secured to a pole stuck into the riverbank. When the pole begins to agitate the woman leaves her washing, draws in the line to remove the fish, baits the hook again and throws the line back into the river before returning to her washing. When finished she may have sufficient fish for a family meal.

After men return from the forest they frequently go fishing in the river or a nearby lake. They stand on the front of the canoe and throw the net into the water. These nets are similar to those used by the Galilean fishermen who followed our Lord. The round circular net is weighted at the edges and when thrown properly it opens fully on the water's surface, and as it sinks it closes in on everything in its span.

Just as in the time of the Lord Jesus many of these fishermen become fishers of men. While living in Canutama on the River Purus I was invited by the family next door to accompany three brothers on a fishing trip. During that day I learned so much from their angling skills and knowledge of the river. Better still, within a few weeks, those three brothers trusted Christ as Saviour and immediately became fishers of men. Like our Lord's fisherman-disciple, Andrew, they brought other family members to their Saviour.

He called His followers to be fishers of men.

Christian Soldiers

"Fight the good fight of faith ... I have fought a good fight."
1 Timothy 6:12, 2 Timothy 4:7

Throughout Paul's letters, he was always conscious that he was in a spiritual conflict. For that reason, he addressed the Christians in Ephesus about the provision and protection the Lord has made for all Christian soldiers.

The enlistment of the Christian soldier. Every child in God's family is enlisted into God's army.

The enablement of the Christian's strength. We can be strong in the Lord. This is the resurrection power of the Lord Jesus by which He overcame principalities and powers. It is the power that defeated Satan and death when Jesus died on the cross.

The engagement of the Satanic foe. Satan is a destroyer and a deceiver. The Lord will bruise him under our feet.

The equipment for the Christian's strife. We must be prayerfully clothed with the whole armour of God.

The endurance of the Christian's service. Keep going on until the battle is won. Endure hardness as a good soldier of Jesus Christ.

The enjoyment of the Saviour's victory. No provision was made for defeat for a Roman Legionnaire. Through Jesus Christ, we are assured of victory.

I spent two profitable years at the Worldwide Evangelization Crusade Missionary Training College in Glasgow where we were challenged by the exploits of C. T. Studd who founded the WEC. Studd was a famed English cricketer who deserted the playing field for the battlefield of worldwide evangelization. He used to upbraid Christians for being what he called, "Chocolate Soldiers" who melt in the heat of the battle. In his *"Quaint Rhymes of a Quondam Cricketer,"* he included this ditty:

Get up, get up for Jesus, ye soldiers of the Cross,
A lazy Sunday morning surely does harm and loss;
The Church of God is calling; in duty be not slack;
You cannot fight the good fight while lying on your back.

Be ready to serve where and when He calls.

When Jesus Comes

"After that John was put in prison, Jesus came into Galilee."
Mark 1:14

The late Dr. Oswald J. Smith, pastor of the famous People's Church in Toronto, Canada, was a gifted Bible teacher, an effective evangelist and a man with a clear missionary vision. Besides all these talents Dr. Smith was also a very accomplished hymn writer who composed some greatly-loved and enduring Gospel songs of our time. One of these tells the story of the blind beggar, Bartimaeus. Besides spending all his life in darkness, Bartimaeus sat each day at the gates of his hometown, Jericho, in the hope that pilgrims on their way to Jerusalem, might toss him a few coins. His life was forever changed when Jesus came. The refrain is based on those words, "then Jesus came."

> When Jesus comes the Tempter's power is broken,
> When Jesus comes the tears are wiped away.
> He takes the gloom and fills the life with glory,
> For all is changed when Jesus comes to stay.

After John the Baptist was seized and imprisoned, his short but effective ministry was terminated. With John gone Mark simply states, "Jesus came." What beautiful words! Like the emergence of the sun after the darkness has run its course, so Jesus came. After John the Baptist had fallen to the tyranny of Herod Tetrarch, Jesus came to Galilee from Judea. What a blessing for the Galileans.

He came as the *Master* calling His disciples by the seashore.
He came as the *Holy One* who cast out demons from an unclean man in the synagogue.
He came as the *Healer* who touched multitudes at Peter's home.
He came as the *Intercessor* who spent time on the mountain alone with God.
He came as the *Sympathising Saviour* preaching throughout Galilee.
He came as the *Friend* of the despised when He touched and cleansed a despairing man who had been afflicted with leprosy.

As in the case of blind Bartimaeus, when he could not go to Jesus, Christ came to him.

When I could not go to Him, He came to me.

Thankful

"One of them ... turned back, and with a loud voice glorified God.'"
Luke 17:12-13

I wish every Christian could have met Alberto. His charisma exuded from his bright personality despite his physical deformities. Alberto was a patient for almost sixty years in a leprosarium. During those decades leprosy took its toll on his emaciated body. As Alberto sat on his bed his toothless grin lit up his sunken cheeks and disfigured face. Any visitor soon discovered that he was blind, the result of repeated infection and scarring on his eyes. Added to this, Alberto had no hands and no feet, again the result of repeated infections on his extremities. When I first met Alberto he had only two teeth, one on the upper gum and the other on the lower. Alberto used to say, "Thank God they meet."

Alberto, like many leprosy patients, was able to feed himself with a spoon tied to the stump of his hand, but he did not use his two teeth for chewing. They were his "hands" for turning on his radio and tape-recorder had been generously supplied by Fred Orr and some friends.

When I took any visitor to meet Alberto, he would give them his customary warm greeting with that smile on his face. His deformities could not hide his love for Christ and God's people. He was always quick to offer his visitors a portion of the Scriptures. One day, through interpretation, he told me he wanted to quote a chapter of the Bible for my friend. I asked which chapter. To this, he promptly replied, "Psalm 119!"

"All of it?" I asked. "It has 176 verses." Alberto had memorised the whole chapter by using his teeth to switch on and off his tape-recorder. I asked him to just quote the first sixteen verses. He did this without hesitation, and then, with his lovely tenor voice, he gave us a beautiful rendition of *How Great Thou Art.*

I think of Alberto when I read how the Lord Jesus healed ten lepers. Only one of them returned to thank Him. Alberto went to be with Christ in 2016. I can almost hear him praising His Lord.

Every day we ought to be thankful.

I Love My Bible

"O how love I Thy law! It is my meditation all the day."
Psalm 119:97

Geraldo lived on the outskirts of Lábrea, isolated from most of the community because he had leprosy. Every Sunday afternoon we accompanied Fred Orr and a church group to conduct a meeting outside Geraldo's simple forest home. One day he lifted his Bible between the stumps of what used to be his hands, and said, "I love my Bible. When you go to your land, please thank the people who sent the missionaries so we could hear the Gospel and thank those who sent Bibles, so we read God's Word. Tell them we will never see them here on earth, but one day in the tabernacles of glory we will greet them with a Brazilian hug."

The Bible is the most remarkable book. It was the first book ever printed, the most popular and best-selling book of all time and the most valuable book ever sold. Though enemies have tried to destroy it, God has preserved His Word through the sacrifice of many saints who gave their lives in its defense. Today the Bible is loved, read and obeyed by millions.

Samuel Chadwick said, *"I have guided my life by the Bible for more than sixty years, and I tell you there is no book like it. It is a miracle of literature, a perennial spring of wisdom, a wonder of surprises, a revelation of mystery, an infallible guide of conduct, and an unspeakable source of comfort.*

Pay no attention to people who discredit it, for they speak without knowledge. The Bible is the Word of God. Study it according to its own direction. Live by its principles. Believe its message. Follow its precepts. No man is truly uneducated who knows the Bible, and no one is wise who is ignorant of its teachings.

This book contains the mind of God, the state of man, the way of salvation, the doom of sinners and the happiness of believers. Its doctrines are holy, its precepts are binding, its history is true, and its decisions are immutable.

Read it to be wise, believe it to be secure and practice it to be holy.

Sit, Walk, Stand

"Having done all, to stand. Stand therefore,
having your loins girt about with truth."
Ephesians 6:13,14

During the Battle of Waterloo when the fight was grim, an officer galloped up to the Duke of Wellington and reported on behalf of his superior officer that they were being destroyed and could not hold the position unless reinforcements arrived soon.

The "Iron Duke" said to the soldier, "Tell him to stand."

The soldier rushed back and delivered the message to his senior officer. Within moments another officer came with the same request for reinforcements. The Duke's answer was the same again, "Tell him to stand."

That soldier returned to the battlefront, and a third soldier came begging in the name of his superior for the needed help. "I have no help to send you," said the Duke, "Tell him to stand."

The soldier saluted and said, "You will find us there, Sir." When the battle was fought and finally won, the Duke found them, all of them, dead in their place. They were prepared to stand and to die in their place for the "Iron Duke."

Paul spent two years preaching and teaching God's Word in Ephesus. He knew that it was not easy to be a follower of Jesus Christ in such a promiscuous and superstitious city. Merchant seamen from all over the world disembarked at the magnificent Ephesian harbour on the Cayster River. They not only brought their cargoes of gold, silver, ivory and precious stones to add to the luxuriant life-style of the Ephesians, but they also indulged and contributed to the moral pollution and decadent corruption of the great city, which was known as the "Market of Asia." Superstition and witchcraft, practiced by both Jews and Greeks, abounded among this people. The majority of the Ephesians venerated the greatness of the Greek god Jupiter and "Diana of the Ephesians."

For that reason Paul taught the Ephesian Christians that although they are seated with Christ in heavenly places, they must walk with Christ in the midst of a perverse world and stand for Jesus Christ against the wiles of the devil.

Failing to stand for Jesus will cause you to fall into temptation.

10th July

Christian Conflict

*"Finally, my brethren, be strong in the Lord, and in the power of His might.
Put on the whole armour of God, that ye may be able to stand
against the wiles of the devil."*
Ephesians 6:10, 11

Sadly, we live in a time when there is little sense of Christian conflict. There are some who want to remove all the hymns with militant themes from our songbooks. They maintain that hymns such as *Onward Christian Soldiers, Hold the Fort for I am Coming* and *Who is on the Lord's side?* are too aggressive. Yet one cannot read the New Testament and fail to sense the clear call to spiritual warfare.

Consider the following verses:

"The weapons of our warfare are not carnal, but mighty through God to the pulling down of strong holds; Casting down imaginations, and every high thing that exalteth itself against the knowledge of God, and bringing into captivity every thought to the obedience of Christ" (2 Corinthians 10:4).

"This charge I commit unto thee, son Timothy, according to the prophecies which went before on thee, that thou by them mightest war a good warfare" (l Timothy1:18).

"Fight the good fight of faith, lay hold on eternal life, whereunto thou art also called" (1 Timothy 6:12).

"Thou therefore, my son, be strong in the grace that is in Christ Jesus ... therefore endure hardness, as a good soldier of Jesus Christ" (2 Timothy 2:1-3).

"For I am now ready to be offered, and the time of my departure is at hand. I have fought a good fight ..." (2 Timothy 4:6,7).

Repeatedly in the Scriptures, the Christian life is depicted in terms of warfare. Living for Jesus Christ has always been a conflict, and it will never cease to be. Whether you are at the beginning of your Christian experience or mature in your Christian walk, the conflict remains. Furthermore, I find the more effective a Christian becomes, the more Satan will oppose him. However, it is also true that the longer we fight and the more victories we gain, the more our faith will be strengthened.

In this conflict, we are assured that the Lamb prevails.

A Jammy Story

"I have commanded the ravens to feed thee there."
1 Kings 17:4

God has a thousand ways of supplying the needs of His children. Maizie Smyth gave another account of how God not only cares for His children but delights to bless them:

"Even though we had an abundance of fresh tropical fruit in Kisangani, it was always a special treat to buy a pot of strawberry jam imported from home. I will never forget someone in Kenya sent me a jar of strawberry jam for Christmas. It was a touching treat, but because many visitors passed through my home, I tried to keep it hidden at the back of the cupboard for when I was alone. In that way, I was able to make one pot of jam last for months.

Just before Easter 1998, I was in one of the small shops buying bread when I noticed they had strawberry jam from Kenya, but it was over £4.00 for a small jar. At that price, there was no way a Ballymena woman was going to part with that amount of money for a little drop of jam.

At a young people's rally on Easter Saturday a young fellow who came from a distant village gave me a packet that his mother had sent for me. I put it aside to open at break time in the afternoon. When I did open the parcel I discovered the lady had sent me two eggs, some money and a letter which read as follows:

'You will not remember me, but several years ago I came by your house for a drink of cold water. We chatted together, and I told you I was moving house to another village. You gave me some seeds for my garden and some money to buy soap and oil. God has blessed my family, and we are very happy here. This year we had a good harvest, and I am sending you something for yourself. Do not give it to anyone else. You may want to buy yourself a pot of jam to eat with your bread.'"

No good thing will He withhold from His children.

Unfurling the Banner

"Thou hast given a banner to them that fear thee, that it may be displayed because of the truth."
Psalm 60:4

The opening of the Olympic Games is an awesome spectacle when competitors of all participating countries parade around the arena carrying the flags of their respective nations. The flags not only identify the nations, they also become a rallying point for their athletes and fans. Rapturous applause erupts from the supporters of each country as their team goes by with the flag waving back and forth.

The most important thing flags or banners do, however, is mark victory. It is well understood that the conquering army in any battle has the right to remove the defeated country's flag and replace it with their own, usually in the highest spot possible for all to see. It means that the country with the conquering flag has won and was in control.

We read that after the defeat of the Amalekites, Moses built an altar to thank God and called the name of the place, Jehovah Nissi -- The Lord Is My Banner. Each tribe in Israel had their individual ensign that was displayed wherever they camped. That flag identified their Lord, unified the people, defied their enemies and testified to victory.

Here are a series of compound Names for Jehovah by which believers can identify with their Saviour:

Jehovah-jireh	-	*The Lord will provide.*	- Genesis 22:14
Jehovah-nissi:	-	*The Lord our Banner.*	- Exodus 17:15
Jehovah-shalom	-	*The Lord our Peace.*	- Judges 6:24
Jehovah-shammah	-	*The Lord is There.*	- Ezekiel 48:35
Jehovah-Tsidkenu	-	*The Lord our Righteousness.*	- Jeremiah 26:3
Jehovah- Rapha	-	*The Lord our Healer.*	- Exodus 15:26
Jehovah-Raah	-	*The Lord is our Shepherd.*	- Psalm 23:1
Jehovah-Sabaoth	-	*The Lord of Hosts.*	- 1 Samuel 1:3

He brought me into His banqueting house, and His banner over me is love.

Christians

"And the disciples were called Christians first in Antioch."
Acts 11:26

The deacons of a country church met to discuss necessary renovations to accommodate their growing congregation. One informed deacon proposed that the church should purchase a chandelier to improve the image of the sanctuary. Jake, the secretary of the church and a local farmer who resented city life, spoke up, "Brethren, what do we need a chandelier for? First of all, we don't have the money to buy it. Secondly, I can't spell it, and furthermore, no one in the church can play it. What we really need around here is more light."

Just as there was confusion about a chandelier in that country church so also in Christendom, there are a lot of fuzzy ideas of what a Christian is. Some have the impression that a Christian is a person who has a Christian name and was born in a Christian country. There is no such a thing as a "Christian country." Salvation is an individual matter. Therefore, a person is not made a Christian by nationality.

Others postulate that a person is considered to be a Christian because they were born in a Christian home. A Christian home is a great privilege, but we do not become Christians by the merits of our family. Each individual needs to be "born again."

Some religious people sincerely profess to be Christians because they belong to a Christian church. A church does not have the power to save or regenerate anybody. We are not converted to Jesus Christ by the rite or ritual of a church no matter how orthodox that church may be.

A Christian is:

A son in God's family. Entrance to God's family is by a new birth by which a sinner becomes a new creature in Christ.

A stone on God's Foundation. Built on Christ and united to all who are in Christ.

A saint in Christian fellowship. Made holy through Christ's blood.

A soldier in the good fight. Serving under the Captain of our salvation

A servant in the field. The field is the world in which we are God's servants.

A Christian is in Christ, and Christ is in the Christian.

14ᵗʰ July

God Provides

"For I know the thoughts that I think toward you."
Jeremiah 29:11

Maizie Smyth testified of how God gave her the grace to step out in faith to serve Him:

On the day I gave my notice to the Down Education Committee that I was leaving my employment at the end of August, no one had any idea I was going to Bible College. The Director summoned me to his office and protested, "You cannot possibly leave now. We are reorganizing the system and need your experience. Could you please delay leaving for one year?"

It is amazing the number of escape routes that appear when God calls. I declined the Director's plea, and soon the word got out and colleagues were whispering, 'That piece of furniture is going to Bible College.'

One Christian colleague from another department asked me to stop by his office. I was taken aback with what he told me and how emotional he became. He said years earlier his son had indicated that God was calling him to go to Bible School, but he had counselled the young man to seek a career first. He was broken when he said that the son was now far from God and that he blamed himself for the son's waywardness. The colleague went on to say that he felt God was giving him another chance to help a friend go to Bible School and with that, he gave me an envelope saying, 'That will help you some way along the line. May God bless you."

I was a little embarrassed but felt sorry for the broken-hearted man. Back at my desk, I opened the envelope and out fell a cheque for a sizeable sum. I wept with joy. Not only did I know God had called me, but within a few hours of giving notice to terminate my employment, my first term's fees had already been provided. I remembered what I had read in Jeremiah 29:11; "For I know the thoughts that I think toward you, saith the Lord, thoughts of peace, and not of evil, to give you an expected end."

The Hand that guides, is the Hand that provides.

Never Give Up

"For consider Him that endured such contradiction of sinners against Himself, lest ye be wearied and faint in your minds."
Hebrews 12:3

Rathlin Island, a green and rocky landmass just off the North Antrim Coast, is mostly noted for its beautiful scenery, its warm and welcoming community and the steep and rugged cliffs which provide a nesting place for thousands of puffins.

Another great feature of the Island goes back to the 13th Century. The famous Robert the Bruce of Scotland was hunted by the English, but he escaped across the Irish Sea to find refuge in a cave on Rathlin. His brother had already been executed, and for seven years his wife and daughters were held captive. Bereft of family and friends, he was low in moral. He wondered if he should remain in exile or try again to free his home village and land from his enemies. He had already tried and failed.

While pondering these options, his attention was drawn to a tiny spider hanging from the roof of the cave. It was trying to swing to fix a line to a nearby rock. Robert noticed that the tiny spider tried six times and failed. Finally, on the seventh attempt, it was successful. The spider's determination and perseverance was not lost on Robert. He returned home to Scotland to win the famous battle of Bannockburn and regain his wife and family.

I am reminded of this story when I read today's text. It is easy to grow weary in our Christian work and become faint in our spiritual walk. It happened to some Bible giants.

Abraham became dispirited in a time of famine and forsook the Promised Land.

Elijah conquered his foes on Mount Carmel, but could not conquer his fears and fled more than 100 miles away from Jezebel.

Jonah dejectedly huffed under a gourd and wanted to die after the great revival in Nineveh.

Do I need to mention Peter who denied his Lord and returned to his boat?

The Psalmist understood the antidote to fainting: *"I had fainted, unless I had believed to see the goodness of the Lord in the land of the living"* (Psalm 27:13).

Let us stay focused on Jesus and keep on following Him.

They Came To Christ

"And they came to Him from every quarter."
Mark 1:45

Mark gives an account of a full twenty-four hours in the Saviour's life in the Galilee region. It began in the bright sunshine of a Galilean morning when Jesus walked by the lake and called fishermen to follow Him. It moved into a mid-morning visit to the synagogue in Capernaum to teach the Scriptures. In the afternoon, He visited Peter's home where He healed Peter's mother-in-law. That evening multitudes of needy people found their way to Jesus for His help and healing. Mark's account concludes in chapter 1 with the Lord Jesus on a solitary prayer-vigil in the hills during the lonely hours of the early morning. This twenty-four-hour period shows how our Lord's was life full and busy.

The Jewish historian, Josephus, tells us that at the time of our Lord there were over 200 cities and villages in the region of Galilee. Because the land was so fertile, it was a booming area for farmers; in fact, farming was the number one occupation of that day. He estimated that the smallest villages and cities contained at least 1,000 people. Galilee probably contained at least three million people.

Mark ends his first chapter with these words, *"they came to him from every quarter."*

All sorts of people came to Christ. Rich people like Zacchaeus came to Him. Religious people like Nicodemus sought Him. The rebellious like the Demoniac from the Gadarenes needed Jesus. We all need the Saviour.

All sorts of places from which they came. Matthew left his business desk to follow Christ. Fishermen left their boats and Zacchaeus came from up a tree to take Christ home. Leprous men emerged from their isolation to ask for His touch.

All sorts of problems they brought. The Bible speaks of diverse diseases. The people's problems were many. They were afflicted with diseases, tormented by demons, whipped by despair and fearful of death.

The only Person to whom they came. They did not go to the priests in the Temple. They sought Jesus--the only One who could help and heal them.

Where else can we go but to the Lord?

A Gideon Bible

"Create in me a clean heart, O God; and renew a right spirit within me."
Psalm 51:10

Peter and June Wright, friends of Keith and Karen Lindsay, had a remarkable conversion. Thirty years ago their lives were falling apart. On their doctor's advice they went to York to try to sort out their lives. Although Peter had already received absolution for sins from his parish priest, he could find no peace for his troubled heart.

While June was making coffee in the hotel room, Peter, always a keen reader, picked up a Bible from the bedside. In the index he noticed that it offered "Bible Helps" and decided to find a reading that might fit their situation. The index pointed him to Psalm 51:10-14. He found it hard to set the Bible down. Every time he read something interesting he shared it with June, but she showed no interest. Finally, in exasperation she said, "If you think we have come away for religion, forget it. It is no good going to W. H. Smith's for your own Bible as these Gideon Bibles are presented to you."

In spite of this rebuff, Peter continued reading the Scriptures. Five days later, before leaving the hotel, Peter asked the manager if he could take the Bible home. The request was declined but the manager told Peter to get in touch with Gideons International when he arrived home.

On arrival home, Peter discovered that a Christian couple, members of Gideons International, lived nearby. Later that same day, the couple arrived at the Wright's house with a gift of a Gideon Bible. Over a cup of tea they shared their testimony with Peter and June and then invited them to a home Bible study. Before leaving, they said to June, "In the meantime, prayerfully read this Bible."

After the couple left, June said to Peter, "I don't know about you, but I'm going to that Bible study as I have arrived home from holiday the same way as I went."

At the Bible Study they learned the Scriptures. On Palm Sunday of the following year Peter and June called upon God for mercy and received Christ as personal Saviour.

The Bible is a living and life-giving book.

18th July

Jesus at Home

"Martha received Him into her house … Mary …
sat at Jesus' feet, and heard His word.
Luke 10:38-42

Our Saviour loved the home of Mary and Martha in Bethany. He esteemed the warmth of the family, the loyalty of their friendship and probably enjoyed the good food. On five occasions in Luke, we find people at the feet of Jesus. Of all these individuals, none speaks more to us than Mary. Each time she is mentioned in the Scriptures she is at Jesus' feet. It was her favourite place. In Luke 10 she seems to be saying, "I want You, Lord." In John 11 she is saying, "I need You, Lord." In John 12 she says, "I love You, Lord." Mary wanted to live close to Jesus and learn more from Him.

Martha opened her home to Jesus. He was always very close to Mary, Martha, and Lazarus, and was always gladly welcomed by Martha. She was thrilled to have Jesus in her home. He ought to be welcomed as a guest in any life and made at home with every family and church.

Mary opened her heart to Jesus. While Martha desired to have Jesus present, Mary delighted to be in His presence. Martha was thrilled to entertain Jesus in her house, but Mary wanted to sit at His feet. Martha's desire to have Jesus in her home was good, but Mary's desire to be close to Him and learn of Him was better.

Martha was encumbered with many things. "Martha was cumbered about much serving." To be "encumbered" is to be "distracted, pulled in different directions." She was too busy in her primitive kitchen, trying to do several things but neglecting the most important thing.

Mary was content with one thing. There were many things that Mary could have been doing, but Her priority was to spend time with Jesus. She decided to lay aside the lesser things to sit at the feet of Jesus. Martha was serving while Mary was sitting. Martha was the worker while Mary was the worshipper. Martha's work was important, but Mary's worship was better.

Work is spending time for God; worship is spending time with God.

Christ is Adequate

*"Blessed be the God and Father of our Lord Jesus Christ, who hath blessed us
with all spiritual blessings in heavenly places in Christ."*
Ephesians 1:4

I remember in 1958 travelling down through the length of England from Heysham to Lydd in Kent on a 600 Norton motorcycle. It took us the length of England from north to south. This meant we had to pass through numerous towns and villages en-route.

Big changes were made the following year when the M1 motorway was inaugurated on July 4, 1959. It was Britain's first motorway, 100 miles long from London to the Midlands. For its opening, newspaper editors hired leading motor racing drivers to drive Jaguars, Aston Martins, and Ferraris to see who could be the fastest in travelling from London to Birmingham.

Stirling Moss and Mike Hawthorn took off in their sports cars and reached speeds of 150 miles an hour and got to Birmingham in less than an hour. There was a buzz around the country. A new day had dawned for family motoring. Here was a road without traffic lights or speed limits.

The following Sunday thousands of people took their saloon cars for a family outing on the M1. The drivers put a heavy foot on the accelerator and got up to maximum speed. It proved to be a disaster. Those cars didn't have the power or resources to maintain top speed. Previously those family cars barely travelled faster than forty-five mph. They were inadequate for the potential speeds on the motorway. Consequently, the hard shoulder of the M1 was littered with broken down cars. The road repair services never had so many calls for assistance, and the government was compelled to introduce the 70 mph speed limit.

On occasions, Christians also break down, run out of fuel and even try to run on empty. The pressures and challenges of daily life can crowd in on them, and they become aware of their inadequacy without Christ's presence. Paul found his adequacy in the riches of the Christian's resources in Christ.

We also need to draw on these heavenly resources in our walk with God as we work for Him.

Jesus Christ is all we need.

Wondrous Grace

"Thou art great, and doest wondrous things."
Psalm 86:10

Vinyl records are becoming popular again. While engaged in river evangelism in Brazil we frequently played a 78LP record of Antonio Silvino, formerly one of Brazil's most notorious gangsters, telling his testimony. People sat spellbound as they listened to his amazing story of God's grace.

Antonio, fast shooting and accurate with his gun, was feared by most people in Northeast Brazil. They knew that he had already murdered more than sixty people, besides inflicting many other atrocities. Antonio told how he was hired to assassinate Solomão Ginsburg, a very zealous missionary who was leading multitudes to Christ. Ginsburg's story is in his book, *A Wandering Jew in Brazil.*

Very early one morning Ginsburg left home on horseback to go to Moganga for evangelistic meetings. On the way, he spotted a man at the roadside with a double-barrelled gun in his hand. It was the assassin, Antonio Silvino. The missionary, not knowing the stranger, greeted him heartily. The criminal responded indifferently.

The people in the village were aware of the plot to kill Ginsburg and were surprised to see him arrive alive. The meeting was packed that night, and afterward, Ginsburg retired to his hammock completely exhausted. Just as he lay down someone called for him. The voice said, "I am Antonio Silvino, and I want to talk with Senhor Solomão."

Ginsburg, now aware of the planned assassination, trembled. He knew he had escaped the bandit that morning, but now he had come to kill him. He sent a telegramme prayer to heaven for protection.

"Do you know who I am and why I have come here?" asked Antonio. Solomão responded that he knew the criminal had been hired to kill him.

"That is true," said the gangster. Ginsburg closed his eyes waiting for the worst. "I've decided not to kill you. Early this morning you spoke to me kindly. Tonight I went to your meeting in disguise. While you were singing, praying and preaching, I realized you are doing a good job. I'd rather kill the man who hired me."

In the small hours of the morning, Ginsburg led Antonio to faith in Christ.

Praise the God of wondrous grace.

A Word in War

*"Fear thou not; for I am with thee: be not dismayed; for I am thy God:
I will strengthen thee; yea, I will help thee; yea, I will uphold thee
with the right hand of my righteousness."*
Isaiah 41:10

Maizie Smyth recalled how one Sunday night while living alone in Kisangani, Congo, she lay on her bed, protected by her mosquito net. She read until nearly midnight before deciding it was time to go asleep. The reverberating noise of trucks rumbling down the streets wakened Maizie. *What could it be?* she thought. Suddenly the house seemed to shake with a loud burst of gunfire.

Maizie courageously opened her bedroom window and spied several soldiers. She asked what was happening, but they ignored her questions. No sleep came for the rest of that night. When dawn broke, convoys of soldiers invaded the town. The local population was terrified when the armed forces recklessly fired their automatic weapons into the air. No one dared leave their homes. Soon shops and houses were being pillaged and looted.

At such times Maizie always found comfort and courage from God's Word. She kept doors and windows closed as she read her Bible in the dim light. Her eyes fell on Isaiah 41:10; *"Fear thou not…"*

While people were plundering and ransacking shops the soldiers had already stolen most of the vehicles in town. Maizie's Land Rover was hidden from public view at the back of her house. Fearing she might lose her precious vehicle, she prayed for the Lord's protection, "Lord put a hedge around us." She reasoned with the Lord that the Land Rover was vital for her work.

While she was praying, she was also watching. When a group of soldiers was passing her door, one said to the other, "Isn't that a Land Rover there?"

The other soldier replied, "Land Rover? What would you do with a Land Rover? Sure you wouldn't even know how to drive it." With that, they marched farther up the street.

Maizie found that reading the Bible in the midst of danger helped her focus her attention and trust on God's promises. She proved that they never fail.

God is our refuge and strength.

Jesus our Saviour

"Lord, if it be Thou, bid me come unto Thee on the water."
Matthew 14:28

The Sea of Galilee is forever related to the name of the Lord Jesus Christ. He not only did many mighty miracles beside the lake, He also performed miracles in the water, with the water and on the water. One of the most remarkable miracles was on the night when Jesus stilled the storm and answered Peter's request to go to Him on the water. Peter had made countless crossings of the Sea of Galilee, but he would never forget the night the Saviour invited him step out of the boat.

I have heard that in ancient Egyptian hieroglyphics the essence of any impossibility was represented by the figure of a person walking on water. I am sure Peter never forgot the Saviour stilling the storm, but his mind especially must have focused on the moment he stepped down from the boat and started walking to Jesus. It took a lot of courage to place one foot on the sea. It took a lot of faith and courage to put the second foot on the water, even though the boisterous storm was raging, and the frenzied waters were greatly agitated.

Peter's action undoubtedly caught the attention of the other disciples. We do not know what interrupted Peter's walk of faith. One preacher suggested that maybe it was Thomas who called out in the darkness, "Watch out Peter! Here comes a big wave!" We do know that everything suddenly changed. Water and waves obscured Peter's sight of the Lord Jesus, faith gave way to fear and instead of walking on the water, Peter was sinking into the waves. In sheer panic he called out, "Lord save me!"

When Peter called for help he was not addressing the disciples. His plea was to the only One who could save him. When Peter called, "Immediately Jesus stretched forth His hand and caught him."

This is a beautiful illustration of how the Lord Jesus saves all who call upon Him. He is never far from anyone of us, and He is always near to help.

We still must walk by faith in spite of boisterous storms.

Crazy for Christ

"We are fools for Christ's sake"
1 Corinthians 4:10

In May 1855, an 18-year-old boy who had recently moved to Boston for employment went to the deacons of a church in the city. Although he had been raised in ignorance of the Gospel in a Unitarian church, he had begun to attend this Bible-believing church. The young man told the deacons that a month earlier a member of their church, Mr. Edward Kimball, had gone to the store where he worked, shared the Gospel with him and then pointed him to faith in Christ. Impressed with Mr. Kimball's zeal, the fellow told the deacons that he wanted to join their church.

As the church officers interviewed the boy, it became apparent that although this young man had been converted, he was ignorant of the basic truths of the Gospel of Christ. They, therefore, recommended that he attend instruction classes to learn more about the Bible. After some instruction, the deacons concluded that although this lad was a shoe salesman, he was not all that bright and a was a slow learner.

Notwithstanding the deacons' conclusion, the young man became active. He hired four pews in a church, and then he went out on the street to invite young men to fill these seats. After several months the young Christian started a Mission Sunday School. The attendance grew dramatically and had soon expanded to between 1,200 and 1,500 young people attending each week.

The deacons and other people sat up and took notice of what this young man was doing. His zeal, earnestness and sincere enthusiasm for people impressed everybody. He helped a Sunday School teacher visit her pupils, and one-by-one he led them all to Jesus Christ. Later, the people of that Boston church looked back with amazement when they realized that the slow-learning young man had become the renowned American evangelist, Dwight L. Moody. Initially, people laughed at him and called him "Crazy Moody." Rather than take the nickname as an insult, Mr. Moody replied, "Yes, that's me, crazy about souls and crazy for Jesus."

A Christian with no concern for others is backslidden.

Undaunted

"I am with thee...I have much people in this city."
Acts 18:10

On one of Billy and Agnes Jones' first visit to this small rural community in Brazil's Rio Grande do Norte, a lady said to them, "There are two places where believing Christians will never be found. One is in hell and the other in São Bento." This certainly was not a welcoming speech, but it made Billy and Agnes aware that they faced an uphill battle, and they needed to be sure that going to live and work there was in God's will.

That assurance came while reading Acts 18:10: *"I am with thee...I have much people in this city."* When Paul received that promise, there were only two believers in Corinth. Billy and Agnes knew of only one believer in São Bento but armed with God's promise, they embarked on their mission in that town.

Initially, they encountered opposition from some and indifference from most people. Undaunted, they organised Gospel meetings even though only a handful of children turned up. They saw this as an opportunity to reach boys and girls for Christ, and within a few months, several children had become believers. These enthusiastic new converts were soon impacting their parents and breaking down many suspicions about the missionaries. Better still, some parents not only began to attend the meetings, several of them trusted Christ.

During their second year in São Bento, the town's mayor offered Billy a daily time on the local radio. Each morning Billy broadcast "The Royal Message." Even though people would not attend meetings, the message was going out, and the feedback in town indicated that many were listening.

Barriers were slowly broken down, opposition decreased, and people came to church. Billy embarked on a series of open-air meetings and conducted several evangelistic missions. God poured His blessings on these efforts. In one weekend, twenty-five people trusted the Saviour.

There were setbacks along the way, but Billy and Agnes continued steadfastly in their Gospel outreach. Besides meetings, there were special social events and food distribution to the poorest families in town. All this resulted in people trusting in the Lord nearly every Sunday during a three-month period.

As promised, God did have many people in that town.

Power With Progress

"Then had the churches rest … and were edified; and walking in the fear of the Lord, and in the comfort of the Holy Ghost, were multiplied."
Acts 9:31

When the Crystal Palace Exhibition opened in 1851 people flocked to London's Hyde Park to behold the marvels of the latest inventions. Back in those days, steam was the in-thing. There were steam ploughs, steam trains, steam looms, and musical organs empowered by steam. The Exhibition's first prize that year went to a marvellous contraption that was made up of seven thousand parts. When the heat got to a certain temperature and the steam pressure was just right, they turned it on, and everything began to move. Gears engaged, wheels turned, pulleys ran back and forward, bells rang, and whistles blew. The noise of the apparatus was tremendous, and the sight was awesome. Thousands flocked to see it. There was only one draw back - it did not do anything. The machine had no practical use. It was only a demonstration on the uses and power of harnessed steam. There was an abundance of energy and action, but it was not put to any effect.

That perhaps is a fitting illustration of Christendom today; there is lots of activity, everything is well organised, the proper sounds are made, church departments run like clockwork, but there is one big drawback, just like the Crystal-Palace prize winner – the church is not productive. There is plenty of function but little accomplishment.

This was not the case with the church of the first century. You cannot read the book of Acts without realising the early Christians were both energetic and effective. The first-century saints had no financial resources, and no political clout. There were not many highly educated members or nobles amongst them. They faced the imperial might of the Roman Empire in persecution, the derision of the sophisticated Greek culture and the fanatical bigotry of Judaism, and yet they accomplished so much. Their weapons were mighty through God: the Word of God to preach, the throne of God in prayer and the Spirit of God upon them.

The same weapons are available today, and yet we accomplish so little.

26th July

Profitable to God

"He is profitable to me for the ministry."
2 Timothy 4:11

Born and raised in East Belfast, as a teenager, Eric Smyth succumbed to the deception of Mormon missionaries who targeted vulnerable young people in his area. Even though Eric had embraced their bizarre, false teachings, he never gained the assurance that his sins had been forgiven. Even though he engaged in Mormon enterprises recruiting others to the cult, he wrestled with personal doubts and confusion in his heart.

The bewildered young Eric was invited by Eric Moore to attend meetings at Everton Hall. That night at the meeting, in the company of lads from the local Boys Brigade, he listened attentively to Pastor Will Hibbert preach the Gospel. Despite the earlier resistance of his heart, Eric was so broken he requested to speak with the preacher at the end of the meeting. After some counselling, Eric knelt beside Pastor Hibbert and received Jesus Christ as his Saviour.

From his earliest days as a Christian Eric wanted to serve his Saviour. At school, he was told that he would accomplish very little in life, for he was dyslexic and had little education. Despite these drawbacks, Eric aspired to be used by God. After he married Frances, they opened their house in Glencairn housing estate for weekly cottage meetings. God blessed their successful Gospel outreach to lead people to Christ.

Although busy for the Lord beyond his daily employment, Eric felt constrained to devote more time to Christian work. To step out into Christian work was daunting for Eric and Frances and their six children. He had to opt out of secular employment, but Eric felt that God was calling him to full-time Christian ministry.

Initially, Eric was recruited by the Martyrs' Memorial Free Presbyterian Church for the work in Aughrim Street Mission Hall in Sandy Row. Eric gave himself wholeheartedly to work among the working class people of that area, and within a short time, he became well known in the district. His wide acceptability opened the way for Eric to be elected to the Belfast City Council in May 1981. Civically and spiritually he served God faithfully.

Little is much when God is in it.

A Sensible Missionary

"I am made all things to all men, that I might by all means save some."
1 Corinthians 9:22

A veteran missionary said, "A good missionary needs a good sense of humour and a bad sense of smell." I am not sure about any defects in Maizie Smyth's olfactory receptors, but she certainly did have a good appreciation for humour, and she needed it.

While travelling on the River Congo to conduct Bible Seminars for isolated believers, she had plenty of reason to draw on her sense of humour. This was especially so early one morning when they were due to leave by canoe to visit another village. One of the seminary students travelling with them fell down the dry toilet. They had to haul the poor fellow out and plunge him into the river. No one was keen on drinking river water for the rest of that day.

No villager ever remembered a white woman staying overnight with them. It was a novelty to have Maizie sleep on an improvised bed in a clay hut. She was the talk of the villages but was glad to identify with the people. Some locals did not realize that Maizie spoke Lingala as well as Swahili, and when they began to speak about this white lady staying with them, Maizie had quite a laugh to herself. "Look at her. Her legs are just like ours; look at her feet, they are so tiny. Take a look at her soft hands. Doesn't her hair look like the soft grass?"

One old man was so concerned that the hot sun would burn the top of Maizie's head that he ordered someone to bring a hat for her. A man brought a variety of hats; most of them were too big, and some even fell over her ears. There was one hat she liked, but the old man insisted that the verandah (the brim) was too small. He chose a ridiculous hat for Maizie, and she had to wear it.

Another necessity for any effective missionary is a readiness to be what God wants and to do anything God chooses. Maizie Smyth was that sort of missionary.

It makes good sense to serve God.

28th July

Extraordinary

"The people that do know their God shall be strong, and do exploits."
Daniel 11:32

Many years ago I had the privilege of sharing in a meeting with Gladys Aylward. Besides being a missionary, she was an extraordinary woman who accomplished so much. Her life was so amazing that Hollywood made a movie about her involving top film stars, *The Inn of the Sixth Happiness*.

Gladys' work in China was compassionate and courageous. Besides rescuing scores of Chinese children from premature death and prostitution, in 1938 she led almost a hundred children, between the ages of four and eight, on a 100-mile trek to safety from the advancing Japanese invaders. After a twenty-seven day tramp over treacherous terrain, she finally arrived with her children in a region controlled by allied soldiers.

Gladys' tiny stature made her a most unlikely heroin. After her conversion at an open-air meeting, she felt constrained to serve God in China and applied to several missionary Societies. They all concluded that she was not suitable for their work and that she did not have the physical strength to face the rigors of life in China or the intellectual capacity to learn Chinese.

Disappointed by the rebuff of established missions, Gladys took a job as a chambermaid to earn enough money to pay her way to China. From the most unlikely beginnings, and contrary to all expectations, Miss Aylward overcame all of the obstacles to do a great work for God.

In 1930 Gladys told her parents: "Never try to get me out or pay ransom for me. God is sufficient." She then set out from London to China with a bedroll, a kettle, a saucepan, a suitcase of canned food, a small amount of money and a heart full of zeal. In the sight of men she was overlooked and spurned, but she was the material God used to save boys and girls in China.

Gladys went to be with Christ on 4th January 1970. Summing up her life she said, "I have been a fisher of men. I went, to China because God asked me. I did not have missionary training or missionary status. I was answerable to Him and no one else."

Exceptional exploits are possible with God.

Serving in the City

"They have addicted themselves to the ministry of the saints."
1 Corinthians 16:15

When we applied for our first visa for Brazil, Alderman Albert Duff, J. P. signed our papers verifying that we were lawful citizens of Belfast. His daughter, Olive and her American husband, John Sessoms, was already serving God with UFM in Brazil.

Mr. Duff was colloquially known in the Sandy Row area as "Da Duff" or "the wee man with a big heart." He had been a Captain in the Salvation Army in County Armagh before becoming a missionary in West Belfast. He founded a new mission work in Belfast's Sandy Row.

It was not uncommon for Mr. Duff to carry drunkards into the hall, talk some sense to them and then give them the Gospel. He saw many of these alcoholics trust Christ as Saviour. During the war, he ran a soup kitchen in which Mrs. Duff and their three daughters helped a team of ladies prepare large caldrons of Irish stew and loaves of bread for the needy neighbours in Sandy Row.

Da Duff was so encouraged by the blessings on this work that he opened a similar mission hall near Brown's Square on the Shankhill Road. Besides his very fruitful work, he also maintained involvement in local politics and served for many years as a Belfast City Councillor for the Sandy Row Ward. In time Albert Duff became an Alderman of the Council and was nominated as a Justice of the Peace.

After Mr. Duff's home-call to heaven, the Aughrim Street Mission became a City Outreach Mission of the Martyr's Memorial Free Presbyterian Church. At that time Eric Smyth was offering himself for full-time Christian service with the Martyr's Church. He was subsequently commended to the work in Aughrim Street.

Like Albert Duff before him, Eric gave himself wholeheartedly to God's work in Sandy Row. With his winsome ways, Eric became well known in the district within a short time. Local people were converted, and soon the numbers attending the Mission Hall increased. Also, like Mr, Duff, Eric was elected by the people of Sandy Row to serve on the Belfast City Council.

Render to God the praise due to His Name.

30th July

Precious Memories

"Wheresoever this Gospel shall be preached throughout the whole world, this also that she hath done shall be spoken of for a memorial of her."
Mark 14:9

We all miss the missionary, Maizie Smyth. Those of her generation will tell you she was the epitome of Christian zeal, enthusiasm, warmth, humour and sacrificial love for her Lord. She left a large imprint on many lives wherever she went but possibly nowhere more than in the Congo and other African countries.

She told of the time when she combined with the church in Kisangani to conduct Bible seminars at interior churches on the Congo River. Just before they were due to leave news came through of several foreign workers who had been injured at a Catholic Mission down river. The church leaders were hesitant about Maizie travelling in that area, but teachers and students assured the leaders they would look after her.

On the canoe, Maizie was exposed to the elements. At times, she had to take shade from the hot tropical sun or take shelter from the torrential rainstorms. Another hazard was embarking and disembarking from the canoe on muddy, and slippery river banks. The Africans were quick to hold Maizie's hand to make sure she did not fall.

Hundreds gathered each evening for the sing-along and sharing the Gospel. Before light the next morning they gathered for an extended prayer meeting followed by a cup of sweet tea. The Bible seminars through the day were enhanced with prolonged and profitable times of questions and answers. In between the two-hour sessions, Maizie joined the groups to munch through roasted corn on the cob, sugared peanuts, and sweet bananas or plantains.

At the end of the day, Maizie collapsed into an improvised bed the locals had prepared for her. When she pulled the four-legged bed out from the wall, it suddenly became a three-legged bed. The fourth leg was a stack of mud bricks over which were crawling dozens of large cockroaches. Maizie quickly propped up the bed again, and despite the menacing cockroaches, collapsed on to the straw mattress totally exhausted but grateful for the opportunity of sharing God's Word with those people.

Constrained by love for Christ.

God's Word Prospers

"My word … shall not return unto Me void, but it shall accomplish that which I please, and it shall prosper in the thing whereto I sent it."
Isaiah 55:11

The Bible is unique. It is the living, life-giving and everlasting Word of God. He said that His Word would not return unto Him "void," i.e. it will never come back to Him empty or in an empty condition. Sermons may not live very long or accomplish very much, but when God speaks to the human heart, it accomplishes an eternal effect.

God adds that His Word will *"accomplish"* and *"prosper"* in all He intends. That means it will perform and execute God's purpose. To "prosper' is to succeed. Success may not happen the way we want it to happen, but God is working through His Word to accomplish His purpose. His Word always hits the mark and is never unsuccessful.

Six years had passed before Adoniram Judson baptized his first convert in Burmah. Someone asked him about his lack of success, "Do you think this is going to pay off?" To this Judson replied, "As much as there is a God, Who will fulfill all His promises!" Subsequently, thousands were converted through Judson's ministry.

Sunday School teacher Edward Kimball shared God's Word with D. L. Moody. Mr. Moody invited Dr. F. B. Meyer to preach in the United States, and at those meetings, Wilbur Chapman was converted. Chapman became an evangelist with the YMCA, and through his ministry baseball player, Billy Sunday, was saved. Billy Sunday also became a noted preacher, and during his evangelistic campaign in Charlotte, North Carolina, he had to leave early for another engagement. Mordecai Ham took his place as the evangelist. At Mordecai Ham's meetings, Billy Graham was converted. God's Word prospered and accomplished so much.

Henry Moorhouse, a noted British evangelist, impressed upon D. L. Moody the need for preaching the Word more than his own thoughts. Moorhouse said to the American evangelist, "If you will stop preaching your own words, and preach more of God's Word, He will make you a great power for good."

Read the Bible yourself, and relay the Bible to others.

August

Dark Hedges, Co Antrim

A Faithful Scotsman

"He which persecuted us in times past now preacheth."
Galatians 1:23

"Where's the wee Scotsman who plays the accordion?" That was the question many people asked when we did door-to-door evangelism in Belfast's Short Strand during our years at Templemore Hall. The Scotsman they were referring to was the late Raymond McKeown, a good friend and my predecessor as pastor at Templemore hall. Raymond was a multi-talented servant of God; he was a musician, a soloist, a Bible teacher and undoubtedly, the best open-air evangelist I have ever heard. Every Friday morning he attracted the attention of the residents in the Short Strand area as he and a few friends sang and preached the Gospel.

Although his strong and winsome Glaswegian accent earned him the name "the wee Scotsman," Raymond was born in Belfast. His family left for Scotland when he was a young boy. Living in Glasgow's deprived Gorbels helped equip him for the adversities of life. His mother and father and two sisters were converted after their arrival in Scotland and attended the Tent Hall where well-known evangelist, Jock Troup, was superintendent. It broke his mother's heart that Raymond neglected attendance at the Tent Hall in pursuit of other interests. He enrolled for voice training, played football, enjoyed the musical entertainments and engaged in public debates or heckling the speakers on the city's streets. He saddened his parents' heart when he espoused atheism and agnosticism and entered into public debate to prove evolution. This heartbreak helped focus their prayers for their wayward son.

Initially, it seemed their supplications were not making any headway. However, one day after listening to an open-air preacher at Glasgow Cross, he was so moved that he decided to go to the Tent Hall that night to hear Jock Troup preach. When the appeal was made for people to accept Christ, Raymond did not respond publicly. He made his way to a side room and there on bended knees he accepted the Saviour. A mother's prayers were answered, and another miracle of grace had happened. Not only had a prodigal come home, an antagonist against the Gospel surrendered to the claims of Christ.

Who can measure the value of a praying mother?

2nd August

Kindness

"Charity suffereth long, and is kind."
1 Corinthians 13:4

When I think of kindness, I recall our colleague Emily McFarland. Before she was married, Emily (nee Gilchrist) had served God for almost ten years in Nigeria. While there she was kidnapped by Biafran rebels during the infamous Biafran War and held captive for six weeks. Some time after her release, she returned to Nigeria and worked in a Mission hospital. After her service for Christ in Africa, Emily went to Brazil with Acre International where she plied her skills to care for her leprosy patients. Her dedication was obvious to all who knew her, but most of all to her patients. They loved her gentle ways and kindness as she patiently listened to their fears and problems. Emily, always gracious and obliging, slipped into the presence of her Lord on 29th July 1999.

Kindness is becoming increasingly scarce in today's self-seeking society where rudeness and crudeness prevail too often. This is in contrast to what the Saviour taught about *turning the other cheek, going the second mile and giving a cloak.*

Kindness manifested by Christ. Jesus Christ was the epitome of kindness. He poured kindness into countless lives. He was kind to children, to widows, to the sick, to the blind and to those who mourned. Of course, that kindness is poured out upon us, for "In ages to come He might shew the exceeding riches of His grace in His kindness toward us through Christ Jesus."

Kindness modelled in the Bible. Think of Joseph who modelled kindness toward his brothers who had planned evil against him. Consider David asking, "Is there yet any that is left of the house of Saul, that I may shew him kindness for Jonathan's sake" (2 Samuel 9:1)? Consequently, David showered kindness on Mephibosheth.

Kindness ministered by Christians. We can show kindness by our lives, with our lips and by exhibiting the love of Christ to others. The old saying goes, *"Do all the good you can, to all the people you can, every time you can, and in every way you can."* That is a challenge.

Kindness is like a boomerang – it will always come back to you.

3rd August

Sowing

"Blessed are ye that sow beside all waters."
Isaiah 30:20

A convention met in the United States to discuss "How to Reach the Masses." During that week, a young man was preaching on a soapbox at a street corner. Workmen, on their way home from their employment, gathered to listen. Many of them were so deeply moved by the preaching, they forgot their hunger and weariness and continued listening.

The crowd became so dense that they had to go to the nearby Academy of Music where the convention was due to be held. The men filled the main floor of the building, many of them with lunch boxes still under their arms, while the man continued to preach with such power that many were moved to tears. The preacher had to conclude when the clergy began to arrive for the "How-to-Reach-the-Masses" Convention.

When the convention started hundreds of clergy were inside discussing how to reach people while the young preacher was doing exactly that on the city's streets. That young preacher was D. L. Moody. He was preaching the Kingdom of God, and many were believing his message.

General Booth of the Salvation Army prayed, "Lord close up hell for one year and help us win the lost." It is not possible to close hell, but reaching the lost was a divine compulsion and constraint in the heart of a young man named Ernie Allen. It was that zeal and vision that led him to found the Revival Movement out of which grew the Every Home Crusade. True revival is a practical matter. While others talked about revival, Ernie Allen did something about it. While revival is for the glory of God and the edifying of the church, it should result in the salvation of the lost. Revival is God moving through His children with mighty power to accomplish His purpose.

The Every Home Crusade has been experiencing an unheralded revival for decades. Who can ever measure the impact their tracts, leaflets, posters, and booklets have made on thousands of lives in many lands and different cultures? Tens of thousands of people have responded by letters to register their conversion to Jesus Christ.

Enjoy the blessings of the harvest.

4th August

The Open-Air Preacher

"The common people heard Him gladly."
Mark 12:37

Raymond McKeown was a man of many hats. He was a carpenter, a respected shop steward, and union delegate at Clydeside Shipyards and a pastor at Templemore Hall. For all that, Raymond is best remembered as an exceptional open-air evangelist. He was at his best when surrounded by a crowd at Epsom Downs Racecourse, Trafalgar Square, or at a factory gate preaching the Gospel with wit, humour, and eloquence. His musical talents and plain language helped him hold the crowds spellbound, and his keen intellect meant he was ready to answer the occasional heckler.

I still remember joining Raymond and his friends at Glasgow Cross, and at the famous Barrowland Market for a rousing open-air rally. In Glasgow, Raymond was always surrounded by a group of talented musicians. Bob Hamilton, who played his saxophone or clarinet, had played for some of the world's top jazz bands; he even accompanied the famous Ella Fitzgerald. Bobby Handyside, also an accomplished musician with several leading dance bands, played his piano accordion. Willie Massie led the trumpet trio. Davie and John strummed their guitars while a drummer provided the percussion.

Raymond picked up his old battered trombone, affectionately called his "shove me off the pavement." When Bobby Hamilton nodded, "One, two, three, four," the ensemble swung into an up-beat rendering of "Hold the fort for I am coming." Feet were still tapping to the tempo even when they played, "Abide with Me," or "The Old Rugged Cross."

I know from first-hand experience that Raymond was not slow to call on a few from his group to testify of how they had been converted. He always added, "Keep it short sonny." After one or two solos, Raymond gave a short but clear presentation of the Gospel. I remember an atheist heckling Raymond about sin and salvation. Raymond appealed to the crowd, "Listen to him deny the existence of sin. Ask him does he have any locks on his door at home. Keys and locks are evidences of our sin. I am here to tell you about the Saviour from all sin."

Heaven will reveal the outcome of every ministry.

My All-Sufficient Shepherd

"The Lord is my Shepherd."
Psalm 23:1

No portion of Scripture is more universally loved, more widely known and more frequently used than Psalm 23. This Psalm is the first we learn in life and frequently the last we quote at death. The same Psalm is good for every valley of life. With good reason, it has been called, "The pearl of Psalms."

The Psalm's initial words, "The Lord is my Shepherd," identifies the Shepherd of whom King David spoke is JEHOVAH. This covenant name, which God revealed to Moses at the burning bush, denotes that JEHOVAH is the great "I AM," the unchanging and faithful God of Israel. In the Old Testament, seven words are added to JEHOVAH, each giving different but assuring aspects of His character. These seven portrayals are evident in David's affirmation of Jehovah as His Shepherd:

Jehovah-Jireh: -- The Lord will provide, *"I shall not want."*

Jehovah-Shalom: -- The Lord our Peace, *"He leads me beside the still waters."*

Jehovah- Rapha: -- The Lord our Healer, *"He restoreth my soul."*

Jehovah-Tsidkenu: -- The Lord our righteousness, *"He leadeth me in the path of righteousness."*

Jehovah-Shammah -- The Lord is there, *"Yea, though I walk through the valley of the shadow of death."*

Jehovah-Sabaoth -- The Lord of Hosts, *"You prepare a table before me in the presence of my enemies."*

Jehovah-Nissi: -- The Lord our Banner, *"I will dwell in the house of the Lord forever."*

Christians can look back and trace how the faithful hand of the Shepherd has guided them and how His goodness has provided for them. Be thankful that the unchanging JEHOVAH, the great "I AM," and our Shepherd grants goodness and mercy to His sheep every day, and He will do so until that day when they arrive in the house of the Lord, to rest in that home forever.

How He has blessed me, tongue can never tell.

6th August

M.K.s

"The grace of our Lord Jesus Christ be with you all. Amen."
Romans 16:24

Missionary children (M.K.s) are exceptional individuals. They can enhance the life of their parents and help in moments of loneliness. At times, they can be their parents' best language instructors and experts in local food, culture, and customs. In foreign countries, their distinctive appearance often opens up a conversation in shops and market stalls, and their smiles can melt the heart of the most awkward officials. They can fill their homes with friends and often attract others into activities in the work their parents are pioneering.

At the same time, M.K.s can be subject to a complex mixture of cultures; they feel out of place in their parents' homeland, but they are not accepted as nationals in the country in which they live. Being looked on as "missionary kids" they can suffer from many unreasonable expectations that might be put on them, but they are ordinary boys and girls who grow up through their infancy, childhood, and adolescence in a fishbowl.

I remember when our two girls joined seventy other M.K.s at a jungle boarding school. Ages ranged from seven years old to eighteen, and they were divided into three dorms: senior, middle and junior. The school had many excellent advantages such as a keen Christian ethos and spiritual emphasis, great camaraderie among the children and the exemplary dedication of the teachers who devoted their lives to these children. Although the rustic school was surrounded by forest, they had good facilities which included a soccer field, a basketball court and the Amazon River for swimming or fishing. The only access was by riverboat, and the city was three hours away.

At the November, "American Thanksgiving Dinner" each child around the table had to say something for which they were thankful. A seven-year–old boy said, "When my Mom brought me to this school I cried every night because I missed my parents. Auntie (dorm parent) told me to ask the Lord to help me in this. I did ask Him, and I thank God for answered prayer, for now, I never even think of my Mom and Dad."

Funny? But it is not funny.

Pray for all M.K.s.

7th August

Counting the Cost

*"Which of you, intending to build a tower,
sitteth not down first and counteth the cost."*
Luke 14:28

I spent eleven great years in Banbrige, County Down. The town's most famous landmark is the Crozier Monument near the Bann River. It was erected in 1862 in honour of Captain Francis Crozier, a commander on Sir John Franklin's Royal Navy ill-fated expedition to the Artic in 1845.

Sir John Franklin and 138 officers and men embarked from England to find the Northwest Passage across the Canadian Arctic to the Pacific Ocean. They sailed in two three-masted ships. Captain Francis Crozier was the Master on one of these vessels. Each craft carried an auxiliary steam engine and a twelve-day supply of coal for the entire trip, which was projected to take two or three years.

Instead of additional coal, each ship made room for a 1,200-volume library, china place settings for the officers and men, cut-glass wine goblets, and ornate silver tableware. Engraved on the handles were the individual officers' initials and family crests. The expedition carried no special clothing for the Arctic, only the light uniforms of Her Majesty's Navy.

The ships set out from England with enormous glory and fanfare. Two months later a British whaling captain met the two ships in Lancaster Sound and reported back to England on the high spirits of officers and men. He was the last European to see them alive.

Years later, Eskimos reported they had seen men pushing and pulling a wooden boat across the ice. Other Eskimos later found the boat with the remains of the thirty-five men who had been dragging it. At another place Eskimos found a tent on the ice and in it were thirty bodies. Over the next twenty years, search parties recovered skeletons from all over the frozen wastes. Another search party found two skeletons in a boat on a sledge. Beside the two skeletons, they found chocolate, guns, tea, and table silver.

Franklin and his men perished because they underestimated what was required for Arctic exploration. They had exchanged necessities for luxuries, and this led to disaster.

Jesus made it clear that discipleship, though worthwhile, is costly.

Discipleship costly? Think of Calvary!

Props and Prayer

"Thou, Lord, only makest me dwell in safety."
Psalm 4:8

Maizie Smyth was ready for anything. This was evident when she wrote about her trip from Ubundu to Kisangani.

Late on Sunday it began to rain heavily and continued right through the night. At dawn, a heavy mist hung over the forest, and the road was a quagmire. Believers wanted us to stay, but we needed to get back to Kisangani. We knew there were four slippery log-bridges ahead of us. After praying for protection, we cautiously set out, careful not to slide off the road. At the first bridge, the nine passengers got out of the Land Rover as I gingerly tried to manoeuvre the vehicle across the rustic bridge, which had no barrier rails on either side. Furthermore, the bridge spanned a very deep gorge. Everyone was greatly relieved when I was able to safely steer the vehicle to solid ground on the other side.

Similar breathtaking experiences followed on the next two bridges. On each occasion, the Land Rover performed admirably. When we arrived at the fourth bridge, I was horrified to find that the drop below the slippery logs was about a hundred feet deep. I put the vehicle in the lowest gear and slowly edged on to the logs, fearful of falling over the unprotected sides of this improvised structure. Suddenly, the greasy logs separated, and the Land Rover's four wheels slipped between them. Now what? We tried to jack the vehicle up and wedge logs below the wheels, but when we removed the jack we heard the logs crack under the weight of the heavy Land Rover.

"Pray, pray," I shouted as perspiration ran down my back. One man offered his help; "The Catholic Mission truck comes by every month, and they could pull us out. They passed here last Thursday and will be back in three weeks' time." Three weeks?

We all prayed earnestly and worked frantically. Finally, a young man said, "Cut down some tall trees to prop up the other logs. It took a few hours to do this, but we finally made it across the bridge with a prop and a prayer.

There are no emergencies with God.

9th August

Joy

*"There is joy in the presence of the angels of God
over one sinner that repenteth."*
Luke 15:10

Walter Burrell, a Seamen's Christian Friends' missionary in Cork, arrived at the Faith Mission meeting in Ballymena. Always enthusiastic and zealous for the Lord, Walter asked prayer for two Mormon missionaries he had witnessed to on his way to the meeting. One of those Mormons, Martin Quiqley, told his side of the story:

My colleague and I, both of us Mormon missionaries in Belfast, were doing our usual house-to-house visitation. Walter, who was on his way to a meeting, felt compelled to stop when he noticed us walking on the sidewalk in a rural area outside Belfast. Walter was shocked to hear that I was from Dublin and was a recent convert from Catholicism to Mormonism. He witnessed to us before continuing on his journey. I later learned that everywhere Walter went, he asked people to pray for the young Mormon missionary from Dublin. I returned to Dublin in December 1977 after serving the Mormon Church on a two-year mission.

A few years later after some personal struggles and much searching, I was converted to Christ. Seven years after that first encounter with Walter, I took my family to a meeting in a small fellowship on the north side of Dublin. During the service, a man called Walter was invited to share about his work in Cork. As soon as this small man stood up, I recognized him immediately. He had a very distinctive gray beard and a pronounced Irish accent. I turned to my wife, Carole, and said, 'That's the guy who stopped me many years ago near Belfast when I was a Mormon missionary and told me that no Church could save me. He said that only Jesus Christ could save.'

I couldn't wait until the service was over to tell Walter my story. What a meeting that was! I will never forget Walter's reaction. While he hugged me, tears of joy flowed down our cheeks. Walter told me he had never stopped praying for me after he had met me on the street near Belfast.

Our part is to witness and pray. God gives the increase.

10th August

Israel

"Brethren, my heart's desire and prayer to God for Israel is,
that they might be saved."
Romans 10:1

We have been privileged to live in the generation that has witnessed the restoration of Israel as a nation and the "aliyah" - "the returning to Israel" from the four corners of the earth. This happened even though the Jewish people were scattered for 2000 years. Despite the Holocaust, repeated wars initiated by her enemies and international prejudice against them, the Jewish nation, the Jewish people and the land of Israel are modern-day miracles.

Israel is an amazing place. Speaking of the Promised Land, the Scriptures say, *"It is a land the LORD your God cares for; the eyes of the LORD your God are continually on it from the beginning of the year to its end"* (Deuteronomy 11:12). This was the land promised to Abraham and given to his son Isaac, but the land was never promised to Ishmael. The land was conquered by Joshua and became Israel's homeland.

Israel is looked upon as the crossroads of the world, and Jerusalem is its crown. The Via Maris, the trade route from Africa to Europe, passes through the heart of Israel. Over Israel, migratory birds make their seasonal intercontinental flights. This small land, similar in size to Northern Ireland, has the topography of Africa, Asia, and southern Europe rolled into one. It is an amazing place.

Israel is an amazing race. The Jewish people are the most unusual and special people in the world. God declared the same in Scripture, "The LORD your God has chosen you out of all the peoples on the face of the earth to be his people, his treasured possession" (Deuteronomy 7:6). God does not have His favourites, but He chose Israel to execute His redemptive purpose as promised to Abraham. For that reason the Bible is a Jewish book, the Saviour was born under Mosaic Law, all the apostles were Jews, and the first Christians were Jews.

Israel shows amazing grace. Although Jewish elders crucified the Lord of glory, God has not cast off His people. For that reason, He asks us to pray for them. He still has His purpose for Israel.

Pray for the peace of Jerusalem.

11th August

Glad Encounter

"Our friends salute thee. Greet the friends by name."
3 John 14

Martin Quigley, Vice President of The Faith Mission in Canada, and a former Mormon, gives an amazing testimony:

My first encounter with The Faith Mission was on a beautiful Sunday evening at the harbour front in Burlington, Ontario in 1993. We were conducting our weekly outreach to the local community. Following a time of prayer, some songs, and a Gospel presentation, we mingled with the crowd to hand out evangelistic literature and witness to individuals.

My family and I had emigrated from Dublin, Ireland to Canada the previous year. After we had preached the Gospel, I approached someone who seemed very interested in what we had been saying and asked if he was a Christian. When he assured me he was, I detected his Irish accent. I enquired what part of Ireland he came from and he told me he was from the South. He also added that he and his wife, Isabel, and their family, had emigrated from Ireland to be Director of The Faith Mission in Canada. This was the first time I met John and Isabel Bennett.

John also perceived my Irish accent, and straightaway we began to talk about the Gospel and life and happenings back in Ireland. He asked me when I had become a Christian. After I had shared my testimony from Mormonism to Christ, he said, 'We have prayed for you for more than eight years.'

John had led the Faith Mission meeting in Ballymena when Walter Burrell had asked prayer for two Mormons. I was one of those Mormons. I told John that after my conversion to Christ, I had met Walter in Dublin.

Meeting John Bennett on that Sunday in 1993 was the beginning of a lasting friendship with him and The Faith Mission. After sharing how I had met Walter Burrell and how God had answered prayer, we rejoiced together. I realize that our meeting that evening was no coincidence. I thanked John for his prayers for me all those years ago.

That encounter resulted in Martin becoming President of The Faith Mission in Canada.

Amazing!

Heaven's Glory

"Thou shalt guide me with thy counsel, and afterward receive me to glory."
Psalm 73:24

It was a fine spring Sunday evening in April 2003. Boys and girls snuggled up close to their parents in the comfortable pews of the wide church building for another evangelistic service. None of those present knew the uniqueness of the circumstance. Margaret Craig climbed a few steps to the microphone as she had done many times before, to sing another Gospel song to the listening congregation.

The huge pulpit made Margaret seem quite a diminutive figure, but she took her place behind the large reading desk. Without speaking a word, she nodded towards her eldest daughter, Patricia, who was at the piano, as a cue to play the introductory bar for, *"I dreamed I searched Heaven for You."*

Although Margaret initially appeared to be so inconspicuous in her surroundings, she now seemed to stand tall. The volume of her rich and sweet soprano voice swelled to its highest tones until it echoed from the lofty wooden ceiling, filling the building and absorbing the congregation. Her diction was rounded and precise. Besides seeming to reach the notes with consummate ease, she also expressed the significant lyrics with deep emotion and solemnity;

> I dreamed I had gone to that city,
> That city where never comes night,
> And I saw the bright angels in glory,
> I saw the fair mansions of light.
> I gazed for long, long years of rapture
> On the face of my Saviour so true,
> And I sang with the servants in holy,
> Then I dreamed I searched heaven for you.

After the last chord was sounded a serene silence filled the building. Margaret returned to sit by her husband. What no one in that meeting realised was that this would be the last time this renowned Gospel singer would sing in public and the last time her daughter Patricia would play for her. By the following Sunday Margaret had joined the choir of heaven to employ her redeemed voice to sing the praises of the Saviour she loved and served so well earth.

God's guidance here leads to God's glory there.

13th August

Safety in His Promises

"Thou shalt not be afraid for the terror by night."
Psalm 91:5

In Kisangani, rumours ran rife that rebel soldiers would soon be returning. Tensions were high, and planes had already stopped flying. Many locals fled down-river on canoes. Maizie Smyth was tempted to follow them, but the church leaders assured her that all would be well. Government soldiers marched through the town every day. It was then she remembered Psalm 118:8; *"It is better to trust in the Lord than to put confidence in man."* Instead of depending on the army, Maizie was looking to the Lord and God's Word for support. She wrote:

"That night I went to bed even though neighbours were shocked that I should even think of sleeping. I told them that if anything happened to me, I would be going home to glory. I went to bed, but sleep was intermittent. As soon as dawn broke, I searched my Bible again to see what the Lord had for me that day. When danger is near it helps us focus our attention on God's promises. The reading was from Psalm 91 "Thou shalt not be afraid for the terror by night; nor for the arrow that flieth by day." I read and read and reread these verses throughout that day. I remained indoors, but hundreds of soldiers ran up and down the road firing their automatic weapons into the air.

Church members arrived to tell me that soldiers were looting houses and ransacking the Catholic Church. They were planning to come to our street. I thanked them for letting me know but told them that God had promised to take care of me. They stared at me in silence and disbelief. After escorting them to the gate, I returned to the house and fell on my knees to pray. My Bible opened at Colossians 3:16: "Let the word of Christ dwell in you richly in all wisdom … singing with grace in your hearts to the Lord." God's peace flooded my soul, and I knew He was in control. I quietly sang praises to Him.

Not one soldier came near my door. God kept His promises. He always does.

You can kneel on God's promises.

14th August

Satisfied

"The Lord is my Shepherd."
Psalm 23:1

So many precious nuggets of golden truths have been quarried from this beautiful Psalm 23. It is such a deep mine of treasured and heart-warming teachings. Consider the following:

The Shepherd. This is Jehovah. This Good Shepherd not only hand-picked His sheep, but He also laid down His life for them. He knows all His sheep by name, secures them in His hand and pledges that none of them shall ever perish. We could never belong to a better Shepherd than Jesus.

The Sheep. Sheep become part of a shepherd's flock either by birth, being bought at a price or being brought into the flock. This Good Shepherd did exactly this for His sheep. They are born again of the Holy Spirit, purchased by His precious blood and translated into God's heavenly flock.

The Satisfaction. In this Psalm, it seems as though the sheep is looking back on one day with the Shepherd and Bishop of our souls and is satisfied with who He is and what He does. Starting the day knowing you belong to this great Shepherd is gratifying and assuring. Early in the morning He takes His sheep to graze in green pastures, and when they have eaten, He then makes them lie down beside still and refreshing waters. If any sheep goes stray, His crook is near to restore them.

After nourishment in the pastures, He leads His sheep in the right paths, for the sheep does not know the way. His paths may lead the sheep through dark valleys where predators lurk, but His presence and protection reassure them. With His rod He will ward off any beast, and with his staff He will guide His flock.

Once through the dark valley, the Shepherd leads the sheep to higher pastureland for more rich nutrition. At the end of the day He examines each sheep, and where needed, He pours on fresh oil for healing. This Shepherd then provides troughs overflowing with refreshing water.

The Safety. At the end of the day, all His sheep are gathered into the secure sheepfold, safe and satisfied. Goodness and mercy follow us every day, and up ahead, we shall abide in the Father's house forever.

Saved and Satisfied.

15th August

Meet In Heaven

"She hath wrought a good work on Me."
Mark 14:6

In my book, *Blue Skies Over Africa*, missionary Maizie Smyth told some amazing stories:

I met an elderly lady at a meeting one snowy evening in Ireland. Only the bravest dared risk the elements that night. As I prepared to show slides of the Congo, the lady asked me where I worked. After telling her it was the Congo, she asked, "That's in Africa, isn't it?

I confirmed that her geography was right. The lady went on to explain that she had prayed for a man in Africa for over thirty years, but could not remember the name of his country. No matter how many questions I asked about the nationality or location of her friend the only answer was, "He is from Africa, love. That is all I know."

"Africa is a very big continent," I answered and continued to set up my equipment. As I did, it struck me to ask the lady an improbable question, "What is the name of the man you pray for?"

She answered, "Magundi Paul." I almost collapsed, for I was going to show a slide of his family in the presentation that night. When I enquired how she had heard of Magundi Paul, the lady told me that many years earlier she had seen his picture in the Mission's magazine, and God had put it into her heart to pray for him, and she had done so ever since.

Magundi Paul was a faithful servant of the Lord, and no doubt, this was due to this lady's prayer support. All who serve the Lord know the value of faithful prayer warriors who often do the "real work." We certainly could not continue in His service without them.

When I got back to the Congo, I went to see Magundi Paul and his family. The servant of God was deeply humbled and emotionally broken when I shared with him about this unknown lady who had prayed for him for so many years. He said, "What a glorious place heaven will be when we shall meet up with God's children from around the world who made an impact on our lives."

What rejoicing there will be.

16th August

Calvary Covers it All

"Blotting out the handwriting of ordinances that was against us, which was contrary to us, and took it out of the way, nailing it to His cross."
Colossians 2:14

While living in remote areas of Brazil's interior, we depended so much on shortwave radio for news and Christian ministry. Every week we enjoyed the broadcast of "The Old Lighthouse," a programme from Pacific Garden Mission in Chicago. This work was founded by Mr. and Mrs. William Taylor who had opened this rescue mission to reach the hopeless and homeless people on the streets of their city. One radio broadcast told the story of a man named Mac.

Mac attended the mission every night and always sat two rows from the back. Night after night Mac sat through the Gospel service but left unmoved, unsaved, and unchanged. The Mission's workers were concerned over Mac's condition, so they began to work with him.

They discovered that Mac was a professional dancer with the reputation for having the fastest feet in that part of the country. He attended the mission when he was between bookings. They also discovered that Mac had a serious drinking problem. He later admitted that he was bound by *"Satan, sins, and the suds on the beer."*

Finally, one night, Mac was moved and responded to the Gospel invitation. He knelt at the mourner's bench to seek God. Mrs. Taylor had been playing the piano that Billy Sunday had donated to the mission. When she saw Mac kneeling, she went down to him. As she got closer, she heard him praying, *"But, God you just don't understand. With everything that I have done in my past life, surely you can't save me."*

Mrs. Taylor remembered a testimony that an Indian had given a few weeks earlier in which he said, *"Calvary covers it all."* Mrs. Taylor knelt beside Mac and said, *"Mac, it doesn't matter, because Calvary covers it all!"* Mac looked up at Mrs. Taylor and realized that Calvary did cover it all. That night he was gloriously born again into the family of God. As a result of Mac's conversion, Mrs. Taylor wrote the hymn, *Calvary Covers It All.*

Christ's cross covers our sins.

Neighbours

"But he... said unto Jesus, 'And who is my neighbour?'"
Luke 10:29

All the following people have something in common.

Borrow Bill, so called because he was always borrowing something, was a war veteran who had fallen on hard times. His meagre pension was not enough to sustain him, and he lived in virtual poverty. Worse still, at eighty years of age, he had never heard the Gospel or ever met anyone to explain the simple way salvation through Jesus Christ. However, on Borrow Bill's first hearing the Gospel, he accepted the Lord, and his life was transformed spiritually. Materially he continued to live up to his name, Borrow Bill.

Eufrasio was a murderer, a man greatly feared in Canutama as a hard drinker and tough fighter. He would never attend a Gospel meeting, but one day his daughter got saved, then his wife; two of his sons trusted the Lord, and finally, Eufrasio yielded to the Lord Jesus. This former murderer became as tender and gentle as a lamb.

Billy and Norah kept a spotlessly clean house in East Belfast. Norah was good living, but not saved. Billy was a hard worker; earned good money, but was a hard drinker and when under its influence, was a terror of a man. It was a happy day when they both called on the Saviour's name. First Norah was converted at church, and then redemption came to Billy on his knees in what we used to call "the parlour."

Matt, also from East Belfast, was retired and confined to a wheelchair. His paralysis was compounded by loneliness. The emptiness of his home was too much for him, so he sat in the wheelchair outside a shop at a street corner in all sorts of weather all the year round. His physical condition prohibited him from going to church. Life changed for Matt when we brought him into an informal meeting to hear the Gospel, and he accepted the Lord Jesus.

What did they all have in common? At different times and in various locations, they have all been our next-door neighbours, either next door to our home or next door to the church.

Across the street and across the world, they need to hear that Jesus saves.

Jesus Loves the Little Children

"Jesus called a little child unto Him..."
Matthew 18:2

Children can say the most amusing things that adults would not even dare to mention. Here are a few:

"Dear God, Please send Dennis Clark to a different camp this year. Peter"
"Dear God, I went to a wedding in Church and they kissed each other right in the church. Is that ok? Neil."

"Dear God, We read that Thomas Edison made light, but in Sunday school they said You did it. He must have stolen your idea. Sincerely, Donna."

"Dear God, In Bible times did they really talk like that? Jennifer."

"Dear God, I am British. What are You? Robert."

"Dear God, I'm sure it's hard to love everybody in the whole world. There are only four in our family and I can never do it. Nan."

"Dear God, If You watch in church on Sunday I will show You my new shoes. Mickey."

"Dear God, If we have to come back as somebody else - please don't let me be Jennifer Horton, for I hate her. Denise."

"Dear God, I would love to live for 900 years like that man in the Bible. Love, Victor."

We cannot read the Bible without being impressed how much God invested in the lives of children. He promised and provided Isaac for Abraham and Sarah and that boy carried all the promises of God on his small shoulders. All the hopes of Israel were risked when Jochebed laid baby Moses in a basket to float down the Nile. Baby Samuel was an answer to his mother's prayer, and through her influence he was one of the greatest prophets. What more can we say of David, Daniel, and Timothy?

There is no doubt that God loves the little children and has great purposes for their lives.

Pray for all the children of the world.

19th August

God Makes a Way

"His Word runneth very swiftly."
Psalm 147:17

Belfast-born missionary, Dr. William Scott, founder of the India Bible Literature Mission, agreed to become a distributor of Every Home Crusade's literature in India. When the first supplies of Christian booklets arrived from Belfast, the Indian Customs and Excise Authority impounded the eight tea chests and levied a very heavy duty to be paid to release the literature. The India Bible Literature Mission refused to pay the significant amount of money.

Although prayer was requested both in India and Ireland for the release of the evangelistic material, the literature remained in the custody of the Customs. God's ways are not our ways, and He overruled in another way. The Custom and Excise Authority finally decided to auction all unredeemed parcels and boxes. Dr. Scott and friends of the India Bible Literature Mission attended the auction and were able to purchase all the consignment at a significantly reduced cost than if they had paid the tax that had been demanded of them.

After that, the Every Home Crusade and the India Bible Literature Mission were able to streamline their operation so that today the shipments are released with the minimum delay and expense.

Dr. Scott sent a report soon after the first containers arrived in Madras:

Dear Brother Adams, India Bible Literature Mission's Management Committee takes this opportunity to thank you and your dedicated members who have been untiringly working and have made it possible for us to receive millions of copies of the Gospel of John, the Scripture and Gospel booklets.

The blessings we see today in the Lord's work in India commenced in the 1970s. At that time we did not have to go out to distribute the Gospel literature to the people. The people were coming to us for the Scriptures. Their demand was greater than we could supply. In the 1980s this growth accelerated, and now we are living in a time of God's visitation in India.

God by His Spirit is moving in India. He has raised up and anointed thousands of evangelists and Bible women and has equipped them to do the work of the Gospel.

Pray for the Word and the workers.

A Bible Barnabas

"He was a good man, and full of the Holy Ghost."
Acts 11:24

Dr. Bill Woods was always greatly encouraged by Cecil and May Harvey from Crossgar, County Down. Cecil was a Christian businessman who had been converted through the ministry of Ulster evangelist, W. P. Nicholson. Cecil's Christian life was ignited by Mr. Nicholson's enthusiasm and evangelistic fervour. He was appointed Captain of the Boys Brigade (BB) at Lissara Presbyterian Church, Crossgar, and afterward served as an elder at the same church. His keen interest and involvement in sports enhanced his leadership in the BB Company. His wife May, who was appointed Captain of the Girls Brigade, was a godly, warm, hospitable and kind lady.

Representing pharmaceutical products, Cecil travelled all over the country, and with his broad smile and pleasant disposition he gained many friends. These contacts also provided numerous invitations to speak at various meetings.

In 1951 Cecil and May became foundation members of Crossgar Free Presbyterian Church in which Cecil again served as an elder. This move initiated a life-long friendship with Dr. Ian and Mrs. Paisley. Cecil was soon appointed to be the minister of the new congregation at Whiteabbey. He helped the church negotiate the purchase of the village's former Courthouse and Police Station to establish the church. It was with poignant significance that the congregation sang, "Free from the Law, Oh, happy condition."

Dr. Paisley asked Bill to help Cecil by playing the organ at the weekly services in Whiteabbey. Bill willingly committed to this request in spite of being nervous about his abilities as an organist. The church's heating was generated by a large fire at the front of the room where the meetings were conducted. While Bill played the organ, it seemed as though the burning coals whistled to the tune of the rousing hymns.

Bill's close association with Cecil and May Harvey forged a lasting friendship, and the couple was later responsible for circulating Bill's prayer letters when he went to Brazil.

Cecil, a political ally of Bill Craig, Ian Paisley and Enoch Powell. Cecil and May Harvey reached beyond Ulster and encouraged missionaries all around the world.

Like Barnabas, they were always encouraging others.

Jesus and the Outcast

"Her sins, which are many, are forgiven; for she loved much: but to whom little is forgiven, the same loveth little."
Luke 7:47

One of our Saviour's outstanding qualities was the way He pursued and cared for outcasts and outsiders. His mercy and grace were demonstrated when a nameless woman, referred to as a "sinner," entered the home of Simon the Pharisee where Jesus was a guest. Perhaps she was a prostitute who walked the streets of Nain in southwest Galilee. The self-righteous Pharisees despised such a woman. Furthermore, no proper woman would enter such a gathering in the house of a prominent Pharisee uninvited.

She knelt at Jesus' feet and began to cry. Her warm tears dropped one by one onto His feet. She then undid the long tresses of her hair with which she wiped Jesus' dusty feet, washed them, and kissed them. She removed an alabaster flask of perfume from around her neck and poured the costly, fragrant oil on Jesus' feet. This was an act of worship.

Simon, the host, denounced Jesus and questioned the Prophet's integrity for allowing a woman of such notorious reputation to touch and disgrace Him. While the Pharisees looked only at the woman's outward actions, Jesus saw her heart, lonely and sad, penitent and loving; she honored Him as Lord and sought forgiveness for a sinful, wasted life.

Simon's lack of love was evident by his blindness. He was blind to who Christ was, blind to his need of Christ and blind to his own pride.

The lady's love was seen in giving. Great grace gives great gratitude. This nameless woman who came in disgrace departed Simon's house in peace. Jesus publicly forgave her sins, and she reciprocated with a demonstration of love for Him. She went her way with a freshly cleansed heart and a new life in Christ.

Jesus' love was seen in forgiving. To the men's astonishment, Jesus defended the woman. He reminded them that Simon had neglected to wash His feet, nor had he offered a welcoming kiss or to anoint His head with oil. The woman, humbly and graciously, offered Him all these welcoming acts.

We love Him because He first loved us.

Good News from Jerusalem

"Glorious things are spoken of thee, O city of God."
Psalm 87:2,3

There is no other city on earth quite like Jerusalem. Christians, Jews, and Moslems attribute the origins of their religions to the Holy City. Today Palestinians claim the Holy City to be the capital of their State. Israel declares it to be their ancient capital, given to them by God's Covenant 3,000 years ago. God loves Jerusalem and is jealous for the city. He speaks: *"Thou shalt also be a crown of glory in the hand of the Lord, and a royal diadem in the hand of thy God"* (Isaiah 62:3). *"Jerusalem, the city where I have chosen for Myself to put My name"* (1 Kings 11:36). Israel may be prepared to compromise on other things, but Jerusalem is not on their agenda. It is their avowed eternal capital.

With this conflict being fermented almost daily, it is no wonder that there are bombs, bullets, and killings. The victims of this violence are all too common and greatly lamented. Keep in view that Jerusalem features greatly in God's plans for the future: *"And in that day will I make Jerusalem a burdensome stone for all the people. All that burden themselves with it shall be cut in pieces though all the people of the earth be gathered together against it"* (Zechariah 12:3).

It is somewhat ironic that from this troublesome city came the greatest news the world has ever heard, the glad tidings of the Gospel of Jesus Christ. We may hear a lot of bad news from Jerusalem. What is the good news from that city?

In Jerusalem, "Christ died for our sins according to the Scriptures..." The Good News about who died -- Christ, how He died – crucified, and why He died for us and for our sins.

In Jerusalem, Jesus Christ was buried. His burial was the proof that He died. On the cross, He bore our guilt. In death, He defeated our great enemy.

In Jerusalem, "He rose again the third day according to the Scriptures." The best news comes from a graveyard in Jerusalem, "He is not here for He is risen."

This is Good News indeed.

23rd August

Prison Praying

"For this cause I bow my knees unto the Father... "
Ephesians 3:14

Incarcerated in a cold and filthy Roman dungeon, Paul had chains on his arms and shackles on his feet; he was guarded by Roman soldiers. In spite of all the discomfort and contrary circumstances, Paul not only penned his famous and fruitful prison letters, but he also engaged in prayer for the churches he had founded and he prayed for the saints he knew.

Writing of his times of prayer Paul wrote, "I bow my knees…" I wonder what kind of impression that made on those Roman soldiers. They must have been captivated. Better still, think of the impact his prayers made on those for whom he prayed.

You can never truly chain the person who knows how to pray. When Paul prayed he changed that dungeon into a chamber of prayer and praise. His heart and soul were freely lifted toward heaven as he prayed to God. No prison bars or closed frontiers can hinder effectual praying.

During my years of pastoral ministry, I have known saints who have been confined to home due to physical ailments. Some of these have been able to transform a bedroom into a sanctuary of prayer. While visiting one lady, in particular, I borrowed her Bible to read the Scriptures to her. As I lifted the Bible small oval-shaped pieces of paper fell to the floor. I apologized, but to that, she said, "Don't worry, those are the eggs I am praying for." On each piece of egg-shaped paper, a name was written, "I am praying for these people, and already twelve of these eggs have hatched, and the people have been saved." The room had been transformed into a sanctuary of prayer and praise.

Although Paul bowed his knees to pray, no particular posture for prayer is commanded in the Scriptures. Abraham prayed standing up. David prayed sitting. Perhaps, bowing is an acknowledgment of your deep need of God. Sometimes the burdens are so heavy, and the needs are so great, that we fall on our knees in prayer. Whatever the position, it is important to pray – at all times.

Circumstances can be transformed into opportunities to serve God.

Best Text Book

"For ever, O Lord, Thy word is settled in heaven."
Psalm 119:89

When the missionary, Lucimar, returned to Rio Branco, Acre, in 2001, she was invited to teach Religious Education (R.E.) in a local school. Due to the misconduct and violence of the pupils, the school authority had lost control of the children, and police were constantly on duty. Sadly, their behaviour only reflected the lawlessness of the whole district.

Each week, Lucimar had the opportunity to teach the Scriptures to 520 students ranging in age from six to fourteen years. She maintained that she had the world's best curriculum for R.E., the Word of God. However, one teacher in the school did not share Lucimar's estimation of the Bible. She complained to the school's Director that the missionary's curriculum was too restrictive and it would be better to adopt one that was approved by the government.

Consequently, Lucimar was called before the Director to answer this complaint. She told him that she still maintained that the Bible was the best textbook on the problems of human nature and for the correction and training of children. She further protested that none of the teachers had ever attended her classes to be in a position to judge the value of her teaching.

After listening to Lucimar's defense, the Director suggested to the faculty that they attend Lucimar's class alongside the children to evaluate the instruction she gave. God overruled that potentially precarious situation so that both teachers and pupils were present for Lucimar's weekly R.E. class. One teacher even came to her afterward and purchased a Bible.

When Lucimar told the local Gideon International representative of what had happened, he organised a visit to the school to present a copy of the Scriptures to all the students and staff.

After that initial venture, Tom and Lucimar Geddis established a ministry of thirty-six teachers who lead CEF Bible courses in the city's schools each week. More than 2,000 students and teachers are enrolled in these courses, and they have made a marked behavioural difference in some schools. Among those many who have been converted is the lady who made the original complaint.

More Bible makes for better behaviour.

25th August

Burdens Are Lifted

"Mine iniquities are ... as an heavy burden they are too heavy for me."
Psalm 38:4

While I was editor of the *Life Times* Christian magazine, I was in correspondence with Dr. John Moore, who had formerly been superintendent of the Seamen's Chapel in Glasgow before immigrating to Canada. Besides sharing his testimony, Dr. Moore sent us the story behind his famous hymn, *"Burdens Are Lifted at Calvary."*

I wrote "Burdens Are Lifted at Calvary" after a most interesting experience. The secretary of a large shipping company telephoned the Seaman's Chapel and requested that I visit a young merchant seaman, who was lying critically ill in a Glasgow Hospital. After getting permission from the nursing sister, I visited the young sailor and found him glad and eager to hear what I had to say. For a few moments, I talked about general things before putting my hand into my case for a tract, not knowing which one I would pull out. It happened to be a tract based on "Pilgrim's Progress" with Pilgrim coming to the cross with a great burden on his back. I showed the young seaman this picture and told him the story, in brief, adding that Pilgrim's experience had been my experience, too.

The more I told him, the more anxious he became. I explained that, when I came to the cross of Christ, my burdens rolled away, and my sense of sin and guilt before God was removed. By this time, the tears were running down his cheeks, and he nodded his head when I asked him, "Do you feel this burden on your heart today?" We prayed together, and never shall I forget the smile of peace and assurance that lit up his face as he said that his burden was lifted!

Later that night, sitting by the fireside with paper and pen, I could not get the thought out of my mind – his burden is lifted! I started writing, and the words flowed on to the paper. The tune was written at the same sitting, but never for a moment did I imagine that this little hymn would become a favourite in many languages throughout the world.

Jesus, the Sin-bearer, is also the Burden-bearer.

26th August

Guilt and Grace

"Blessed is he whose transgression is forgiven, whose sin is covered."
Psalm 32:1

The worst trip we can ever experience is a guilt trip. Guilt will take us farther than we want to go, keep us longer than we want to stay, and charge us more than we can pay. Psychologists may address guilt feelings, but they can never deal with our guilt.

Adam did not have the ability to cope with guilt because he was created not to sin. After he had sinned he tried to hide his sin and then tried to hide from God. Only Jesus Christ through grace can take away our guilt.

Psalm 1 opens with the word *"Blessed"* referring to the godly man who does not walk in the way of the ungodly. This Psalm also opens with the same word, *"Blessed,"* the blessedness of a guilty man who has been forgiven.

Psalm 32 is very much related to Psalm 51. In both Psalms, David not only repented from sin, but he also remembered how he had tried to cover his sins. David was fully aware of the nature of his sin. He called sin "transgression" --"stepping over the mark." This was his sin in relation to his rebellion against God. He also called it *"sin,"* -- "falling short or missing the mark." This was his sin in relation to God's Law. We have all come short. He acknowledged his sin was "iniquity," – *"unequal or twisted."* It is our sin in relation to our corrupt condition.

He was glad his sin was forgiven. Forgiveness is the Scapegoat *"carrying the burden away."* God sent our sin away as far as the east is from the west.

He was glad his sin was forgotten. *"For I will forgive their iniquity, and their sin I will remember no more"* (Jer. 31:34). Our sin was cast into the depth of the sea, never to be remembered any more.

He was glad his sin was forsaken. *"To whom the Lord does not impute iniquity."* To impute is to charge to someone's account. Jesus paid it all, and God will never charge our sins to our account. Christ's righteousness was imputed to us.

Sweet forgiveness.

The Shepherd

"I am the Good Shepherd."
John 10:11

One of the most frequent presentations of our Lord in the Scriptures is that of a Shepherd. Jacob looked to the Lord as the "Stone and Shepherd of Israel" (Genesis 49:24), and Israel was His flock (Psalm 100:3). In one of the best-loved Bible chapters, David declared, "The Lord is my Shepherd." How beautiful are the words and images of Isaiah 42:11, *"He shall feed his flock like a shepherd: he shall gather the lambs with his arm, and carry them in his bosom, and shall gently lead those that are with young."*

The Lord Jesus spoke of Himself as the Good Shepherd who knew His sheep and gave His life for them. Adding to this affirmation he said that not one of His sheep would ever perish, and no one could ever pluck them out of His hand.

Even in heaven the Lamb of God will still shepherd His people. *"For the Lamb which is in the midst of the throne shall feed (shepherd) them, and shall lead them unto living fountains of waters: and God shall wipe away all tears from their eyes"* (Revelation 7:17). When David's first words in Psalm 23 are joined to the final word of the short Psalm, it reads "The Lord is my Shepherd … forever."

The Good Shepherd gave His life for the sheep (John 10:11). In the Old Testament the sheep gave their lives for shepherds. Now the Lamb gave His life for the sheep.

The Great Shepherd was brought again from the dead by the power of His own blood (Hebrews 13:20). The Great Shepherd defeated our greatest enemy, death, and lives to give eternal life to His sheep.

The Chief Shepherd will soon appear again in glory (1 Peter 5:4). He will give crowns of glory to His sheep.

In the trilogy of Psalms 22-24 we have a composite image of our Lord as Shepherd. Psalm 22, the Shepherd on the cross dying for His sheep. Psalm 23, the Shepherd with His crook leading His sheep. Psalm 24, the Shepherd's coronation when He comes again.

You call Him "my Shepherd." He calls you "My sheep."

Surprised

"He Himself knew what He would do."
John 6:6

The story of Ernie Allen and the Every Home Crusade suggests that God is full of surprises. Although God is never taken by surprise, we are frequently surprised at what He does. God is never frustrated, knows no barriers and entertains no fears. He is omnipotent, but we are weak; He is infinite, but we are finite. When we try to gauge God by our earthly and limited reason, then we are in for surprises.

On one occasion, our Lord's disciples, Philip and Andrew, employed their human reason to gauge how impossible it would be to feed a large multitude with their insufficient resources. They were astonished when the Lord took a boy's lunch, which consisted of five loaves and two fishes, blessed it, and fed a multitude of more than 5,000 people. I am sure the boy who gave up his lunch was also astonished.

I like to think how that boy's mother got the biggest surprise of all when her son arrived home to tell her how the Lord Jesus had been able to use the lunch she had prepared to feed so many people.

As a young man in Hillsborough Ernie Allen gave his all to the same Lord Jesus. Through that dedicated life, the Lord has fed even greater multitudes. I like to think that when Ernie arrived in heaven on December 2002, his mother was greatly surprised when he told her of the millions of people that have been fed with the Bread of Life because of how she had prayed for her son in their simple home in Annahilt.

Ernie Allen maintained his passion and vision for the ministry of Every Home Crusade to grow and produce Gospel Literature until the Lord called him home. Early in 2003, the Directors of Revival Movement Association appointed Samuel Adams and Clive Allen as joint Mission Directors and Heather Mercer as Mission Secretary. They have seen that work grow so that every day five tonnes of printed page is prepared to reach millions of souls around the world with the good news of the Gospel Message.

God's way's are beyond finding out.

When God Leads

"These forty years the Lord thy God has been with thee;
thou hast lacked nothing."
Deuteronomy 7:2

Solomon Ginsburg, a converted Jew, was one of the first pioneer Baptist missionaries to Brazil in the late nineteenth century. Life was not easy for him in Latin America. Although he came up against many closed doors and faced much persecution, over several decades, he was mightily used by God in Southern and Northeastern Brazil. He led thousands to faith in Christ and was instrumental in establishing the Baptist denomination in Brazil. Behind his effective evangelistic ministry was his prayer life. Many seemingly impossible situations were transformed in answer to his prayers.

In 1911 he completed a very successful evangelistic tour through Brazil's Northeast, especially in Pernambuco and Bahia, two of Brazil's most idolatrous and crime-ridden states at that time. On several occasions, his life was threatened, but God protected him in marvelous ways. In Pernambuco a notorious gunman had been hired to murder him, but Mr. Ginsburg led that criminal to faith in Christ. In Bahia alone, more than 1,000 people were converted.

When that strenuous evangelistic visit was finished, Ginsburg felt he needed a rest and had to visit his family in the United States. He crossed the Atlantic from Brazil to Portugal, hoping to follow on to England and then to the USA. When he was about to embark on the ship for London, an alert was posted warning of terrific storms in the infamous Bay of Biscay. Solomon wondered should he stop over in Lisbon until these storms had abated and catch the next sailing to England on the following week. As he implored God for guidance he noted a verse on his prayer calendar: *"He knoweth thy walking through this great wilderness; these forty years the Lord thy God has been with thee; thou hast lacked nothing"* (Deuteronomy 7:2).

With this reassuring verse, his heart was at complete rest, and he proceeded to England. On arrival, he booked his passage to New York on the *SS Majestic*. He found out afterward, that if he had delayed his journey in Lisbon, he would have been a passenger on the ill-fated *Titanic*.

God makes no mistakes.

Heavenly Wisdom

"Trust in the LORD with all thine heart; and lean not unto thine own understanding. In all thy ways acknowledge Him, and He shall direct thy paths."
Proverbs 3:5,6

Missionary William Carey adopted a great discipline in life. Every day he read a Psalm to help in his relationship with God. He also read a chapter of Proverbs to guide him in his relationship with men. The Psalms provide us with the lyrics of life while Proverbs give us laws for living. The Psalms will deepen our devotional life with God, and Proverbs equips us daily to cope with people.

Proverbs is a collection of heavenly sayings for earthly sinners. Its thirty-one chapters are equal to the number of days in most months, perhaps suggesting for us to read a chapter each day. The book of Proverbs offers us simple but profound, hands-on wisdom, encouragement, and advice.

Proverbs 3 is one of the best-loved chapters. The opening verse teaches us not to forget God's Word: *"My son, forget not my law…"* (3:1). Verse 6 teaches us not to forsake God's will: *"He shall direct thy paths."*

Two words that frequently occur in Proverbs are *"way"* and *"path."* The Christian life is a pathway – *"The path of the just is a shining light that shineth more and more…"* When we accepted Christ, we left the "broad road" and entered by "the narrow gate" to the narrow way that leads to life.

For the Christian that way of life is to be a confident way, trusting in the Lord; a committed way, acknowledging Him, and a controlled way, for God directs the paths of those committed to Him. Note the following:

Obeying God's will protects our path. *"He keepeth the paths of judgment, and preserveth the way of his saints…*(2:8). God will protect the Christian's path.

Obeying God's will directs our path. *"He shall direct thy paths"* (3:6). God will direct, supervise, govern and make our way plain.

Obeying God's will perfects our path. *"The path of the just is as the shining light, that shineth more and more unto the perfect day."* The way gets brighter, better and higher. Doing God's will perfects us.

Earthly sinners need this heavenly wisdom.

Publish Abroad

"Because I will publish the name of the Lord:
ascribe ye greatness unto our God."
Deuteronomy 32:3

One of the most productive programmes of the Every Home Crusade has been their use of the writings of Dr. J. C. Ryle, the former Anglican Bishop of Liverpool and one of the foremost bishops of the Church of England during the eighteenth century. As well as being a faithful and fruitful preacher, Dr. Ryle was a prolific author. He wrote many books on evangelistic themes, practical Christian living, historical biographies of the great English Reformers and Bible commentaries. Most of these publications became classics and best sellers.

It is not so well known that the godly Bishop produced a series of Gospel tracts. He was justly called "the prince of tract writers." As a young curate, he zealously distributed leaflets of the Religious Tract Society in Southampton. In 1845 he produced a tract based on a sermon he had preached from Luke 7:40, "*I have somewhat to say unto thee.*" He distributed this tract everywhere he went and tried to enthuse others to do the same. He wrote almost 300 tracts which sold at one penny each and were widely circulated in the British Isles and throughout the British Empire.

William Hunt of Ipswich published Dr. Ryle's tracts in seven small volumes with the title, *Home Truths.* It is believed that about 12,000,000 of these tracts were distributed during Dr. Ryle's lifetime. They were translated into more than a dozen languages.

It is difficult if not impossible to improve on Bishop Ryle's tracts. Early in Ernie Allen's ministry he began printing and circulating copies of these tracts, first in Britain and then all over the world in different languages. It is estimated the presses of the Every Home Crusade have published more than 100,000,000 of Dr. Ryle's tracts.

Although the godly and zealous bishop has been with the Lord since 1916, his tract ministry still reaps a great harvest of precious souls through the agency of Every Home Crusade. Many letters arrived at Ernie Allen's desk asking him to give their greetings to Dr. Ryle. Ernie has now joined him in heaven.

There will be some party in heaven.

September

Rio Negro, Brazil

1st September

The Seed Story

"The seed is the Word of God."
Luke 8:11

Jesus was the greatest storyteller of all time. When He spoke, people listened, for He spoke the truth with authority. His stories were not "once-upon-time" tales. Jesus spoke in parables. More than a third of the Saviour's teaching was done by parables, and on one occasion He only taught in parables. While we were still children, we learned that "a parable is an earthly story with a heavenly meaning." All of the Saviour's parables weigh heavily with eternal and practical teachings.

Jesus told stories about soil and seed, shepherds and sheep, servants and sons, and suffering people and selfish people. All of them are classics. Perhaps the best known of all the Saviour's parables is that of the Sower, the seed, and the soil.

Throughout the Scriptures, the Word of God is likened to seed, good seed, precious seed and incorruptible seed. The purpose and aim of seed is to produce fruit. In like manner, the Bible also is productive. Peter spoke of the Scriptures as the *"incorruptible, by the word of God, which liveth and abideth forever"* (1 Peter 1:23).

The Seed is the Incorruptible Word of God – "not of corruptible seed, but of incorruptible, by the word of God." Many despise God's Word; for they hate it. Others deny the Bible because they do not accept its authority. False teachers seek to distort the Scriptures and change the Word. Be sure to not disregard or desert God's Word.

The Seed is the Incontestable Word of God – "the Word of God... liveth." Nobody can ever overcome the Word of God because it is the word of God. Many names are given for the Scriptures in the Bible, but its most frequent name is "the Word of God."

The Seed is the indestructible Word of God -- "the Word of God ... liveth and abideth for ever." The Bible is not the book of the month. It is the book of the ages. Heaven and earth will pass away, but His Word shall live forever.

This Seed is indispensable for our lives.

2nd September

Reaching Homes and Hearts

*"Joseph is a fruitful bough, even a fruitful bough by a well;
whose branches run over the wall."*
Genesis 49:22

I will always remember delivering mail in Omeath Street, Belfast back in 1958. The front window of nearly every house displayed a green plant in a brass flowerpot, flanked on either side by net curtains. All these windows were in stark contrast to that at 95 Omeath Street. Advertised in this window were Gospel texts, Bible slogans and Revival Movement publications of soul-stirring revivalists Charles G. Finney, Rueben A. Torrey and D. L. Moody.

I soon discovered that behind the window was a small desktop printer/duplicator being used to churn out revival literature. The material was circulated to hundreds of Christian leaders to motivate and inspire them to seek God for revival.

Behind the window was the small printing press, but behind the printing press was a man with a big heart that was so burdened for revival that he embarked on an endeavor to reach every home in Ireland, North and South, with the Gospel of Jesus Christ. This was Ernie Allen, a man with a passion for revival and a vision to make it happen.

When the Allen family moved to a new residence in Oakland Avenue, Ernie acquired a larger press to enhance his printing capacity. Thus, Every Home Crusade was initiated. From the Allen's family home, the work expanded to a former church building, then to purpose-built premises at Clara Street and when they became too small, they took possession of a large warehouse at Kinallen, County Down, its present home.

A team of twenty-four workers, plus volunteers, operate modern printing presses and accompanying up-to-date machinery to produce five tons of literature every day. This literature ranges from Bible portions, Gospel booklets and tracts, flash card Bible stories and choruses, and the publication of classic Christian books in multiple languages to be sent to ninety-five countries around the world.

Like Joseph, Ernie's fruitful ministry has crossed walls of cultural and linguistic frontiers to bring in a great harvest of souls all around the world.

God chose to reveal Himself through the written and printed page, the Bible.

A Precious Colleague

"Her children arise up, and call her blessed."
Proverbs 31:28

The Lord blessed us in Acre International with great colleagues at home and abroad. They became our role models and our dearest friends. Space does not allow me to write of their love, talents, sacrifice, and service for the Saviour. The Lord knows all about them.

In 1978 we were introduced to Jovita Mesquita. Before joining us in Amazonas, she had been a missioanry with World Missions to Children and a co-worker with Millicent Baillie in Recife, Brazil. We were immediately impressed with her warm gentleness and gentle disposition that endeared her to everyone.

Jovita was the youngest of twelve children in a traditional Roman Catholic family in Northeast Brazil. The light of the Gospel shone into that home when her oldest brother, Francisco, was the first in the family to trust Christ as Saviour. That light soon spread through the whole household as one by one the whole family, including Jovita's grandparents and parents, put their trust in Jesus Christ. Jovita was converted when she was fourteen years old.

Benedita, Jovita's oldest sister, became a missionary with World Missions to Children. Challenged by her sister's step of faith, Jovita, aged twenty-five, followed Benedita to serve God in an orphanage with the same mission. There she used her many skills to help the children; she taught them embroidery and cooking, and she shared with them the message of the Gospel with warmth and grace.

Although Jovita loved all the children at the orphanage, she adopted one little six-week-old boy, George, who had been abandoned by his mother. George became the light and joy of her life. Today George is a businessman in Manaus with many in his employment.

Jovita joined Millicent in Manaus to continue reaching boys and girls for Jesus Christ. Their child evangelism took them to schools, correctional centres, churches, houses and open-air meetings. They also taught in various theological seminaries. Auntie Jovita never lost an opportunity to witness for the Saviour with a warm word in season, a tract to a fellow passenger on a bus or even singing to the taxi drivers. Many today are walking with Christ because of Jovita's bright witness for Christ.

Jesus had a heart for boys and girls.

Shipyard Saints

*"They received the Word with all readiness of mind,
and searched the Scriptures daily."*
Acts 17:11

Belfast's Titanic Centre is a global attraction, and the nearby former Harland and Wolff Planning Office is being transformed into a luxury hotel. No longer are the shipyard's slipways and dry docks being used to construct great ships to traverse the oceans.

The lasting legacy of this famous shipyard is not only in the tonnage of great vessels of the past. Under the shadow of high cranes, a more enduring construction work took place. All over the "Island," in the Boiler shop, the Plumber shop, the Engine works, the East Yard, and on board many uncompleted structures, workers met daily at lunchtime with a mug of tea in one hand and a Bible in the other. While non-Christians huddled together for card schools, Christians met to pray and study the Scriptures.

Laymen led these interdenominational gatherings in systematic Bible studies. Discussion and interaction frequently followed, and not infrequently, a difference of opinion was expressed in a Belfast manner. The meetings were short and had to finish promptly and sometimes abruptly.

Billy Lavery was highly respected in the classes he conducted. His work took him all over the shipyard's sprawling complex. Being well-known, Billy attracted large gatherings to his insightful studies in the shadows and types of Christ in the Old Testament.

Alfie Stewart was a legend in his day with his warm-hearted manner and the gentle reverence with which he spoke of the Saviour. Andy O'Hara conducted a Bible Class in the Electrician Shop; Jimmy Bailey led his group in the Boiler Shop, and Sam Rea held another class in the Blacksmith Shop. Every shop and department had its leader.

Some men obtained permission to form the "Shipyard Gospel Witness." They organised weekly open-air meetings for Friday lunchtime. Local preachers were often invited to address the shipyard workers. Visiting evangelists such as Peter Brandon, Jack Shuler, and Hyman Appleman were also asked to preach at these meetings.

Our colleague in Brazil, Fred Orr, also worked at Harland and Wolff's Shipyard before going to serve God in Brazil.

There was Bible building at the shipyard.

In Christ

"For by grace are ye saved through faith…"
Ephesians 2:8

While travelling on the River Tarauacá, Padre Humberto, a German priest, followed a day's journey behind us seeking to undo all we were endeavouring to accomplish. Although I built a friendship with him in later years, he often remonstrated with new converts. He even stood outside a meetinghouse to impede anyone from going in to hear us preach the Gospel. One day I spoke with him, and he said he was going to attend. He did.

In conversation one day he said to me. "Victor, you evangelicals talk about 'being saved.'" He then went on to allege, "No one can be sure they are saved until they enter heaven." I took the time to point out to him that the Apostle Paul wrote in Ephesians 2:8; *"By grace, you are saved..."* I reasoned with him that Paul did not say we might be saved, or hope we will be saved. He used the present tense, "you are saved." The Gospel is not about a "hope-so salvation." We can enjoy blessed assurance on all that God has done for us.

What Has God done? In Ephesians 2 Paul focused on what God did for Jesus Christ: He raised Christ from the dead, made Him sit down in heaven, and exalted Him in glory. Paul then identified the same spiritual parallels in those who are saved. They also, through Christ, have been raised from the dead. They have been made to sit with Christ in heavenly places, and they share in His glory.

"He hath quickened us together with Christ." J. I. Packer vividly explains, "Between us sinners and the thunder-clouds of divine wrath stands the cross of the Lord Jesus." Jesus transferred us from death to life.

"He hath raised us up together with Christ." Sin brought death and put us in the tomb, but Jesus raised us out of that tomb by His resurrection.

"He hath made us sit together in heavenly places in Christ Jesus." Jesus Christ sits at the Father's right hand, and we are seated with Him in heaven. Being "in Christ" makes the Christian distinct from the unbeliever.

All that Christ has done is to be appropriated by faith.

God Opens Doors

"A great door and effectual is opened unto me."
1 Corinthians 16:9

When Mr. Maxton, the leader of Every Home For Christ in India, was invited to Northern Ireland for deputation meetings, everything seemed to go wrong. It was the wrong time of year, and few meetings were available. His visit seemed to be a waste of time until a friend introduced him to Ernie Allen at the Every Home Crusade Factory (EHC) in Clara Street, Belfast. Mr. Maxton was unaware that Every Home Crusade existed in Northern Ireland.

Ernie Allen and Samuel Adams were touched as they listened to the visitor tell of the great need for the Scriptures in his country. Literature stocks were very low, and they had few resources. Mr. Maxton explained that he worked with 600 evangelists who distributed Christian literature all over the country.

Mr. Maxton's face glowed when Ernie and Samuel promised to send literature to India on a regular basis. What he had thought was a waste of time turned out to be God's way opening a door for Christian literature for India.

During that visit, Mr. Maxton told Ernie and Samuel about Dr. William Scott and the India Bible Literature Mission. Dr. Scott, from Belfast, had gone to India over forty years earlier with his American wife, Dr. Joyce Scott. They had founded the India Bible Literature Mission to provide Bibles and Christian books in all Indian languages. Their vision was rooted in the question, *"Is anything too hard for the Lord?"*

During a trip home, Dr. Scott met Ernie and Samuel at Clara Street and was pleasantly surprised to discover what EHC was doing in many countries. After sharing his burden for Christian literature with Ernie and Samuel a bond and alliance were formed that would lead to supplying container loads of literature for distribution in India. Dr. Scott explained that he had a team of over a thousand evangelists engaged in the distribution of God's Word and a school of evangelism to train evangelists.

God used two men as the hinges to open the door of supplying a container load (18 tonnes) of Gospel literature for India each month.

There is nothing too hard for the Lord.

7th September

Broken

"And (they) brought the ass, and the colt, and put on them their clothes,
and they set Him thereon."
Matthew 21:7

Traditional Brazilian holidays always attracted people from the interior and brought some excitement to Santa Inêz where Wesley Gould lived. One event that stood out in Wesley's memory was "Dia De Mansar Os Cavalos," or "Taming the Horses Day."

Professional vaqueros (cowboys), rode untamed horses through the village. To "break" the horse, they rode it at speed up and down the main street for about 200 metres in each direction. The cowboys lashed and whipped the poor horses and dug their spurs into their bodies until they bled. The on-looking crowd roared and cheered as each horse galloped past. The spectacle seemed to go on endlessly until some of the blood-soaked horses collapsed on the street.

Wesley was fascinated to see all the excitement. Foolishly he asked one of the trainers if he could mount and ride his horse. The man placed a whip in Wesley's hand, helped him up onto the horse and gave it a gentle tap. The horse immediately dashed down the road at great speed, and Wesley was able to hang on until the horse suddenly stopped at the end of the street. The abrupt stop threw Wesley out of the saddle, but his foot was caught in the stirrup. The horse then ran around in circles dragging and kicking at Wesley. The people gathered round to see the horse making a fool of the foreigner.

When the horse finally stopped, Wesley was able to free himself from the stirrup. After he had dusted himself down, he walked home, thankful to the Lord for his protection.

That night, Wesley used the incident to contrast his experience with that of Jesus Christ riding a donkey colt into Jerusalem. He emphasized that no one had ever ridden or tamed that colt. However, when Jesus sat on the animal, He changed its nature so that it meekly bore Him through the thronging multitudes crying "Hosanna" to the Saviour. Wesley told the people that Jesus Christ was still able to change the nature of people.

Jesus makes new creatures through the new birth.

Grace and Mercy

"He is the propitiation for our sins."
1 John 2:2

I recently noticed a large poster prominently displayed outside a building that read, "JUSTICE FOR THE POOR." I think I have seen similar placards carried in various protest demonstrations with people calling for "justice." While there may be a worthy cause behind the sign, justice is the last thing sinners need. What we all need is mercy. Justice gives us what we deserve. Mercy does not give us what we do deserve.

Instead of God dispensing justice to us, He gave us Jesus. When the Lord Jesus came into the world, He did not come to give sinners what they deserved. He came with grace and to give grace. Justice gives us what we deserve. Mercy spares us from what we deserve, but grace bestows upon us what we do not deserve. The Apostle John wrote, *"The law was given by Moses, but grace and truth came by Jesus Christ."*

The broken Law of God calls out to all transgressors, "Guilty, guilty, guilty." God is a God of love, but He also is a God of justice and holiness. In our natural condition, we have no hiding place from the broken law of God.

When Christ died on the cross, God's mercy completely made a covering for man's sin. God's Son came between the broken law and the holiness of God. The just wrath of God fell upon Jesus Christ; divine justice was executed, and God was fully satisfied by the Saviour's atoning death on the cross. God's wrath fell upon Christ at Calvary. Forgiveness was made possible through the shed blood of Jesus Christ. The prophet spoke of Christ 700 years before Christ died: *"He shall see of the travail of his soul, and shall be satisfied"* (Isaiah 53:11).

When Jesus intervened at Calvary, the justice of God was satisfied, and the throne of judgment became a throne of mercy. *"Whom God hath set forth to be a propitiation through faith in his blood…"* (Romans 3:25). Calvary's cross calls out to us, *"Mercy here is rich, and grace is free."*

Kneel at the cross. Jesus will meet you there.

9th September

A Timely Word

"Thou art come to the kingdom for such a time as this."
Esther 4:14

In the Congo Maizie Smyth had to learn to speak French, Swahili, and Lingala. She recalled how her teacher in Ballymena had refused to let her enter an English exam saying, "It would be a waste of the government's money." Maizie proved that when God calls His servants, He also equips them for His work.

Maizie knew she needed more than the ability to speak these languages. She also needed the assurance that God was with her. When she arrived in Kisangani great doubts assailed her. Her original plan was to work alongside other colleagues, but they had to go home unexpectedly. Maizie was left alone. She recalled that time:

"Easter Sunday morning is always a special time of celebration in the Congolese church. Believers joyfully greet each other with the words, 'Christ is risen!' I always rose early on that special Sunday, but during this Easter great doubts disturbed my mind. I was left alone and wondered, 'Have I made a mistake? What is wrong with me?' I read God's Word but had no peace of mind. I knew God's promises but wondered if I was in the right place. I continued to prepare to go to church even though my mind was in turmoil. Not to go to God's house would have been disastrous, for the believers would have come to my door to find out why I had not been there.

At the morning service, I received a message to go to Pastor Bo's home immediately after church. Seven Christians crowded into my Land Rover as we sped off to visit him. At his house, he put them all out and said he wanted to speak with me alone.

'Maizie, did you bring your Bible?' He asked me to read from Esther 4:14. When I did, he told me to note these words, "Thou art come to the kingdom for such a time as this." He lifted his eyes and said, 'I don't know why God has told me to give you this verse, but I know you need it.'

I knew the reason why."

God's Word is sure and assuring.

Bring Them In

"And he brought him to Jesus."
John 1:42

When I was editor of the "Life Times" magazine I wrote an article that was commended by Francis Dixon's daughter for writing the following story about her father. While Francis Dixon was pastor at Lansdowne Baptist Church for many years, he told an amazing story. While on a mission trip to India he heard a lady missionary tell of her conversion through a tract that had been given to her by an anonymous man in George Street, Sydney, Australia.

Sometime later, Pastor Dixon was on another trip to the West Indies and in another meeting where a Christian worker gave testimony he said that he had been converted through a Gospel tract that had been given to him on George Street, Sydney. This story grew momentum when the same Pastor Dixon visited the north of England and yet again heard a person relate of their conversion attributing it to a Gospel leaflet given to him in Sydney. The pastor was so impressed that he told the story at his Sunday evening service. Two people came to him afterward and told the preacher they also had been converted through the impact of Gospel tracts given to them on George Street, Sydney.

Sometime later Francis Dixon was invited to preach in Perth, Australia. Before travelling to Sydney, he prayed that the Lord would let him meet this mighty soul-winner on the city's streets. On arrival in Sydney, he searched in vain for the anonymous man. However, while he was looking in a shop window, there was an unexpected tug on his sleeve. When Pastor Dixon looked round an elderly white haired man offered the preacher a Gospel tract saying, "Excuse me sir, but if you died today, do you know if you would be going to Heaven or Hell?"

At last, the preacher met Frank Genner, the anonymous evangelist. Pastor Dixon recounted to him the various testimonies he had heard. The old saint began to cry and said, "For twenty-five years I have been giving out tracts on these streets and never heard of one person being converted."

The greatest service we can render to others is to bring them to Jesus.

11th September

Links In the Chain

"Having therefore obtained help of God, I continue unto this day..."
Acts 26:22

The conversion of the Apostle Paul on the Damascus Road was undoubtedly one of the greatest turning points of church history. Although he had blasphemed the name of the Lord Jesus, feverishly opposed the Gospel and cruelly persecuted Christians, yet he became one of the greatest Christians that ever lived. As an Apostle to the Gentiles, he became the church's most outstanding missionary. His multiple gifts, his untiring energy, and his abounding zeal revealed that he was God's man for that early generation. To him was given the inestimable privilege of carrying the Gospel to many Orthodox Jewish synagogues, to crowded marketplaces in Asia, to the proud European cities of the Roman Empire, and people throughout the world.

For all the qualities of this man of God, he was always grateful for the help he received from many others in the body of Christ. Paul was surrounded by a host of Christian colleagues with whom he enjoyed friendship, fellowship, and partnership in the Gospel. In Romans 16 he mentioned more than thirty names of people who had aided him in his great ministry.

Consider the people who influenced Paul's life:

The faith of Stephen convicted him. On the day that Saul of Tarsus presided over the death of Stephen, he heard Stephen's prayers and saw Stephen's face. This testimony pierced Saul's stony heart and pricked his conscience. Little did he know that one day, like Stephen, he also would wear a Christian martyr's crown.

The faithfulness of Ananias charged him. Even though Ananias had heard frightening reports about this notorious persecutor, he courageously extended a welcoming hand to this new convert with the words, "Brother Saul..."

The fellowship of the disciples compassed him. The very Christians Saul had intended to persecute became his helpers, as they held the ropes to enable their brother, God's servant, escape.

The friendship of Barnabas comforted him. When doubtful believers were afraid to receive Saul in Jerusalem, Barnabas befriended and introduced him to the apostles. Barnabas went to Tarsus sometime later and brought Saul to Antioch where he was introduced to Christian service.

Every link counts in God's chain.

Joy in Jesus

"All my springs are in Thee."
Psalm 87:7

During a visit to Peru I had opportunity to visit Machu Picchu. Not far from the ruins of the famous Inca village is a small freshwater lake. Water descends from the lake, down through a mountain gorge and gathers momentum as it flows to the valley below. In the valley the original stream becomes a wide and fast flowing river. That river is the beginning of the great River Amazon which flows past towns, villages and cities on its way to the Amazon Delta, three thousand miles away. The river supplies food and livelihood for tens of thousands of people who live along its long course. At the Amazon Delta millions of gallons of muddy water gush into the Atlantic Ocean where the Amazon current reaches out for almost a hundred miles off shore. All this life, force and power begins in a small lake which is hidden high up in the Andes Mountains.

That is the best illustration I know of what David said in Psalm 87:7: *"All my springs are in Thee."* The heavenly springs of love, joy, peace, contentment, strength and provision flow from God to us by His Holy Spirit.

That is what the Apostle Paul experienced when he wrote to the Philippians. Although he was shut up in a Roman jail he wrote a letter that was filled with joy--joy that hangs alongside love in the cluster of the fruit of the Spirit.

Opening Paul's prison letter is as if he were opening a window to a gust of fresh air that brings the fragrance of heaven. This little book pulsates and radiates with joy. This was not an ordinary joy. It was supernatural joy--the joy of Jesus Christ in our hearts. In Paul's letter, he repeated the words "joy' "rejoicing" and "gladness" nineteen times. In the same letter, he mentioned "Jesus" on twenty occasions. Christ was the fountain of his joy.

It is interesting that the New Testament begins with joy on earth when Jesus was born, and the Bible ends with joy in heaven. This joy flows from heaven to our hearts.

In God's presence is fullness of joy.

Where Is the Mission Field?

"Suffer the little children to come unto Me."
Mark 10:14

When Maizie Smith worked in Belfast, she initially boarded at the Presbyterian Hostel and worshipped at Berry Street Presbyterian Church. Both places contributed to Maizie's deepening interest in missions. Joe Wright, a former missionary in Brazil and Irish Secretary for Unevangelized Fields Mission, had his office nearby. Joe quickly befriended newcomers to the hostel and introduced Maizie and other Christian friends to his monthly missionary prayer meeting. At these meetings, Maizie met many frontline missionaries. She loved to pray for them and financially support them: soon she was corresponding with several.

At the Berry Street Christian Endeavor, the missionary convener, Dorothy Moffat, frequently invited missionaries to tell of their work. At the hostel, Maizie had been challenged by "foreign" missionaries. When Fred and Violet Rainey, Child Evangelism Fellowship (CEF) missionaries in South Belfast, were invited to speak of their work, Maizie learned that night that the mission field was not only in some distant land. The mission field began immediately outside the doors of the church in Belfast.

Fred and Violet's visit was in October 1966 when the whole nation was in mourning over the horrendous disaster in Aberfan in the Welsh Valleys. A slagheap had suddenly moved and swamped the village's primary school. More than 140 children and their teachers perished in the disaster. As Fred concluded the meeting, the sombre mood deepened even further when he posed the question, "If Aberfan had happened on your street, how many boys and girls would be in heaven today because you had led them to Christ?"

At the end of the meeting, Maizie spoke with Fred. She knew she had to do something. Within a few weeks, Maizie was enrolled in a teacher-training programme at the Rainey's home. This was a milestone in her life, for she realized that to teach children the Scriptures, she would have to study her Bible. This helped her develop a deepening love for God's Word.

Maizie was allocated to be a CEF worker at McClure Street City Mission. That first step would soon take her to reach boys and girls in Africa.

Be sure to bring them in.

Power With Progress

"Then had the churches rest … and were edified; and walking in the fear of the Lord, and in the comfort of the Holy Ghost, were multiplied."
Acts 9:31

When the Crystal Palace Exhibition opened in 1851 people flocked to London's Hyde Park to behold the marvels of the latest inventions. Back in those days, steam was the in-thing. There were steam ploughs, steam trains, steam looms, and musical organs empowered by steam. The Exhibition's first prize that year went to a marvellous contraption that was made up of seven thousand parts. When the heat got to a certain temperature and the steam pressure was just right, they turned it on, and everything began to move. Gears engaged, wheels turned, pulleys ran back and forward, bells rang, and whistles blew. The noise of the apparatus was tremendous, and the sight was awesome. Thousands flocked to see it. There was only one draw back - it did not do anything. The machine had no practical use. It was only a demonstration on the uses and power of harnessed steam. There was an abundance of energy and action, but it was not put to any effect.

That perhaps is a fitting illustration of Christendom today; there is lots of activity, everything is well organised, the proper sounds are made, church departments run like clockwork, but there is one big drawback, just like the Crystal-Palace prize winner – the church is not productive. There is plenty of function but little accomplishment.

This was not the case with the church of the first century. You cannot read the book of Acts without realising the early Christians were both energetic and effective. The first-century saints had no financial resources, and no political clout. There were not many highly educated members or nobles amongst them. They faced the imperial might of the Roman Empire in persecution, the derision of the sophisticated Greek culture and the fanatical bigotry of Judaism, and yet they accomplished so much. Their weapons were mighty through God: the Word of God to preach, the throne of God in prayer and the Spirit of God upon them.

The same weapons are available today, and yet we accomplish so little.

15th September

The Saviour and the Sabbath

"The Son of Man is Lord also of the sabbath."
Mark 2:28

The end of Mark 2 and beginning of Mark 3 highlight two Sabbath-day events in the life of our Lord. The first was a secular matter that concerned our Lord's disciples plucking corn in the fields. The second was a sacred matter when Jesus healed a man with a withered hand in the synagogue on the Sabbath. In both events, Jesus Christ displayed His deity. He also displayed His fury toward the religious zealots and legalists who held the people in fear and bondage to their traditions.

In the Jewish Mishnah, there were 1521 laws relating to the Sabbath. These laws were both extensive and excessive. For example, Jews were forbidden to eat eggs that were laid on the Sabbath. If a man were bitten by an insect on the Sabbath, scratching his body was prohibited. No false teeth could be used on the Sabbath, and shoes with nails were not to be worn on the Sabbath day.

The Pharisees frequently clashed with our Lord on two matters: the first was that Jesus Christ claimed to be God, and the second concerned His actions on the Sabbath. Our Lord taught these hypocritical Pharisees several lessons about the use of the Sabbath.

Concerning work on the Sabbath, He gave them a lesson on liberty.

As regards the word of the Law, He gave them a lesson on His Lordship.

By doing good on the Sabbath to a poor lady in the synagogue, He gave them a lesson on love.

What does the Lord's Day mean to you? It is a day in which we should enjoy His presence, engage in His worship, express our praise, explore His Word and edify our bodies. Do not let the spirit of the world invade the Lord's Day and rob you of honouring God in the way He instructed us. There is no better way to begin the week than by meeting with the saints to remember the Lord Jesus and the miracle of His resurrection.

We use our rest day best when we meet with our Lord.

Bargaining

"As for God, His way is perfect."
Psalm 18:30

Broughshane missionary, Maizie Smith, touched many African lives. Perhaps for that reason, the Congolese children named her "Sifu" (praise). According to Maizie, her work in Africa all began with Ballymena bargaining. She related that when she went to live in Belfast, she found it strange that people did not bargain for a better price in shops as had been her custom in Ballymena.

One day Maizie began to haggle with God. First, there was the matter of a sum of money that she had saved to purchase a car. Three times God had spoken to her about surrendering the substantial sum to His work. She reacted: I want to buy a mini car. I worked to save this money. She said, "I was in great turmoil, and the conflict finally came to a head when I surrendered everything to Him, as best I knew how. I spent a long time in God's presence sorting this out."

At a missionary conference, several weeks later a friend asked Maizie, "If you ever think of Bible School you might consider going to the Bible Training Institute in Glasgow." Maizie quickly replied, "I have no intention of going to any Bible College, thank you." She chuckled at the thought: *Maizie Smith go to Bible College? Never. The Lord would never ask me to do a thing like that.*

As the missionaries reported on their work, God spoke to Maizie again. The Lord wanted more than her money. He wanted her. She spent a sleepless night on the Liverpool boat returning to Ireland. This time she was wrestling with the thought: *Could God be asking me to be a missionary?* Still trying to bargain with God, Maizie made a pact that night: "If God wants me to become a missionary, He will either put me out of my job or out of our lodgings." Both of these were very secure – so she thought.

On returning home, she learned that her landlady had unexpectedly put her house up for sale, and Maizie and her flatmates had to get out. Maizie reeled at the news. God wanted her to be a missionary.

Let the Lord have His way.

Thank God for those Who Pray

"Brethren, pray for us."
1 Thessalonians 5:25

Wesley Gould often travelled by small launch at night to conduct Gospel meetings in the scattered settlements along the shores of the Amazon Delta. Sometimes the scene seemed idyllic with the reflection of the full moon shimmering on the vast expanse of the Amazon. The people climbed the muddy banks of the river and left their paddles at the door before squatting on the bamboo floor of a simple house for a meeting. Wesley's Tilley lamp attracted thousands of flying insects, including mosquitoes and other bloodthirsty bugs.

One such place they occasionally visited was about six hours up river. They had many good meetings there and had the joy of pointing quite a few to faith in Christ. Wesley will always remember his visit to that place:

Our return journey depended on the tide. If the tide were out, the small river inlet would be too shallow for our launch to pass. That meant we would have to wait until about midnight for the tide to begin our journey home.

To make matters worse I took a severe pain in my stomach after the meeting that night. I don't know what could have caused it. I did not eat much of the boiled pork that was provided for our evening meal, but I was in agony, and we had no medicines to relieve the pain.

When we finally got on our way, I was still suffering. I tried lying down in a hammock to see if it would help, but it only seemed to make it worse. I found that the only way to get a little bit of relief was to stand up and hold on to the side of the launch as it chugged along in the darkness. About two o'clock in the morning, the pain suddenly and completely disappeared. It was a moment of unforgettable relief.

The next day I was telling a Christian friend about what had happened. He said that he woke up during the night and felt a strong urge to pray for us on our return journey on the launch. God does hear and answer prayer.

Those who pray play their part.

18th September

Your Life

"He hath set the world in their heart."
Ecclesiastes 3:11

A few years ago I shared a meeting with Canadian missionary and anthropologist, Don Richardson, author of the best-selling book Peace Child. He spoke on the theme of his new book, Eternity in Their Hearts, and based his remarks on today's verse, emphasising that all people groups in the entire world have a consciousness of eternity.

We were all made for God and eternity. Although our hearts may cease to beat one day, that will not be the end of you or me. The Bible teaches that our bodies are like tents, *"For we know that if our earthly house of this tabernacle were dissolved, we have a building of God, an house not made with hands, eternal in the heavens"* (2 Corinthians 5:1).

There are two questions we ought to face up to in the light of eternity. The unconverted need to ask and answer, *"Where am I going?"* The Christian should ask, *"What am I living for?"* Our sense of destiny should determine our attitude to life and to influence our goals and priorities. Eternity was a motivation for the Saviour. He said, *"I must work the works of him that sent me, while it is day: the night cometh, when no man can work"* (John 9:4).

Life is a Trust. We are owners of nothing and stewards of all that we receive. Paul reminded the Corinthians that they were not their own, for they were bought with a price. He said, *"What hast thou that thou didst not receive?"* He reminded them that they were stewards and followed with, *"It is required in stewards, that a man be found faithful."*

Life is a Test. Throughout history testing and temptation have been common to all men. Adam was tempted in the Garden of Eden – *a test of integrity.* Abraham was tested at Mount Moriah – *a test of faith.* Joseph was tempted about purity.

Life is temporal. The Bible reminds us of the brevity of life – it is as vapour, like grass and passes as quickly as the weaver's shuttle. Make the most of it.

Make your days count.

19th September

Flee Pride

> *"A man's pride shall bring him low:*
> *but honour shall uphold the humble in spirit."*
> Proverbs 29:23

An mythical story tells of a frog enviously gazing at elegant geese rising into the sky with the majestic flap of their wings and soaring at great heights. One day the little frog said to two geese, "I have a brilliant idea. If we get a long stick and each of you secures either end of it in your bill, I can close my mouth in the middle of the stick so that when you take off into the sky, I will hold on with my mouth and soar away up there with you."

The geese agreed to the frog's request, and soon they were airborne, each goose securing the stick in its bill while the frog held on with its mouth. The proud frog was enjoying the ride as he soared far up above the marshes below.

Just then a farmer below saw the unusual spectacle flying overhead--a frog between two geese. He removed his cap as he looked up and said, "I've never seen the like of that before." He called out, "Whose idea was this?"

The little frog could not resist the proud moment. He unwittingly opened his mouth and answered, "Miiiiiiine" as he fell to earth.

If humility is the highest virtue, pride is the first of the deadly sins. Twice in the New Testament, we read, "God resisteth the proud, but giveth grace unto the humble." (James 4:6; Peter 5:6).

Pride is a very dangerous sin. It does more harm to hold back revival than any other sin. 2 Chronicles 7:14 begins, "If my people, which are called by my name, shall humble themselves…"

Pride is such a deceitful sin. Many who are infected and infested with pride have no idea that they are proud. A drunkard knows he is a drunkard, a thief knows he is a thief, but a proud person is often unaware of his pride.

Pride is a destructive sin. It did not originate in the Garden of Eden. It was pride that cast Lucifer out of heaven, and we ought to resist it and run from it.

Pride often results in a downfall.

Christ is All we Need

"For to me to live is Christ, and to die is gain."
Philippians 1:21

Audrey and I were honoured to have William and Margaret McComb, founders of the Acre Gospel Mission, at our wedding. Willie McComb, challenged by the dedication and sacrifice of the famous cricketer, C. T. Studd, had gone to serve God in the heart of the Amazon in 1926. At our wedding reception, he gave us some advice and encouragement before our impending departure to serve God in Brazil. He went on to give us a cursory summary of Pauls' epistle to the Philippians and urged us to prove what Paul had written centuries earlier: that Christ is adequate for all we need.

From chapter 1 he indicated that Christ was Paul's life. In chapter 2 Christ was his mind. In chapter 3 Christ was Paul's goal, and in chapter 4 he spoke of Christ as Paul's strength. Mr. McComb applied the summary to us – "Make Christ your life – live for Him; make Christ your mind – rest in Him; aim to have Christ as your goal, strive to please Him and in it all I pray you will find that Christ is your strength. Jesus Christ is adequate for all you need."

That outline was probably not original, but it did under-gird us for the years ahead and made Philippians my favourite book in the Bible.

Dr. Daniel Poling was editor of the American *Christian Herald* and for many years president of Christian Endeavour International. His son, Clarke Poling, was one of the four chaplains who went down on the troop carrier. The *Dorchester*, in the Sea of Labrador on 3rd February 1943. The Four Chaplains, also sometimes referred to as the "Immortal Chaplains" or the "Dorchester Chaplains," gave their lives to save other civilian and military personnel on the ship.

Clarke Poling loved his wife and children, and before he left he wrote a letter to his family and his parents; and in that letter he said, *"I know I shall have your prayers; but please don't pray simply that God will keep me safe. War is a dangerous business. Pray that God will make me adequate."*

Adequacy is the ability to cope with life.

Treasures and Tragedy

"I will give thee the treasures of darkness."
Isaiah 45:3

Wesley and Winnie Gould opened a new work in Dom Pedro, and during the first year there, many people were converted. Sadly, near the end of that year, a terrible tragedy befell the church. Dona Otília heard believers singing on their way to church and was so impressed by their joy that she enquired who they were and where they were going. She wanted to have whatever made these people so happy.

As a result, Dona Otília made her way to the meeting that night. On hearing the Gospel for the first time, she trusted Christ as Saviour. Winnie was moved when she heard Otília's circumstances. She had had seven children, but only one had survived, Maria. The other six had died early in life.

After her conversion, Otília began to witness to her daughter Maria and son-in-law, José, who also had seven children. Within a short time, Maria and José waited after the meeting one evening, desiring to become Christians.

Maria showed considerable signs of genuine conversion to Jesus Christ. José was a different story. Wesley always sensed there was something sinister, even satanic about him. He eventually stopped coming to the meetings.

The situation deteriorated rapidly. José started to make false accusations against Maria, including being unfaithful to him. This led to arguments, and José began physically beating Maria in front of their children. It became a very unhappy home.

One lunchtime, Maria was sitting at the kitchen table when José arrived home in another fit of furious rage. Without warning, he violently attacked his wife in a demonic rage plunging a sharp knife into Maria's chest and stomach eight times. She died almost immediately. José ran out onto the street in an attempt to escape but was apprehended. In due time he was sentenced to a lengthy jail term at the State Penitentiary.

Consequently, Dona Otília gained the custody of her daughter's seven children. Ironically, she inherited seven grandchildren in place of the seven sons and daughters she had lost. During the next years, Otília was able to raise her grandchildren in the paths of righteousness.

Wheat and weeds always occupy the same field.

22nd September

Embarrassed

*"Unto every one of us is given grace according to the measure
of the gift of Christ."*
Ephesians 4:7

Have you ever been embarrassed and then dumbfounded? I have – many times. I was the acting administrator of the small hospital in Tarauacá during the absence of Dr. Geddis. The hospital was an old wooden structure which was in constant need of repair. While tropical downpours and the hot sun took their toll on the building, white ants did the greatest damage. They seemed to have had a ferocious appetite for the hospital wood.

One day I discovered that part of the hospital's exterior wall was hollow. An army of ants had obviously feasted on the upright boards, and they needed to be replaced. Our usual skilled carpenter was not available, so someone recommended Arnaldo, a man I did not know. I outlined to him the work that needed to be done and left him to it.

When I returned later that day, I was aghast to find that the newly installed "upright boards" were anything but upright. In exasperation I loudly said to the nurse, "Whoever told me that man was a carpenter? All those boards are crooked and lying to one side." Just as I was finishing my rant, Arnaldo put his head around the doorway and said with a wide smile on his face, "Hello Pastor Victor. I did it."

I was completely taken aback to realise he had heard me complaining, especially since I had witnessed to him about the Gospel and invited him to church on Sunday. He readily admitted that the boards were off plumb and soon rectified his mistake. What dumbfounded me was that he and all his family arrived at church on the following Sunday. Not only did they attend, but at the end of the Gospel meeting he and his wife, Marlene, accepted Jesus Christ as Saviour.

Arnaldo developed a great love for the Word of God and zeal for God's work. He attended classes that I organised for potential Christian workers. After we left Tarauacá, Arnaldo and his wife became missionaries on the frontier of Brazil and Bolivia, and his children are still very active in God's work.

God's grace confounds us.

*"He that believeth and is baptized shall be saved;
but he that believeth not shall be damned."*
Mark 16:16

After the famed Baptist preacher, Charles Haddon Spurgeon, was converted, he wrote to his parents, asking permission to be baptized. Although his father cautioned him not to trust in his baptism, his mother wrote to her son:

Dear Charles, I have often prayed for the Lord to make you a Christian, but I never prayed that you would become a Baptist. Love, Mother.

To this the young Spurgeon playfully responded:

Dear Mother, The Lord has answered your prayer with His usual bounty and has given you exceedingly abundantly above what you asked or thought. Love, Charles.

There is no virtue in water. It can never wash away our sin, nor will it ever drown the devil. However, there is virtue in obedience.

Naaman was a highly respected commander in the Syrian army, but he was a leper, considered to be unclean and loathsome. A young Israeli slave girl in his household took pity on her master and said, "If only my master were with the prophet who is in Samaria! For he would heal him of his leprosy." She was not only concerned for her master, but she was also confident that God could heal him.

Naaman took great riches and a letter from his king and eventually arrived at the doorstep of Elisha the prophet in Israel. Not wanting to touch the unclean leper, Elisha sent his messenger to tell Naaman to wash in the River Jordan seven times to be cleansed.

Naaman was insulted that Elisha did not come out to lay hands on him. Why he should go to the Jordan when the rivers of Damascus were just as good as the Jordan. But his servants persuaded him to go down to the Jordan. After immersing himself seven times, Naaman was cleansed. The Syrian commander learned that obedience is the secret of blessing.

I say again, there is no virtue in water, but there is blessing in obedience. Jesus said, *"He that believeth and is baptised shall be saved."* In the New Testament, everyone who believed was baptised, except the thief on the cross.

There is no other way but to trust and obey.

24th September

His Words and Works

*"But that ye may know that the Son of Man hath power
on earth to forgive sins."*
Mark 2:10

The Gospels are a record of the words and works of our Saviour. However, what is most important about our Lord Jesus Christ is not the words He spoke or the works He did. These are important, but not the most important. The most important thing about our Saviour is Who He is. He is God. Unless we have a right view of Who He is, then the value of what He did and what He said will be lost on us.

If Jesus Christ is not Who He claimed to be, then all He did and all He said was in vain. With unclouded simplicity the Gospel writers amply display who Jesus Christ is. Our Saviour perceived the need of a paralytic, saw the faith of his four helpers, read the thoughts of His critics and was attacked because He exercised His divine prerogative to forgive sins. He called Matthew to the Kingdom and declared Himself to be Lord of the Sabbath. Who but God could do these things? Jesus Christ is God.

Grace and authority characterised the ministry of our Lord. In Mark 2 His power was manifested by two great miracles. The first was the miracle of raising a paralytic man. A generation ago The Coalmen's Mission in Belfast was a favourite place for Saturday evening gospel rallies. "Wee Sammy" (Dodger) Spence was one of the effective leaders of those Christian Coalmen. He often spoke of the miracle of the man sick of the palsy and how he was healed. Sammy summed up the miracle in typical style, "Here is a man who when he came to the Lord Jesus, he had his head on the bed, but when he left, he had the bed on his head. That was a miracle that raised the roof!"

The second miracle was even greater. The deepest need of the human heart and the greatest gift that we can receive are summed up in that sweetest of words - forgiveness. Forgiveness for the sinner is a miracle of grace.

Forgiven? Oh, the bliss of this glorious thought.

25th September

Catching Fish

"Go thou to the sea, and cast an hook, and take up that first cometh up, and when thou hast opened his mouth thou shalt find a piece of money: that take, and give it unto them for Me and for thee."
Matthew 17:27

In 1962 I was with a group of students conducting a Gospel Mission at the Fisherman's Hall in Brora, on Scotland's northeast coast. It was a busy but blessed time. Several of those converts went into Christian work, including Anna Sutherland who became a missionary to the Jews.

On a morning off, Anna's brother loaned me a fishing line to try my hand at fishing at the nearby estuary to Brora harbour. I had never fished before, so this was a novelty and might have been a futile exercise. However, after more than an hour casting out the line as I stood on the rocks I was about to give up. Just then I spied a fish coming near me. I could see that it was still alive, but barely. It seemed as though it had taken pity on me, and gave up in surrender. I wrapped the line around its mouth and pulled it in. I wasn't even sure what sort of fish it was until I arrived at Anna's home. There I learned I had caught a ten-pound salmon. Apparently, someone had illegally detonated something in the river to stun the fish, including my catch.

The incident reminded me of Peter when the Lord sent him to catch a fish that would have a coin in its mouth sufficient to pay temple tax for Jesus and him. Peter was used to fishing with nets but went line fishing because Jesus had sent him. Imagine someone watching Peter fishing with a line and the conversation that ensued. "Why are you fishing?" "To pay the taxes for two people," Peter answered. "Pay taxes with fish?" "No, the fish will have a coin in its mouth." "Tell me another story!" Just then out popped the fish. Peter removed the coin and tossed it in the air. The onlooker asked, "What sort of bait did you use?"

His creation knows His voice and He knows our needs.

Don't Pass by on the Other Side

*"And by chance there came down a certain priest that way:
and when he saw him, he passed by on the other side."*
Luke 10:31

On 26th September 1944, Ray Hamley, a 21-year-old RAF officer, and his crew dropped bombs on the town of Kleve in Germany. His bombs hit the railroad station, some Nazi factories, and the town church. He had an inkling that one of his bombs hit the church, but justified it by thinking war was war.

Ray Hamley went home to England after the war, married his childhood sweetheart, and became the head of a primary school. In 1983, someone handed him a newspaper clipping that showed how the people of a small town in Germany named Kleve were rebuilding their church that had been bombed during the war. Something triggered in Ray's memory. He found his old logbook in the attic and suddenly realized that it had been his bomb that had destroyed the church back then.

He thought about that tiny town, and how the loss of their church must have touched those people. He was tempted to *"pass by on the other side,"* reasoning, *"The Nazis bombed innocent children in London; it was wartime, and it was years ago."*

Ray Hamley could not forget it. He wrote to the Mayor of Kleve, asking for forgiveness of the townspeople and requesting that his letter be read at the dedication of the new church building. In 1984, Ray got a reply from the people of Kleve, requesting that he and his family come and see the new church building. Second thoughts about the gesture frightened Ray, and he could not even answer the letter.

Another letter arrived, this time signed by 500 parishioners offering their forgiveness to him in the name of Jesus Christ.

Ray Hamley went to Kleve. His visit not only healed old wounds in his life but brought about an incredible reconciliation between Ray's hometown in England and the people of Kleve in Germany.

And it all happened because, by the power of God, Ray Hamley could not pass by on the other side.

Forgiveness is divine.

27th September

Forever

"So shall we ever be with the Lord."
1 Thessalonians 4:17

Family reunions can be great times. Too often we have been separated from family and friends, but prolonged absences only added to the joy of reuniting. Annual Field Conferences in Brazil were special times for exchanging news and renewing friendships. Also, returning home from Brazil to meet family after four or five years abroad was exciting for everyone.

Family reunions on earth cannot compare with the gathering of the ransomed in Heaven. It will be for all those who were born again of the Holy Spirit into His family and redeemed by the precious blood of Christ. Family reunions on earth often end with sad farewells, but in Heaven, no one will ever say "Goodbye."

When Christians meet on earth, it is never for the last time. They shall meet in heaven. Bible commentator, Matthew Henry, was engaged to a very rich young lady. Her father objected to his only daughter marrying a preacher. "You see," he said, "he may be a perfect gentleman, a brilliant scholar, and an excellent preacher; but he is a stranger, and we do not even know where he comes from."

"True," replied the daughter, "but we know where he is going, and I should like to go with him." When we know Christ as our Saviour, we will spend eternity in Heaven with our loved ones who also know Him.

Our Saviour prayed: "Father, I will that they also, whom Thou hast given me, be with me where I am; that they may behold my glory, which Thou hast given me: for Thou lovedst me before the foundation of the world" (John 17:24). That prayer will not go unanswered.

Our Lord has planned for our perfect reunion to take place when He returns. Then we will be with Him in our new bodies, and will enjoy the reunion with all of our redeemed loved ones. "Then we which are alive and remain shall be caught up together with them in the clouds to meet the Lord in the air: and so shall we ever be with the Lord."

What a gathering that will be.

28th September

But for His Mercy

"The God of my mercy shall prevent me."
Psalm 59:10

Wesley Gould tells of his long trip to Belem:

To visit our daughter in Belém, Pará, I had to ride on the back of an old lorry with wooden benches down its sides. The first 150 kilometres was over a dirt road full of potholes. For twenty-four hours we crawled and bumped until we got to the State frontier. I planned to catch another bus to Belém on the following morning.

I discovered that there was only one little boarding house in the village, and I could have a single bed in a room with another man. I gladly accepted for I was exhausted. After something to eat, I went to bed early. My unknown roommate did not return until late. He was a cattle rancher who had sold his animals and was going home. He held a large bag that, no doubt, contained a lot of money.

Soon after he lay down, he was asleep. In my deep sleep I had a dream in which I saw a Christian friend in our room, and for some strange reason, I felt I had to put him out. While still sleeping, I got up from my bed, went over to the stranger in the other bed and put both my hands around his throat. Without knowing, I was literally strangling him. At that stage, I woke up to find the man's eyes were bulging out of his head, and he was trembling from head to foot. The rancher was frightened out of his wits, no doubt, thinking I was trying to kill him to rob him.

Travelling men are generally armed for self-protection. He could have easily killed me with a good case of self-defense. I tried to convince him it was just a dream, but he would not believe me.

The frightened man sat up on his bed and kept watching me. He made the sign of the cross across his body and then began to pray for the Virgin Mary's protection from this maniac.

I shuddered to think what might have happened if God had not protected me.

His mercies protect us.

Job's Conclusions

"I know that Thou canst do every thing, and that no thought can be withholden from thee. Who is he that hideth counsel without knowledge? therefore have I uttered that I understood not; things too wonderful for me, which I knew not."
Job 42:2, 3

Job is one of the oldest books in the Bible, yet its lessons are right up to date. A cursory summary of his life could be stated as Job's test, his trouble, and his triumph. However, these trite words cover a lot of pain and anguish. Job endured losses like few other people, if indeed any other person, has known. He lost his business when his farm was destroyed, and his finances were wiped out. He lost his family when all his children perished. He lost his health and the respect of his wife. He lost his friends when they questioned his godly life.

Although Job was a holy man, he was also human. He felt pain and heartache. He wrestled to understand what his sufferings meant. However, below all his pondering with the mystery of suffering he had this confidence, *"The LORD gave, and the LORD hath taken away; blessed be the name of the LORD.* Job was able to progress beyond asking the *"Why"* of suffering to have the confidence to see *"Who"* is in control when we suffer.

For thirty-four long chapters after Job 2, God was silent. That was the hardest thing to take – God's silence. For Job it even seemed at times as if God were absent. God did not answer Job's questions. In His time he broke His silence and took Job on a tour of the universe and asked Job dozens of questions.

In the final chapter, after Job listened to God, he concluded:

The power of God cannot be limited -- "I know that Thou canst do every thing…"
The purpose of God cannot be thwarted -- "No thought can be withholden from Thee…"
The plan of God cannot be explained -- "Who is he that hideth counsel without knowledge?"
The praise of God should not be withheld -- "I have heard of Thee by the hearing of the ear: but now mine eye seeth Thee."

Our best place before God is surrender and submission.

Out and Out for Jesus

*"And daily in the temple, and in every house,
they ceased not to teach and preach Jesus Christ."*
Acts 5:42

One of the greatest investments of our time in Manaus was teaching students at the Regular Baptist Seminary five nights each week. Added to this, Audrey and I worked alongside Januário and Tereza to establish Calvary Regular Baptist Church. Although Januário and Tereza earn their living by teaching at a Japanese School, they have dedicated their energies establishing new Gospel centres in the expanding districts of Manaus. Until now they founded twelve new churches, and we had the privilege of working with them in three of these. Several converts from that work also trained at the Baptist Seminary and are serving God as missionaries and pastors.

While living in Manaus, we swung between two social extremes every Saturday afternoon. First of all, Audrey conducted a Good News Club in a slum area of town. The poverty was overwhelming, the squalor unbelievable and the stench of stagnant water below the houses was foul. Nevertheless, for almost two hours, boys and girls sang choruses, learned Bible verses, listened to the Gospel and then enjoyed some goodies Audrey provided for them.

After a shower and a quick change of clothes, we travelled to an upper-class residence in a more opulent part of town. At the side of a beautiful swimming pool and under the idyllic setting of overhanging palms, we conducted a Bible study for a group of professional people. Following the study, a substantial meal was served. Most of those present did not attend any church, so it was a great opportunity to present the Gospel.

The meetings in the slums were very responsive. Several children and parents trusted the Lord. The study at the side of the pool seemed to be unproductive. That is, until a young man who was totally unchurched, sought the Lord. Conviction of sin had taken sleep from his eyes and finally led him to repentance and faith in Jesus Christ. His conversion was followed by that of another professional who discovered that life without Christ was empty and aimless.

Jesus is the Saviour of the world.

October

Harvest Time

Steadfast

"Be ye steadfast, unmoveable, always abounding in the work of the Lord."
1 Corinthians 15:58

A few believers from Piracuruca accompanied Wesley and Winnie Gould when they went to Batalha, a village about twenty miles from Piracuruca. They quickly found that, like in Piracuruca, the local priest dominated the town.

Even though a good number of people gathered at the town square to hear the Gospel, they could hear the all-too-familiar chant of an organised mob led by the priest. As they approached, four men carrying an image of the local patron saint, shouted, "Death to the Protestants."

The hostile crowd continued to mill around for some time, undoubtedly hoping that the believers would run off. However, the team stood firm until the mob finally dispersed.

The following week, the priest and his followers repeated the same opposition, but on this occasion, the mob was bigger and the people more agitated than the week before. Wesley and his friends carried on with their meeting regardless.

At the end of the meeting, Wesley gave an invitation for anyone who wanted to accept Jesus Christ as Saviour to step forward. Even Wesley was surprised when four men stepped to the front. All of them were hearing the Gospel for the first time. Among these was Senhor Gonzalo who later became a deacon in the little church in Batalha. Over the next few years, every member of his family also trusted Jesus Christ as Saviour.

In spite of many verbal threats, slanderous insults, and public processions, Wesley and Winnie refused to be drawn into any form of retaliation. They majored on preaching that Jesus Christ was the only Saviour from sin. God honoured their faithfulness, and people responded to the Gospel.

Miracles of mercy continued in Batalha. José Lucimar, a sixteen-year-old altar boy, paraded at the front of the angry mob opposing those open-air meetings. Even Wesley was surprised when young Lucimar arrived at the meeting one evening. It was a happy night when he trusted the Lord Jesus.

Today Lucimar is a pastor, a Christian journalist and broadcaster in Brazil and the founder of many churches in Piauí.

Monuments of mercy and trophies of grace.

God Speaks

"The heavens declare the glory of God … There is no speech nor language,
where their voice is not heard."
Psalm 19:1, 3

Travelling on the tributaries of the Amazon gave us a deeper appreciation of the grandeur and beauty of God's vast creation. Not only did we see a wide variety of wild life and splendour of virgin forest by day, but were able to gaze at the vast expanse of the night sky. How awesome and spectacular is the dust-like appearance of the Milky Way and the brightness of the mariner's friend, the Southern Cross. It made us cry out, "How Great Thou art."

It is obvious that when King David was a shepherd boy, he was overwhelmed with the beauty of God's handiwork. God's great creation was a revelation to him of how great and near God is. In Psalm 19 David enlarges on the glory of God's threefold revelation.

The revelation of His glory in the skies. David recognized that with the rising of the sun each morning, nature preached a new sermon every day. The grandeur of God's creation is a testimony of God's existence, His wisdom and His power. His revelation by creation is unmistakable, unspoken, unceasing and is a universal language. God used the revelation of the heavens to bring the Wise Men to Bethlehem.

The revelation of His grace in the Scriptures. Creation reveals that God exists but does not introduce us to a relationship with Him. We can see His work, but not His will, His wisdom but not His holiness, His glory but not His grace. David turns from the skies to the Scriptures with five different titles for God's Word. Added to this he enlarges on these titles with adjectives describing His Word as perfect, powerful, prudent, pure, permanent and precious. His Word has the power to challenge us, change us, and cheer us.

The revelation of His goings in our souls. By His Spirit God speaks into our souls. He makes us conscious of our secret and presumptuous sins, but also assures us that with Him there is mercy and grace.

The Mighty God of the sky and Scriptures is our Refuge and Redeemer.

3rd October

Jesus on Board

"He went into a ship with His disciples."
Luke 8:22

While visiting Israel we ask the group where they might like to have been present at any time during the ministry of our Lord. We nearly always have the usual variety of answers: "the Mount of Transfiguration, Calvary, the Garden Tomb, etc." I have never had anyone say they would like to have been in the boat during the storm on Galilee. Like our Lord's disciples, none of us like storms, yet in the school of Christ, they are part of the course.

The Master's presence on the ship. Jesus had spent an extremely busy and exhausting day performing miracles and ministering to multitudes when He said, "*Let us pass over unto the other side.*" Crossing to the other side of Galilee was not the disciples' plan. The greatest decision taken that night was to make sure that Jesus Christ was on board. He guided them in the darkness, governed the circumstances, and guaranteed their arrival on the other side.

The menacing peril of the storm. "*There came down a storm of wind.*" The storm was *a surprise.* These disciples had frequently crossed that stretch of water, but on that night they were in for a big surprise. *The storm was severe.* The storm was so severe that seasoned fishermen were sure they would die. *Was the storm Satanic?* Some commentators suggest that the storm was a diabolical attack on our Lord, and I tend to agree with them.

The miraculous power of the Saviour. "*He arose and rebuked the wind and … the water.*" The Saviour was sleeping in the storm, but when the wind came down Jesus stood up. He is greater than all our storms. The word "*rebuked*" can be replaced to read, "*Jesus muzzled the wind.*" Our adversary may be a roaring lion, but Jesus is well able to muzzle him. He muzzled the storm and mastered the sea.

The marvellous peace on the sea. "*And there was a great calm.*" Is it any wonder they asked, "*What manner of Man is this?*"

With Christ in the vessel, we can expect the storms and smile.

A Blessed Conjunction

"But God, who is rich in mercy, for his great love wherewith he loved us."
Ephesians 2:4

Perhaps the most precious and dramatic conjunction in the Bible is the word "but," especially when used about God, *"but God..."* On these two words hang the turning point of human history. The same two words have changed countless lives. Joseph reminded his brothers, *"Ye thought evil against me; but God meant it for good."* Stephen also said, *"Patriarchs, moved with envy, sold Joseph into Egypt: but God was with him"* (Acts 7:9).

Of David, on the run from Saul, we read, *"Saul sought him every day, but God delivered him not into his hand"* (1 Samuel 23:14). Perhaps for that reason, he later wrote, *"My flesh and my heart faileth: but God is the strength of my heart, and my portion forever"* (Psalm 73:26).

Of course, the same two words can make a difference to the person who leaves God out. We read that rich farmer calculated his personal worth, *"But God said unto him, Thou fool, this night thy soul shall be required of thee: then whose shall those things be, which thou hast provided"* (Luke 12:20)?

Of the Saviour, the Apostle Paul said, *"They took him down from the tree, and laid him in a sepulchre. But God raised him from the dead"* (Acts 13:29-30).

Paul reminded the Corinthians that God did not choose many wise, many mighty or many noble *"But God hath chosen the foolish things of the world to confound the wise; and God hath chosen the weak things of the world to confound the things which are mighty"* (1 Corinthians 1:27).

We are unworthy, unmerited and undeserving, but when we were dead in our sins, He made us alive; when we were helpless slaves, He raised us up, and when we were down and out in disobedience, He made us sit in heavenly places in Christ.

This little conjunction "but" makes such a difference, *"But God commendeth his love toward us, in that, while we were yet sinners, Christ died for us"* (Romans 5:8).

Life would be aimless and despairing if it were not for, "But God."

The Race

"Seeing we also are compassed about with so great a cloud of witnesses,
let us lay aside every weight, and the sin which doth so easily beset us,
and let us run with patience the race that is set before us."
Hebrews 12:1

The Olympics are not a new phenomenon. Almost 2,500 years ago the Olympics were held on Mt. Olympus in Greece. The Pythian Games took place in Delphi, and the Ismeian Games took place at Corinth. These events were so important that they were held at staggered intervals throughout the year so that the wealthy could attend all three. The athletes who participated were hailed as being more important than military generals, learned philosophers or successful business people. People almost worshipped the ground on which they walked.

The Apostle Paul enjoyed many sports, or he was closely acquainted with them in his day. He made many illusions to various sports in his letters. He alluded to boxing when he wrote, *"I therefore so run, not as uncertainly; so fight I, not as one that beateth the air."* He was referring to shadow boxing. Of competition, Paul wrote, *"If a man also strive for masteries, yet is he not crowned, except he strive lawfully."* The author to the Hebrews also drew an incredible lesson from sports in his time. Observe these:

Ready, steady, go. If you are saved, you are in a race. Salvation is not a prize to be gained by winning the race. Salvation by grace is the gift that puts you into the race.

Never give up. Great heroes of the faith have already finished their race, and from heaven, they cheer us on.

Don't slow down. Nobody runs a race in an overcoat and with a suitcase in each hand. We must lay aside every weight that would slow us down.

Don't fall down. If it is harmful to slow down, it is disastrous to fall down for any reason.

Never give up. We should never stop running until we finish the course. It does not matter how far ahead we think we are or how near the finish line we are.

The key to success in this race is – "Looking unto Jesus."

Good Samaritan

"A certain Samaritan, … when he saw him, he had compassion on him, and went to him, and …and took care of him."
Luke 10:33,34

Neighbourliness can be a good subject. We often hear people ask, "What's your neighbour like?" It is important that we learn to be good neighbours rather than look for good neighbours. Someone has written: "To love the whole world, for me it is no chore; my only real problem, is my neighbour next door."

When a lawyer accusingly questioned the Lord Jesus about the Law, he asked who our neighbour is. The Lawyer's question was good, but his motives were wrong. He tried to find fault with the Saviour. In reply, the Lord Jesus told one of the best known of all His parables--the story of the Good Samaritan.

This is the story of a man who took a treacherous journey from Jerusalem to Jericho. The way was rough, steep and threatening. It was sometimes called "The Bloody Way" because robbers often lurked in the shadows, and without fear of intervention, they frequently mugged or even murdered pilgrims.

The misery of the hurting man's condition. The traveller fell among thieves, who stripped him of his clothing, wounded him, and left him half dead. The Saviour showed what a godless society could do to the travellers of life. This man took the wrong direction, leaving Jerusalem, and fell into danger.

The motives of two holy men's contempt. A passing priest, possibly leaving the Temple, looked over, and he saw the victim and then passed by on the other side. A Levite arrived on the scene, looked at the same injured man, and passed by on the other side. These two religionists deliberately avoided the bleeding man lying in the dirt for fear of becoming unclean. Neither of them had any heart for the needy. They saw a need but felt nothing.

The mercy of the Samaritan's concern and care. In contrast to the two religious men, a certain Samaritan saw the injured victim, and at his own expense, cared for him even though he was of a different persuasion. The Samaritan proved that he was a most worthy neighbour.

Look beyond people's labels and see their needs.

Our Keeper

"The Lord shall preserve thee from all evil."
Psalm 121:7

James and Dorrie Gunning, our Field Leaders in Brazil, were excellent role models of dedication to God's work and love for the Saviour. Invariably, before we would leave on a journey James would read Psalm 121 and then pray with us for the protection promised in that reading. We are glad to say that God answered those prayers.

Bill Woods has been travelling by small single engine planes for more than fifty years. Ten of the pilots with whom he travelled died in various airplane disasters over the forest. We also are thankful for God's protection during many scary episodes.

I remember travelling to Canutama on a small plane, normally a three-hour flight. After two hours we landed in Tapuá where a passenger disembarked. After an hour we took off again for the rest of the journey. Just as the plane was climbing to a few thousand feet into the air, smoke began to pour from the cockpit's instrument panel. The pilot panicked and told us to be ready for a rough crash. He banked the airplane to the left in an attempt to circle back to the grassy runway in Tapuá. The smoke continued to pour from the panel accompanied by the smell of burning rubber or plastic. After a few tense minutes, the pilot was able to land the 'plane. When he brought it to an abrupt stop all four of us scrambled out in case the aircraft would catch fire.

The pilot and a local electrician worked on the faulty panel for a few hours while we took shade from the hot sun. Eventually, the pilot had a few men wrap a rope around the cone of the propeller and then pull the rope in an attempt to crank the plane's engine into life. After several vain attempts at cranking the engine, we had to abandon the flight. I was not too keen on boarding that plane again.

That night I recalled Psalm 121. *Our Lord is a sure Helper (v.2), a sleepless Watcher (v. 3), a strong Upholder, a sheltering Protector (vs. 5, 6), and an all-sufficient Preserver.*

He that upholds the universe will keep you.

A Family Postcard

"Paul, a prisoner of Jesus Christ, and Timothy our brother, unto Philemon our dearly beloved, and fellowlabourer, and to our beloved Apphia, and Archippus our fellowsoldier."
Philemon 1, 2

Paul's letter to Philemon is considered by many to be a masterpiece of literary art for both its grammar and grace. It overflows with the bonds of friendship and fellowship between Paul, Philemon, and his family.

The letter has also been likened to a postcard more than a letter. In its opening verses, Paul provided us with a picture postcard of the Christian life by the names he accorded to his colleagues.

Timothy was a brother in the fellowship. On four occasions Paul referred to his companions as "brothers" in this postcard. It is the language of God's family. While Paul was writing to a family, he referred to this wider and greater family of God. In this postcard, Paul also enlarges on the two things that should characterise God's family: the life of God in the soul and the love of God in the heart.

Paul was a prisoner in fetters for Jesus Christ. Philemon is one of Paul's prison letters. In it, we can discern Paul's submission to the will of God. Paul did not consider himself to be a prisoner of Emperor Caesar. He was a prisoner of Jesus Christ. God gave him a fetter. Samuel Rutherford said that God takes the best wine from the deepest cellars of suffering.

Paul was in prison by God's appointment. He had planned to go to Rome as a preacher, but God took him as a prisoner. Paul had gone looking for fruit, but God gave him a fetter. He knew he was there in God's keeping, under His training, and for His time.

Philemon was a beloved fellow-labourer in the field. The work of the Gospel makes us fellow-servants to the Lord of the Harvest and fellow-workers to reach the lost.

Archippus was a fellow-soldier in the fight. To engage in Gospel ministry is to enter the sphere of spiritual battle. The enemy of souls is busy, but the Captain of our salvation has already won the victory.

We are children of the King.

Divine Sovereignty

"Who hath known the mind of the Lord?"
Romans 11:34

In 1976 I visited the HCJB radio station in Quito, Ecuador and met many of the missionaries involved in *The Voice of the Andes ministry*. Although it was a blessing to meet God's servants, it was also sobering to learn the following story.

On 15th February 1974 an Avianca Airline flight bound for Quito, Ecuador, crashed into the 14,000 foot-high towering peak of El Tablazo, not far from Columbia's Capital, Bogota. The sound of the aircraft smashing into a mountainside must have been deafening, but no one was near enough to hear it. News of this catastrophic crash ultimately echoed around the world. No passenger ever knew what happened for they all died instantly. Among those on board was a young man, Glenn Chambers who had planned to begin his ministry with *The Voice of the Andes* team. Glen's lifelong dream had been turned into a terrible nightmare.

Before leaving Miami Airport earlier that day, Glen hurriedly scribbled a note to his mother on a piece of paper he had picked up in the terminal. The pamphlet was an advertisement, which bore one single word sprawled across its center, "WHY?" Glen had written on the reverse side, put the note into an addressed envelope and mailed it from the airport.

Between the mailing and the delivery of that note, Glen Chambers was killed. When the letter did arrive, after his mom read her son's last communiqué, she turned the page and was shocked with the single word staring up at her, "WHY?"

Of all the questions we might ask, this is the most searching and tormenting. There are no easy answers. We do not understand why God's servant, the Apostle James, was beheaded by Herod while the Apostle Peter was spared execution.

The only thing we know for sure is; God is too kind to do anything cruel, too wise to make mistakes and too infinite for us to explain His ways.

When our *"Why"* is replaced by *"Who,"* it helps us rest in God's sovereignty, even when our hearts ache with the deafening sound of a crashing aircraft.

He keeps our tears in a bottle.

Precious to Me

"Unto you therefore which believe, He is precious."
I Peter 2:7

The Apostle Peter wrote of *"the trial of our faith being much more precious than of gold,"* a faith founded on *"a living Stone...elect of God and precious."* This is undergirded by "great and precious promises" and fully secured by the "precious blood of Jesus Christ." Peter's repetition of this adjective *"precious"* sums up his personal estimation of the Lord Jesus. His use of the word *"precious"* conveys being *"highly valued or worthy of honour."* The adjective is most appropriate to our great Lord and Saviour, for He is worthy of honour.

Jesus is precious because of the price He paid for us. He did what no one else could do when He redeemed us by His precious blood. *"There was none other good enough to pay the price of sin. He only could unlock the gate of heaven and let us in."*

Jesus is precious because of the power He displayed for us. Jesus, *"the Great Shepherd of the sheep, was brought again from the dead by the blood of the everlasting covenant."* Having paid our debt on the cross, our Saviour entered into death and destroyed death by the blood of His cross.

Jesus is precious because of the place He has prepared for us. The Lord Jesus was known as the Carpenter of Nazareth. He always was a builder. He created the universe and upholds it still. Jesus was the Architect of the first home, and built the first marriage when he brought Adam and Eve together, bound them together and blessed them together. He is not only building His church, but He has also gone to prepare a place for us in the Father's house.

Jesus is precious because of the promises He has given us. Great and precious Bible promises are undergirded by God's faithfulness, and they assure us of His presence with us and His provision and protection for us. Best of all, we have His promise that He will return and take us to be with Him forever.

Jesus, whom having not seen we love, is more precious than words can tell.

His name is like precious ointment.

Following Jesus

"A certain man said unto him, Lord, I will follow Thee whithersoever Thou goest."
Luke 9:57

Jesus often issued the call, "Follow me." Three anonymous men must have heard Him say those words and each answered Jesus, "I want to follow you."

His desire to follow Jesus. The first man said he wanted to follow Jesus wherever He went. Followers of Christ should not say to the Lord, "I want to follow you," until they are ready to say, "wherever Thou goest." Another wanted to follow Jesus whatever the cost. Jesus responded to this man *"Foxes have holes, and birds of the air have nests; but the Son of man hath not where to lay his head."* Jesus was telling him that serving God is seldom without sacrifice. To follow Jesus can be costly. Not the same sacrifices and costs are required from everyone. However, complete surrender to the Saviour means to go wherever He leads and do whatever He commands.

His delay in following Jesus. The second man wanted to follow Jesus but wanted to postpone his commitment until after he buried his father. Too many believers fall into this category. When Jesus asks us to follow, it is to follow Him promptly. It is never right to delay doing what is right.

His distraction from following Jesus. The third man said, *"Lord, I will follow thee; but let me first go bid them farewell, which are at home."* There was nothing wrong with saying goodbye to his family, but Jesus knew the man's problem. His words betrayed him, *"Lord, I will follow thee; but let me first…"* The man had a divided heart, *"follow Thee, but me first…"* It is impossible to be a follower and have a *"me first"* attitude. There are too many *"me first"* Christians. There is only one way to be a follower of the Lord Jesus – full surrender to Him.

Jesus calls for devoted hearts. Jesus called for a personal, prompt and total commitment to Him *"Jesus said unto him, Let the dead bury their dead: but go thou and preach the kingdom of God."*

"No reserve, no retreat, no regrets." William Borden.

12th October

Truth and Love

"Grace be with you, mercy, and peace, from God the Father, and from the Lord Jesus Christ, the Son of the Father, in truth and love."
2 John 1:3

The words "fundamental" and "fundamentalist" have fallen on hard times. Between 1910 and 1915 a series of twelve books containing ninety essays were published by the Bible Institute of Los Angeles. Amongst the editors and contributors were many evangelical leaders of that time including, Drs. R. A. Torrey, B. B. Warfield, A. C. Dixon, Campbell Morgan, and A. T. Pierson. The books were distributed freely to pastors, missionaries, and many Christian workers.

The publications, known as *The Fundamentals - A Testimony to the Truth*, were written to provide a Christian worker resources as a robust defense of the essential Christian doctrines:

> *The inspiration and inerrancy of the Holy Scriptures.*
> *The Virgin birth and full deity of the Lord Jesus Christ.*
> *The sinless nature of Christ and His substitutionary death on Calvary.*
> *The efficacy of the precious blood to atone and to cleanse us from sin.*
> *The bodily resurrection of Christ.*
> *His ascension to glory and present ministry as our heavenly Advocate.*
> *The literal future return of the Lord Jesus to the earth*

In our day of reckless faith, doctrinal compromise and social perversion, there is still a great need to reaffirm the fundamental doctrines of Christianity, especially when a host of groups claiming to be Christian deny the core truths of the Gospel.

This was also a concern to the Apostle John. Light and love were twin themes in all three of his epistles. In 2 John he wrote to a lady who had let her misguided love spill over the boundaries of God's truth and had given hospitality to enemies of the Gospel. If we allow the borders of truth to become eroded, we can fall into a perilous state. Love cannot be separated from truth and neither can truth be separated from love. One must balance and counter-balance the other. Truth and love are eternal qualities which blend and eternally co-exist in God.

If we divorce truth from love we won't have Christian love.

Early Grace

"But Noah found grace in the eyes of the Lord."
Genesis 6:8

Mention the flood of Noah's day, and dozens of questions arise. Did it really occur? How widespread was it? Was it universal? Did the ark hold all those animals? Where did all the water come from? Instead of focusing on these details, the Bible concentrates on Noah and the *favour -- "the grace"* he received from God. Genesis 6:8 gives us the first mention of "grace" in the entire Bible. The ark was a symbol and shadow of the Lord Jesus Christ, the channel of God's grace to Noah as Christ is to us.

The flood of Noah's day was a historical fact to which archaeologists and geologists agree touched all civilisations, everywhere. However, the veracity of the story of Noah, the ark, and the flood do not depend on archaeology or geology. Jesus Christ said, "As it was in the days of Noah, so shall it be also in the day of the coming of the son of man" (Matthew 24:37). Jesus Christ not only spoke of the flood but the social conditions that prevailed in the days preceding the flood.

It was a time of great apostasy. The sons of God took the daughters of men and there was an inter marrying between the sons of God and the daughters of men. Some Bible commentators believe these *"sons of God"* were demon spirits that actually took human wives and their offspring were giants, half-demon and half-human. Others say that the *"sons of God"* were the descendants of the godly line of Seth, who intermarried with the ungodly line of Cain. Whichever, it was a time of unholy alliances.

It was a time of anarchy. "And God saw that the wickedness of man was great in the earth." Mighty men were renowned for their wickedness and sin.

It was a time of apathy. In spite of Noah's preaching, people lived as though tomorrow was going to come just like yesterday had come.

Jesus said, *"As it was in the time of Noah, it will be in the end of the age."*

It must be near the dawning of that day.

14th October

Discouragement

"Blessed is he, whosoever shall not be offended in Me."
Luke 7:23

Discouragement is not only an occupational hazard of the Christian ministry, but it is also a trap into which we can fall too easily. Hudson Taylor said, "Every day, almost every hour, the consciousness of failure and sin oppressed me." No less a figure than John the Baptist seemed to succumb to soul-weakening thoughts of doubt and discouragement.

While he was in prison, John the Baptist's friends told him about the extraordinary works Jesus was doing. Things were not going the way John the Baptist had expected. He possibly thought that he had failed, and his ministry was frustrated. We all feel like that at times. However, when John got discouraged, he did the right thing. He took his problems to the Lord Jesus and waited to hear what Jesus had to say. His messengers asked the Lord Jesus, *"Art thou He that should come? Or look we for another?"* It seems strange that this is the same John who had confidently identified the Lord Jesus by crying, *"Behold, the Lamb of God, Who takes away the sin of the world."*

Did John wonder why Jesus had not mounted a spectacular rescue mission to free him from prison? We are not told, but the very fact that John had questions is helpful to us. It shows us that in spite of his tremendous ministry, John was a man just like us. He knew what it was to be anxious, unsure and discouraged.

After the Lord Jesus heard from John, He did not give the two messengers a lecture in theology or prophecy. He invited them to listen and learn.

The Lord Jesus confirmed John's mission was not in vain. The works that Jesus did vindicated John's ministry. Jesus said. *"Go your way, and tell John what things ye have seen and heard; how that the blind see, the lame walk, the lepers are cleansed, the deaf hear, the dead are raised, to the poor the gospel is preached."*

When discouragement comes, do what John did, take it to the Lord and then listen to His word.

Discouraged? Take it to the Lord in prayer.

15th October

An Open Door

"A great door and effectual is opened unto me,
and there are many adversaries."
1 Corinthians 16:9

The Mission leadership in Brazil invited Wesley and Winnie Gould to open a new Gospel work in Piracuruca, Piauí's second largest city. Although they arrived trusting in God, they soon discovered they were in for a spiritual battle.

No welcome mat was rolled out for their arrival. From the outset, the town's two priests opposed them for speaking about the Bible and were intolerant at the arrival of these new missionaries. This became obvious when the new arrivals tried to rent a house in town. The priests threatened revenge on anyone who dared rent property to these "Protestant heretics."

Wesley and Winnie employed the only means they knew to counter such hostility and spiritual opposition--they prayed and asked friends to pray with them for an open door in the town. In a short while, God answered prayer in an unexpected way. The town's Notary Public was leaving Piracuruca for another place. He was not a religious man and cared nothing about the priests. He offered to rent his large house to the new missionaries. Wesley and Winnie rejoiced at this, for it was in the centre of the town. The priests were furious, but they could do nothing about it.

After taking possession of the property and arranging their living quarters, Wesley turned the property's largest room into a small mission hall. When they started to invite the local people to the meetings Wesley knew that this was the next big spiritual battle. No one dared to venture through the door of their property. The priests had been successful by instilling great fear and intense prejudice in the people's hearts.

Wesley and Winnie decided that if the people of Piracuruca would not come to their house, then they would go to the people. Armed with Gospel literature and a lamp, the two missionaries conducted open-air meetings all over town. There were no Christians to stand with them as yet, and the opposition persisted. In God's time, converts came to Christ, and a church was soon established.

Spiritual darkness can never withstand the glorious light of the Gospel.

Reasons to Love the Lord

"I love the Lord, because he hath heard my voice and my supplications."
Psalm 116:1

A popular song of yesteryear begins, "I could give a thousand reasons as to why I love you." I thought of those words when reading the first line of Psalm 116; "*I love the Lord because…*" Every Christian should have a thousand reasons to love the Lord. It is a worthwhile exercise to sit and ponder on reasons why we love Him.

We love Him because He created us. God created us in His own image. We were created not only by Him but for Him, to know Him and have a loving relationship with Him.

We love Him because He commands us to love Him. The first and great commandment is to "love the Lord thy God with all *thine heart, and with all thy soul, and with all thy might.*" In so doing we can enjoy that full relationship with God.

We love Him because of His concern for us. He pays such attention to us that He knows our thoughts, the number of the hairs on our heads and is aware of everything we need.

We love Him because He came for us. The greatest verse in the Bible reminds us, "For *God so loved the world that He gave His only begotten Son.*" The Father sent the Son because He loved us, and Jesus came because He loved us, too.

We love Him because He was crucified for us. Consider the words of the Apostle Paul, Jesus was "*the Son of God, who loved me, and gave Himself for me*" (Galatians 2:20).

We love Him because of the confidence that He is our heavenly Advocate. He prays for us, and in Him, we are accepted. Before the throne of God above, we have a strong and perfect Priest.

We love Him because He is coming for us. He has prepared a place for us in His Father's house and has promised to return for His redeemed.

Above all else, we love Him because He first loved us.

Is there any reason why people should not love Him?

Standing Firm

"I am doing a great work, so that I cannot come down."
Nehemiah 6:3

Nehemiah was not a preacher, a prophet, or a miracle worker. He was simply a worker who was faithful at his job, a cupbearer to the King. While living in Shushan and serving the king in the palace, his thoughts were back in his homeland, Jerusalem, which was in a mess. In 586 BC Jerusalem had been destroyed and burned, and the people had been carried away to Babylon. Some had returned to rebuild the temple with Ezra and to worship Jehovah. The new temple did not have the former glory of the latter.

The walls of the city were in total disrepair. City walls were critical to keep marauders out and give protection to the population. When Nehemiah heard about the state of Jerusalem, his heart was heavy. He not only prayed, he felt that he needed to do something. He was not obliged to do anything, but felt he could not continue drinking wine for the King when Jerusalem was in such disarray. God opened the door for him to return to Jerusalem and rebuild those broken-down walls.

Why is the story of Nehemiah from 2000 years ago important to us today? We may be trying to rebuild our lives, our families, or our churches. Rebuilding is hard work, and too often too many people give up too soon. If God has called you to do a job, finish what you have started and refuse to lose heart. God will never give up on you.

Stay focused on what you are doing. Nehemiah had to conquer two challenges--He had to obey God and build Jerusalem's walls, and he had to contend with his enemies and defend God's cause.

Stay faithful to who you are. Nehemiah refused to compromise the principles of his godly life or be diverted from God's calling. Who we are is more important than what we do.

Stay firm in what you believe. Nehemiah kept at the work at Jerusalem's walls because he believed Jehovah's word. As soon as the work was completed, Ezra read the Word of God to the people.

To stand firm, stand on God's promises.

Reconciled

*"Esau ran to meet him, and embraced him, and fell on his neck,
and kissed him: and they wept."*
Genesis 33:4

The above text is in the middle of a wonderful story of repentance, forgiveness, and reconciliation. Two brothers, Jacob and Esau, had been at odds with each other for more than twenty years. This was a moment of reconciliation.

Imagine the scene. Esau was sitting on his horse looking down the road at his brother approaching. Jacob took a few steps towards Esau and then bowed. He took another few more steps and bowed again. With every step and with every bow, Jacob without words was saying, "I am sorry. Please forgive me. I have done wrong." It was a humiliating experience for Jacob. His wives were watching: his children and servants were observing his every move. But it was what he had to do.

How tragic it is when spiritual brothers and sisters are divided? How troubling when someone carries a bitter grudge and an unforgiving attitude for years. It is sad when Christians fail to get along with one another.

It is said that when the British and French were fighting in Canada in the 1750's, Admiral Phipps, commander of the British fleet, was told to anchor outside Quebec. He was given orders to wait for the British land forces to arrive, then support them when they attacked the city. As the admiral waited, the statues of the saints that adorned the towers of a nearby cathedral annoyed him. He commanded his men to shoot at them with the ship's cannons. No one knows how many rounds were fired or how many statues were knocked down. When the land forces arrived, the admiral was of no help. He had used up all of his ammunition shooting at the "saints." Many believers are so busy shooting at other believers they are useless in the real battle of life.

Jesus Christ said, *"If ye forgive men their trespasses, your heavenly Father will also forgive you: But if ye forgive not men their trespasses, neither will your Father forgive your trespasses."*

Solemn thought; we will not be forgiven of God if we fail to forgive others.

Heavenly Son Shine

"We are ambassadors for Christ."
2 Corinthians 5:20

There are no mistakes with God. Someone *"by mistake"* left a Bible at a petrol station. Glen Bowden, on the night shift, picked it up and began to read the Scriptures through the night. The next day, he shared the incident with a customer who had recently been converted after a lengthy stretch in prison. This friend invited Glen to Templemore Hall on the following Sunday and arranged to meet him before the service. Glen turned up as had been agreed, but the convert did not. Not to be deterred, Glen went to Templemore Hall alone and found an inconspicuous place to sit.

At the end of the evangelistic service, while others filed out, Glen remained seated. After approaching him and asking his name, I enquired if he was a Christian. When he answered in the negative, I further asked if he wanted to trust Jesus Christ. It was a joy that night to hear Glen Bowden call upon God for mercy and trust Christ as Saviour. The *"mistake"* of losing a Bible resulted in Glen's conversion.

After *"finding his feet"* with the young people in Templemore Hall, he made Newtownbreda Baptist Church his new church home. Fired with zeal to share his faith with others, Glen travelled to Camp Sonshine, Maryland, USA, to train as a Christian counselor. During the next five years, Glen developed his communication skills and progressed from being a counselor to become the Camp's Assistant Director.

In 2001 Newtownbreda Baptist Church invited Glen to become youth pastor alongside Pastor Fred McClaughlin. His first three years in this role were concurrent with his studies at the Irish Baptist College. The skills learned in the USA prompted Glen to conduct similar annual camps in Northern Ireland. God richly blessed this work, and dozens of young people were converted.

Amazingly, God opened the door for Glen to visit his friend, Mark Loney, in the Algarve, Portugal, to engage in more camp ministry. After twelve years as youth pastor, Glen became a missionary with Acre International, and at the annual Camp Sonshine in the Algarve, hundreds of young people are reached with the Gospel.

Let the Son shine.

Weak Vessels

"We have this treasure in earthen vessels, that the excellency of the power may be of God, and not of us."
2 Corinthians 4:7

Numerous Brazilian merchants travelled on wood-burning river-launches for hundreds of miles to the upper River Xingu buying rubber latex and Brazil nuts as they went. Sometimes Wesley Gould travelled on these vessels to reach the people who lived in small and isolated settlements. Wherever the launch stopped to take on firewood he conducted a Gospel witness for the passengers and people who lived nearby. Sustenance on board was always the usual rice and beans. Drinking water came straight from the river without being filtered.

With hygiene being virtually zero, Wesley and the other passengers were vulnerable to picking up intestinal infections. After a few days on one of these trips, he became ill with amoebic dysentery. He had planned to travel as far as a Kayapo village, evangelising as he went. However, this tummy bug changed his plans.

When the launch arrived at a village at the mouth of the River Fresco, Wesley could go no farther. Due to the constant and severe pains in his stomach, he was forced to stay in the village while the boat continued upriver. A kind and elderly lady offered a room to Wesley in her humble home and cared for him while he waited for the launch to return.

In spite of this lady's attention, Wesley continued to deteriorate. He was suffering so much pain he was sure death was imminent. He called upon God, and as he did, he knew that friends and supporters back home would be praying for him without knowing his plight.

God answered those prayers. Out of the blue, a man arrived who just happened to have medicine for dysentery. Wesley gladly took what was offered to him, and in a few days, he improved. By the time the launch arrived, Wesley was feeling a lot better and well enough to travel to Altamira.

When he arrived back in town, the believers at the church could scarcely recognize him since he had lost about seven kilos of weight.

The treasure is precious, even though the vessel may be weak.

God's Work Is not Easy

"Salute the beloved Persis, which laboured much in the Lord."
Romans 16:12

While living in Altamira, Wesley Gould invited Chico to travel down river with him to preach the Gospel at the "Gold Mines." He knew these men needed God more than they needed gold.

The swift current helped them travelling downstream, but they faced danger while passing through the perilous rapids where rocks and submerged trees were a constant hazard. Although they survived the rapids, water got into their outboard motor making it splutter and cough until they finally arrived at the Gold Mines.

They were welcomed to a friend's simple house. After an evening meal, Chico and Wesley brought the outboard motor into the house to dry it out. Chico poured the petrol out of the motor into an open can while Wesley held a Tilly Lamp to throw light on the operation. Suddenly, there was a burst of flames as the petrol fumes ignited. Everyone in the house screamed and ran for the door, except the man of the house. He darted to his bedroom to retrieve his suitcase where he undoubtedly kept his money and other valuables.

Wesley dragged the outboard motor outside into the night air. When he saw flames licking around the bottom of the petrol cans, he bravely ran in again and dragged them outside. Wesley escaped serious injury when the cans exploded and threw flames into the air.

People rushed with pots and tins of water to help put the fire out. Sadly, everything inside the house was destroyed. Wesley felt sorry and quite embarrassed about the incident, but he was also touched by the man's kind reaction. Even though he was not a Christian, the man still showed goodwill and gave them hospitality. Wesley tried to recompense the friend for his loss as best he could.

Without fuel, Wesley and Chico had to paddle their canoe upstream for several days to Altamira. It had been a hard and eventful trip, but they were glad they had taken the risk to plant the precious seed of God's Word in the hearts of these people.

Missionary mishaps are not uncommon.

Hardness

"Endure hardness, as a good soldier of Jesus Christ."
2 Timothy 2:3

Step by step Wesley and Winnie Gould's practical work in Piracuruca helped them establish their Gospel witness. Late one day, some people arrived from Brasileira, a village more than forty kilometres away, to ask Winnie for urgent help. A lady in their village was experiencing some complications in childbirth. The only means of transport for Wesley and Winnie was on a railway trolley, hand-operated by two men pushing levers up and down. They were cautioned to be careful of jaguars coming out of the forest to drink in a stream at night, as they often did.

Thankfully, the journey was uneventful and without any danger. Furthermore, Winnie's aid was greatly appreciated by the family when a baby was safely born.

Wesley's dental skills helped relieve some people from toothaches. These gestures enabled them to build some local friendships, but even then these friends were hesitant to attend any meetings.

Wherever the missionaries went the two priests followed with a mob to disrupt the open-air meetings. They incited the crowd to create a racket to try to drown Wesley's voice. They also retrieved any Gospel literature the missionaries might have distributed, and on several occasions, burned Bibles, Gospel booklets and leaflets on a public bonfire--such was their hostility to the Gospel.

Wesley and Winnie's next-door neighbours were supporters of the priests. Their children followed the Goulds around the town and then ran to inform the priests where the missionaries had an open-air meeting. The priests soon arrived to disperse anyone who might be standing nearby. Some people ran away for fear of them, and those who remained were harassed by the clerics.

Through all this persecution Wesley was mindful of Paul's exhortation to Timothy to *"endure hardness . . . Preach the word; be instant in season, out of season."*

Preaching God's Word was certainly out of season in Piracuruca, but God honoured their work and witness. Dona Francisca was the first person to trust the Lord in Piracuruca, and many followed. She is still looked upon as the mother of that church.

Christians are chosen to be soldiers.

23rd October

My Strength

"I will love Thee, O Lord, my strength.
Psalm 18:1

The Psalms have been likened to a mountain range in the centre of the Bible. They take us to high mountains of praise and joy, guide us along the paths of righteousness and comfort us through the dark valleys of suffering and sorrow. God gives us melodies for sunny days and songs for dark nights.

Like all mountain ranges, some peaks are higher than others. For that reason, we all have our favourite Psalms that have met us in particular circumstances or expressed our emotional or spiritual condition.

Psalm 18 is one of those mountain-top songs. Here David not only praises God for victory and deliverance from his enemies, but he also speaks of repeated affirmations and assurances. In the opening two verses, he uses the personal pronoun *"my"* nine times and descriptive words for his relationship with God seven times: *"I will love thee, O Lord, my strength. The Lord is my rock, and my fortress, and my deliverer; my God, my strength, in whom I will trust; my buckler, and the horn of my salvation, and my high tower."* It is true to say that true religion is made up of personal pronouns.

God is Almighty. To say the Lord is my strength is to experience His omnipotence in our lives.

The Lord is my strength for worship: -- *"I will love thee, O Lord, my strength"* (v.1). Love for Christ is the pinnacle of our worship.

The Lord is my strength for the way. -- *"It is God that girdeth me with strength, and maketh my way perfect* (v.32). His way and wisdom are always perfect, and He perfects our ways.

The Lord is my strength in warfare. -- *"For Thou hast girded me with strength, unto the battle"* (v.39). Our adversary, the devil, is out to steal and destroy, but Jesus Christ is stronger than Satan and sin.

The Lord is my strength for witness. -- *"The Lord liveth; and blessed be my rock; and let the God of my salvation be exalted"* (v.46). Our witness is that Jesus Christ is alive today.

Strength for today is mine all the way.

Martyrs

"And thou, son of man, be not afraid of them … be not afraid of their words, nor dismayed at their looks … Thou shalt speak my words unto them."
Ezekiel 2:6

Wesley Gould felt honoured and challenged when he went to live in Altamira, the principal town on the River Xingu, one of the five tributaries of the Amazon that are over 1,000 miles long. Not only did his hero, Horace Banner work with the Kayapo Indians on a tributary of the Xingu, but it was among the Kayapos that three UFM missionaries were martyred.

The Kayapos are the largest indigenous group and are distinguished by the men having large disks inserted into their lower lips, colourful paints on their bodies and feathers in their hair.

In the 1930s three missionaries, Fred Dawson, Fred Roberts, both from Australia, and Fred Wright from Northern Ireland, spent more than a year trying to make friendly contact with this tribe. In May 1935, they travelled upriver from Altamira for four days then fifteen more by canoe on the River Nova Olinda to reach the Indians. They never returned.

Fred Wright wrote to his family in Northern Ireland:
At the moment of writing, we are at the last outpost of civilisation. Within two days we shall be up to the Riozlnho. We have been two weeks travelling up the Xingu River, and we are lumps from head to foot from the bites of terrible insects.

Fred Roberts wrote home to Australia:
Within a few weeks we shall be outside of civilisation; then we shall purchase a canoe, fit the motor, don coats of galvanised iron, and the search for Indians will begin. We shall be the first white men to intrude upon the freedom of these Indians. Therefore, we are fully aware that, humanly speaking, we are already as good as dead men.

Horace Banner and Willie (Jock) Johnston eventually found some belongings and the battered canoe of the three martyred missionaries.

In the wake of this martyrdom, God spoke to Horace Banner by today's verse. He and his wife Eva, dedicated the rest of their lives taking the Gospel to the Kayapos.

Treasures of great worth.

25th October

On the Mat

"From a young child thou hast known the Holy Scriptures."
2 Timothy 3:15

When a ground sheet was spread on the grass in the middle of a housing estate one summer's evening, children from the surrounding houses rushed to squat and secure their place on the sheet. The local CEF evangelist quickly got their attention by holding up high a large chorus book and leading the children in heartily singing a Gospel song.

The evangelist and his workers also taught Bible memory verses each night and for five consecutive evenings gave them a Bible lesson. Those Christian workers could not have known that amongst the children God was speaking to the heart of young Karen McKibben, and He had a special future for her. Her Sunday school teacher was also praying for her, and a friend took her to the weekly children's meetings at a local church.

Through time this sowing of the Gospel resulted in Karen's mother and two sisters trusting Christ as Saviour, but Karen was resistant to the message. She knew she needed Christ and that her mum and friends were praying for her. A crisis arose when news came through that her eleven-year-old cousin had been killed in a tragic road accident. Karen and all the family were stunned and saddened beyond words.

That sense of loss and alarm about the nearness of eternity touched the fourteen-year-old Karen deeply. Still influenced by all she had heard at the CEF meetings, she attended a Youth Challenge Camp in Kilkeel. Former missionaries, Bob and Alma McAllister, shared their testimony of the tragic times they had experienced in Africa, but how God had delivered them. Karen could hold out no longer, and at that camp, she asked the Lord Jesus to save her.

Her family was greatly helped and influenced in their Christian lives by Rev. Robert and Mrs. Jasmine Courtney in Ballynahinch. Many young people in their church were zealous for the Saviour, and some entered Christian work. Karen qualified as a nurse before going to the Faith Mission Bible College. After many fruitful years of Christian service, she and her husband, Keith Lindsay, continue to serve God with Acre International.

A simple seed can give a great harvest.

A Great Price

"For My name's sake hast laboured, and hast not fainted."
Revelation 2:3

Wesley Gould and Charlie Thompson finally arrived at the Indian village in Sapucaia. They were disappointed to find only a handful of Indians in two separate villages. Most of them were sick. Sadly, over the years, repeated epidemics of various sicknesses without medicines had resulted in most of the Indians dying.

After treating the sick, the missionaries were able to give a simple Gospel message. Most of them had never heard of Jesus and probably would never hear again. The missionaries' hearts went out to these dear souls who were living in spiritual darkness: they were reluctant to leave them. There was no one else to give them the message of salvation through Christ.

While there Wesley and Charlie searched in the forest for the graves of Mrs. Roberts and Fenton Hall, missionaries who had died while trying to evangelize this tribe. Their search was in vain. The Indians had no idea where the missionaries had been buried.

Fred Roberts had written home to his friends in Australia of the rigors and dangers of their early days when he and his wife tried to reach these people for Christ:

Many times I have had to make a journey with a high fever and a splitting headache. Then one often comes to a swamp that takes half an hour to cross. We are glad when we get to the other side, to be able to crawl out of the foul-smelling water, often infested with the cannibal fish, electric eels, stingrays, and the dreaded Anaconda snake, so huge that it can swallow a man with ease.

But, for the missionary travelling alone, except for the company of an Indian guide, there is a harder experience still. As the night closes about him there is an awful sense of loneliness and dread. We have known missionaries in such conditions to throw themselves on the ground, and sob after sob would break forth from an overwrought heart.

Wesley and Charlie bowed their heads and remembered the great price that had been paid and the sacrifice of devotion to reach the lost for Christ.

Jesus Christ is worthy.

In Christ Alone

"The just shall live by his faith."
Habakkuk 2:4

In an Art Museum in Switzerland hangs a painting that arrests the attention of many. A monk is stooped over an Open Bible. A ray of sunlight streams into the cloistered room illuminating the page where the monk has placed his bony finger at a Bible verse: *"The just shall live by faith."* That statement, repeated only four times in the Bible, was the verse that transformed the life of that monk and ushered in the great Protestant Reformation.

That monk, Martin Luther, was born on 10th November 1483 in Eisleben, Germany. His father was a copper miner. Luther studied Law at the University of Erfurt, but in 1505 he decided to become an Augustinian friar. After he was ordained in 1507, he began teaching at the University of Wittenberg and in 1512 was made a Doctor of Theology.

In 1510 he visited Rome on behalf of some Augustinian monasteries. While there he was appalled by the corruption he found in the "Eternal City." Luther ascended the steps of the Scala Sancta on his knees, repeating the Lord's Prayer and kissing each step in the hope of finding peace with God. As he ascended the staircase, the Scriptures kept resounding in his conscience, *"The just shall live by faith."* Halfway up he stopped and walked back down in protest at the veneration of such relics. He became increasingly angry about corrupt clergy selling "indulgences" by which were promised the remission from punishments or forgiveness of sins for someone still living or for one who had died and was believed to be in purgatory.

Luther had discovered that Christians are saved through faith in Christ and not through their own efforts.

In 1534, he published a complete translation of the Bible into German, underlining his belief that people should be able to read it in their own language. Luther's fame and influence spread across Northern Europe and made Wittenberg an intellectual centre. The great Reformer died on 18th February 1546 in Eisleben, his hometown.

The hallmark of the Reformation was this: Salvation is by grace alone, through faith alone, in Christ alone.

That same message still stands today.

God is Sovereign

"Why dost Thou shew me iniquity, and cause me to behold grievance?"
Habakkuk 1:3

The prophet Habakkuk has been called "the grandfather of the Reformation." He introduced the phrase that moved the heart of Martin Luther – *"The just shall live by faith."* The same text is repeated three times in the New Testament: in Romans, Galatians and Hebrews.

Little is known about the life and background of the prophet who lived more than 500 years before our Saviour's birth. He had priestly origins and was a singer in the Levitical Choir. His name means "embrace" or "to wrestle." This was an appropriate name for this man who wrestled with a series of questions about the mystery of God's plan after Israel had been invaded and overrun by the Chaldeans.

At the end of World War II, Dr. Martyn Lloyd Jones preached a series of messages based on Habakkuk's prophecy in response to the anguish of the nation in the aftermath of war. These were later published in a book named *From Fear to Faith.* He set in place some principles:

God has a Plan. - regardless of how it seems to us. In the turmoil of our times, things are not always as they appear to be. The events of history are not accidental. They are following God's plan.

God has a timetable in His Plan. "Lord, how long shall I cry..?" God answered with, *"The vision is yet for an appointed time"* (2:3). God has a timetable, and it is just on time.

God has power to accomplish His plan. "I will raise up the Chaldeans..." Every nation is under the control of the hand of God. There is no power in the world that is not controlled by Him. Never lose sight of the fact that the nations before God are as grasshoppers in His sight, as dust on the scales, as a drop in a bucket" (Isaiah 40:13-15).

God has a place for you in His plan. Each of God's children is His workmanship created unto good works that God foreordained.

God is still on the throne, and He will remember His own

When Jesus Is At Home

"It was noised that He was in the house."
Mark 2:1

After communion with the Father in secret the Lord Jesus returned to Capernaum, and Mark wrote of Him, "He was in the house." The Portuguese Bible we use in Brazil says, *"He was at home in the house."* This does not suggest that it was His house. This was possibly Simon Peter's house where Jesus had healed all the sick at the close of the previous day. We need not speculate about whose house it was, for that was not vital. The most important thing is that Jesus was there and that He was at home in that house.

When Paul prayed for the Ephesians he asked "that Christ may dwell in your hearts by faith." Paul's prayer is exactly what Mark conveyed, that Jesus might be "more and more at home in your hearts."

Because Jesus was at home:

The Son of God was present. It is always a great thing when Jesus is the chief attraction in a home, in a church or in a life. The hungry came to hear Him, the hurting came for help, and the religionists were there to hinder, but the Priest who is greater than the Temple was there. Here is a Prophet who was greater than Jonah and a King who was greater than Solomon. His presence was central in the house.

The Word of God was preached. "And He preached the word unto them." Before the healing of a body there was the hearing of the Word. The miracle that followed involved the body, but our greatest and deepest needs are not physical, they are spiritual. Note that it was not only preaching, but preaching of the Word of God.

The power of God was seen. Luke wrote, *"the power of the Lord was present to heal"* (Luke 5:17). Jesus majored on the forgiveness of the man's sin more than on the healing of his sickness.

The glory of God abounded. *"They were all amazed, and glorified God."* "Unto Him be glory in the church by Christ Jesus throughout all ages, world without end. Amen" (Ephesians 3:21)

Man's chief end is to glorify God.

Privileges Wasted

*"For the Lord will not forsake His people for His great name's sake:
because it hath pleased the Lord to make you his people."*
1 Samuel 12:22

Samuel's first book ends an era of more than 300 years when the Judges ruled in Israel and begins the 500 year period of the kings. Samuel himself was the last of the judges, and he introduced Israel's first king.

One feature of his book is that it is mostly about great men with great beginnings but poor endings. We can see this in the aged priest Eli who served in God's house but failed to control his own family. Likewise, King Saul, Israel's first king, was tall and good looking, but he ended his life in shame. King Solomon, the wisest man in all the earth, played the fool with his life.

It broke Samuel's heart that Israel demanded a king to rule over them so that they could be like the surrounding nations. Samuel maintained that God was the true Ruler of Israel, and that He was sufficient. God allowed the people to have their choice and Saul was designated to be king.

At the coronation, Samuel gave some assurances and advice to Israel and the king:

A great promise to lean on. God's promise assured them that they were the Lord's choice: "*It pleased the Lord to make you His people.*" Israel was also the Lord's concern, "*For His great namesake…*" They were assured of the Lord's company, "*He will not forsake His people.*"

A great principle to live by. In your heart, "*Only fear the Lord.*" With your hand, "*Serve Him in truth.*" With your head, "*Consider how great things He hath done for you.*"

A great part he would play. Samuel was not cutting them adrift; He saw there was a vital role for him to play: "*God forbid that I should sin against the Lord in ceasing to pray for you.*"

King Saul was an enigma: called of God, anointed with holy oil, given another heart, and numbered among the prophets, but he played the fool, died in shame and was nailed to the city walls at Beth-shan.

Count your blessings and don't waste your life.

The Fiery Furnace

*"Our God whom we serve is able to deliver us
from the burning fiery furnace."*
Daniel 3:17

Daniel 3 tells the story of the three Hebrew children, Shadrach, Meshach, and Abednego. Although called, "children," these Hebrew boys were men of faith and valour. The great lesson of this chapter is that faith always conquers the fiery furnaces of life. The Apostle Peter wrote, "Think it not strange concerning the fiery trial that is to try you."

King Nebuchadnezzar constructed a golden image for everyone to bow down and worship. This was an act of rebellion against God to unify all religions, a form of syncretism.

To disobey the King's command brought instant death in a fiery furnace. The threat certainly helped people make up their minds about what they should do. When the King gave the word, all Babylon turned out to obey - all except these three Hebrew boys. While multitudes grovelled to a man-made image, these three worshipped the God of heaven.

Their devotion - they would not bend. Often to stand up means to stand out. These three stood out by refusing to bow down to the image. We live in an age of peer pressure on young people. Pray that God will help them stand up for Jesus.

Their determination - they would not budge. They answered the king, *"Our God whom we serve is able to deliver us from the burning fiery furnace … But if not, … We will not serve thy gods, nor worship the golden image which thou hast set up."*

Their deliverance - they would not burn. The king was astonished, *"Lo, I see four men loose, walking in the midst of the fire, and they have no hurt; and the form of the fourth is like the Son of God."*

Although they were bound when they were thrown into the furnace, they were walking in the midst of the flame. The only things that burned were the fetters that bound them. Three men went into the furnace, but four were seen. Four people were seen in the flame, but only three emerged.

The Son of Man is always with us in the fire.

November

Elephant Rock, Ballintoy

Balance

"I therefore … beseech you that ye walk worthy of the vocation wherewith ye are called."
Ephesians 4:1

E ver hear about the man who thought something had gone wrong with his gait until he discovered he was walking with one foot on the high footpath and the other on the road. Balance is a wonderful thing. We need it every day in our lives. It is what children learn when they begin to walk or ride a bicycle. We are all encouraged to eat a balanced diet. While it is true that we all need balance and equilibrium, sadly, we do not always display such balance when it comes to our Christian lives. We all can be guilty of pushing some things to such an extreme that may cause instability and failure.

All of Paul's letters contain a beautiful equilibrium between doctrine and duty, a healthy balance between belief and behaviour. Ephesians is the perfect example of this. The first three chapters address doctrine--our riches in Christ Jesus. The last three chapters explain our duties--our responsibilities in Christ.

Paul wrote of the Christian life as a "walk". In this we must consider balance. Our spiritual experience springs from and should be governed by the great truths of the Scriptures. Our daily progress of life in Christ is made by taking simple and practical steps, one after another, following the Saviour. As in every walk, some steps will be greater than others, a few may be harder than others, and some may lead to higher ground than others, but each step must always be made by stepping on Gospel truth.

Since we as believers have been adopted as God's own children, sealed with His Holy Spirit of promise unto the day of redemption, given a great inheritance in Christ our Lord, made part of the glorious body of Jesus Christ who is Lord over all, lavished by God's incomparable love, saved by His amazing grace and brought into fellowship with all God's family, Paul taught that we ought to have a balanced walk to fully live out the glorious truths of the Gospel in mature relationships--in our homes, in our work place, in the Christian fellowship and in the world.

Blessed are the balanced.

Striving for the Gospel

"Yea, so have I strived to preach the Gospel, not where Christ was named."
Romans 15:20

Wesley Gould and Charlie Thompson planned to visit the Guajajara Indians in the Sapucaia on the upper River Pindaré Mirim, Brazil.

As far back as the 1930s, there had been a mission station there. Mr. and Mrs. Fred Roberts from Australia had arrived there in 1925 and had worked with these Indians. Sadly, Mrs. Roberts had been struck down with fever and had died while working with the tribe. She was buried there. Her husband joined Fred Dawson and Fred Wright to reach the Kayapo Indians with the Gospel. The Kayapos killed these three missionaries in 1936.

Fenton Hall, also from Northern Ireland, before becoming a missionary, had been a champion boxer in the British Army. He also died amongst these Guajajara Indians less than six months after arriving in Brazil.

Wesley and Charlie expected the trip would take about six days. Paddling the canoe against a strong upstream current and cutting their way through fallen trees was hard work. At night they slung their hammocks between the trees and lit a fire to ward off wild, and prowling animals. A strange feeling of isolation and loneliness was accentuated by the unsettling sounds of insects, and the agonizing cries of the howler monkeys echoing in the night.

By day swarms of sand flies tortured the intrepid travellers as they sat in the canoe in the hot sun hour after hour. Each bite left a little bump on the victim's skin, and this soon began to itch. Wesley got so many of these bites, he thought he would go crazy. At sunset, the sand flies were replaced by dreaded malaria-carrying mosquitoes.

Wesley and Charlie's troubles were compounded when they ran out of rice and beans. To survive, they caught fish, monkey, and tapir which they cooked over an open fire. At midday and before dark they stopped to cool off and wash in the river, careful not to disturb an unsuspecting crocodile or a school of piranha fish.

All this effort to reach the Guajajara Indians with the Gospel.

In Jesus Name and for His sake.

The Scapegoat

"But the goat, on which the lot fell to be the scapegoat, shall be presented alive before the Lord, to make an atonement with him, and to let him go for a scapegoat into the wilderness."
Leviticus 16:10

When we read of the "wilderness," we generally imagine a barren and desolate place. Moses spent forty years tending his father-in-law's sheep in the desert. It was there he met God at the burning bush. For forty years he led the children of Israel through the desert. Our Saviour spent forty days and nights fasting in the wilderness where He was tempted by and overcame the devil.

Tourists to Israel occasionally visit Jebbel Muntar in the Judean Desert. It is the highest peak in the Judean Wilderness. Jebbel Muntar is Arabic for "lookout mountain." Amongst Jews it is believed to be the "Cliff of the Scapegoat" and is associated with Yom Kippur, the Day of Atonement. On that most holy of days, a "sacred lottery" took place. This involved two goats and two lots, one assigned to each goat. One lot read, "for the Lord." That goat was sacrificed in the Temple.

The other lot read, "for Azazel," "for the wilderness." Over that goat, the high priest confessed his sins and those of Israel. The goat was led out of the Temple courtyard, through the Eastern Gate, up and over the Mount of Olives.

The goat was led out into the wilderness of Judea carrying all the sins of Israel. At Jebbel Muntar, it was hurled over the precipice so that it took with it all the sins laid upon it.

This ritual was an alteration of the earlier Israelite practice of releasing the goat out into the wilderness, as taught in Leviticus 16. Some think that the priests feared that the goat bearing all the sins of Israel would wander back to haunt them. So they hurled the scapegoat over this precipice.

This ritual reminds me that the people of Nazareth led the Lord Jesus "to the brow of the hill whereon their city was built, that they might cast Him down headlong" (Luke 4:29).

Our Saviour's blood cleanses us from all sin – forever.

4th November

Why Worry?

"Be careful for nothing; but in every thing by prayer and supplication with thanksgiving let your requests be made known unto God."
Philippians 4:6

Although the word "worry" does not occur in the KJV Bible, other words are used – anxiety and care. Worry is probably the most universal of all addictions. Anxiety has become so acceptable we can hardly imagine a life without it, and sadly, we fail to recognise worry as a sin. The Lord Jesus did. In the Sermon on the Mount He made an assault on worry and worriers when He repeatedly said, "Take no thought for your life … for your raiment … for what you shall eat … for the morrow" (Matthew 6:25-34). His Word is an antidote to our worries.

Paul wrote in the same vein in Philippians 4:6, "Be careful for nothing; but in every thing by prayer and supplication…" Someone penned these words, "Whenever you are in a fix, remember Philippians 4:6." This is a good rhyme to memorise.

Worry can gnaw at our hearts until it destroys our lives and steals our joy, strength, and energy. However, worry evaporates when we cast our burdens on Him. Instead of carrying these cares, it is to better to carry them to God in prayer.

Paul's prescription for a troubled heart -- Be anxious for nothing. The Bible does not downplay our problems. In fact, it tells us quite plainly that problems will stalk us as long as we live in this world. We battle with them every day, but we must learn to let the Lord carry the pressure. Worry insinuates that God is not adequate, and it doubts His ability.

Paul's Prayer with a trusting heart -- Be prayerful in everything. It is good to turn your worry list into a prayer list. Whatever agitates, frightens, or becomes a burden to us, we can place in God's hands.

Paul's Praise with a thankful heart -- Be grateful for anything. Regardless of the situations we may face, we can learn to praise the Lord through them all. Nothing drives the devil away any faster than a genuinely thankful heart.

The trusting heart is a grateful heart.

A Bereaved Widow

*"When the Lord saw her, he had compassion on her,
and said unto her, 'Weep not.'"*
Luke 7:9

As a young preacher, Dwight L. Moody was invited to conduct a funeral. He studied how Jesus conducted funerals, and to his surprise, he discovered that the Lord Jesus interrupted every funeral He attended. He reversed death to raised people to life again. It happened to Lazarus in Bethany and to a twelve-year-old girl in Capernaum.

Jesus also stopped a funeral procession on the way to the cemetery in Nain when He raised a widow's only son to life again. On that day no one knew that the Lord was coming to town. He had not been invited, but thankfully, He arrived just in time.

There was a peculiar sadness in the bereavement of this nameless widow. This was "the only son of his mother." Mourners accompanied the lone woman, but they could not help her. Jesus approached: ignoring circumstance and ceremony, He touched the dead boy and commanded him to sit up.

The Saviour's compassion for the widow. Looking at the widow Jesus said, "Do not weep." His words might sound inappropriate in her circumstances. Having already suffered the loss of her husband she was left destitute. Any hopes for the future were dashed with the death of her only son. Her home was empty, and all hope was gone. The compassionate Christ knows all about our sorrows.

The Saviour's command to the dead son. "Young man, I say to you, arise." In full view of many witnesses, Jesus asserted His authority over sin and death and called for resurrection. Fear and awe must have swept through the onlookers as the young man sat up and began to speak. Jesus presented him alive to his mother. With that same voice, the Saviour will command the dead in Christ to be raised.

The Saviour's conquest over death. Two lines of people met head-on that day. The followers of Jesus, the Prince of Life, encountered the procession of death. On that day the Prince of Life conquered death.

Why fear death when you know the Prince of Life.

Bonds Across Borders

"Fervent in Spirit, serving the Lord."
Romans 12:11

Over a cup of coffee at the Rio Sul Shopping in Seixal, Portugal, Keith Lindsay and I met Barry and Raquel Henry. We soon discovered that this young couple had a passion to serve God in Portugal even though it would mean a big adjustment for them and their three children.

Barry was born and raised in Southern Ireland. Although his parents had been associated with the Jehovah Witnesses, they were converted to Christ later by the grace of God. Anxious for their family's spiritual welfare, Mr. and Mrs. Henry taught the Scriptures to their four children at home and in church. Barry trusted Christ as Saviour as a young teenager and showed initial signs of spiritual growth. Alas, he strayed from that early Gospel fervency when he moved out of the family home. However, his parents never ceased to pray for him.

In September 1995 Barry's father said to him, "Pity you weren't at the meeting yesterday. A good-looking exchange student from Portugal was there. I would love you to meet her." The mention of "a good-looking girl" was enough to kindle an immediate encouragement in Barry to attend church the next Sunday.

Raquel was that overseas student who had arrived in Limerick to develop her language skills. Born into a Christian home in Portugal, Raquel had trusted Christ as Saviour as a young girl. During her teacher training studies she was sent to Ireland to develop her use of English. Besides acquiring a good Irish accent, Raquel also met her Irish sweetheart. By the end of her four months study assignment, Barry and Raquel had fallen deeply in love, committed to each other and to the Lord.

After their marriage on 10th August 1998, they moved to Portugal where Barry obtained a degree in modern languages. Although Barry engaged in Christian work in Seixal, he was deeply challenged by his involvement in the annual Bible Camp ministry in the Algarve. Consequently, they stepped out of their employment to serve God.

Barry and Raquel and their children, Matthew, David, and Rebecca, are fully serving the Saviour with Acre International at the International Church in Loulé, Portugal.

Pray for them.

Compassionate

"The Lord is gracious, and full of compassion."
Psalm 145:8

North Belfast has produced some great missionaries. Five members of the Munn family from York Street went to serve God in Europe and Africa. Lily Boal from the same area went to India with WEC, and Nell Shannon went to Brazil. Cathy Cowan grew up on Belfast's Shore Road in a family of four brothers and four sisters. The family belonged to the nearby Saint Paul's Church of Ireland, where Mr. and Mrs. Pitt greatly helped and influenced Cathy and other young people.

After listening to several missionaries at the Christian Endeavour, Cathy felt challenged to do something. She spoke with Robert Munn who told her about the Bible College of Wales in Swansea. Although her father was not pleased with the thought of her leaving home, Cathy packed her bags and with several other Irish students headed to Swansea. When she began to study the Scriptures with 100 other students and listened to their testimonies, Cathy realized that she had never been born again. Cathy had been religious but had never been regenerated. This was quickly remedied when she asked the Lord Jesus into her heart.

At College, the students studied deeply, prayed fervently and worked hard. The Director, Rev. Rees Howells, frequently called for days of prayer. When World War II started in 1939 and Hitler's troops relentlessly advanced across Europe, all lectures were suspended. Staff and students engaged in days of prayer and fasting. To help the war effort, some students joined the army. Others worked in the coalmines, and several ladies became nurses. Cathy joined the Fire Brigade Service. Each evening she returned to College for prayer meetings that went from 7:00 p.m. until midnight.

Cathy needed this training for future days. After the war, she trained as a nurse. When she heard that General MacArthur (USA) was asking for missionaries to return to Japan, Cathy volunteered. After some years learning Japanese, she was invited to work with World Vision in Korea, caring for thousands of child refugees fleeing from communist North Korea. She spent fourteen years caring for these orphaned children.

Compassion is love in action.

Sent and Spent for Christ

"None of these things move me, neither count I my life dear unto myself, so that I might finish my course with joy, and the ministry, which I have received of the Lord Jesus, to testify the Gospel of the grace of God."
Acts 20:24

The word "missionary" is akin to the word "apostle." Although the New Testament "Apostle" was a particular office for a given time to a limited number of chosen men, the word fundamentally means "sent one." A good missionary is a good messenger, sent with good news for lost sinners.

When we survey the last eighty years of Acre International, we thank God for the early pioneers and those who followed; they are a group of dedicated servants of God who did their utmost to discharge their responsibility of taking the good news of Jesus Christ to a lost world.

The Apostle Paul was aware that his primary mission in life was obedience to the will of God. When he recalled the formidable challenge, he had faced in Ephesus, he reminded his colleagues of why he had persevered there. His principles find parallels in our missionary colleagues.

He was sent in the will of God. Paul had initially encountered persecution in Ephesus. What kept him going was the assurance that God had sent him. God's providence and Paul's perseverance enabled him to stay there for three years – a long time for Paul's itinerant ministry.

He served in the work of God – "Serving the Lord with all humility of mind and many tears." Paul's service was characterized by humility of mind and heaviness of heart: humility like that of his feet-washing Saviour, and heaviness of heart as manifested by the Lord Jesus weeping for Jerusalem. Such service brought in the harvest of souls.

He spoke the Word of God - "I kept back nothing that was profitable unto you, but … taught you publicly, and from house to house." Paul's passionate preaching and teaching ministry established the Ephesian church.

He shared the grace of God – "Testifying both to the Jews, and also to the Greeks … the Gospel of the grace of God."

Paul was a pattern for God's servants.

Fiery Darts

"Above all, taking the shield of faith, wherewith ye shall be able to quench all the fiery darts of the wicked."
Ephesians 6:16

I was invited to conduct a Bible Conference for the Tikuna Indians near Tabatinga on the borders of Brazil and Columbia. The Tikunas are the largest indigenous tribe in Brazil numbering more than 40,000. They live on either side of the Brazil/Columbia/Peru frontiers. Our Baptist missionary friends have worked with these people for decades. As a result, more than a thousand Tikunas have trusted Christ as Saviour. Today they have their own indigenous churches and Bible institutes.

We conducted a study on the "Christian Soldier," and in one of these we focused on, "the shield of faith," and "all the fiery darts of the wicked." These Indians are experts in using their famous blowguns which can measure up to two metres long. The blowgun is carved from wood with a bamboo tube used as the barrel in the centre. Darts are made from thin lengths of "paxiuba" palm leaves. One end of the dart is sharpened so that it can pierce an animal. The other end of the dart has cotton from the kapok tree wrapped around it. The sharp end of the dart is placed on the skin of the poisonous frog or poison is collected from a plant. These poisons contain extremely powerful toxins that are lethal to any animal. With a quiver full of these darts, the Indian is ready to hunt for birds, monkeys, and other animals.

Poisoned darts are the nearest thing these Indians can relate to the fiery darts of which Paul spoke. Roman soldiers contended with enemy archers who shot sharp arrows to which were attached flaming rags which had been dipped in pitch and ignited. On hitting its target, the burning pitch splattered all over the soldier's armour.

Satan has a quiver full of fiery and poisonous darts that he accurately fires at every child of God. He did it against Eve in the Garden of Eden, and we should not be ignorant of the devil's target or his tactics. He will attack the Christians heart, accuse our minds or make an assault on our faith.

Satan's arrows can be quenched by faith in Christ.

A Widow's Praise

"Anna ... gave thanks ... unto the Lord, and spake of Him to all them that looked for redemption in Jerusalem."
Luke 2:38

The Annual Service of Remembrance each November at the Royal Albert Hall in London is a very emotional experience. The whole programme is carried out with military precision and focused on men and women who had served Queen and country, especially those who had made the supreme sacrifice. The most poignant moment for us was when military widows in single file, descended the staircase into the arena accompanied by the music of a military band. Everyone spontaneously rose to applaud these ladies as they bravely took their place. Tears ran down many faces and goose bumps were aplenty. Young men had laid down their lives, but these widows, young and older, and their families were still paying a high price.

The Scriptures give great consideration for those who have suffered the loss of a spouse and plainly teach how these special people should be treated. God cares for them and exhorts us that we do likewise (1 Timothy 5:3).

Seventy-six Bible verses refer to widows, and some of these were outstanding ladies; the widow of Zarephath who fed Elijah and the anonymous widow who gave her last two mites are but two. Another widow who quietly displayed God's grace in her affliction was Anna who expressed her praise at the birth of the Lord Jesus. Her married bliss had lasted for only seven years, but when she appears in the Scriptures she was eighty-four years old.

Her dedication in sorrow. We are not told what early struggles she may have experienced, but to have reached this great age with dignity, dedication and contentment is amazing.

Her devotion in service. It seems that Anna had her home in the temple area, lived close to God and sacrificially served Him "... with fasting and prayer."

Her discovery of the Saviour. Anna's hope was rooted in God's promises recorded in the Old Testament scriptures. Her long years of widowhood were supremely crowned when she saw Jesus. This filled Anna with thanksgiving and public testimony.

Our greatest day will be when we shall see Jesus.

The Heart of the Gospel

"For God so loved the world, that He gave His only begotten Son, that whosoever believeth in Him should not perish, but have everlasting life."
John 3:16

The twenty-five words of John 3:16 condenses the whole message of the Gospel into one verse; this verse is considered to be the most precious verse in the Bible. There are 66 books in the Bible, 1,189 chapters, and 31,175 verses. All these books, chapters and verses can be compacted together into this one simple verse. It provides news of the rich remedy of redemption for the maladies of mankind, pardon for the guilty and free salvation for the lost.

While travelling on the Amazon tributaries, taking the Gospel message to those who had never heard it before, I asked myself how I could present the Gospel in such a way that everyone would understand it at the first hearing, They should also never forget it, should this be the last time they heard of Jesus. I could find no better verse than John 3:16 to leave with the people. It is simplistic in its language, sublime in its love, sweeping in its length, and so sure in its offer of everlasting life. Why did I use it?

Because it begins with God: It was not hard to convince people in the forest of the reality of God. The beauty of His handiwork was all around them, and the clear night sky spoke to them of the immensity of the great Creator. Furthermore, each person had a God-consciousness in their hearts.

Because it speaks of God's love: Creation reveals that God is good, but Jesus revealed how good God is. He is the fountain of love.

Because it tells us who God loves: The world – men and women of every generation, race, status. He loves the literate and illiterate, rich and poor, rebels and religious.

Because it tells us how much He loves us: He gave His only begotten Son. He did not spare His Son but sent Him to the cross to bear our sin.

Because it tells us why He did it: That those who believe might have everlasting life.

The Gospel is the grandest theme in the whole world.

12th November

Goodness

"Goodness and mercy shall follow me all the days of my life."
Psalm 23:6

Wesley Gould and Charlie Thompson, both from Portadown, were colleagues in Brazil. They were returning on horseback from a meeting when they were told of a shortcut by crossing a shallow lake. They accepted the advice but were not very sure where this shallow area was.

Charlie's horse was calm and steady, and he easily crossed the lake. Wesley's horse was very easily frightened. As soon as it entered the lake, it began to buck and struggle, and this took them into deeper water and mud. Suddenly, the horse threw Wesley off its back--dumping him and the saddlebag into the dirty water.

Wesley struggled to his feet and managed to retrieve the saddle from the lake. He placed the sodden saddle back on the horse and secured it as best he could. He then mounted the steed once more, but after a few yards, the horse threw him and the saddle back into the water. There was no way he was going to try to ride the horse in the water again, so he grabbed the halter and dragged the frightened horse behind him to the other side of the lake.

After he had made it to solid ground, he secured the horse to a tree before throwing off his muddy and wet clothes. He then started back into the lake to retrieve the saddle. On his way, he bumped into a bush and upset a hornet's nest. Immediately a swarm of angry hornets flew out to attack him. Poor Wesley, already feeling a little sorry for himself, was stung on his head, arms and shoulders. Notwithstanding his discomfort, he got the saddle out of the lake, placed it on his head and returned to his shivering horse.

While all this had been going on Charlie had been sitting at the side of the lake enjoying the whole episode at Wesley's expense. He teased Wesley by quoting from Psalm 23; *"He makes me to lie down in green pastures; he leads me beside the still waters."*

The two men arrived home that night, tired, hungry and dirty, but they were happy to be serving God.

God is good!

God's Fortress

"I will say of the Lord, He is my refuge and my fortress."
Psalm 91:2

A missionary on furlough told his home church in Michigan the following story:

"While serving at a small field hospital in Africa, every two weeks I travelled by bicycle through the jungle to a nearby city for supplies. The journey took two days; I had to camp overnight at the halfway point. When I arrived in the city I observed two men fighting, one of whom had been seriously injured. I treated him for his injuries and at the same time talked to him about the Lord.

"I travelled two days home, camping overnight, and arrived safely. Two weeks later I repeated my journey. On arrival at the city, I was approached by the same young man I had treated earlier. He told me that he knew I had been carrying money and medicines. He then said, 'We followed you, knowing you would camp overnight. We planned to kill you and take your money and drugs. But just as we were about to attack, we saw that you were surrounded by twenty-six armed guards.

"At this, I laughed and said that I certainly was alone that night. The young man insisted and said, 'No, sir, I was not the only person to see the guards, my friends also saw them, and we all counted them. Because of those guards, we were afraid and left you alone.

"At this point, one of the men in the church congregation jumped up and interrupted the missionary. He asked for the exact day on which this happened. After the missionary told him the date, the man who had interrupted said, 'On the night of your incident in Africa, it was morning here and I was preparing to play golf when I felt a strong urge to pray for you. In fact, the urge of was so strong; I called men from our church to meet with me to pray for you.'"

He asked all the men who had met on that day to stand up? The missionary looked around and counted how many men he saw. There were exactly twenty-six!"

When we intercede, God intervenes.

God's Ways

*"Delight thyself also in the Lord; and He shall give thee
the desires of thine heart."*
Psalm 37:4

When many young soldiers were returning from World War II, Wesley Gould knew that the Lord was recruiting him for another conflict, a spiritual one. With that conviction in his heart, he applied to and was accepted to study at Belfast Bible School in September 1944.

Although at first, he was a little apprehensive, Wesley soon found that he had much in common with other young people at the college who had felt a similar call on their lives. Among his newly found colleagues were Robert Mackey who went to Liberia and became the international leader of the Worldwide Evangelization Crusade, Billy McIlfatrick who went to India with OMS, Minnie Bell who went to Syria with the Reformed Presbyterian Church, Donald Wilson who served God with WEC and David Ross who later became Wesley's colleague in Brazil.

These students soon found that the principal, Mr. McKnight, was a very strict disciplinarian. He encouraged the students to be totally focused on their calling to God's work. Any romance between students was not permitted, and relationships outside college were discouraged.

These restrictions posed no problem for Wesley until he visited Lisburn Road Methodist Church one Sunday morning where he was introduced to Winifred Dundas from County Fermanagh. Years later Winnie became Wesley's wife.

Back at the college, some banter ensued among the students about "the girl" Wesley had met at church. When news of this got to Mrs. McKnight's ears, she lectured Wesley about not being distracted from his calling and to put this nonsense out of his head. She said, "You are going to Brazil. Look at Horace Banner. He has sacrificed marriage that he might be able to devote his time to the Kayapo Indians. He will be here next week."

On the following week, when Horace Banner got up to speak to the students, the first thing he said was, "I have just become engaged, and Eva and I hope to be married soon. She is looking forward to working in Brazil, and I am really pleased to have a wife." There were some hidden smiles.

Trust God for each step.

Forgiven

"Jesus said unto her, Neither do I condemn thee: go, and sin no more."
John 8:11

The early dawn sun rose over the Judean hills as our Lord descended from the Mount of Olives where He had spent the night, crossed the Kidron Valley and entered the precincts of the Temple, His Father's house. His teaching session was suddenly interrupted by a hostile group of men who burst through the crowd to accuse a terrified and dishevelled woman of flagrant adultery.

A trap was set. Everyone recognised these accusers as self-righteous Scribes and Pharisees. They forced their frightened victim to stand in the midst as they addressed Jesus, "Teacher, this woman was caught in the act of adultery. Moses commanded us to stone such women. Now what do you say?" Although the question appeared to be legitimate, a sinister motive lay behind it. They were attempting to trap the Lord Jesus. Failing to endorse the woman's death would contravene the Mosaic Law. Condemning her would contravene the Roman authorities that prohibited Jews carrying out capital punishment. Either way, they reasoned that Jesus would be trapped.

The trial was sinister. Repeatedly in the Gospels, we read that Jesus knew the thoughts and intentions of people's hearts and minds. He knew exactly the implications of this carefully planned and cunning question.

Without a word, the Saviour bent down to write with his finger on the dusty ground. As He wrote the questioning continued, persistent and arrogant. The Lord Jesus straightened up and challenged the accusers. "If any of you is without sin, let him be the first to throw a stone at her." He stooped down again and continued to write.

We do not know what Jesus wrote, but the accusers, smitten in their conscience, receded one by one.

The tenderness of salvation. After the accusers had gone Jesus turned to the trembling woman and enquired about her accusers. "Has no-one condemned you?" He asked. She had been used to the criticism and hostility of many. The Saviour's gaze was different. She must have melted when Jesus said, "Neither do I condemn you. Go and sin no more."

Forgiveness is not cheap. It was paid for at Calvary

From Fishermen to Fishers of Men

"Now as He walked by the sea of Galilee, He saw Simon and Andrew his brother casting a net into the sea: for they were fishers. And Jesus said unto them, Come ye after Me, and I will make you to become fishers of men."
Mark 1:16, 17

There are many lessons to be learned from the Lord Jesus when He called His disciples from their nets to become fishers of men.

These fishermen wove their nets. As James and John wove their nets, they tied knots in cords to string a bunch of holes together. A hole is a "nothing." That is exactly what our Lord required of His disciples, a collective group of nothings that He would use.

These fishermen washed their nets. After toiling in vain all night without a catch, it might seem surprising that they were mending the nets. Some people might have sold them or left them. Fishermen are patient. Their nets had picked up debris and dirt and needed to be clean. Dirty nets might stink in the boat, rot the cords and thereby make their work harder. We also need to constantly keep our lives clean from the filth of sin and things that would hinder our testimony.

These fishermen worked their nets. Jesus said to Simon Peter, *"Launch out into the deep, and let down your nets for a draught. And Simon answering said unto Him, Master, we have toiled all the night, and have taken nothing: nevertheless at Thy word I will let down the net."* We are not on earth to sail through the sea of humanity and keep our nets on the boat. We must cast and draw the Gospel nets to bring others to Jesus.

These fishermen worshipped the Saviour. Peter and his fishermen colleagues learned that the Lord Jesus is Lord of all. They had loaned their boat to the Lord, launched into the deep at His word, and now they left their nets to follow Him.

Most fishermen catch fish to kill, but these fishers of men brought souls out of death into everlasting life.

Following the Saviour involves fishing for souls.

My Shepherd – My Sheep

*"Surely goodness and mercy shall follow me all the days of my life:
and I will dwell in the house of the Lord for ever."*
Psalm 23:6

King David's son, King Solomon, wrote, "A word fitly spoken is like apples of gold in pictures of silver." When he wrote this, I wonder did he have in mind Psalm 23 that flowed from his father's pen. No words could better describe this sweetest of all songs by the Shepherd-King of Israel. In six short verses David left us a classic of literature, a masterpiece of genius and a well proven testimony of the relationship we, the sheep, may have with our great Shepherd, the Lord Jesus Christ.

This Psalm is sometimes referred to as "The Shepherd's Psalm," but in truth, it is David assuming the role of a sheep to speak of the contentment, confidence, company and contemplation the sheep enjoys with its Shepherd.

Think of those who do not know or belong to this great Shepherd. For them Psalm 23 reflects a negative message that would read as follows:

The LORD is not my shepherd; I shall want.

He does not make me to lie down in green pastures: He does not lead me beside the still waters. He doesn't restore my soul:

He does not lead me in the paths of righteousness for His name's sake.

Yea, when I walk through the valley of the shadow of death, I will fear evil: for Thou art not with me; Thy rod and Thy staff do not comfort me.

You do not prepare before me a table in the presence of my enemies: You do not anoint my head with oil; my cup does not run over.

Goodness and mercy may follow me all the days of my life: but I will not dwell in the house of the LORD forever.

That's pretty startling! How different for the Christian! For the Christian, the best is yet to be. Every day on earth with Jesus is sweeter than the day before, and the Father's house awaits us.

Jesus said, "These are my sheep."
The Christian says, "Jesus is my Shepherd."

18th November

Pray

"I exhort therefore, that, first of all, supplications, prayers, intercessions, and giving of thanks, be made for all men."
1 Timothy 2:1

Who can measure the value of Christian parents who pray? Mr. and Mrs. Gould lived a short distance from Thomas Street Methodist Church. Their three children, James, Wesley, and Margaret, were taken to the Sunday services, Sunday School and other activities in the church.

Wesley's life nearly came to an abrupt end at that Sunday School. As soon the lesson finished the boys dashed for the door to see who could be out of the building first. On one Sunday, an eager ten-year-old Wesley was first out through the door. Instead of rushing down the staircase, he jumped at the bannister to slide down to the ground floor. Sadly, he missed it and plunged to the stone floor below. He was knocked unconscious and remembered nothing until he opened his eyes in the doctor's surgery sometime later. Although he sustained a nasty cut inside his mouth, the doctor told Wesley he had escaped serious injury and might have been killed. The Lord had preserved his life for a purpose.

After Wesley left school, he forsook Sunday School, church attendance and anything related to religion. He and his friends became engrossed in outdoor activities and frequented the local cinema on Saturday evenings.

Although he did not attend church, he knew that his mother never gave up praying for her children. After Wesley had celebrated his nineteenth birthday, he recalled hearing a preacher say, "If you are not converted before you are twenty years old, your heart will become so hardened that the chances of becoming a Christian will be greatly diminished." This sobering statement played on Wesley's mind.

With his twentieth birthday quickly approaching Wesley decided to attend an evangelistic mission conducted in Portadown by two Brethren evangelists, Duff and Allen. Everything he had learned at church and Sunday School about sin, eternity and salvation came flooding back to his mind. At the end of the meeting, Wesley asked the Lord Jesus Christ to save him. This only convert of that mission went on to serve God at home and abroad for more than seventy years.

Keep on praying.

19th November

A Blessed Mother-In-Law

*"He stood over her, and rebuked the fever; and it left her:
and immediately she arose and ministered unto them."*
Luke 4:39

Sometimes mothers-in-law are branded with an unenviable reputation, especially if they discordantly share the same house as their married offspring. On the other hand, many couples enjoy a good relationship with their in-laws and depend on them for babysitting, helping out in emergencies or giving sound advice.

Although the Scriptures do not tell us much about Peter's mother-in-law they give us a glimpse into her Capernaum home where Jesus visited with His first followers.

Her Son-In-law. Simon was a fisherman. His parents are not mentioned in the gospel story, but his brother, Andrew, obviously lived with Simon and his wife's mother. It was Andrew who introduced his brother to Jesus Christ who changed Simon's name to Cephas, or Peter.

Peter's conversion brought an immense change to his home. Can you imagine the reaction of his family as he and Andrew related how they met the Saviour? They not only believed on Him but had decided to follow this Stranger. How could they think of such a thing when they had a family to support?

Her Sickness. Dr Luke tells us that Peter's mother-in-law was sick with a "great fever." None of the usual remedies had proved effective, and her relations became very concerned.

By this time Jesus was well known in Simon's family for He had been teaching, preaching and healing throughout Galilee with great multitudes of people following Him. On that very day, Jesus had taught in their synagogue and had delivered a man from an unclean spirit. When he arrived at Simon Peter's house, they implored Him for the fever-ridden patient.

It was a dramatic moment when Jesus stood by the bedside, took the fevered hand in His and raised the lady to immediate health and strength. Dr Luke says the Lord rebuked the fever, the same word used also about His mastery over devils and the storm.

Her Service. Any doubts this lady might have had about Jesus were dispelled as she sensed His compassion and experienced His power. Now all she wanted to do was to serve Him. Wouldn't you?

Jesus deserves the highest honour.

Triumph and Testing

"And Abram journeyed, going on still toward the south. And there was a famine in the land: and Abram went down into Egypt to sojourn there; for the famine was grievous in the land"
Genesis 12:9,10

Our missionary colleague, Dorrie Gunning, was a prolific letter writer. She always headed her letters with meaty quotations. One of those was this, "The will of God will never lead you where the grace of God cannot keep you."

That would have been a good maxim to send in a letter to Abram and Sarah in their day. They had arrived in the land God had promised them and had probably expected to settle down and enjoy their new tent. God did not let them. Instead, He permitted a famine to come to the land. There is no record that Abram had ever faced a famine back home in Ur or during his stay in Haran, but when he arrived in God's land he had no food for his family or fodder for his flocks.

God allowed them to face the famine because they were in the "school of faith." Our greatest tests often follow great triumphs.

Alas, Abram fell flat on his face when he went down to Egypt. He ran away from the first test. The same temptations that Abram faced then, we may face today.

Disappointment. It must have been a great disappointment for these early pilgrims. They did not know that God was testing their faith. He wanted to know if they were trusting in the land or trusting in their Lord. Instead of remaining where God had called them, they went down to Egypt.

Downward steps. Whenever you go to Jerusalem, you go up. Whenever you go to Egypt, you go down. Egypt is always a picture of the world. Abram forsook pitching tents and building altars to trust in worldly ways.

It is easy to make the wrong choices. Jonah chose Joppa when he should have gone to Nineveh. Samson lingered with Delilah instead of being with God's people. David sat on the rooftop instead of going to the war.

True faith is always tried.

Sowing and Growing

"For he that soweth to his flesh shall of the flesh reap corruption;
but he that soweth to the Spirit shall of the Spirit reap life everlasting."
Galatians 6:8

One of the welcoming sights returning to Northern Ireland after a few years absence is to view the Province from the airplane and see the patchwork of multiple farm lands below in "forty shades of green." In September these are punctuated by the sight of golden harvest fields that remind us how blessed we are by a bountiful supply and variety of crops.

The same cannot be said while flying into many other countries including the Middle East. The view from above reveals the bareness of the terrain except for chosen cultured plots. Even so, harvest time is important in those countries also.

This is reflected in the Bible where much emphasis is put on sowing and reaping. The Lord Jesus told several parables based on sowing and reaping and the apostle Paul also wrote frequently of the same principle as did the Psalmist. In these Bible references, it can be observed that God established several unalterable and universal laws for harvesting.

We reap what we sow. It is impossible to sow potatoes and reap pumpkins. Paul indicated that we must make one of two choices: sow either to the flesh or to the Spirit. Our sowing will determine the kind of harvest we shall reap. To live for the flesh is to live to satisfy self and temporary pleasures. To live in the Spirit is to enjoy His life through us and please God.

We reap more than what we sow. This means you must sow to grow. A handful of seed can produce an abundant harvest. When Jesus spoke of the harvest he said that the seed of the Word produced thirty, sixty or even 100 times more than what was sown.

We reap later than when we sow. Impatient people do not make good farmers. There is a season to sow and a season to reap. The final reaping will be when the great Lord of the Harvest appears, and then all shall be revealed.

Sow to the Spirit in the soil of your life.

Remember Me

"He said unto Jesus, Lord, remember me when Thou comest into Thy Kingdom."
Luke 23:42

Early in his missionary career, Wesley Gould accompanied a group of believers to visit and conduct meetings in Bom Futuro, a small village in Maranhão, Brazil. Wesley engaged in door-to-door evangelism. As he arrived at one door, the owner of the house was leaving to sow rice on his plantation. Wesley engaged the man in conversation about the Gospel. Their exchange continued for quite a while with the result that the man was detained too long and had to defer planting rice until the following day. He became very angry about the delay and blamed Wesley for wasting his time.

Afterwards Wesley learned of a sequel to this incident. Senhor José Madeiro, who later became a pastor, was among the group that took Wesley on his first visit to Bom Futuro. Years later, José was visiting the same village when he met a man who asked him if he did not recognize who he was. José admitted that he could not recollect ever meeting the man before.

At this, the man said, "Do you remember back in 1949 when you and a wee missionary came to visit Bom Futuro. He came to my house and talked with me for a long time about salvation. Well, I was so furious with him that day, for he had upset my plans to sow rice, and I felt I had lost a whole day. I was so angry that I made up my mind to harm both of you that night. With my machete well sharpened, I circled round and round the house during the meeting, hoping for an opportunity to attack you and that missionary, but it did not work out. I want to tell you that I am a Christian now and all my family has also accepted Jesus Christ as Saviour."

Wesley had no doubt that someone, in some place and at that very moment must have been praying for them. The Lord not only restrained the murderer's hand, God's glorious grace brought the man to repentance and faith in Jesus Christ.

God's grace abounds to the chief of sinners.

The Vital Link

*"And the Syrians brought away captive out of the land of Israel a little maid
and she waited on Naaman's wife."*
2 Kings 5:2

The story of Naaman is one of the most fascinating in the entire Bible. While the Scriptures underline his greatness, it also emphasises Naaman's weakness. He was a captain in the Syrian army, a conqueror, and hero in his nation, yet he had a physical flaw, he had leprosy. It had spread in his body, spoiled his life and separated him from his friends.

That was not the end of the story. Naaman discovered that God's mercy was as vast as the ocean and His grace was as free as the sunshine. In an amazing way, he heard about the God of Israel and His servant, the prophet Elisha. Commended by his own King and armed with bullion of gold, silver, precious stones and beautiful Syrian garments, he went to Israel in search of healing.

Naaman was disappointed when he found that the prophet Elisha was not interested in the Syrian treasures but curtly told him to go and wash seven times in the river Jordan. At first, he refused to obey the prophet judging that the rivers of his own country were better than the Jordan. Pride is a terrible thing. It can rob us of God's blessings, and it hinders many from coming to the Lord Jesus.

Although hurt and humbled, Naaman finally obeyed God's servant, and after he dipped in Jordan's muddy water seven times his leprosy was cleansed.

In the golden chain of God's providence that led to Naaman's healing, there is a vital but almost unnoticed link. In the shadow of this great man's life, there was a young girl who said, *"Would God my lord were with the prophet that is in Samaria! for he would recover him of his leprosy."*

Here was a young girl whose name and age we don't know, and yet God used her to point Naaman to a life-changing experience that would free him from leprosy. She is the real heroine of this story, for she brought a shaft of golden sunlight to an alien home.

Shine for Jesus everywhere you go.

Preserved

"O Lord: let Thy lovingkindness and thy truth continually preserve me."
Psalm 40:11

After Wesley Gould and Edmund Norwood had retrieved their submerged van from the lake where they had suffered an accident, they were relieved to discover that they were able to crank up the engine again. Wesley confessed that his nerves were at the breaking point and there was no way he could drive. Even though it was late, they set off towards Piracuruca with Ed in the soggy driver's seat. The road was even more hazardous in the dark, but Edmund drove slowly along the narrow gauge and treacherous road all through that night. They were too upset for sleep, and their adrenaline kept them alert until daybreak. Finally, they saw Piracuruca in the early dawn.

When Edmund drove up to the house, both men lifted their hearts to God in praise for His protection through the night. Wesley's wife, Winnie, had expected the men to return on the previous day and was anxiously waiting for this moment. When she emerged from the house, she was shocked to see the filthy condition of the van and even more shocked to see the bedraggled appearance of Wesley and Edmund. She was all the more taken aback when Wesley got down on his knees and kissed the ground. Undoubtedly she was expecting him to kiss her first.

When Winnie opened her arms to give her husband a welcoming hug she was repelled by the stench. She asked if they had been to a pig yard, for they stank of pig slurry. Winnie asked, "What did you kiss the ground for?"

"I was never so glad to get back home again," said Wesley. "I thought I would never see you or Piracuruca again."

Winnie asked about the goods they were supposed to buy in Fortaleza. Wesley held up what had been left of the sack of sugar. The contents had melted away in the lake, and the other supplies were totally ruined.

Before retiring that night, all three missionaries lifted their hearts to God in praise and prayer. They also recognized that someone must have been praying for them.

He is our Keeper.

The Other Prodigal

"These many years do I serve thee, neither transgressed I at any time thy
commandment: and yet thou never gavest me a kid,
that I might make merry with my friends."
Luke 15:30

As children, we used to sing, *"Seek them out, get them gone all the little bunnies in the fields of corn; envy, jealousy, malice, and pride these must never in my heart abide."* Later I wondered why they ever related these ugly attitudes to bunny rabbits. They are more like ravenous wolves that do so much damage to people and God's work.

The story of the prodigal's elder brother reveals too much envy, jealousy, malice, and pride. These traits robbed him of much joy. They always do. In the parables of the lost sheep, the lost silver, and the lost son, there was a lot of joy and singing: joy for the shepherd who found his sheep, joy for the woman who found her silver and joy for the father who welcomed home his repentant son. The only one who had no joy was this elder brother. He was immersed in bad attitudes.

Pharisees might well have been able to draw parallels between the wayward son and publicans and sinners, but they were blind to those hidden and hypocritical sins of the spirit of which they were guilty. Pharisees defined sin in terms of outward actions but not inward attitudes.

There were plenty of commendable traits with the elder brother. He stayed at home with the father; he worked hard in the field and never brought public disgrace on the family. However, he had harboured hidden resentments. The Lord Jesus said that the two greatest commandments were to love the Lord with all our hearts and to love our neigbours as ourselves. Sadly, the elder brother displayed little love for his father and no love for his brother.

Could it be that such elder brothers and sisters are still alive today? A Christian was asked, "Who was the elder brother?" to this he replied, "I met one yesterday." When asked who it was, he replied, "I discovered, to my shame, that I was the elder brother."

Seek them and get them gone.

Excitement in Nain

"'Young man, I say unto thee, Arise.' and he that was dead sat up,
and began to speak. And He delivered him to his mother."
Luke 7:14, 15

No one knew that the Lord Jesus was going to Nain that day, but it is just like Him to arrive in the nick of time. On this occasion, Jesus came to break up a funeral procession.

A nameless but distraught widow led a large crowd of mourners from Nain on the way to a cemetery. She had not only lost her husband; now her only son was dead leaving her destitute and despondent.

As Jesus approached the city, a crowd also followed Him. When the two multitudes converged, Jesus approached the bier, ignoring circumstances, ceremony or even contamination by contacting a dead body. He stilled the people, comforted the widow, touched the bier, and spoke to the dead boy. Upon hearing the Saviour's voice, the young man sat upright. Nain had never seen anything like it. What shouts of joy and excitement must have rung in the streets of the city that day.

In this wonderful miracle several things should be noted:

The Saviour's compassion for the grieving widow. When Jesus looked at the mother and said, "Weep not," His words must have sounded absurd under the circumstances. The widow's heart was broken, her husband was dead, her home was empty, her heritage and standing in the community were zero, and her hope was gone. Jesus knew all of this, and He had compassion on her.

The Saviour's command to the dead son. In full view of many witnesses, Jesus again asserted His authority over sin and death and commanded, "Young man, I say unto thee, Arise." Fear and awe must have swept across the crowd as the young man sat up and began to talk. Jesus then presented the boy to his mother. The Lord of life had demonstrated His power and compassion.

The Saviour's conquest over death. Two crowds of people met that day. One was led by the Prince of Life – Jesus Christ. The other by the King of death. Jesus Christ prevailed, Satan and death were conquered.

The Saviour will command all the dead in Christ to rise.

Grace and Mercy

"He is the propitiation for our sins."
1 John 2:2

I recently noticed a large poster prominently displayed outside a building that read, "JUSTICE FOR THE POOR." I think I have seen similar placards carried in various protest demonstrations with people calling for "justice." While there may be a worthy cause behind the sign, justice is the last thing sinners need. What we all need is mercy. Justice gives us what we deserve. Mercy does not give us what we do deserve.

Instead of God dispensing justice to us, He gave us Jesus. When the Lord Jesus came into the world, He did not come to give sinners what they deserved. He came with grace and to give grace. Justice gives us what we deserve. Mercy spares us from what we deserve, but grace bestows upon us what we do not deserve. The Apostle John wrote, *"The law was given by Moses, but grace and truth came by Jesus Christ."*

The broken Law of God calls out to all transgressors, "Guilty, guilty, guilty." God is a God of love, but He also is a God of justice and holiness. In our natural condition, we have no hiding place from the broken law of God.

When Christ died on the cross, God's mercy completely made a covering for man's sin. God's Son came between the broken law and the holiness of God. The just wrath of God fell upon Jesus Christ; divine justice was executed, and God was fully satisfied by the Saviour's atoning death on the cross. God's wrath fell upon Christ at Calvary. Forgiveness was made possible through the shed blood of Jesus Christ. The prophet spoke of Christ 700 years before Christ died: *"He shall see of the travail of his soul, and shall be satisfied"* (Isaiah 53:11).

When Jesus intervened at Calvary, the justice of God was satisfied, and the throne of judgment became a throne of mercy. *"Whom God hath set forth to be a propitiation through faith in his blood…"* (Romans 3:25). Calvary's cross calls out to us, *"Mercy here is rich, and grace is free."*

Kneel at the cross. Jesus will meet you there.

A Shepherd Meets the Good Shepherd

*"Ye were as sheep going astray; but are now returned
unto the Shepherd and Bishop of your souls."*
1 Peter 2:25

The Yorkshire Dales are best known for its outstanding scenery and natural beauty, and all this is enhanced with flocks of grazing sheep and skipping lambs scattered over the hills. However, it was not the natural beauty of the area that drew newlyweds, Keith and Karen Lindsay, to that area in 1992. As workers with the Faith Mission, they accompanied Trevor Matthews, the Mission Director in England, to conduct an evangelistic mission at Westhouse Methodist Church. It was the spiritual needs of the region that weighed on their hearts.

Among the many young people attending those meetings was a young shepherd, Matthew, who spent most of his time caring for his sheep that were scattered over the surrounding hills. Matthew and his sheepdog were firm companions, but he was shy and retiring in adult company. Being surrounded by the splendour of God's handiwork on the open Dales made Matthew acutely aware of his need of the Greater Shepherd. Through the preaching of the Gospel at those evangelistic meetings, Matthew, with many other young people, trusted Christ as Saviour.

Although still quite bashful, almost immediately Matthew joined the other new converts in serving God in his community. With plenty of time on his hands, while caring for his sheep, his Bible became his firm companion. He read and devoured the Scriptures and often arrived at the church with a tattered but well-read Bible.

A close bond developed between him and the Lindsays, and it was a happy day when he announced to them that he felt God was asking him to go on a mission trip. In the course of the required medical for that trip, the doctors discovered that Matthew had terminal cancer. Even though the news was a shock to him and his family, Matthew accepted it with amazing grace. The evidence of this grace touched his friends and community. Although he had the various courses of chemotherapy, Matthew, was called home to meet the Shepherd and Bishop of his soul.

He now dwells in the house of the Lord forever.

Christ and the Ark

*"While the ark was a preparing, wherein few, that is,
eight souls were saved by water."*
1 Peter 3:20

God gave us a multitude of pictures that foreshadow the Lord Jesus in the Old Testament. One of the most vivid of these is Noah's ark. The Apostle Peter indicated that it was a magnificent Old Testament type of the Lord Jesus and our salvation through Him.

Christ and the substance of the ark. *"Make thee an ark of gopher wood."* Scholars tell us that this was cypress wood which did not easily rot. Ancient coffins were made of cypress wood because cypress was reckoned to be indestructible, a symbol of Christ and His indestructible humanity.

"Thou shalt pitch it within and without with pitch." This inner and outer covering of sticky pitch was to make the ark watertight. The word used here for pitch is translated seventy times elsewhere in the Scriptures as *"atonement."* Thank God for the atonement, the covering of Christ's precious blood for us.

Christ and the size of the ark. *"The length of the ark shall be three hundred cubits, the breadth of it fifty cubits, and the height of it thirty cubits."* This large ship had an estimated capacity of three million cubit feet which was sufficient for all. The size and immensity of this great work are God's way of saying to us that there is room for all. There is room at the cross for you.

Christ and the structure of the ark. *"A window shalt thou make in the ark… and the door of the ark shalt thou set on the side thereof …"* The door and the window were necessary. God controlled the closing of the door while Noah was to open the window. Noah could also look up through the window. The Lord Jesus is the door to salvation and God's window to heaven.

Christ in the sustenance of the ark. *"And thou shalt take unto thee all food that is eaten."* The Lord Jesus not only saves, He also satisfies.

Sheltered by the work of Christ's cross.

Fighting with Fleas

"After whom dost thou pursue? after a dead dog, after a flea?"
1 Samuel 24:14

A lot of insects, flying and jumping, emerged every night in the Amazon forests. Worse still, fleas were abundantly present day and night. I have never met an animal lover who had a fondness for fleas. It is estimated that there are approximately two thousand different species of these annoying pests. Some fleas feed only on one host, as the case with rabbit fleas, whereas cat fleas can turn up on dogs, rats, squirrels, chickens, and even humans.

These minute beasties are the best jumpers in the world. They have unique springy legs that enable them to take off faster than any other creature, and they jump up to 150 times their body length. That would be equal to a human jumping over thirty single-decker buses lined up end to end. Furthermore, fleas lay more eggs than any other creature. A female cat flea, for example, may lay one egg every hour during its adult life, which is usually about three months.

These little pests not only irritate their hosts, but they have also been responsible for a major disaster. In the Middle Ages twenty-five million people died, one out of every four citizens in Europe, because of the Bubonic Plague, a terrible disease caused by bacteria that was carried by rat fleas.

In today's text we have the first mention of fleas in the Bible. It is a question posed by David to King Saul with a sense of sarcasm. Samuel had anointed Saul as king to rule over Israel with integrity. Alas, instead of reigning, he became so consumed with jealousy that he abandoned his royal duties to pursue and kill David. David's sarcasm was that the king had forsaken the more important responsibilities of his office to give attention to eliminating him.

Saul was reduced to tears. He pleaded for forgiveness from David, but he still failed to shake off his jealousy. There were more important battles to fight than to fight with God's anointed.

Too many people get taken up with fighting the wrong battles. Maybe they are just itching for a fight.

Do not major on minors.

December

Winter Snow

1st December

Our Saviour's Lament

*"O Jerusalem, Jerusalem ... how often would I have gathered thy children
together, even as a hen gathereth her chickens under her wings,
and ye would not!"*
Matthew 23:37

A thousand years before our Saviour's lament over Jerusalem King David ascended the same Mount of Olives as he fled from Jerusalem in the wake of the revolt of his son Absalom. The Bible reminds us that he "went up by the ascent of mount Olivet, and wept as he went up, and had his head covered, and he went barefoot: and all the people that was with him covered every man his head, and they went up, weeping as they went up" (2 Samuel 15:30).

Absalom's revolt ended when his long hair was caught on a branch as his mule ran under a tree. Then David's right-hand general, Joab, finished him off with a spear through his heart. When David heard the news he wept again, crying "O my son Absalom – my son, my son Absalom. If only I had died in your place! O Absalom my son, my son!"

Although David and Jesus traversed the same ground, they did so in a very different manner. David fled the city in defeat, whereas Jesus entered the city in triumph. When the Lord Jesus made His entry into Jerusalem on the same route by which David fled, the company that greeted Him did not have their heads covered or engaged in widespread grief and tears as did David's friends. On the contrary, His followers spread their cloaks and palm branches to make a smooth path for this, *"King David's greater Son."*

Enthusiastically they cried, *"Hosanna to the Son of David! Blessed is He who comes in the name of the Lord! Hosanna in the highest heaven!"* The cheering crowds were greeting Jesus as their King and Liberator.

During His descent of the Mount of Olives, the Saviour stopped and looked across the Kidron Valley at Jerusalem with its gleaming temple. In a lament that reminisced of David's heartbreak over his rebellious son, Jesus cried, *"O Jerusalem, Jerusalem..."*

Our Saviour's compassion for Jerusalem was in view of His prophecy of its coming judgement.

"Knowing therefore, the terror of the Lord, we persuade men."

"In labours more abundant … in journeyings often, in perils of waters…"
2 Corinthians 11:23, 26

Wesley Gould and Edmund Norwood were making their 400-kilometres return trip from Fortaleza to Piracuruca. Tropical downpours had increased the danger of the already perilous slippery road. Conditions worsened when unrelenting rain churned the roads into virtual rivers of mud. Wesley found it difficult to drive at any speed as the van slid, swerved and skidded on the slippery surface. Edmund's adrenaline was running high as he helplessly looked on, giving only occasional advice or suggestions to Wesley.

Their worse nightmare happened after Wesley's attention was diverted. When he looked round again, the vehicle swerved towards a clay embankment. In a frantic attempt to rectify this, he pulled the steering wheel in the counter direction, but it was too late. The van skidded, careened through a low verge and toppled over on the driver's side before plunging into a lake that was brimming full from the heavy rain. Foul smelling and filthy water gushed into the cabin as the vehicle quickly sank. Both men struggled to get out through the passenger-side window which was still above the water level. Edmund was able to scramble out onto the vehicle's side first. Wesley, now standing above his waist in the filthy water, also struggled to climb up over the seats and steering column to emerge out through the open window.

Both missionaries were soaked, bewildered and dumbfounded. Edmund remarked to Wesley, "This is the worst yet." It certainly was. Not only was the van submerged, it was not their vehicle. They wondered how they would ever be able to retrieve it from the lake.

Several men emerged to secure a rope from their car to the van. The rope tightened, the wheels of their vehicle spun in the mud, but the sunken van did not budge.

Darkness quickly fell on them. The next morning, workmen arrived with heavy machinery to pull the van from the lake. Wesley was fearful that they might damage the van. Edmund was just too glad to be alive. He was grateful that family and friends at Keswick Street Mission Hall had been praying for them.

Perils, protection and prayer are related.

The Blood and the Book

"In that day there shall be a fountain opened ... for sin and for uncleanness."
Zechariah 13:1

In October 1973, under cover of darkness, the armed might of the Syrian army secretly converged on Northern Galilee while Israel was observing one of its holiest days - "Yom Kippur" the Day of Atonement. All commerce was closed; soldiers were on leave, and emergency services were on skeleton staff. For twenty-four hours Israel reeled as it suddenly awakened to the invasion, but when it did the Israelis not only defeated the Syrian army but also conquered the Golan Heights and afterward annexed that region to be part of Israel.

The feast of Yom Kippur reminds us that atonement is at the heart of the Bible. It was prophesied, promised and prefigured throughout the Old Testament. When Adam and Eve sinned, God shed the innocent blood of animals to cover their nakedness.

Adam and Eve's two sons, Cain and Abel, wanted to worship God. Cain sacrificed the fruit of the ground, but Abel brought a lamb. God accepted the blood of the lamb, but He rejected Cain's offering because "without the shedding of blood, there is no remission of sin."

In Genesis 22 God told Abraham to sacrifice his promised son, Isaac. Before Abraham could plunge the dagger into his son, an angel stopped him. At that moment, he saw a ram caught by the horns in a thicket. Isaac was spared, but the blood of the ram was shed in his place.

To deliver His people from the land of Egypt God instructed each house to slay a lamb and put the blood on their doorposts, for He said, *"When I see the blood, I will pass over you"* (Exodus 12:13).

Tens of thousands of animals were sacrificed on the altars of the Tabernacle, and the Temple and their blood were spilled as sacrifices for sin.

Full atonement was realized when Jesus Christ died upon Calvary's cross. His death was the fulfillment of all the prophecies and promises that had gone before. Jesus was born to die; He planned to die, and He lived to die;

He was the Lamb slain from before the foundation of the world.

4th December

Belt Up

"Stand therefore, having your loins girt about with truth."
Ephesians 6:14

When Paul was in a Roman prison he observed that the soldier's belt was an essential part of his armour. In fact, it was more than a belt; it was an apron that secured every other part of the armour in place.

The Roman soldier's toga was a large square piece of material that hung loosely over the body with openings for the head and arms. A loose toga would flap in the breeze and hinder a soldier's mobility and combat capacity. To avoid this the soldier pulled the four corners of his tunic through the belt, allowing him to move freely.

Although Paul mentioned the girdle first in describing a Christian soldier, it was the last piece of armour to be put on. After the soldier hung his sword and possibly a dagger on the belt, he was ready for combat.

The Lord Jesus spoke of *"girding your loins."* This carried the same the idea of gathering up all the loose material, tucking it into the belt and preparing for the conflict.

Readiness should be a watchword for all Christians:

Readiness for a sudden departure. Paul said that he was ready to be offered, and the time of his departure was at hand (2 Timothy 4:6). Death for Paul was a departure from earthly limitations to be with Christ which was incomparably better.

Readiness to suffer for the Saviour. Paul also indicated his readiness "not to be bound only, but also to die at Jerusalem for the name of the Lord Jesus" (Acts 21:13).

Readiness to speak for the Saviour. Although Peter had denied His Lord he wrote, "Sanctify the Lord God in your hearts: and be ready always to give an answer to every man that asketh you a reason of the hope that is in you with meekness and fear" (1Peter 3:16).

Readiness to serve the Saviour. Paul signalled his flexibility in serving Christ: "So, as much as in me is, I am ready to preach the gospel to you that are at Rome also" (Romans 1:14).

Peter once said, "Lord, I am ready to go with thee … to death."

Long and Full

*"Remembering without ceasing your work of faith, and labour of love,
and patience of hope in our Lord Jesus Christ."*
1 Thessalonians 1:3

It seems that longevity is becoming more common. Experts tell us that we are living longer. When I took part in the funeral of Wesley Gould, I was reminded that there is a difference between a long life and a full one. Wesley had a long innings. He was ninety-six years old when he went to be with Christ. He died one week short of his sixty-fourth wedding anniversary and more than seventy years after stepping out in faith for full-time Christian service. His certainly was a full life.

He was saved by the grace of God. Wesley was associated with Thomas Street Methodist Church throughout his life. His father was a lay-preacher in the Portadown circuit. It was at a Gospel mission in 1941, conducted by two brethren preachers that Wesley trusted Christ when he was nineteen years old. He was the only convert of that mission.

He lived and walked by faith in God. After conversion he became a Sunday school teacher, a Boys' Brigade Officer, and a lay preacher in Portadown. Challenged by missionary biographies, Wesley stepped out of secular employment in 1945 to study at Belfast Bible College and the Missionary School of Medicine in preparation to serve God in distant Brazil. It was a decisive step.

He served God by love. During his thirty years in Brazil Wesley and Winnie Gould served God in establishing churches in various towns, often in the face of danger, stern opposition and persecution. There are many in heaven today and others on the road because of their service for Christ. They did it for love of the Saviour.

He lived and died in the blessed hope of the Gospel. The Christian's hope is not based on speculation. Rather, as Wesley learned at the Boys' Brigade, it is a hope that is sure and steadfast, anchored in our Saviour's atoning sacrifice. This living and lasting hope is guaranteed by the resurrection of Jesus Christ, and it leads to an inheritance, incorruptible and undefiled, reserved in heaven for all who trust in Him.

Blessed assurance.

Corn From Heaven

"He … opened the doors of heaven, and had rained down manna upon them to eat, and had given them of the corn of heaven."
Psalm 78:23,24

Goodness and mercy followed God's people through the wilderness for forty years. Every day He opened the windows of heaven and fed them with heavenly manna. God still showers goodness and mercy upon us each day and seeks to bless us. We do not gather manna daily in baskets like those Israelites, but we should glean heavenly corn daily from God's Word. Jesus said, *"Man shall not live by bread alone, but by every word that proceedeth out of the mouth of God"* (Matthew 4:4).

Dr Stephen Olford produced a little booklet called, "Manna in the Morning" in which he emphasised the benefit Christians derive from a daily quiet time and gave helpful suggestions how to make the most of it. Dr Olford likened that devotional time to the Israelites gathering their manna each day.

I must confess that throughout my Christian life, although I have endeavoured to maintain a daily devotional time, it has not always been easy. Too frequently I have let pressures, programmes, moods and people press in upon me and steal away a time with God.

I felt rebuked when I read of Bertha Smith, a missionary to China in the last century, who wrote about her time with God. It was bitterly cold in her part of China. During the day she wore layers of clothes that weighed thirty pounds, and at night she slept under heavy bedding and with a hot water bottle. Her greatest challenge came in each early morning hour when she wanted to rise before others so she could have her quiet time before the scores of interruptions that each day brought. She would struggle in the darkness to put on her thirty pounds of clothing, and then she would break the ice to wash her face in the cold water. She quietly slipped out to a particular haystack where she raked aside the frosted hay, knelt down and spent time with the Lord before the sun came up. That was her manna in the morning.

You can meet God each day in His Word.

Sweet Or Sour

"Looking diligently lest any man fail of the grace of God; lest any root of bitterness springing up trouble you, and thereby many be defiled."
Hebrews 12:15

When we lived in Brazil, we enjoyed a wide variety of juicy home-grown fruits: mangos, coconuts, limes, oranges, guavas, passion fruit, carambola, and jambo. To enjoy the sweetness of these fruits much attention had to be given to their roots.

There is nothing so bad as a bitter life. Bitterness is a root that produces all sorts of trouble. Bitterness may begin with a tiny seed that quickly grows beneath the surface. It is invisible to the eye, requires very little soil and needs very little cultivation. Although it grows quickly, it is exceedingly difficult to weed it out.

Sometimes a seed of bitterness takes root in a heart because of something that has been done to us or because of something that was said about us or because of something that was taken from us.

Concerning something that may be said about us. Jesus said, *"Blessed are ye, when men shall revile you, and persecute you, and shall say all manner of evil against you falsely, for my sake. Rejoice, and be exceeding glad: for great is your reward in heaven..."* They did the same thing to Jesus.

Concerning any wrong that may be done to us. Jesus said, *"Ye have heard that it hath been said, An eye for an eye, and a tooth for a tooth: But I say unto you, That ye resist not evil: but whosoever shall smite thee on thy right cheek, turn to him the other also."* It is not what happens to you that matters to God, but how you react to it.

Concerning anything that may be taken from us. Jesus said, *"If any man will sue thee at the law, and take away thy coat, let him have thy cloak also."* It is better to be wronged than to wrong.

A root of bitterness can produce only poisonous fruit, and that is totally alien to the fruit of the Spirit.

Be sure to cultivate your heart so that your life is better and not bitter.

Walking With God

"The steps of a good man are ordered by the Lord: and he delighteth in his way. Though he fall, he shall not be utterly cast down: for the Lord upholdeth him with His hand."
Psalm 37:23,24

M editate on these two verses phrase by phrase:

"The steps of a good man," not the leaps. Walking with God means taking one step at a time. To walk with Him says a lot about *the direction* we are travelling, *the pace at which we are going* and *the company we are keeping.* God has a plan for our lives, and we are not to live a haphazard sort of life like a rudderless ship on a stormy sea and without a compass. The life of faith is an ordered life controlled and planned by God.

"Are ordered by the Lord and he delighteth in his way." It is a joy to walk with God. Years ago I enjoyed walking out with my wife Audrey – I still do. I like to think that Audrey also enjoyed walking with me. While Enoch enjoyed walking with God, the Bible also suggests that God was pleased to walk with him. God said that He enjoys walking with the Christian and *"delights in his way."*

"Though he fall, he shall not be utterly cast down." The Lord knows that we are weak. He knows our frame and that we are likely to stumble and fall. Some people have the mistaken idea that if the Christian is in the will of God, he will never fall and should never shed a tear. Old Testament patriarchs, prophets and New Testament saints were flesh-and-blood humans just like we are. They also stumbled and fell, but the Lord never forsook them. Take courage; although God knows that we might sometimes stumble, He will not let us remain cast down.

"The Lord upholdeth him with His hand." Have you ever tried to teach a little baby how to walk? That child needs a hand to uphold it. How comforting to know that God holds our hands.

He walks with me, and He talks with me.

What to Do With Burdens

"Bear ye one another's burdens, and so fulfill the law of Christ."
Galatians 6:2

Burdens come in all shapes and sizes. To these Galatians, Paul was speaking of a crushing weight. He was familiar with such burdens. From Asia Minor, he wrote to his praying friends in Europe, *"For we would not, brethren, have you ignorant of our trouble which came to us in Asia, that we were pressed out of measure, above strength, insomuch that we despaired even of life."* That was a crushing burden.

To those same friends, Paul expressed his gratitude for sharing in his heavy burden, *"Ye also helping together by prayer for us, that for the gift bestowed upon us by the means of many persons thanks may be given by many on our behalf."* Joy shared is joy doubled. Sorrow shared is sorrow halved.

It should not surprise us that the Lord has joined us one to another both as a body and a building – cemented to each other. "One another" is one of the key phrases of the New Testament. We are commanded to *love* one another, *accept* one another, *encourage* one another, *pray* for one another, *build up* one another, *comfort* one another, *serve* one another, *forgive* one another and *bear* one another's burdens.

Everybody is laden with burdens, young and old, men and women, believers and unbelievers. What are we to do with these burdens?

We need to shoulder the burdens of those who fail (Galatians 6:1). Too often we put down those who fall and fail. Like the Good Shepherd, love gives a shoulder to the erring saint.

We should share the burdens with the fellowship. Paul was grateful for those around him whom he called fellow-helpers, fellow-labourers, fellow-soldiers and fellow-servants. In Romans 16 he mentioned thirty-two Christians and commended them for their service, succour, and sacrifice for him

We can shed all our burdens unto the Saviour. He carried our sins, He carried our sorrows, and He will carry our burdens: "Cast thy burden upon the Lord, and he shall sustain thee: He shall never suffer the righteous to be moved" (Psalm 55:22).

You do the casting; He will do the carrying.

Faithfulness Required

"Moreover it is required in stewards that a man be found faithful."
1 Corinthians 4:2

We sometimes admire the talents of other Christians and wish we had their abilities. At such times it is good to remember that God is not looking for anything else other than faithfulness in the talents He has given us.

It is reputed that the great evangelist Dwight L Moody was very limited in oratorical grammar. One evening after he had addressed a congregation, an elderly lady approached him and complained, "I noticed you made eleven grammatical mistakes in your message tonight."

Mr. Moody smiled at the lady and replied, "Yes, I'm sure that's true. My education is limited. I wish I could have had more, but I'm simply using the grammar I have to win all the people I can for the Lord." Mr. Moody was faithful.

A faithful steward is required to be faithful at all times in every part of his life. That means being *faithful to his family*: his wife and children, *faithful in his finances* with integrity and *faithful to his friends.* According to Acts 2:42 the early Christians were *faithful to the Christian fellowship* – to the church of the Lord Jesus Christ. Believers ought to be in the house of God on a regular basis, participating in prayer, contributing tithes, sharing in Bible studies and demonstrating their love for other believers.

Early Christians were also faithful to their faith. They were faithful to the Word of God continuing steadfastly in the apostles' doctrine. In our time when Christianity and Christians are under attack, we need to faithfully stand for the great truths of the Word of God.

Our greatest motive for faithfulness is God's faithfulness. *"Know therefore that the Lord thy God, He is God, the faithful God…"* (Deuteronomy 7:9). God is faithful and just to forgive us (1John 1:9). He is faithful to help us in the hour of temptation (1 Corinthians 10:13). With the rising of the sun, each morning comes an eloquent testimony to His faithfulness, and this is accompanied with His loving kindnesses (Lamentations 3:22, 23).

Faithfulness should govern the small and the secret areas of life.

Youthful and Useful

"Let no man despise thy youth; but be thou an example of the believers, in word, in conversation, in charity, in spirit, in faith, in purity."
1 Timothy 4:12

Young people are the most priceless asset of any nation. It has been well said, "Treat your children well for they will not only inherit the national debt; they will also choose the nursing homes for our old age."

The Bible does not discriminate when it comes to age. Samuel was a young boy when he began to serve God, and David was a youth when he was anointed King. Likewise, God used many young women like Moses's sister, Miriam, the beautiful Queen Esther and a nameless slave girl in Naaman's home. God will use anyone who is will¬ing to learn from Him and is prepared to serve Him.

Youths are like the players in a stadium. Older people are the spectators cheering them on while children are on the subs' bench waiting to take to the field later. Young people change our language, dictate our fashions, compose the music and write the lyrics of the songs.

Young people are vulnerable, and the pressures on them are very great. They not only live in developing bodies where hormones are racing like galloping horses, but they may also be pressurized or bullied by their peers at school or stressed by the demands of secular society.

Young people may be the thinkers and leaders of tomorrow, but today they are trying to come to grips with spiritual and eternal values. They grapple with the fundamental questions about life: *Who am I? Why am I here? Where am I going?*

The Bible is not silent when it comes to adolescence. David asked the question, "Wherewithal shall a young man cleanse his way?" He also gave the answer, "By taking heed according to Thy word."

Being young is exciting and the best time to start a relationship with God. A life without Christ is an empty and hopeless life. King Solomon, the wisest of men, said, "Remember now thy Creator in the days of thy youth."

Beginning life with Christ guarantees a bright and blessed future.

Our Lord's Pattern

"Jesus went about all the cities and villages, teaching in their synagogues, and preaching the gospel of the kingdom, and healing every sickness and every disease among the people."
Matthew 9:35

Preaching, teaching and healing--this threefold ministry pretty much summed the activity of our Lord during His three years of public ministry. He established the pattern that sums up all Christian ministries for today--a pattern we try to follow. For years our missionaries have been engaged in a wide front of preaching, teaching and healing. Pioneer evangelism in towns, on rivers, and reaching boys and girls on the streets has been the objective of leading souls to Christ and planting local churches. Churches were established; Christian leaders were developed, and many believers matured through the faithful teaching of the Word of God. For more than fifty years our missionary nurses and doctors have dedicated their lives to bring help and healing to thousands of victims of horrendous diseases.

Jesus' pattern indicates that God cares for the whole person. Teaching the Bible ministers to a person's mind--an intellectual ministry for his soul. Preaching the Gospel ministers to a person's heart--a spiritual answer to his sin. Healing ministers to a person's body--a physical ministry for his sickness.

I think it is also important to notice the order of our Lord's ministry pattern. Healing was last in order, not because it is not important, but because it is not the number one priority.

In the work of missions our two primary roles must be the teaching of the Word and the preaching of the Gospel. Jesus did not primarily come to heal the sick, perform miracles or raise the dead. As Lord of the Harvest He came because He loved the harvest; He gave His life for the harvest, and now He sends His servants to gather in the harvest. Jesus came to seek and to save the lost.

Let's keep our Lord's pattern in view. Dr. Vance Havner said, "If they had a social gospel in the days of the prodigal son, somebody would have given him a bed, a sandwich and a welfare allowance, and he never would have gone home."

The harvest pattern still matters today.

Your Enemy

*"Your adversary the devil, as a roaring lion, walketh about,
seeking whom he may devour."*
1Peter 5:8

I remember Miss Moore, our teacher at Linfield Intermediate School, excitedly reading to us from C. S. Lewis's book, *The Screwtape Letters*. At that time we could not have cared less, but later I understood her excitement over this iconic classic on spiritual warfare. Screwtape was Satan and Wormwood his nephew. Together they plan to sabotage the church. In his strategy, Screwtape says to Wormwood, "The church is a fertile field if you just keep them bickering over details, structures, money, property, personal hurts, and misunderstandings. One thing you must prevent – don't let them look up to see the banners flying. If they see the banners flying, you have lost them forever."

The church of Jesus Christ is not a trophy cabinet of perfected and heroic saints. Rather it is a company of vulnerable, unworthy and forgiven sinners who are saved by God's grace.

Speaking to the House of Commons in 1913 Winston Churchill gave this advice: "We must always be ready to meet our average moment, the thing that any possible enemy could hurl against us at his selected moment." Christians also must be aware that Satan studies us and knows us thoroughly. He could hurl a deadly temptation at any given moment.

Be Alert. Peter must have remembered His anguished Lord in the Garden of Gethsemane when He said, "*Watch and pray, that ye enter not into temptation*" (Mark 14: 37). Maybe he also remembered how he fell asleep at that vital hour.

Be aware. Satan is your enemy. Peter put together two titles for Satan, "adversary", which simply means Satan, and "the devil," which denotes the accuser. These two titles sum up all that Satan is. Here is our foe, forever the devourer. Do not treat him lightly. Jesus is praying for us.

Be Armed! Recognise him as your enemy; resist him by the Word of God as our Saviour did. He might roar, but the Lion of the Tribe of Judah will always prevail.

The best way to resist our adversary is to submit to the Lord

Viewing Christmas

"Christ Jesus came into the world to save sinners."
1 Timothy 1:15

I remember as a boy going to the local cinema for the cheap matinee every Saturday afternoon. One Saturday we were intrigued when we were issued with a pair of paper spectacles to wear during the movie. When we did, we nearly jumped out of the velvet seats. Dinosaurs and snakes seemed to be flying out of the screen right at us. It was our introduction to 3D movies.

3-D vision is quite interesting. Unlike horses, our human eyes are located side-by-side at the front of our head. This allows each eye to take a view of the same area from a slightly different angle. Each eye picks up the visual information that the other doesn't, and the two separate images are relayed to the brain for processing. These two images arrive in the brain simultaneously where they are fused into one picture. The result is a three-dimensional, width, height, and depth. It is these dimensions that make 3-D viewing so special.

Sadly, the majority of people in our world only have only a one or two-dimension view of Christmas. They are more often taken up with when it is, what gifts they are going to give or get, and what foods they are going to eat.

This limited and distorted view of Christmas misses the real reason for the season. Herod and the religious people of Jerusalem missed that first Christmas when angels stood in the sky above the fields of Bethlehem and announced to humble shepherds, "Fear not: for, behold, I bring you good tidings of great joy, which shall be to all people. For unto you is born this day
in the city of David a Saviour, which is Christ the Lord."

Look beyond the "when" and the "what" of the Christmas season. Be sure to add the dimension of "why" Jesus came. By Christ coming into the world we can discern the width, height, and depth of the love of God for us.

Love came down at Christmas.

15th December

An Early Christmas Promise

"I will put enmity between thee and the woman, and between thy seed and her seed . ... unto you is born this day in the city of David a Saviour, which is Christ the Lord."
Genesis 3:15 and Luke 2:11

The name Waterloo is big in history even though it is a small town in Belgium with a population of fewer than 30,000 people. Most people associate "Waterloo" with the famous battle in 1815 when the armies of the Iron Duke of Wellington met and defeated the resurgent armies of Napoleon and changed the course of history. Since then the name *"Waterloo"* has assumed an importance that has little to do with its physical size or geographical location.

Likewise, we do not know the measurements of the Garden of Eden, but its place in history is immense. Eden was home for our first parents, the site of the first temptation, and sadly, the location of the first human transgression and rebellion against God. It was also there that the evil-one, the old serpent, met his *Waterloo* and learned that he had made a monumental blunder in attacking Adam and Eve.

In Genesis 3:15 God made a promise in the presence of Adam, Eve and the devil. He promised that one day the Seed of the woman, not the seed of Adam, would be the Saviour. That Seed was Jesus Christ, who was born of the Virgin at Bethlehem. He also said to the serpent, "He shall bruise your head, and you shall bruise His heel."

It was at the cross that the serpent bruised Jesus' heel, but by the merits of His shed blood and His resurrection, Jesus Christ bruised the serpent's head. By His death, He took the sting out of death and the power out of sin. Adam and Eve's failure in the Garden of Eden was fatal, but because of the Seed of the woman, it was not final. The Seed of Eve is traced from Adam to Abraham, to the tribe of Judah, to a king called David and to the baby born in Bethlehem, Jesus Christ, the Saviour of the world.

Everyone on our planet is a sinner who needs a Saviour

Christmas "Fear Nots"

"But the angel said unto him, Fear not, Zacharias: for thy prayer is heard; and thy wife Elisabeth shall bear thee a son, and thou shalt call his name John."
Luke1:13

Although Christmas is a wonderful time of the year, it can also stir many negative emotions. It is at this special season that loneliness can be most acute, grief can be more painful, and uncertainty can create greater fears. Take time to look out for neighbours and friends who may grapple with these unwelcome sentiments during this season.

Throughout the New Testament account of the Christmas story, God sends several "fear nots" for various people who were undergoing a whole range of human emotions during the Advent season.

The story of Zacharias is very human. He lived with the seeming problem of unanswered prayers. He found out that God is full of surprises. We just have to remember Abraham and Sarah having a child in their hundredth year. That was more than a surprise - it was a shock. Zacharias and Elisabeth received a similar shock, for although they had prayed for a family for years, they seemed to have had finally resigned to having a childless home - that is until God stepped in.

I find it interesting that Luke's Gospel begins with a couple who walked with God, Zacharias and Elisabeth, and ends with a couple with whom Jesus walked on the Emmaus Road. Both couples needed God's comfort and enlightenment.

This story reminds us that no prayer remains unanswered even though it may not be the answer we expect. How does God answer our prayers?

At times God gives us the things we desire in prayer. He puts His desires in our hearts.

At times God denies us the things we ask. When God says "No" it is always for our good and His glory.

At times God delays to give us the things for which we pray. Delays are not necessarily denials.

At times God diverts us from the things we desire. He may not give us what we ask because He wants to give us what is best.

The "fear nots" of long ago still speak to us today.

"Fear Not Mary"

"And the angel said unto her, Fear not, Mary: for thou hast found favour with God. And, behold, thou shalt conceive in thy womb, and bring forth a son, and shalt call His name JESUS."
Luke 1:30.31

I believe in miracles because I believe in God. Not only did the Lord Jesus perform many miracles, He was a miracle. Not only was the virgin birth the greatest of all miracles, it also presented the greatest human impossibility.

When Mary, possibly only eighteen years old, was startled by the appearance of the angel Gabriel and the announcement of God's plan for her life it not only seemed improbable, it was humanly impossible. That is why she frankly asked of Gabriel, *"How can these things be?"*

Gabriel was quick to answer with reassurance, *"The things that are impossible with man are possible with God."* This reassurance for Mary echoes the words of Jeremiah; *"…There is nothing too hard for thee."*

The visit of the angel was followed by the testimony of Mary's salvation, Mary's submission and Mary's salutation of praise. Through Mary's submission God used her as the human instrument to bring Christ to the world; *"And Mary said, Behold the handmaid of the Lord; be it unto me according to thy word. And the angel departed from her"* (Luke 1:38).

In Romans 12:1 Paul indicates that our worship should involve the sacrifice of our body, the transformation of our mind and proving the good, and acceptable, and perfect, will of God. Mary's submission included all these elements.

Mary surrendered her body for the Lord's use. She gave her body to bring Christ to the world and the Gospel to every creature.

Mary surrendered her mind to the Lord's mystery. Mary was not asked to understand all the mysteries of God's providence but rested in God's faithfulness,

Mary surrendered her will for God's purpose. Her response to God was full of enthusiastic surrender to God's will. She was prepared to be part of God's plan and in God's good time.

Mary withheld nothing from God.

Fear Not Joseph

"While he thought on these things, behold, the angel of the LORD appeared unto him in a dream, saying, Joseph, thou son of David, fear not to take unto thee Mary thy wife: for that which is conceived in her is of the Holy Ghost. And she shall bring forth a son, and thou shalt call his name JESUS: for He shall save His people from their sins."
Matthew 1:20, 21

Joseph, the carpenter of Nazareth, is the first real living person we meet on the pages of the New Testament. In the volume of words, the Bible tells us very little about him, but we learn that he was betrothed to Mary.

After the angel Gabriel visited Mary and made the startling announcement that God would send His Son through her, she must have hurried to Joseph to tell him the incredible news. We can only imagine what his reaction might have been. It was then that the angel must have appeared unto him to reassure him that he was in God's plan. He had already planned to marry Mary, but they could never have imagined what God had planned for their home.

At the same time, there were some issues that they young couple had to face. The stigma of a child conceived out of wedlock might have caused tongues to wag. To explain the mystery to others might have been met with unbelief.

Through it all, Joseph's character remained upright.

His holiness was expressed, for he was just and walked with his Lord.

His tenderness was exemplified, for he refused to allow any shame to fall on Mary.

His faithfulness was evident, for he was obedient in everything God commanded him to do.

He was full of faith, for he believed everything that God said, and when the Christ-child was born he gave the name, *"Jesus"*, the only word Joseph ever spoke that is recorded in the Bible.

Go look over Joseph's shoulder into the manger and see the Child he saw. This Christ-child had abandoned His golden throne room for a dirty stable, and worshipping angels were replaced with bewildered shepherds.

We worship Him who Joseph presented to the world.

Meet Mary

"And Mary said, My soul doth magnify the Lord, and my spirit hath rejoiced in God my Saviour."
Luke 1:46, 47

In all the drama surrounding the Saviour's birth, no one played a bigger part than the young girl from Nazareth whose name was Mary. There are five other Marys mentioned in the Bible. Although sometimes referred to as "the virgin Mary," Elizabeth called her "the mother of our Lord."

There has never been a person outside the Lord Jesus who has been more misrepresented than Mary. Many magnify her to the point of mistakenly deifying her and wrongly teaching that she is a mediatrix between men and God. Others go to the other extreme and are guilty of ignoring her. The truth is that no other person was ever closer to our Lord than Mary. What secret hours of unseen and unhurried communion she must have had with the Lord Jesus. Is it any wonder that the angel Gabriel said that she had received great grace?

As a young girl, Mary brought Christ to the world. Think of the shame she had to handle with the news that though still a virgin, she was not only pregnant, she was carrying the Christ child. How did she convince her parents, her family and neighbours? She was ready for whatever God asked her to do, no matter what the price or the shame.

As a mother, Mary was there to guide the infant Jesus during the years of his childhood. Observe Mary as a mother caring for the Lord Jesus in Nazareth.

Mary was there in the silent years to shape and mould the career of Christ. View her and Joseph taking the Lord Jesus to the temple in Jerusalem for His Bar Mitzvah.

As a widow, Mary stood with John at the cross watching the Lord Jesus Christ. Surely, a painful sword of sorrow must have pierced her heart as she watched the Saviour suffer and die.

Mary knelt in the upper room with other believers of the early church to support the furtherance of the Gospel.

"He that is mighty hath done to me great things; and holy is His name."

Adore Him

"The glory of the Lord shone round about them: and they were sore afraid. And the angel said unto them, Fear not: for, behold, I bring you good tidings of great joy, which shall be to all people. For unto you is born this day in the city of David a Saviour, which is Christ the Lord."
Luke 2:9-11

Christmas is a great time for exchanging gifts, it is also a perfect time to visit and receive guests. The Bible reminds us that we should not forget strangers, for some even entertained angels unawares. When the anonymous shepherds received a visitation of angels, it most certainly was a momentous and memorable visit.

It may seem that shepherds were the most unlikely people to visit. Shepherds were probably considered to be the least influential people of first-century society. They were treated as social outcasts because they usually were dirty, smelly and unkempt. They were looked on as religious outcasts because they were defiled and unfit to be in the Temple. Separated from both God and man, they seemed to be hopeless, but hope is what they received that night.

Shepherds were the first to receive the angelic news that the Lamb of God had come into the world. God is not impressed with human prestige. The King of Kings was welcomed to earth by lowly shepherds in a stable rather than to a sovereign in a palace.

The shepherds received the heavenly guests. One angel appeared to announce the Saviour's birth, then a host of angels joined in the great song that accompanied the news of the Jesus' birth.

The shepherds received heavenly guidance. They were told where to find the Christ child - *in the city of David,* Who the child was - *Christ the Lord,* and how to recognize Him - *you shall find the Babe wrapped in swaddling clothes and lying in a manger.*

The shepherds witnessed the heavenly glory - The glory had departed from Israel according to Ezekiel. The Shepherds could say with John, *"We have seen His glory, the glory of the only begotten…"* - the Shekinah glory of God's presence.

Humble shepherds met the Great Shepherd who was God's Lamb.

Colourful Characters

"When the fullness of the time was come, God sent forth his Son."
Galatians 4:4

The characters of Christmas are as colourful as the lights on our Christmas trees. Most of these individuals burst onto the pages of the Bible, play their part and then silently disappear into history. That is certainly true of the shepherds and the wise men; and even Joseph and Mary soon fade into the misty background. The only enduring and always central character is Jesus.

There is much to learn from the response of characters to the coming of our Lord Jesus Christ to earth.

Joseph teaches us to obey God when circumstances seem inexplicable. The background to the angel's visit to Joseph suggests that he must have been puzzled by the news that Mary had been chosen to bear the Christ-child. He refused to hesitate at obeying God's command and faithfully stood by Mary.

Mary teaches us to trust God when the future seems impossible. She was only a teenage girl from the back streets of Nazareth, but God knew He could entrust her with this amazing role and gave her grace to accomplish it. Mary refused to limit God.

The shepherds teach us God is not impressed with celebrities. It was to shepherds in the fields that God sent news that Jesus was born. These shepherds, ordinary workmen, were not out of place in a stable. Not priests in a temple, but the most unlikely people worshipping Christ in a most unlikely place.

The wise men teach us that God is gathering His redeemed from all over the world. The magi were not Jews. Study of the Scriptures indicated that Christ would be born in Bethlehem. Priests and Pharisees also knew these Scriptures, but they had no desire to seek the coming Christ. The wise men were concerned, and God guided them by His star.

Their worship was exclusive and extravagant. Their hearts were not satisfied until they saw Jesus. To Him they bent the knee, surrendered their hearts and presented their gifts.

The heavenly angels teach us that God is glorified in the praises of His people. "Glory to God in the highest…"

Sing with joy the Christmas carols.

22nd December

How Poor?

"Though He was rich, yet for your sakes He became poor."
2 Corinthians 8:9

Wars inevitably produce multitudes of refugees and displaced peoples. Aid agencies, religious and secular, often rush to provide necessary relief to these destitute victims taking what are known as the basic needs of mankind: food, clothing and shelter.

When it comes to shelter, there certainly are some very elaborate and expensive shelters dotted all over our countryside and squeezed into our cities.

These basic needs of human kind remind us just how poor our Saviour became for us. As an infant He was a refugee in Egypt when Mary and Joseph fled the infanticide in Judea. Later He confessed, *"The foxes have holes, and the birds of the air have nests; but the Son of man hath not where to lay His head"* (Matthew 8:20).

When Jesus was born in Bethlehem He had no infant's crib other than a rough feeding trough. He borrowed a boat on the shores of Galilee, and to feed the great multitudes in the wilderness He borrowed a boy's lunch. To pay tax He performed a miracle and borrowed a coin to teach a lesson. At the well in Samaria He had no bucket to draw water, and when they took His crucified body from the cross He was laid in a borrowed tomb.

This same Lord Jesus clothes the flowers of the earth with magnificent beauty, yet He bore the shame of nakedness on the cross. He feeds the birds every day from His bountiful storehouse, and yet on the cross He cried, "I *thirst.*" He never owned a home here on earth, but He has gone to the Father's house to prepare an eternal home for those He has purchased by His own precious blood.

The only thing Jesus ever owned was His cross. John said of Him, *"And He bearing His cross went forth …"* (John 19:17). Paul wrote of the Saviour, *"Having made peace through the blood of His cross, … Blotting out the handwriting of ordinances that was against us, which was contrary to us, and took it out of the way, nailing it to His cross"* (Colossians 1:20, 2:14).

His cross manifests the riches of His grace.

God In Control

"But the Word of God grew and multiplied."
Acts 12:24

When Mollie Harvey arrived back in Boca do Acre after a prolonged furlough she had to be brought up to speed on all the changes. Oil lamps burned well after midnight as the missionaries clustered around a table and talked until the wee hours. During Mollie's absence, there had been considerable growth in the smaller churches in Terra Firme and São Paulo where James Gunning had acquired two properties that were transformed into church buildings.

James related how the purchase of the house at Terra Firme had greatly angered the local Italian priest who vowed that he would make sure that the doors of this new evangelical church would never open. His opposition was so great that he bought the house next door to the church to start evening novenas for the people.

Even as the missionaries were talking about the matter, something happened that dramatically changed the priest's plans. Mollie told the story in the Mission report:

On Christmas Eve we chatted all through that night. Early the next morning, we opened the shutters to let the sunlight stream through the trees. When I looked up the street I realized something was wrong. People ran past our house crying; others were being carried, apparently, they had been injured. I thought it strange that no one had asked us for help since we were usually the first people called in any medical emergency.

We later learned that during the Christmas Midnight Mass a terrible accident had happened at the Catholic Church. To accommodate the expected crowds, the priest had hurriedly built a balcony in his large church. When the gallery became packed with people, the whole structure collapsed under the weight. Many worshippers, including the priest, were seriously injured, and he had to be flown out to São Paulo in the south of Brazil for special treatment. We were stunned and speechless when we heard the news.

When the small church at Terra Firme was opened to the glory of God later that day James prayed for the salvation of the injured, and especially for the priest who had tried to hinder the church opening.

God works and who can hinder?

The Word of God

"All things must be fulfilled, which were written in the law of Moses, and in the prophets, and in the psalms, concerning Me."
Luke 24:44

Messiah's mission on earth did not begin at Bethlehem when He arrived at the manger as a little baby. He was the Lord of glory and was with His Father in the beginning. The pathway from heaven to Bethlehem was prepared and overseen by the Father. Through patriarchs and prophets God gave more than 300 prophecies and promises in the Old Testament relating to the coming of our Lord Jesus Christ. All of these prophecies were fulfilled in the New Testament, and this could not have happened by chance.

A skeptic might say that Jesus, a student of the Old Testament, simply arranged to fulfill all these prophecies in Himself. To this we must answer that it would have been impossible for Him to arrange to be born in Bethlehem, fulfilling the prophecy of Micah 5:2. Furthermore, how could He arrange to be born of a virgin or that the prophet Isaiah should write so many intricate details of His birth centuries before He was born?

Could the Saviour have arranged for the psalmist to describe His death by crucifixion long before that most cruel form of punishment had ever been introduced? Could He have arranged for a Roman soldier to nail Him to a cross, or for Judas to betray Him for exactly thirty pieces of silver, as Zechariah prophesied? Humanly speaking, it would have been impossible for Him to have arranged His own resurrection from the dead three days after His burial.

In another sense, the Lord Jesus did arrange all this. As God, He revealed it all to patriarchs and prophets who wrote the prophecies that Jesus fulfilled. Moreover, so convinced were those who saw that He was the promised Messiah that they were willing to lay down their lives for Him. Surely, no one would lay down his or her life for a lie. Those early Christians knew that Jesus was who He claimed to be. There was no other way to explain three hundred fulfilled prophecies apart from divine inspiration.

God's Word cannot be broken.

An Amazing Promise

But thou, Bethlehem Ephratah, though thou be little among the thousands of Judah, yet out of thee shall He come forth unto Me that is to be ruler in Israel; whose goings forth have been from of old, from everlasting.
Micah 5:2

Many children look forward to Christmas to receive the presents they have been promised with the condition--"if you have been good." Of course, the true message of the season is that God sent His unspeakable Gift to us because we were not good. On the contrary, we are sinners by birth and sinners by choice, but *"God manifested His love toward us, in that while were yet sinners, Christ died for us."*

God's Gift had been promised and prophesied on hundreds of occasions throughout the Old Testament. One of the most interesting prophecies is found in Micah 5:2. This verse not only gives amazing details of the coming Messiah, but it is also the central verse of the eleven Minor Prophets, which, in synagogues to this present time, is considered to be one solitary book. This reveals that the coming Saviour was at the heart of the prophets' message.

Micah, a contemporary of Isaiah, spoke at a time when Israel was longing and looking for a Deliverer, the Messiah.

Micah spoke about the Person of Messiah. In the light of the prophecies that Micah had given, the people feared a foreign ruler. Micah said that the coming would be God's Ruler, the Sovereign, the Shepherd and the Everlasting Ruler.

Micah spoke of the place Messiah would be born. Bethlehem is contrasted with Jerusalem. Jerusalem would be taken captive, but Deliverance would come out of the humble village of Bethlehem. Bethlehem had been the place of weeping for Jacob's wife, Rachel, and the place of Ruth's wedding. David also desired the sweet water from Bethlehem's well, but now, Bethlehem would witness the coming of Him who would be the greatest Wonder of all time, Jesus Christ.

Micah spoke of the power Messiah exercises and the peace Messiah brings.
"For now shall He be great unto the ends of the earth, and this man shall be the peace" (Micah 5:4,5).

Thank God for His inexpressible Gift.

Coming Soon

"This know also, that in the last days perilous times shall come."
2 Timothy 3:1

We are living in momentous days. The Bible calls them "perilous times." I believe with all my heart that the sands of time are running low for our generation and that we are living in the shadows of the end of this age. Everything indicates Jesus Christ is coming soon.

No man has any right to set dates. As a matter of fact, some modern heresies have been propagated because false prophets dared to set dates for Messiah's coming. However, we cannot deny the fact that so much is happening so quickly that our Lord Jesus must be about to return for His saints, and God is about ready to judge the wickedness of this old world.

Paul was concerned for Timothy, and his letters are full of grit and steely determination for him to endure hardness as a good soldier who wages a good warfare. Paul also wrote to warn Timothy of the last days, not just Paul's last days, but the closing days of the church age. It is evident that these days are upon us when we consider the following:

The depravity of the human heart. In 2 Timothy chapter three Paul majors on the depravity of the heart. Today stark depravity and lawlessness parade the streets of our cities and terrify both old and young alike.

The development of events around the world. The modern miracle in the rebirth of Israel and its important role in world affairs. The realignment in Europe. The rise of radical Islam. The resurgence of Russia. The global financial alignment. These are leading pointers that the end of the age and coming of our Saviour is near.

The doctrines of devils and deception of people. The multiplicity of cults under the guise of Christendom increases by the day.

The departure from the faith. In 2 Timothy Paul mentions eight people who had departed from the faith. Some denied the faith; others were deceived by false teachers; some deserted the truth; others defiled the faith, and some declared their opposition to the work of the Gospel.

There is no doubt that Jesus is coming soon.

Your Eternal Inheritance

"To an inheritance incorruptible, and undefiled, and that fadeth not away, reserved in heaven for you."
1 Peter 1:4

Every Christian has been brought into a special family, *"begotten again to a lively hope by the resurrection of Jesus Christ from the dead."* Because the believer is part of that special family God has reserved for him a special future, *an inheritance incorruptible, and undefiled, ... that fadeth not away."* Our minds can never comprehend how rich is that inheritance.

When John described the New Jerusalem, he wrote of the gates of pearl and the streets of pure gold. The foundations of the city were made of precious stones. Our Lord has made us meet to be partakers of the inheritance in that heavenly city. This inheritance deserves our attention.

The saints' inheritance is beyond death. Like eternal life and the saints' glorified bodies, this inheritance will never decay for it is incorruptible. Its value will never diminish, for it will endure throughout eternity.

The saints' inheritance can never be defiled. Rust can never touch it nor moths erode it. Since death entered into the world, everything on earth has been in a state of degeneration with multiple flaws and imperfections. In heaven, nothing will ever defile our reserved inheritance. It is permanent and pure.

The saints' inheritance will never know degeneration. The most beautiful flowers and blossoms on earth fade away, but this inheritance is unfading and incomparable in its beauty. Old photos may reveal that childhood dimples have given way to wrinkles. When we have been 10,000 years In heaven, neither the saints nor their inheritance will have grown old.

The saints' inheritance cannot be destroyed or stolen. It is secure forever. Jesus said, *"Lay not up for yourselves treasures upon earth... where thieves break through and steal: but lay up... in heaven ... where thieves do not break through nor steal"* (Matthew 6:19, 20).

Not only is this inheritance reserved for the believer in Christ, every believer is kept by the power of God for that inheritance.

Heavenly investments will never lose their value.

Changed

"We shall not all sleep, but we shall all be changed, in a moment, in the twinkling of an eye, at the last trump."
1 Corinthians 15:51, 52

There is no greater song than the song of redemption. *Redemption is a commercial term that denotes a purchase price* or a payment of a ransom. It also implies a purchased possession that which has been ransomed. Our great Redeemer came to *"give His life a ransom for many"* (Mark 10:45). Through His death at Calvary, the Saviour provides complete redemption for all who trust Him. Paul wrote to the Ephesians about "being blessed with all spiritual blessings in heavenly places in Christ." He indicated that redemption was at the heart of those blessings; *"In whom we have redemption through His blood, the forgiveness of sins, according to the riches of his grace"* (Ephesians 1:7). We are redeemed by the precious blood of Jesus Christ.

Redemption also denotes a purchased possession. Paul reminded the Corinthians that Christians are a purchased possession; *"Know ye not ... ye are not your own? ye are bought with a price"* (1 Corinthians 6:19, 20). Paul spoke of *"the church of God, which he hath purchased with his own blood"* (Acts 20:28).

This costly redemption has not only purchased our souls, it includes body, soul, and spirit, the totality of all we are. At present, we live in corruptible bodies that are subject to weakness and degeneration. Some saints long to be free from their infirmed, weak and burdened bodies. Paul wrote of this: *"For we know that the whole creation groaneth and travaileth in pain together until now. And not only they, but ourselves also, ... groan within ourselves, waiting for the adoption, to wit, the redemption of our body"* (Romans 8:22,23).

Redemption through Christ guarantees that He will transform weak bodies to be *"fashioned like unto His glorious body."* For that reason, Job said, *"I know that my redeemer liveth, and that He shall stand at the latter day upon the earth: And though after my skin worms destroy this body, yet in my flesh shall I see God."*

Redemption of the body makes us ready for heaven.

Known in Heaven

"Then shall I know even as also I am known."
1 Corinthians 13:12

Many times people ask if we will know our departed loved ones in heaven and if they shall know each other. While the Bible does not tell us everything there is to know about heaven, it does tell all that we need to know. That said, I find there are several assurances that the saints in heaven will know each other in their eternal Home.

We shall know more in Heaven than we do on earth. "Now I know in part; but then shall I know even as also I am known." Our knowledge of each other will be better in heaven.

David expected to meet and recognize his infant son. "I shall go to him, but he shall not return to me" (2 Samuel 12:23). Parents will meet these little ones who are "safe in the arms of Jesus."

The rich man in hell recognized Lazarus, the beggar who had died and gone to heaven. It is a sobering thought that this tormented lost man lifted up his eyes in hell and saw "Abraham afar off, and Lazarus in his bosom" (Luke 16:22, 23).

Jesus promised that He would see the repentant thief in Heaven. "Jesus said ..., Verily I say unto thee, Today shalt thou be with me in paradise" (Luke 23:42, 43). We don't know his name, but it was registered in heaven.

Old Testament saints shall be recognised in the kingdom of Heaven. "Many shall come from the east and west, and shall sit down with Abraham, and Isaac, and Jacob, in the kingdom of heaven" (Matthew 8:11). To sit with them is to recognise them.

Saints will be recognised at the resurrection. The Scriptures assure us that the dead and living shall be caught up together to meet the Lord in the air. We shall meet our saved loved ones and together go to meet the Saviour (1 Thessalonians 4:17).

At our Lord's transfiguration *Peter, James, and John recognised Moses and Elijah* even though they had never met before. Furthermore, Moses and Elijah lived centuries apart on earth (Matt. 17:3, 4).

Rejoice because your name is written in heaven.

Any Moment

"Then we which are alive and remain, shall be caught up together with them in the clouds, to meet the Lord in the air."
1 Thessalonians 4:17

We live in a troubled world. If it is not famines, earthquakes, and tsunamis, it is war, nuclear threats, economic woes, riots, and revolution. Some are tempted to wring their hands asking, *"Whatever is going to happen?"* Christians are not just looking for *"something to happen,"* they are looking for *"Someone who is coming."*

While living in Manaus, we visited the leprosarium on Sunday afternoons. We went from house to house to read, pray and sing with believers who had leprosy. At the end of the visit, we gathered at Pastor Valdemar's home for our final round of singing and praise. We always finished singing, *"Maranata, Maranata, ora vem Senhor Jesus."* (Translated: *Maranatha, Maranatha, so come Lord Jesus*). Although faces were distorted and bodies ruined because of leprosy, these friends were not shaking their heads in despair. Rather, they lifted their voices to enthusiastically sing of the blessed hope that Jesus was coming again. They knew that He would transform their afflicted bodies to be like to His glorious body – what a day that will be.

The Second Coming of Jesus Christ is the most talked about theme of the Bible. It was prophesied by the prophets, promised by the Saviour, preached by the Apostles, portrayed at the Lord's Supper and is the blessed expectation of all believers.

In a moment, in the twinkling of an eye, He will come. Someone reckoned that the average person blinks somewhere between 10,000 to 20,000 times a day. In one of those blinks, the Lord Jesus could return. What an awesome thought.

Imagine a crane with a great magnet hanging at the end of a long cable. As the crane swings round the powerful magnet picks up pieces of iron. Not all metals will respond to the magnet–only iron. Why? Because iron has an affinity with and the same nature as the magnet.

In the same way, those who are Christ's, when He comes again, will be caught up from the grave and the earth to meet their Lord in the air.

Maranatha!

31st December

Confident and Content

"Be content with such things as ye have: for He hath said, I will never leave thee, nor forsake thee. So that we may boldly say, The Lord is my helper, I will not fear what man shall do unto me."
Hebrews 13:5, 6

While walking alone on Brighton's sands in 1865, Hudson Taylor fully surrendered himself to God. "I told Him that all the responsibility must rest with Him." He prayed for twenty-four new workers for China's and Mongolia's inland provinces that were without missionaries. Mr. Taylor then opened a bank account under the name "China Inland Mission" with "ten pounds and all the promises of God." He needed those promises when he buried his eight-year-old daughter, and again when his wife died in childbirth. When Mr. Taylor died forty years later, the Mission had 805 missionaries. Hudson Taylor said, "It was not great faith in God, but simple faith in a great God."

Entering into this New Year, we also need simple trust in the promises of God. That is why God gave them to us; we need to trust, try and prove them. The author of Hebrews finished off his letter with one of the most precious promises for God's people that should help us every day of this New Year.

Be content with His Provision. Contentment is not getting what we want, rather it is being satisfied with what we already have. This is an antidote to coveteousness. Provision = "pre-vision." God sees and knows the way ahead.

Be confident of His Presence. Jesus never used the word "Goodbye." We can be sure every day and in all circumstances that He will never give us up and never let us down.

We are covered by His Protection. Because "He hath said…" we, therefore, can boldly say, *"the Lord is my helper, and I will not fear what man shall do unto me."* We are under the shelter of His hand.

After Hudson had received letters about serious trouble developing in certain provinces, he began whistling, "Jesus, I am resting, resting, in the joy of what Thou art." Someone asked how he could do this. He replied, "I just roll the burden on the Lord."

A Happy New Year.

Acre International is an evangelical faith Mission serving God since 1937 in Brazil, Portugal, Canary Islands and Northern Ireland. Today much of the work is in the hands of national workers who continue to need our guidance and support.

We invite the reader to stand with us in this work:

EVANGELISM

In obedience to the Lord's command (Matthew 28:18-20) we are totally committed to the task of preaching Christ and especially where He is not known, believing that every individual has the right to be confronted with the claims of the Saviour.

CHURCH PLANTING

Preparing the ground, planting the seed, cultivating, harvesting and discipling has led to the founding of churches in various towns and cities.

BIBLE TRAINING

In many places national Pastors have taken over from the missionaries or are working alongside them. A strong national Church necessitates leaders well-grounded in God's Word. Missionary involvement in the training and equipping of such leaders through Seminary/Bible Institute staffing is an ever-increasing opportunity, though limited by lack of personnel.

CHILDREN'S WORK

While missionary work does involve reaching children, there are missionaries fully occupied in this ministry and also seeking to train others for the work.

LITERATURE MINISTRY

As literacy increases around the world the printed page is fast becoming a vital tool in evangelism and spiritual development. Bibles and Christian books are in great demand.

PRISON VISITATION

A difficult yet rewarding ministry- the chaplaincy responsibility for the missionary is a great opportunity.

MEDICAL WORK

Through medical work, occasions do arise when the spiritual needs of the patient can be addressed. The on-going Leprosy program in Brazil is very demanding. Dr William Woods OBE is Co-ordinator of the Leprosy Programme for Northern Brazil.

How you can help us

BE PRAYERFUL

Prayer is absolutely vital in the work of the Lord. Attend, if possible, the Acre prayer meeting in your area. There are monthly prayer groups in various homes in and around the city of Belfast, in or near provincial towns such as Lisburn, Portadown, Ballymena, Bangor, Annalong, Loughgall, and Carryduff. None in your area? Why not start one in your home? The Mission Co-ordinator will be delighted to help you.

BE INFORMED

Ask for "INSIGHT"- published three times per year - this will be sent to your home free of charge. You might even consider distributing copies to interested friends within your church or fellowship. Also, be aware of the latest news/prayer requests by asking for "IN TOUCH" - ten issues annually. You can subscribe to either of these publications, FREE OF CHARGE, bysending us an Email with your NAME, DAYTIME TELEPHONE NUMBER, ADDRESS, NAME OF PUBLICATION and NUMBER OF COPIES REQUIRED. Please enter the words "Mailing List" in the subject field of your message.

BE INVOLVED

Offer to arrange meetings in your church/fellowship/home with missionaries while on furlough. An informal encounter (coffee morning) can be so informative and useful.

Commit to support the work on a regular basis. This can be done by bank draft or by sending periodic gifts to the Mission. Ask for a Missionary Box or Globe available from the Mission Co-ordinator. Ask for the relevant details about the Covenant Gift Scheme.

OTHER BOOKS BY VICTOR MAXWELL

WHEN GOD STEPS IN
by Victor Maxwell

I WANT YOU TO DO SOMETHING
Dr. Bill Woods OBE with Victor Maxwell

TRIUMPHS OF FAITH
by Mollie Harvey

GOD SENT THE WIND
James and Dorrie Gunning

THE LEGACY LIVES ON
Hazel Miskimmin with Victor Maxwell

ACRE INTERNATIONAL OFFICE
30 Carnglave Manor
Spa
Ballynahinch
Co.Down
Northern Ireland
BT24 8XE
Telephone: +44 (028) 97563200
Email: acregospelmission@hotmail.co.uk